Why **Neuroscience Matters** in the Classroom

Principles of Brain-based Instructional Design for Teachers

Kathleen Scalise
University of Oregon

Marie Felde

Boston   Columbus   Indianapolis   New York   San Francisco
Amsterdam   Cape Town   Dubai   London   Madrid   Milan   Munich   Paris   Montreal   Toronto
Delhi   Mexico City   São Paulo   Sydney   Hong Kong   Seoul   Singapore   Taipei   Tokyo

Vice President and Editorial Director:
Jeffery W. Johnston
Vice President and Publisher:
Kevin M. Davis
Editorial Assistant: Anne McAlpine
Executive Field Marketing Manager:
Krista Clark
Senior Product Marketing Manager:
Christopher Barry
Program Manager: Janelle Rogers
Project Manager: Pamela Bennett

Operations Specialist: Carol Melville
Cover Design Director: Diane Ernsberger
Cover Art: Getty Images, Gary Waters
Full-Service Project Management:
Mohinder Singh, iEnergizer Aptara®, Ltd.
Composition: iEnergizer Aptara®, Ltd.
Printer/Binder: RR Donnelley/
Harrisonburg North
Cover Printer: RR Donnelley/
Harrisonburg North
Text Font: Bembo MT Pro

Library of Congress Cataloging-in-Publication Data

Names: Scalise, Kathleen.
Title: Why neuroscience matters in the classroom : principles of brain-based
   instructional design for teachers / Kathleen Scalise, University of
   Oregon, Marie Felde, University of California, Berkeley.
Description: Boston : Pearson, [2017] | Includes index.
Identifiers: LCCN 2015031671| ISBN 9780132931816 | ISBN 0132931818
Subjects: LCSH: Learning, Psychology of. | Cognitive learning. |
   Teaching—Psychological aspects. | Instructional systems—Design.
Classification: LCC LB1062 .S33 2015 | DDC 370.15/23—dc23 LC record available at
   http://lccn.loc.gov/2015031671

10 9 8 7 6 5 4 3 2 1

PEARSON

ISBN 10:   0-13-293181-8
ISBN 13: 978-0-13-293181-6

Preface

As an author of this book, the main question I have been asked is, Why? Why did my coauthor and I write it, why is it needed, and why should teachers and educators learn about the brain?

Why Neuroscience Matters in the Classroom came about because of a course I began teaching at the University of Oregon in 2005. Called "Analysis of Teaching and Learning," the course focused on advanced learning theory for educators. My "students" were primarily school principals and veteran teachers. On average, they possessed 20 or more years of teaching experience each. If they were going to take a course on learning theory, they said, they wanted something new and fresh that was also of high utility and importance in their work.

The course that resulted had at its core a type of scientific literacy for teachers and others in the field of education. True to the name of the course, we analyzed the research literature in teaching and learning. We asked ourselves whether the convergence of cognitive psychology, neuroscience, and educational research offered any utility to teachers. We pondered scientific findings in memory, emotion, attitude, and motivation. Much to my surprise and delight, the educators immediately connected with the material. They couldn't get enough of it.

The educators wanted to know more and more, especially about one thing: the brain and how it worked. From a tiny doctoral seminar, the course doubled and tripled. It soon moved to larger and larger rooms, and was broadcast to multiple satellite sites. New teachers just entering the field began to enroll along with the veterans and principals. They wanted to know what their school leaders and teacher colleagues were learning.

So, this is part of my answer to why my coauthor and I wrote this book. The need for engaging teachers and educators in this body of knowledge about the brain is well-founded. If it is made accessible, not only will they come but they will bring their friends and colleagues. Administrators and teachers, new and experienced, exhibit an almost insatiable desire and they resonate with it. After all, what educator hasn't wondered what is going on in the minds of students? Teachers are on the front lines of learning, so this is exciting for them.

Also, educators find the scientific knowledge is not nearly as challenging as they might at first think. After getting a feel for the field, it becomes second nature to start following the advances. In the time my coauthor and I have been writing, we hardly can finish a chapter without something new coming along. For teachers, when new knowledge starts flowing that quickly and you are a part of understanding it, it is a highly energizing experience.

Another reason to write this book is the current state of the field. Scientific findings on the brain appear in news reports daily. Discoveries are breaking in research journals and academic conferences at blinding speed. As painstaking as brain research is, a new era of knowledge is at hand. For instance, teachers just entering the classroom today can expect to spend a career of 30 or more years surrounded by continuously emerging new information on how students learn. This means every teacher needs a base on which to build future understanding. Providing educators with a frame of reference is imperative.

Educational advisory committees nationally and around the world agree. From the U.S. National Academies to the International Organisation for Economic Co-operation and Development (OECD), scientific and policy advisory reports for teachers recommend learning about the mind and brain. The reports put to rest the idea that knowing about the brain is out of the scope for teachers. While there is more for science to discover about the brain, important findings are already available of which every teacher should be aware. Skepticism also is warranted, and teachers need to be able to evaluate claims.

We have listened to a few important messages in our journey with teachers. First, we find it is important to keep the teacher voice present in communicating. The reader will find teacher narrative a primary focus throughout this book, as well as profiles and interviews with neuroscientists and cognitive psychologists. Story and narrative are a major way in which the brain learns. They are seen by the brain as a type of evidence, or "social proof," that reflects on experiences that have been valuable or compelling to others.

Second, a missing gap for teachers, we believe, is a text that focuses strongly on considering three mind sciences together and alongside each other: neuroscience, cognitive psychology, and educational research. Putting the pieces together is important. Teachers are busy. They don't have time to assemble all the new information themselves. One educator who attended a brain science conference said she was so taken with the two days' worth of lectures and workshops that she knew she wanted to take it back to her colleagues. But nothing had been collected and put together so that it was easy to share the information. This book is intended to provide a richness of information organized for teachers to share, including scenarios to ponder.

Finally, teachers will find this isn't a subject you learn and check off. It stays with you. It is amazing. If you can take this with you, you will be the life of the teachers' lunchroom. When you start sharing what you have learned and it starts to ring bells with your colleagues, it really is astonishing what happens. Teachers will find they bring this significant knowledge not only to their teaching practice but also to their learning practice, which is hugely valuable.

Acknowledgments

We want to thank the many contributors who have helped us, most especially Columbia University's Department of Neuroscience, Columbia's Mortimer B. Zuckerman Mind Brain Behavior Institute, Teachers College at Columbia, and the College of Education of the University of Oregon, which together assisted to sponsor the collaborations that made this book possible. We also thank the many scientists, cognitive psychologists, and educational researchers who contributed to each chapter, including assisting us with profiles and interviews. We also would like to thank the following reviewers of the manuscript who supplied us with valuable suggestions: Anne K. Bednar, Eastern Michigan University; C. Anne Gutshall, College of Charleston; Elizabeth K. Reed, Plymouth State University; and Linda Schlosser, St. John Fisher College.

Finally, we extend our gratitude to the teachers and principals who shared their stories with us, and all the educators who work with our children and young adults every day in our nation's classrooms and schools. We hope this book will prove useful to them, and we invite their stories and feedback so we can grow in our work along with our readers.

Kathleen Scalise, Associate Professor
Educational Methodology, Policy and Leadership, University of Oregon

brief Contents

Contents

Why **Neuroscience Matters** in the Classroom

A **CORE** of **Understanding**

A core of seven guiding principles will be introduced in this chapter: what every teacher, educator, and educational leader should know so that she or he can put brain science to use in the classroom and establish a foundation for a lifetime of learning in this emerging area. The chapter includes research to find common ground. Immediately following this chapter will be a section titled "Framework of the CORE: Seven Guiding Principles and Their Associated Big Ideas." That separate section will summarize guiding principles and explore a set of associated Big Ideas for each principle. The principles explain *why* an educator should be interested. The Big Ideas present *what* educators should know.

Introduction

The kindergarten teacher tapped her foot impatiently. "I can't present this article!" she said. "It's about the brain. What do I know about the brain?"

She was participating in a course on learning theory for educators, and each student presented a class reading. "Can somebody else do it?" the kindergarten teacher pleaded. Her eyes scanned the room. "Maybe a science teacher?" she asked hopefully. "OK," she sighed. "I'll try."

When her time came, the kindergarten teacher held the article high in the air as if showing small children a picture book. "This is very important!" she said. "I didn't want to teach it to you before, but now I do! And I am going to tell you why!"

"A dentist is a type of doctor," she said. "For a dentist, it is very important for him or her to know about . . ." She gestured at her teeth. Everyone looked at her. "Help me out here, people!" she said sharply to the class.

"Teeth?" a few voices in the room ventured.

"Correct!" the teacher said. "A dentist must know about teeth!"

"A podiatrist is a foot doctor," the teacher continued. "A podiatrist must know about . . ."

"Feet!" the class called out.

"Yes!" the kindergarten teacher said. "Very good!"

"Now a teacher," she said, "must know about . . ." She pointed to the sides of her head.

The class hesitated. "Head?" one ventured. Another shouted "Hair!" then looked perplexed. From the class reaction, it seemed many weren't sure what to say.

The kindergarten teacher looked startled. "No!" she roared. "Not head! Not hair! The brain! We are teachers and we must know about the BRAIN!" For example, she described, by knowing how the brain forms memories, teachers understand why focusing on building connections to what is known instead of drilling students on isolated facts is important. It secures new information in memory and makes it useful beyond tomorrow's test.

Of course, she was right. The **brain** and the mind are fascinating subjects to anyone attracted to how we think and learn and act. A number of national and international reports for teachers affirm that neuroscience now has advanced to the point that it is possible to think critically about discoveries important to educators (National Research Council, 2000). An international collaboration of 34 countries, for instance, went as far as to describe incorporating brain science into teaching as an ethical imperative (See CORE 1a; Organisation for Economic Co-operation and Development [OECD], 2007).

Today's educators are in a unique position. They are the first in their ages-old profession in a position to put an awareness of cognitive neuroscience to use in their classrooms and in the

Short Course: Brain Concepts

A
Attention—focusing on certain types of information or stimuli in the environment in preference to others.

B
Brain—biological organ that performs key functions such as to receive, organize, process, direct, store, use, and distribute information and thinking.
Brain-based concepts for educators—providing information on how the brain and mind work as understood by research fields exploring these areas.

I
Instructional design—an extended process of analysis, synthesis, and evaluation in order to produce an effective instructional system.

L
Learning—relatively lasting change in our thinking, attitudes, actions, or behavior as a result of experience.

M
Metacognition—processes involved with monitoring, reflecting on, regulating, and controlling our own thinking.

N
Neuromyth—when a facet of brain science or cognitive psychology research is widely misunderstood or oversimplified to the point of misuse.

P
Plasticity—the ability of the physical structure of the brain to change.

design of educational policy. By bringing an awareness of how the brain learns into their practice, students and teachers both benefit.

The field of brain science is growing rapidly. Every year the amount of information about the brain and how it functions is expanding so quickly that no one individual could possibly keep up. Yet much of this emerging information and new insight is incredibly important for teachers to understand.

Massachusetts Institute of Technology neuroscientists, for example, are using real-time brain imaging to help distinguish brains that are ready to learn from those that are not (Yoo et al., 2012) in recollections of visual scenes. Their research is beginning to identify the conditions that make a brain ready to process and remember information. Just as important, at the University of California, Berkeley, and other institutions, research has begun to identify what interferes with the ability to learn. The field is also bringing important new insights into the roles that sleep and nutrition play in learning that go much farther than simply coming to class well rested and not hungry. Brain science has also illuminated the importance that even brief interactions with others can immeasurably increase cognitive understanding. These and a host of other findings have great potential in assisting teachers and benefiting students.

So, the question has become not so much *whether* educators should learn about brain science, but rather *what* to learn. What, in such a vast and growing field of brain science, would be most valuable for educators to know now to support a lifetime of learning in this emerging field?

To that end, this text identifies a core base of knowledge about brain science for teachers and all education professionals. This foundation, called the *CORE,* is introduced in this chapter and is cross-referenced and expanded throughout the chapters that follow. The CORE is organized into seven guiding principles of brain science for educators. These principles are based on research identifying what has been proposed for teacher practice in the United States and elsewhere in the world by both the teaching community and neuroscientists.

The Power of Three: Three Learning Sciences Are Better Than One

Neuroscience. Cognitive Psychology. Educational Research. Each of these disciplines adds to our understanding of how we learn, each in their unique and worthy way (see Figure 1.1). Where neuroscience looks to the physical functioning of the brain, cognitive psychologists typically study processes such as **attention**, language, memory, and thinking through laboratory experiment and observations of behavior. Educational research often focuses on classroom studies or student and teacher experiences to evaluate real-world practices.

Each field is rightly called a *learning science*. Each can offer invaluable insight into effective learning and human cognition. Until recently, though, as individual disciplines developed and brought new insights to the forefront, the fields and findings often remained segregated and were not able to inform or amplify the work of one another. That is changing

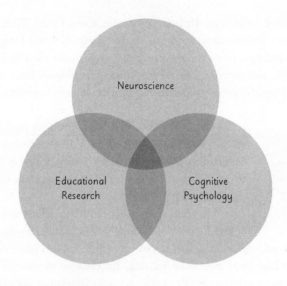

FIGURE 1.1

Three Learning Sciences

quickly, much to the benefit of teachers in classrooms and education policy makers. However, this means pertinent material crossing the three areas is often not available in one spot. As one instructor in human learning and cognition described, "I have to pull [together] so many sources and materials for my course because all of the information cannot be found in just one text, which is why I think the concept of this book is a great one."

In this text, we take a strong stance on use of the term **brain-based concepts for educators**. Some instructors prefer to avoid the term, believing it lacks clarity or can be misused (see the section titled "A Word about Neuromyths" on page 7). As one instructor described it, some people who are interested in the link between neuroscience and education have viewed the term *brain-based* in the past as a trick or device. Here, we think it is important to strongly embrace the term, and to give it a new meaning. This is in order to underscore the importance of scientific literacy for teachers. We define *brain-based* as invoking an understanding of how the brain and mind basically work, according to how this is understood by the research fields exploring an area.

It is true that some experts argue that everything related to learning involves the brain, and therefore is brain-based regardless of approach. Others do not see understanding even the basics of brain science as involved in any fundamental way in how a teacher should approach instruction. We believe brain, mind, and behavior are all vital to learning and education, so the brain-based principles presented in this chapter and throughout the book are those of understanding how the brain and mind work, and relating this to what we know of behavior and learning in the classroom.

More and more brain research is collaborating across fields. Take, for example, the work of the Human Connectome Project (Massachusetts General Hospital HC Project, 2013), aimed at building a first-ever baseline database that can cross-link with personality traits, cognitive skills, and genetics. The project is mapping long-distance neural pathways in the brains of 1,200 healthy people who are also participating in cognitive tests and psychological interviews.

RESOURCE

K–12 teachers can use with students: Gorman, 2014. (See the Citations list at the end of this chapter.)

One segment of this $30 million project funded by the U.S. National Institutes of Health[1] is focusing on the ways that differences in the individuals' brains are related to the way they think by watching in real time how certain memory tasks activate various parts of the brain.

It is the *intersection* of the knowledge and insights from the three fields of neuroscience, cognitive psychology, and educational research that underpins this text: the power of three. When taken together, the fields begin to inform at least some aspects of learning. An essential premise of this text, then, is that these research areas can now begin to offer a powerful triad of understanding. In other words, three mind sciences are better than one.

The Power of Three: A Focus on Reading

Dr. Michael Posner, a cognitive psychologist who has worked extensively with brain research teams for many years, often uses the long-standing challenge of how to teach reading to illustrate the value of bringing learning and the brain sciences together.

Although there is debate on how best to teach reading, there is complete agreement that it is a fundamental skill. Reading has been shown to be critical to discovering new knowledge, expanding creativity, and establishing strong preparedness for career and college readiness. Moreover, as researcher and author Stanislaus Dehaene (2009) describes in his book, *Reading in the Brain: The New Science of How We Read,* neuroscience findings are showing that learning to read effectively may itself induce large cognitive gains. Through studies of readers and nonreaders, Dehaene discusses differences seen in brain organization, some of which may come about through the process of learning to read itself.

According to Posner, there has been a controversy about reading in education for many years. In an interview in his office at the University of Oregon, he describes the controversy as a puzzle for educators: Should reading be taught through approaches to phonics (sound

---

[1] The bibliography at the end of the chapter is organized into two sections to facilitate use of this material. "Citations" lists the research and scientific references; "Resources" lists materials that teachers may want to use more directly in the classroom. Of course, for educators working with pre-service and in-service teachers, either may be appropriate depending on the need and use.

units), as many educators have found effective, or should instruction focus more on the written word, another common approach, which involves the visual processing of symbols?

Posner points out that brain studies now provide vital data and useful findings to answer that important question. Through brain scans, Posner states, we now know that effective reading activates two distinct areas in the brain: One handles visual word forms and one involves phonological processing (the organizing of sounds that gives meaning to language). Indeed, children who were having difficulty learning to read often were found to fail to activate one or the other of these critical areas in the way that successful adult readers do. Although this doesn't answer a separate question about contrasting the use of phonics to a "whole-child" approach that puts the emphasis on meaning, it does glean insights about decoding in the reading process.

Part of the brain chunks letters into a unit, Posner says, whereas another area is involved in auditory sound and is particularly susceptible to phonics training, sometimes responding in as little as a few weeks. Posner maintains that these two parts of the brain have to work together to maximize reading success. He notes that the question on how to teach reading has been an issue of debate for years, but this new research makes clear that there are two parts of the brain—one for each reading function. The finding, Posner adds, is nothing short of fascinating.

A Word about Neuromyths

One unfortunate outcome of the growing interest in brain-based education and the appeal of using brain science to improve learning is that it can be easily subject to misunderstanding, oversimplification, and misuse. There is even a name for this; it is called **neuromyth**.

So much of what is published and said is useless, described Kurt Fischer, founding president of the International Mind, Brain, and Education (MBE) Society and director of the MBE graduate program at Harvard University. According to Fischer (cited in Bernard, 2010), what is described as brain-based learning is not based in neuroscience at all.

RESOURCE

K–12 teachers can use with students: Bernard, 2010. (See the Citations list at the end of this chapter.)

Typical of the neuromyths that educators and scientists try to debunk is the incorrect notion that the brain is a static organ fully developed at a young age and unchanging over a lifetime. Another myth is that some people are left-brained and others right-brained and so must be taught differently. Also, it is a common misunderstanding that we use only 10 percent of our brain capacity, even to the extent that it was the basis for the popular 2014 sci-fi film, *Lucy*. We won't dwell on the subject here (it is addressed again in Chapter 8), but we raise it now to bring awareness of this ongoing discussion within the educational community and to highlight the value of having a grounding in the science and literature of educational neuroscience.

neuroscience. Instructors describe that neuromyths are one of the hardest issues for teachers to accept. To give up old notions and move along to more current understandings is difficult in any profession.

Organization of This Book

We start in this chapter by laying out the foundation of knowledge we are calling the CORE that was developed especially for teachers and other educators. Using a technique called *saturation evaluation* to explore a wealth of research-based resources, University of Oregon researchers, along with the assistance of Columbia University researchers, identified what could reasonably constitute essential understandings of brain science for teachers, as described in Appendix A, "Technical Report on Development of the CORE." This ranges from the basics of anatomy and the function of neurons to emerging research that may inform instructional design well into the future.

Throughout this text, information is presented in a way to capitalize on what learning science is telling us. Science tells us that by integrating new information with what's already known—but in a new or different context—we learn better. Thus, the CORE neuroscience and cognitive science ideas presented in this chapter are revisited in the later chapters through numerous teaching and learning stories.

Narrative accounts from educators, interviews with researchers, and examples drawn from classroom experiences are woven extensively throughout the chapters to provide that key element: relevance. The order in which topics are covered introduces concepts that build on each other. However, readers and instructors are encouraged to use the chapters in the order that best supports their background and needs. Going forward, each chapter will begin with a "Learning Points" introduction to "prime" the reader for what's to come and will conclude with a "Closing Scenario," an activity to summarize the material covered by putting the new knowledge to use to problem solve. All these approaches, as you will see, reflect teaching practices that educational research has shown to be effective and for which brain science provides evidence to show why it works.

By using research methods to examine leading resources concerning education and the learning sciences, common ground was identified and a core knowledge base emerged, called here the CORE. Because brain science tells us that knowledge is better mastered when organized according to principles and big ideas, the CORE is organized into the seven guiding principles abstracted from the research. Associated key information, from basic brain anatomy to complex cognitive systems, accompanies each principle, so the CORE provides teachers with information they may need in this fast-moving field.

The selection of facts, information, and theories that comprise the CORE is based on the survey and evaluation of 62 resources, ranging from scientific reports to book chapters and teacher guides. Five of these are important summary publications generating the outline of principles shared in this chapter; the rest are used to paint a picture in more detail in subsequent chapters.

The first five publications broadly identify a landscape of brain science relevant to educators. These represent the work of major scientific societies (Society for Neuroscience, 2008), international organizations that serve teachers and educators in many countries (OECD, 2007), and national scientific think tanks in the United States and United Kingdom. The U.S. National Research Council (2000) report, for instance, describes a revolution in the "study of the mind" that it says has important implications for education, while the U.K. Economic and Research Council (Howard-Jones et al., 2007) report discusses how knowledge of the brain is growing in power and relevance to areas as varied as economic and political behavior as well as education. A contribution also draws on some ideas for teachers about the theoretical and computer-based modeling of the brain and learning (Hawkins & Blakeslee, 2004). Together, these resources paint a picture of a core of information for educators, explored next through the seven principles and their associated Big Ideas.

The CORE addresses a number of questions, such as, If the brain is remarkably dynamic and built to change, what, then, drives that change? How does the brain judge relevance? What makes it remember some things and not others? Why and how does it make connections? Equally important, if the brain's job is to learn, what can interfere with the neural and cognitive activities essential to successful learning?

Research is starting to provide some answers. With the foundation of knowledge laid in this chapter and the basics of physical change (neural plasticity) presented in Chapter 2, we move into the heart of the educator's world. Chapters 3, 4, and 5 are devoted to the links between cognition and learning through instructional design, including workings of brain systems such as memory. This is followed in Chapter 6 by evolving research into the physical environment of the brain and body, including nutrition, exercise, and sleep. Emotion and attitude play major roles in brain function and are explored in Chapter 7, followed by properties of stress in Chapter 8. Chapter 9 explores what constitutes useful feedback and evidence, both essential to how the brain learns. Sensitive periods of brain development are discussed in Chapter 10. Finally, giving the reader additional practice with CORE ideas, Chapter 11 provides specific examples in subject-matter areas, and Chapter 12 closes with an action plan and what's on the horizon for educators.

Those who are not particularly confident in their science backgrounds may be reluctant to dive into the CORE at first, but if they will stick with it, they will quickly see a move into more familiar territory in subsequent chapters as their study continues. Neuroscience and cognitive psychology cannot tell an educator what she or he should do in the classroom or on the policy front, but these science and research-based fundamentals can provide valuable insight into how we learn—information we can use to improve how we teach. And this, in many ways, is where the hard work for educators begins.

Introducing Seven Guiding Principles

The CORE's seven guiding principles organize brain science concepts into manageable "chunks" for teachers and other educators. Each of the guiding principles is associated with key information called Big Ideas. They are presented in the "Framework of the CORE" section following this chapter and are explored in detail in each of the successive chapters. Each guiding principle describes *why* the Big Ideas of the CORE are important to educators. These Big Ideas are *what* teachers actually need to know to implement the principles. Here, the power-of-three connections among the learning sciences described in this chapter become evident through the principles themselves, which glean many insights from basic neuroscience but also from cognitive psychology and educational research.

As we will see through the following chapters, the information in the section called "Framework of the CORE: Seven Guiding Principles and Their Associated Big Ideas" is essentially an outline of key information from these fields. Each subsequent chapter explores the CORE material in more depth and ties the concepts wherever possible to what teachers do in classrooms.

▓|| Establishing a CORE

From a psychology perspective, **learning** is often defined as relatively lasting change in our thinking, attitudes, actions, or behavior as a result of experience. From education, this learning definition is often applied through schooling or study experiences, but educational research also acknowledges a vast variety of less formal opportunities by which we effectively learn. These include everything from interactions with parents, caregivers, and peers, to our relationships with the physical world, to learning resources we may tap, such as the Internet, books, films, and other stored repositories of knowledge and expression.

Neuroscience describes learning as ubiquitous and very much a defining aspect of the human experience—while we live, we learn. Profoundly, the sciences bring us a truly revolutionary insight, discussed in Chapter 3, that all learning involves actual biological change to the brain. Be it ever so small, learning influences us. We change as we learn.

Because there are varying views and ideas about what is helpful for teachers to know about the emerging understanding of the brain and how we learn, a plethora of suggestions have come from various experts, task forces, institutions, and governments. Much common ground can be seen across resources, and it is helpful to have a summarized picture. The research undertaken for this book was aimed at deriving such a depiction.

The approach taken began by scouring a 17-year span (from 1995 to 2012) of published books, reports, Web resources, and other references to capture the information and knowledge base that the many sources agree all teachers would find useful. The research, technically called *saturation evaluation,* also points out where sources disagree and where basic gaps remain that educators, psychologists, and scientists ponder. (See Appendix A, "Technical Report on Development of the CORE," and Appendix B, "Summary of Sampled Resources of the CORE," for an in-depth report on the approach, methodology, outcomes, and resources.)

Laying Out the CORE

Guiding Principle 1
Teachers play a large role in school experiences that literally shape the brain in the school-age years through the biological properties of neural plasticity.

The first guiding principle of brain science for teachers—that experience and learning directly influence the structure of the brain—is simple but has profound implications.

Until recently, the brain has been slow to give up its secrets. Due in large part to advances in brain scanning and imaging technology, neuroscientists today are increasingly able to actually record inside and observe what happens in the brain. They are able to identify moments of actual engagement—register when some aspects of learning happen—and map where in the brain activity occurs. They can also identify what kinds of stimulation produce long-lasting changes to the brain. With these tools and the wealth of new knowledge they bring, scientists have an ever-growing understanding of complex brain function and networks. Advanced brain-scanning techniques that allow researchers to watch the brain at work are giving rise to a growth in research programs. Some research focuses on the neuroscience of learning; that is, the kind of learning that happens in classrooms, with parents and friends, in front of television and computer screens, and in the exploration of daily life.

One of the first and most important concepts addressed in this text is that the brain is not a static mass of wrinkled gray tissue. In fact, it is highly dynamic, altered in clear physical ways by what it experiences and how it learns. Although recent studies indicate that the ability of the brain to change is life long, much of this reshaping is particularly active in childhood and teen years. Teachers, then, are not simply teaching a curriculum. Along with parents, peers, and caregivers, they play an instrumental role in shaping and changing the brain itself. The changes involved in learning generate long-lasting rearrangement of the brain, as is described in detail in Chapter 2.

The extent to which the physical brain reconfigures and rebuilds itself over time is seen by many as the most important and most exciting topic to emerge for teachers from brain research in recent years. This action is particularly evident in the early and school-age years. The ability of the physical structure of the brain to change is called **plasticity**. It takes place, at least in part, to help optimize what the brain finds itself called on to do. Change can come about via several avenues, such as rerouting brain circuits, eliminating certain neural connections, and adding new ones. The key message of this guiding principle is that substantial change happens in the brain. Our experiences and all that we learn are now known to reconfigure our brains in fundamental ways.

To support this principle, the CORE resources indicate that teachers should understand the ways in which plasticity works. The Big Ideas of neural plasticity are presented in the "Framework of the CORE" section under Guiding Principle 1 and are explored in detail in Chapter 2.

Guiding Principle 2
Mastering the learning sciences empowers teachers to identify, advocate for, and support decisions that impact their professional lives and success for students.

The second guiding principle of the CORE deeply encourages scientific literacy for teachers. Simply put, if you reshape or change brains, as described in Principle 1, then you need to know how the brain changes. The Big Ideas for this principle describe selective but fundamental concepts of brain anatomy and structure. Without this information, teachers will have a harder time understanding and applying upcoming principles. By knowing how the brain works, teachers will increase their effectiveness and their ability to support students, empowering them with the resources they need to argue for and support decisions for curriculum and assessments (Pratt, 2002, p. xiv).

The goal is *not* to turn teachers into technicians. Teachers do not need to know everything about the brain, but they will certainly benefit from knowing some key concepts. Therefore, this guiding principle is specifically written to provide teachers with essential resources—information and knowledge that will allow them to make and support decisions in the classroom. Educators update the deep foundation of pedagogical strategies as they incorporate knowledge about the brain. This impacts their own practice and that of others around them.

Such literacy is needed by all educators these days, not just science teachers. With the fast pace of the Information Age, teachers need to be able to think their way through why certain strategies and approaches are more effective than others in their teaching. In "Framework of the CORE," CORE Figure 2 identifies brain anatomy related to this guiding principle. Teachers should remember in encountering these anatomical ideas, which can get complex and include much new vocabulary, that the concepts need not be memorized. Rather, they should be understood more generally as Big Ideas of brain structure and function. These Big Ideas of brain anatomy and structure (CORE Figure 1) are presented in the "Framework of the CORE" section under Guiding Principle 2 and explored in detail beginning in Chapter 2. They are integrated into each subsequent chapter of this text as they become relevant to the educational information presented.

Guiding Principle 3
How we learn dramatically affects what knowledge we can actually use.
Instructional approaches such as priming, elaboration, extension, and knowledge
integration are key to learning outcomes. In teacher talk, this is about changing
instructional design.

The third guiding principle is about building a functional system of knowledge and skills for students. This principle is focused on the *how* of learning. Research shows that the way we go about learning fundamentally affects what we can do with our knowledge. In everything from "learning to see," which helps us recognize meaningful information, to "transfer," which is applying knowledge in a new context, the *how* of our learning process is key to whether we have actually learned effectively. The issue here is what we can do with what we know.

For instance, our brain's *executive function* is defined as how we control cognitive processes such as planning, attention, selection, rehearsal, and monitoring of information retrieved from memory. Some brain areas become active when we engage with a wide variety of tasks and have a role in the allocation of attention and other brain resources.

Instructional design is an extended process of analysis, synthesis, and evaluation in order to produce an effective instructional system. Emerging perspectives from the learning sciences can help inform this design process; they do not replace it nor can they encompass it. In this guiding principle, cognitive science interacts with fundamental brain ideas. Teaching practices that build on approaches described here have been shown to support brain function. Each of these concepts is an important idea for teachers to understand and employ in appropriate contexts. Cognition and instructional design are presented in the CORE section under Guiding Principle 3 and addressed in more detail beginning in Chapter 3.

Guiding Principle 4
What we learn endures because of memory strongly influenced through persistence
practices that reinforce recall of information and experiences.

The fourth guiding principle is about memory, or *where and how* learning is stored in the brain. Without the brain's memory systems, we would neither be able to acquire new information nor remember past learning. Storing, accessing, and retrieving what we know makes learning work well on our behalf. In terms of what becomes modified in the brain when teachers instruct, research has shown that a reinforced neural pathway is the "fruit" of learning. In other words, some brain processing becomes easier and faster when we learn.

A major complaint of teachers is the limited time that learning may persist, or last, in many cases. Learners work hard to understand. If what students know and are able to do doesn't last, the frustration builds. The high cost-to-benefit ratio when understanding does not persist undermines the efforts of both teachers and learners.

Research shows that teachers can help extend how long memories last, known as the *memory trace,* for students. For instance, intriguing brain research in the area of "forgetting functions," or mathematical descriptions of what we remember, helps tell us how long we recall experiences and under what conditions. Different approaches to learning can have different "decay" rates—the lengths of time when the information remains stored and accessible in the brain. Therefore, the way we go about learning may be key to whether we will have knowledge available when the need arises to put our understanding into action. Encoding strategies and memory are presented in the "Framework of the CORE" section under Guiding Principle 4 and addressed in more detail in Chapters 4 and 5.

Guiding Principle 5
When we effectively learn is influenced by important brain-related factors including emotions. What we filter out matters as much as what we process.

The fifth guiding principle focuses on *when* we learn. To the astonishment of many teachers, the brain itself has a variety of sophisticated filtering systems and emotional pathways in place that are critical for how we learn. These filters appear to allow us to manage the load of information we receive and the stimuli coming at us from all directions. They help us zero-in on important patterns around us, as identified by the brain.

As significant as they are to making our brain successful, the filtering systems and emotional pathways can also strongly impede school learning if not well addressed by teachers. Perceived relevance, for instance, can be a strong motivator to the human cognitive system for successful learning. Conversely, its absence can be a major barrier to learning. Stress also enters into the picture of how the brain functions.

A useful lesson for teachers regarding Guiding Principle 5 is that teacher practices must not only establish pathways to learning, as addressed in Guiding Principles 1 through 4, but must also lower barriers that are a natural, respectable, and important part of human brain function, without which we would not have our high-functioning cognitive capacity. Being aware of the barriers helps us avoid stumbling into them. Emotion and attitude in the brain are presented in the "Framework of the CORE" section under Guiding Principle 5 and addressed in more detail in Chapter 7.

Guiding Principle 6
Physical conditions under which we learn best include aspects of sleep, exercise, and nutrition, and may encompass certain sensitive periods, or times during brain development that are particularly well suited to learning certain types of skills and knowledge.

The sixth guiding principle addresses a range of physical conditions under which we learn best. Here, the entire body's preparedness for learning is important. Actions that support learning include adequate sleep, good nutrition, and sufficient physical exercise. Stress enters into the picture as well. In addition, research shows that for some types of skills and knowledge acquisition, the human brain may have built-in cycles, or "sensitive periods," when more effective learning is taking place. These can be age-related and involve natural developmental processes, although much is yet to be understood about such phases.

Although quite different in nature, being aware of how the brain functions in these aspects of physical preparedness can help teachers more readily identify needs for learners. Nutrition is widely accepted by teachers as impacting how students learn. Perhaps less well understood is the role of exercise, which supplies oxygen to the brain and keeps systems on which the brain depends running and in good order. Growing evidence shows that sleep seems to play unique roles in brain development and in the consolidation of knowledge. Stress is a complex factor, depending on types as well as how much and long-lasting the stress is not only for the learner but also for the teacher.

Sensitive periods are perhaps the most attention-grabbing and the most controversial CORE topic of Guiding Principle 6 for teachers. Sometimes called *critical* periods (though there is a debate about that, too), these are described as times in an individual's development when the brain is being found particularly well-suited to learning specific skills. Basically, scientists are finding that different parts of the brain may be ready to learn at different times, and these times may be systematically somewhat age-related. Sensitive periods have been found in vision, sensory enrichment, language, motor, and emotional development.

Differing opinions exist on whether sensitive-period research is ready at this time to be used by educators. However, there is consensus that teachers should be aware of this aspect of human learning, and should be ready to consider pertinent questions as new research arises. Chapter 6 addresses nutrition and powering the body; exercise, oxygenation, and conditioning; and sleep. Stress is addressed in Chapter 8 and sensitive periods are the topic of Chapter 10.

Guiding Principle 7
The brain is a remarkable pattern-capturing mechanism that regulates the learning process through feedback, including what teachers provide in a variety of forms to effectively support metacognition, the learner's ability to regulate, or shape, his or her own learning.

The seventh guiding principle involves how the brain regulates the learning process by feedback and evidence. This can come in a variety of forms. From the physical ("Ouch! That hurt") to the social ("Wow, all my friends are getting tattoos, so I guess I'd better do it, too"), the brain is constantly searching for decisions to act on in the world around us. Teachers are an important part of that feedback cycle.

Neuroscience research shows that the human brain is an amazing pattern-capturing mechanism. Patterns are treated as evidence by the brain. Feedback allows the brain to tailor how it responds to evidence. In learning situations, depriving the brain of sufficient evidence in the form of feedback strips away one of its most powerful learning tools—**metacognition**. This is the power to regulate our own learning.

Research shows that learners need to know what the goals of the learning are, where they stand on the goals, and how to close the difference between the goal and what they know. This fits the view of the brain as mining information from the world around it. In this principle, we include the concept of neuromyths, or ideas about the brain that may be misconstrued or not well supported by evidence. Thus, feedback and evidence in the brain are the focus of Chapter 9.

Succeeding in the 21st Century

One goal of this book is to provide a base of useful knowledge. Another goal is in part inspirational: to inspire teachers to learn more about how the brain works and to examine whether they see utility in doing so. Utility, of course, means bringing added value. Asking educators to understand how the brain works in the absence of a clear understanding of *why* is an example of poor attention to the modern understandings of brain science: the importance to the brain of relevance. Therefore, the intentions of this text are to be both practical and relevant throughout. By using scientific findings to underpin practices, we hope to provide teachers a better understanding of why some practices work and some fail, or do not achieve the intended result. Providing a scientific basis to support practical and intuitive knowledge of teaching can help decision making and support additional grounds to bring support around the approaches selected.

Although the workings of the brain are far from being fully understood, we have learned a great deal of useful information since the time when an 18th-century Japanese artist depicted a man's brain as a tangle of noodles situated in a head-shaped bowl. Today, for instance, we know that we pay attention to new information and encode it in memory best when it is presented in a way that is meaningful to us, as first described in Chapter 2. This key concept—that a perception of relevance is essential to effectively retain, integrate, and transfer new knowledge to cognition—shows up again and again in learning science (National Research Council, 2003; Schunk, 2003).

From kindergarten teachers to post-secondary educators, encouraging the educational community to have a serious conversation about engaging with brain-based findings is important. So much progress in understanding human cognition is being made today that a 21st-century awareness of how neuroscience fundamentals intersect with well-studied teaching practices will surely become a part of education's future.

A former teacher and school principal wrote in an article for educators that he believes the teaching profession has included some of the first societal leaders to put neurobiology to use (Sitze, 2012). He described that even though there has been some disagreement on particulars, the profession generally embraces the concept of the educational usefulness of neurobiology. For him, "learning" has become a metaphor for something larger about the idea of "change" within human consciousness. Helping educators gain new perspectives on how people change—for instance, understanding how new language is formed—might improve how they educate. Knowing what engenders teens' self-esteem or builds motivation in young children might give teachers more understanding of change related to rich and rewarding environments. Therefore, Sitze says, teachers probably already know more than what they think they do—but they may need to think of knowledge in new ways. And so, a fundamental principle here is *change*. Some educators, excited by the possibilities, are already bringing the power of the learning sciences into their schools.

Bringing Cognitive Science into the Classroom

After more than 20 years in the classroom, Tina K. Lagdamen returned to her teaching roots in San Francisco. A lot had changed since her rookie year as a second-grade teacher in the Bayview district, one of San Francisco's most economically disadvantaged areas. For one thing, Lagdamen is a principal in charge of a 700-student school in another part of the city. For another, her passion for teaching is now amplified by a passion for neurobiology and the science of learning.

Lagdamen says that it was her early experience in the classroom that triggered her interest in how to use the science of cognition to make learning more useful to her students. "I had been teaching for a while. I was about 4 or 5 years into my teaching when we were having all these trainings and reading all these books about how kids learn. But then you talked to people and [they] didn't know how kids learn," she explains in an interview.

"With my own students I kept thinking there was something missing. I knew I was a good teacher, but [the students] were not getting it. The way I was teaching, it was just superficial knowledge; it wasn't learning. They were regurgitating a lot but I wanted to know, How can I have it so that they retain the information and they are able to transfer it?"

Langdamen enrolled at San Francisco State University where she designed her own master's program, combining studies in the departments of education and psychology to focus on metacognition and how it can improve reading comprehension. "That's how I got into the cognitive sciences. It was just like, Wow. Why didn't I get this in my teaching credential program?" she recalls.

Soon, her new understanding of cognitive science began to change how she taught. "In terms of practice, it changed my lesson design, the pedagogy. It just turned it upside down. I understood pedagogical content knowledge. This was huge—revolutionary. This is what teachers ought to be doing."

Asked to give an example, Lagdamen elaborates: "The shift in my practice came from understanding how the brain retains information and creates mental models. The brain likes parts-to-whole thinking. The brain loves metaphors. If you teach that way, the information is retained longer, or retained in permanent memory.

"Say the learning outcome is teaching children how to write summaries. Before this I would say, 'Let's read *Charlotte's Web* and let's write a summary of the story.' And, if the child gave me what happened in the story, I accepted that. That's the pedagogy I got from my methods class and that's what I used. Of course, when it was time for them to summarize in another setting, say social studies, they weren't able to transfer that.

"Now, in introducing how to write a summary, instead of just saying, 'OK, today I am going to teach you to write a summary,' I will take the summary and present it as a parts-to-whole thinking lesson. There are different parts to a summary. First is the title of the book. Second is the author. Third are the important events in the story, which includes the plot. Another part is the author's purpose: Did the author write the text to inform, entertain, or explain? Now the student can easily write the topic sentence of his or her summary. For example, '*Charlotte's Web* by E. B. White describes a friendship between Charlotte and Wilbur.' That's important because that tells me the child understands the main idea in writing his or her summary.

"If students understand all the parts of a summary, then when it comes down to revising, I can sit down with a student in the first draft and I can say, 'You have this part and you have this, but something is missing.' And the child can reply, 'Oh, I'm missing the important events.' It helps in the child's thinking.

"It is the thinking part that I did not get in my teaching credential program. Yes, I was trying to teach how to write an effective summary but what I have learned since is really more about teaching students to think so they are able to retain and transfer the skill."

Lagdamen says she is optimistic that an understanding of brain-based learning will become an important part of teacher training in the near future.

"Most of the teachers I meet are wonderful teachers and they are always looking to find a way to improve their practice, but most of them did not receive training in cognitive science. In all the literature (about California's teaching standards) the focus is on highly trained teachers. They are not highly trained, I believe, unless they have had cognitive development and science. This is because cognitive science to teachers is like anatomy to doctors. We have been operating without this. Would you go to your doctor if you knew your doctor had not had Anatomy 101 and biology? So cognitive science, psychology, and neuroscience—those are our anatomy and biology."

Students too, she says, benefit enormously when they are taught about how their brains work. "I have a brain book and it's all torn up because I used it for years. It has pictures of the brain. I would show it to my students when I gave my introduction at the beginning of the year. I would show it to the parents, too. I'd show them the anatomy of the brain and which parts of the brain retain memory. I'd show them the front of the brain, and what part of the brain controls their senses, and when you are reading which part is activating. They were fascinated. I introduced them to the brain and I asked them, 'Did you know that your brain grows every day? . . . Reading, mathematics, playing music—all this helps your brain grow.'

Brain Imaging

Seeing Is Believing

Improvements in technology that allow scientists to see what's happening inside a living brain are contributing to an ever-growing understanding of how the brain works and ushering in groundbreaking research into memory, cognition, and many other areas. Increasingly, neuroimaging is going beyond identifying where activity is occurring in the brain to addressing questions about what the observed activity reflects.

Neuroimaging is comprised of two broad categories: structural imaging and functional imaging. *Structural imaging* offers static views of the brain to identify lesions or damage, or to monitor changes in brain structure over time. *Functional imaging* provides information on brain activity at a given time or during a specific performance. For instance, in research on autistic spectrum disorder over the last three decades (Salimpoor, 2003), two structural and six functional techniques are described (see Figure 1.2). The lesson for teachers is that depending on the technology used, imaging can directly or indirectly capture structure or activity.

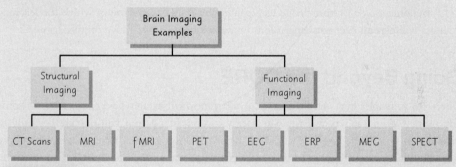

FIGURE 1.2

Examples of Brain Imaging Techniques

- Computerized tomography (CT scan) creates cross-sectional images of the body using X-rays and a computer. It launched the era of advanced brain imaging in the 1970s.
- Magnetic resonance imaging (MRI) is used for both diagnostic and research studies. Entirely noninvasive, it can obtain views of the brain from any angle and can generate images that make selected areas of the brain stand out in sharp details.
- Functional MRI (fMRI) is used to measure real-time brain activity. It is considered the most informative technique for monitoring the brain at work. Because it employs signals that are intrinsic to the brain (as opposed to the use of isotopes and radioactive probes), it allows for repeated observations of the same individual.

- Positron Emission Tomography (PET) maps functional processes, such as blood flow in the brain, by tracking isotopes introduced into pathways.
- Electroencephalography (EEG) is a neurological test that uses an electronic monitoring device to measure and record electrical activity.
- Many other types of brain imaging are also available, including Event-Related Potentials (ERP), Magnetoencephalography (MEG), and Single Photon Emission Computed Tomography (SPECT).

"It excites students because it gives them hope. I would ask them, 'Does everybody here have a brain? Check your head? Yes? As long as you have a brain, you can learn. You might not learn as fast as some others but that's what the brain does. It learns. That's its job. So as long as you have a brain, you can learn.' You can see their eyes popping. They're thinking, 'OK. I've have a hard time in my last grade. I've been struggling, but in this class the teacher is saying, I can learn.'"

It was great to see her students get excited about learning, Lagdamen adds. But she says the real payoff for bringing an understanding of cognitive science into her teaching practice was when she began to see students retain knowledge in a way that allowed them to transfer it from one setting and use it in another. When that happened, she believed they had truly learned.

Building a base of knowledge to prepare educators for a future in which the learning sciences will play an ever-growing role is where we begin as we move on to Chapter 2.

Going Beyond the CORE

The seven principles here and their associated Big Ideas will be new and challenging for some educators. Other teachers will find them easy to understand, and will quickly be ready to extend their knowledge beyond the CORE as they go through each of the upcoming chapters.

In this text, however, we confine our material to stay within the CORE. Our intention is to help establish a base of what every teacher should know, and to introduce a type of framework that might help the learning sciences understand what all teachers could be expected to know. This is not to imply by any means that nothing else is known or verified that might be interesting in the areas of neuroscience, cognitive psychology, or educational research.

Instructors may wish to supplement this material, and students might finish this text and be ready to start on more advanced work. We encourage this with one hesitation. College instructors describe how education students are generally drawn to neuroscience and cognitive psychology, and are eager to add this knowledge base to their understanding. Our focus groups with pre-service and beginning teachers suggest that they are only just starting to knit together their understanding of educational methodology. They have limited knowledge of student patterns of learning in their subject matter or grade-level areas. The focus group participants described how critical they found the CORE brain and cognition information to be at this point in their learning. They also believed they could manage the CORE with effective instructor support—but not much more. So, depending on the student audience, the CORE may be enough for starters.

Science and psychology students exploring this text may do so for the purpose of learning more about what the next generation of teachers will know. For noneducators, making meaning of all the educational terms and examples here can likely be difficult. So those who desire extension may supplement the CORE with original source material, whether in neuroscience, cognition, or educational research. We should all try to design instruction for the students with whom we are working.

Conclusion

What becomes apparent throughout the CORE principles is an important emerging forefront for teaching and learning. Educators should have an awareness of the topics here, and practice making the connection with their work. The CORE calls not for learning *about science* but for the practice *of it*. Teachers themselves are called on to practice making these connections, using their knowledge base and their areas of teaching and learning. They can do this every day as they ponder how their students learn, and what to do next, says cognitive scientist Michael Posner (see more in Chapter 11).

It may be important that teachers, armed with facts, can play the role of "neuromythbuster" from time to time, but teachers do not want to have to become brain scientists to do their jobs. Besides, it might not be terribly helpful anyway. If there is one thing all neuroscientists will say about the brain and learning, it is that they cannot tell an educator how to teach. As we said at the beginning of this chapter, the question is: What about the workings of the brain would be most valuable for educators to know? There are many valid opinions and approaches on this question. Teacher education programs in the learning sciences are now offered at a number of universities. With the "Power of Three" as a premise for this text, the focus here is on the *intersection* of the knowledge and insights from neuroscience, cognitive psychology, and educational research that can inform and enhance classroom learning.

When teaching her students about the differences in these learning sciences, one instructor described it as, "The students compare the type of data that each science studies." The instructor finds that the focus on the three sciences is important. Students need to know how each group builds new knowledge and brings it to the practitioner, and to understand that they are not in a competition. She helps students look at how the various research methods are involved and how they can contribute to understanding each other. This is discussed more in Chapter 3.

Dialogue is also called for so that the shared ideas can be advanced by reflection, reaction, and co-construction of knowledge. The United Kingdom's learning sciences report describes this as moving away from a one-way flow of information of neuroscience to education toward a two-way or larger collaboration. Knowledge of learning and of the brain feed each other. According to Ian Diamond, chief executive of the U.K. Economic and Social Research Council, this will result in new knowledge about both neuroscience and education, and improve learning outcomes.

Seven principles and their associated Big Ideas are more than enough to get a conversation started, but of course as the appendixes "Technical Report on Development of the CORE" and "Summary of Sampled Resources of the CORE" describe, there remain gaps in what educators would like to know. These include underrepresentation of some of the Big Ideas and less discussion in some areas than teachers would like. Partly, this is because much research about the brain is yet emerging. However, the upcoming chapters dive more deeply into many specific areas of the CORE. They present research findings, expert commentary, and narratives to illustrate the ideas presented, and to explore the emerging context for educators.

Resources

K–12 Teachers Can Use with Students

Bernard, S. (2010). Neuro myths: Separating fact and fiction in brain-based learning. *Edutopia.* http://www.edutopia.org/neuroscience-brain-based-learning-myth-busting

Geake, J. (2009). Neuroscience and neuromythologies in education: The ups and downs of an interdisciplinary research. *Faculty of the Professions: Bridging the Gap between Ideas and Doing Research, 4th Annual Postgraduate Research Conference.* http://www.une.edu.au/faculties/professions/Resources/confabstracts/jgeake.pdf

Gorman, J. (2014, Jan. 7). The brain in exquisite detail. *New York Times: Science Times,* pp. D1–D-3. Retrieved from http://www.nytimes.com/2014/01/07/science/the-brain-in-exquisite-detail.html?_r=0

References

Dehaene, S. (2009). Learning to read. In *Reading in the brain: The new science of how we read* (pp. 195–234). London: Penguin Books Ltd.

Hawkins, J., & Blakeslee, S. (2004). A new framework of intelligence *On intelligence* (pp. 85–105). New York: Times Books.

Howard-Jones, P., Pollard, A., Blakemore, S.-J., Rogers, P., Goswami, U., Butterworth, B., . . . Kaufmann, L. (2007). Neuroscience and education, issues and opportunities: A TLRP commentary. http://www.tlrp.org/pub/documents/Neuroscience Commentary FINAL.pdf

Massachusetts General Hospital HC Project. (2013). Human Connectome Project. *Laboratory of Neuro Imaging and Martinos Center for Biomedical Imaging.* http://www.humanconnectomeproject.org/

National Research Council. (2000). Mind and brain. *How people learn: Brain, mind, experience, and school, expanded edition* (pp. 114–128). Washington, DC: The National Academies Press.

National Research Council. (2003). The nature and conditions of engagement. In Committee on Increasing High School Students' Engagement and Motivation to Learn (Ed.), *Engaging schools: Fostering high school students' motivation to learn* (pp. 31–59). Washington, DC: The National Academies Press.

Organisation for Economic Co-operation and Development (OECD). (2007). Understanding the brain: The birth of a learning science. Paris: Author. doi:10.1787/9789264029132-en

Pratt, H. (2002). Introduction. In R. W. Bybee (Ed.), *Learning science and the science of learning.* Arlington, VA: NSTA Press.

Salimpoor, V. N. (2003). Advances in neuroimaging of autistic spectrum disorder and other developmental disabilities. *NADD Bulletin, 6*(3). http://thenadd.org/modal/bulletins/v6n6a3~.htm

Schunk, D. H. (2003). Information processing. *Learning theories: An educational perspective.* New York: Macmillan.

Sitze, B. Creating an appropriate 21st century education: Taking cognitive neuroscience beyond education. (2012, January). *Information Age Education Newsletter, 82,* 1–4.

Society for Neuroscience. (2008). *Brain facts: A primer on the brain and nervous system.* Washington, DC: Society for Neuroscience.

Yoo, J. J., Hinds, O., Ofen, N., Thompson, T. W., Whitfield-Gabrieli, S., Triantafyllou, C., & Gabrielia, J. (2012). When the brain is prepared to learn: Enhancing human learning using real-time fMRI. *NeuroImage, 59*(1), 846–852.

Framework
of the CORE

Seven **Guiding Principles** and Their Associated **Big Ideas**

This special section titled "Framework of the CORE" provides a convenient reference to the seven Guiding Principles introduced in Chapter 1. Each principle and related set of Big Ideas are referenced chapter by chapter.

How to Use This Framework

This material provides two useful tools as a *framework* for building understanding of brain science for educators. As we approach the next chapters, the framework provides a concise overview of the key concepts. Furthermore, all the ideas presented here are more fully explained in the chapters; each time a CORE concept is described, it is cross-referenced to a Big Idea.

For example, in Chapter 4 about memory, a line of text states, "One important concept teachers need to know is the comparison of people's memories for words with their memories for pictures of the same objects. **(See CORE 4g.)**" The reader, having been referred to CORE 4g, consults the Big Idea of CORE 4g. He or she reads:

Comparison of people's memories for words with their memories for pictures of the same objects often shows a superiority effect for pictures. Pictures are retained longer. Due to such findings, teachers should supply multiple ways to present information for all students. Zones in the brain selectively process different categories of information, with often different "forgetting functions" for how they are managed and retained.

The Big Ideas are the foundation of the Guiding Principle under discussion. The ideas we provide are the support of research and scientific discoveries espoused in the Guiding Principle. Scanning the Big Ideas, some teachers like to check off ideas they already understand. Others often underline concepts they want to know more about. In whichever way the Big Ideas of the seven guiding principles are used, readers should refer to the chapters for more vocabulary, definitions, and context, such as research and scientific discoveries in each area.

1. Guiding Principle: Teachers play a large role in school experiences that literally shape the brain in the school-age years, through the biological properties of neural plasticity.

Big Ideas

a. Neuroscience has advanced to the point where it is possible to think critically about how research information can be useful to educators. Educational neuroscience is an emerging area bringing together formal dialogue between neuroscience and education. This is a relatively new conversation to which both scientists and educators can contribute to advance learning. One question being asked is whether it is ethical in reflecting about education *not* to take into consideration what is known about the learning brain. Chapter 1, page 3.

b. The brain is central to learning. Learning changes the physical structure of the brain. Change occurs potentially at a variety of levels, from minute aspects of cellular change and connectivity, to large-scale changes involved with remapping due to injury or developmental processes. Chapter 2, page 41.

c. These structural changes impose new patterns in the brain that organize and reorganize it, thereby encoding learning. Chapter 2, page 41.

d. Such changes occur throughout life and are not solely the unfolding of preprogrammed genetics. Rather, the brain is a dynamic organ shaped to a great extent by experience. Neuroscience research confirms the important role that experience and learning plays in building the structure of the brain. Chapter 2, page 41.

e. Since biology is not destiny and genetic tendencies interact with experience to determine brain structure, every brain is unique. Stating whether nature or nurture is responsible for the process of brain development is overly simplistic, since it is a continuous interaction. For instance, most major diseases that have a genetic basis are strongly influenced by the environment. Heritability studies with identical twins, for instance, one type of evidence for genetic variation, show the probability of a given outcome is often not absolute given the same genes. Chapter 2, page 47.

f. One of the most important findings of brain science for education in recent years is that of "brain plasticity," the concept that the brain modifies its neural structure substantially over time. Forces of plasticity are at work extensively during the school-age years. Plasticity allows the brain to change to better cope with new circumstances. New neurons are not generated in most parts of the brain, only in a few areas, but change comes about through reconfiguring pathways between brain cells that transmit signals in the brain, and by adding and eliminating, or "pruning," connections in the brain. Intentional cell destruction also takes place, along with chemical change. Chapter 2, page 41.

g. At certain stages of life the neural connections grow extensively, but are later pared back (pruning) to create a more efficient system. Brain connections that are active and generating electrical currents are more likely to survive, while those with little or no activity are more likely to be lost. Thus, the brain is crafted by sculpting away less used connections, leading to permanent changes in the brain. Chapter 2, page 52.

2. Guiding Principle: Mastering the learning sciences empowers teachers to identify, advocate for, and support decisions that impact their professional lives and success for students.

Big Ideas

a. The primary organ involved in learning is the brain. Concepts about it need not be memorized by teachers but should be understood as Big Ideas of the brain. The first anatomical concept is that the brain is the seat of a human's mental functions, controlling not only vital functions such as breathing but also reasoning and learning. It can be pictured as a spongy, 3-pound mass of densely folded tissue. The brain and the spinal cord compose the central nervous system (CNS). Chapter 2, page 39.

b. The brain has three basic units: forebrain, midbrain, and hindbrain (see CORE Figure 1). The forebrain is the largest part of the human brain. It consists of the cerebrum and numerous structures hidden beneath it. The cerebrum is divided into two halves, each with four lobes: occipital, parietal, temporal, and frontal (see CORE Figure 2). The surface layers of these lobes comprise the cerebral cortex, believed critical to higher-level thought processes in humans. Chapter 2, page 40.

c. Brain cells come in primarily two kinds: nerve cells, also called neurons, and glial cells, providing support services. There are more glial cells than neurons in the brain, but the neuron will be the primary focus for teachers. Neurons specialize in communication. Chapter 2, page 42.

d. An electrical signal is propagated within a neuron and a chemical process usually transmits from one neuron to the next, across the synapse, or gap between cells. Chapter 2, page 43.

e. The neuron consists of four main parts. These need not be memorized but the overall flow should be understood. For neurons, (1) dendrites are tree-like structures that detect signals, (2) they connect to the main cell body which collects signal information, (3) a cord-like axon extends away from the cell body to deliver the accumulated signal, and (4) the axon ends in a section that can release chemicals to the next neuron. Chapter 2, page 45.

f. The electrical signal involves opening and closing of small channels through which charged substances move. When a signal is sent, or "fired," positively charged substances rush in across the membrane. This produces minute voltage changes, temporarily switching local internal conditions from negative to positive. The result is an "action potential"—a signal—that swiftly passes along the membrane. Chapter 2, page 44.

g. Through learning and more frequent triggering of certain sets of neurons, specific brain activity improves over time via physically changing the structure of the brain. This is one example of the process: "What gets fired gets wired." Chapter 2, page 46.

h. Myelin insulation of neurons makes signals operate faster and more consistently. Some diseases such as multiple sclerosis result from the myelin deteriorating. Chapter 2, page 45.

i. A neuron combines information in order to determine if a signal should be sent. This is like collecting a sample of information rather than relying on a single source. Some information collected may encourage a neuron to fire and some may inhibit it. Chapter 9, page 226.

j. As many as 80 to 100 billion neurons in the human brain are organized in extensively interconnected networks. If neurons were people, a single brain could populate the entire world more than 10 times over. A large and broadly distributed set of neural networks are used even during any routine task we undertake. Chapter 4, page 115.

k. Functions such as vision, hearing, and speech are mostly distributed in certain specific regions of the brain involved with these interconnected networks. Some regions are associated with more than one function. Chapter 11, page 261.

3. Guiding Principle: How we learn dramatically affects what knowledge we can actually use. Instructional approaches such as priming, elaboration, extension, and knowledge integration are key to learning outcomes. In teacher talk, this is about changing instructional design.

Big Ideas

a. Cognition is a set of processes for acquiring, retaining, and applying knowledge. Cognition relies on brain activity. Learning has been found better supported by certain cognitive strategies and environments of which teachers should be aware. Cognitive neuroscience links cognitive models with brain science findings. Chapter 3, page 71.

b. The brain's "executive function" is defined as how we control cognitive processes such as planning, attention, selection, rehearsal, and monitoring of information retrieved from memory. Some brain areas become active when we engage with a wide variety of tasks, and have a role in allocation of attention. Executive function is still developing in the teenage brain, including directing attention, planning future tasks, inhibiting inappropriate behavior, multitasking, and a variety of socially oriented tasks. Chapter 3, page 74.

c. Sufficient stimulation improves brain function. Animals raised in a complex environment may have a greater supply of blood and oxygen to the brain. More cells may support nerve function with nutrients and by removing waste (astrocytes). The weight and thickness of the cerebral cortex may alter, as well as the number of synapses per neuron. Such improvements result when animals are not raised in deprived environments. Chapter 3, page 80.

d. From a cognitive view, intelligence can be thought of as measured by the capacity to remember, predict, apply, and extend patterns in the brain. This is applicable in areas such as language, mathematics, physical properties, and social situations. Chapter 3, page 85.

e. Some learning approaches specifically support memory. These include cognitive elaboration and extension, which are intellectual efforts to discern relationships that add more detail to concepts or ideas. Effective questioning strategies, reflective activities, and problem solving employ elaboration and extension. These support understanding by creating and reinforcing memory and knowledge integration. Chapter 3, page 65.

f. Recognizing relevant features of a situation is one important dimension of learning. The brain creates information experiences through inferencing, category formation, and other ways of processing information. But first, recognition is necessary for segmenting the brain's perceptual field, or "learning how to see." Instructional designs that provide students with experiences to recognize meaningful patterns are helpful to the brain. Learning to recognize similarities and differences has been found to have some of the largest positive effects on student learning outcomes, across a number of subject matter areas. Chapter 5, page 124.

g. For effective learning, knowledge must be "conditionalized" in the brain; in other words, what is learned must be clearly associated with situations for which the new knowledge is useful. Using knowledge in multiple contexts and integrated across subjects is helpful. Relevant knowledge that is "inert," or not activated appropriately in neural processing, is one of the most frustrating challenges for teachers. Chapter 5, page 131.

h. Where supports of learning, or, in teacher talk "scaffolding," is used, teachers should "fade" or systematically reduce the need for it. Examples include environmental cues, hand signals, trigger words, challenges broken down by teachers into fine pieces, and external motivators. Revisiting knowledge to support proficiency helps. Understanding that is associated only with past conditions or teacher-pleasing behavior is not independent learning. Chapter 5, page 134.

i. Social interaction is a constituent component both for early development of cerebral structures and for normal development of cognitive functions and learning. Chapter 5, page 137.

4. Guiding Principle: What we learn endures because of memory strongly influenced through persistence practices that reinforce recall of information and experiences.

Big Ideas

a. Memory traces, or reinforced neural pathways, are an end result of learning. Chapter 4, page 101.

b. Memory is a cognitive process enabling past experiences to be remembered, both through acquiring new information (development phase of the trace, or path of neural prior activity) and remembering information (reactivation phase of the trace, or prior path of activation). The benefits of learning persist because of memory. Chapter 4, page 102.

c. Memory is neither a single entity nor occurring in a single part of the brain. However, the cerebral processes of perception, processing, and integration are facilitated by meaningful consolidation. Information presented first (prime) or last (recent) may be associated with more vivid remembering. Short instructional cycles assist new ideas to be either prime (e.g., the first 10 minutes) or recent (e.g., the last 10 minutes). Such approaches as small-group reflection or hands-on learning help connect primacy/recency cycles. Chapter 4, page 104.

d. Knowledge is better mastered if it is organized according to principles, or Big Ideas. However, approaches currently in place in curriculum design make it difficult to organize knowledge meaningfully for the brain, such as superficial coverage of facts, disconnected ideas, and too little time allocated to develop important organizing ideas. Chapter 4, page 105.

e. When a series of events are presented in a random fashion, people reorder them into sequences that make sense when they try to recall them. This is an example of re-arranging or "meaningfully chunking" information. During learning, memory processes make relational links to other information. Individuals gradually build on the basis of their own experience a set of "representations," or personal viewpoints, that translate the outside world cognitively into individual perceptions. Chapter 4, page 114.

f. Cognitive load involves the brain's executive control and capacity of working memory, and describes the "load" placed on it by a given task. Keeping cognitive load manageable during learning is important for mastery. Strategies can include cognitive supports such as graphic organizers, visuals, tables, glossaries, and tools. "External representations" offload some of the heavy demands on working memory in learning. Chapter 4, page 112.

g. Comparison of people's memories for words with their memories for pictures of the same objects often shows a superiority effect for pictures. Pictures are retained longer. Due to such findings, teachers should supply multiple ways to present information for all students. Zones in the brain selectively process different categories of information, with often different "forgetting functions" for how they are managed and retained. Chapter 4, page 98.

h. The more a memory trace, or prior neural pathway, is activated, the more "marked" it will become, and therefore the less vulnerable and likely to be forgotten. Analogical reasoning is a process by which the brain identifies generalizable patterns, or "schema" in the world, as the brain underscores the relevance of the information. Chapter 4, page 99.

i. Memory involves persistent structural change in the brain. This can be seen as an investment and commitment of brain resources. Teachers should know brain resources are limited for every individual. The brain filters what to remember and maintain based in part on conditions it perceives, consciously or unconsciously, such as relevance. Chapter 4, page 100.

j. Research shows there are at least two basic longer-term memory processes: declarative memory (memory for facts and events), and procedural or nondeclarative memory that involves mastering skills and other cognitive operations. Chapter 4, page 95.

5. Guiding Principle: When we effectively learn is influenced by important brain-related factors including emotions. What we filter out matters as much as what we process.

Big Ideas

a. Recent contributions of neuroscience are revealing the emotional dimension of learning. Emotions arise from cerebral processes and are necessary for the adaptation and regulation of human behavior. Chapter 7, page 168.

b. Different emotions correspond to distinct functional systems in the brain and have their own cerebral circuits often involving structures in the limbic system, known as the "seat of the emotions," as well as cortical structures, mainly the prefrontal cortex, which plays a prime role in regulating emotions. Chapter 7, page 173.

c. If a positively perceived emotion is associated with learning, it can facilitate success, whereas a negatively perceived emotion can be associated with failure. Retention and recall of an event or information in learning also can be changed by a strong emotional state, a special context, heightened motivation, or increased attention. Chapter 7, page 182.

d. The benefits of intrinsic motivation for learning are such that it is of paramount importance for research to orient its efforts at least in part toward this domain. Chapter 7, page 185.

e. The brain is not composed entirely of the cerebral cortex; many other structures are critical for learning, including the hippocampus (critical for consolidating new memories) and the amygdala (playing an important role in emotional responses). The amygdala appears to play a role in attaching emotional significance to otherwise neutral stimuli and events. Chapter 7, page 173.

f. Emotions are complex reactions that can be described in three components: a particular mental state, a physiological change, and an impulsion to act. Chapter 7, page 175.

g. Researchers have gained insight into the mechanism of molecular neuropharmacology, which provides a new understanding of the mechanisms of addiction and other ways brain function interacts with motivation. Chemicals called neurotransmitters and neuromodulators may excite or inhibit actions. The amount of chemical released and the number of receptors involved respond to experience, a cellular basis of plasticity. Chapter 7, page 172.

h. **Newly** discovered molecules responsible for guiding nervous system development **give scientists** a better understanding of youth. An important discovery is that so-called "second messengers" trigger biochemical communication with a cell after the action of neurotransmitters at the receptors. Direct effects of second messengers on the genetic material of cells may lead to long-term alternations in cell function and behavior. Chapter 7, page 172.

i. The prefrontal cortex matures late in human beings, concluding its primary development in the third decade of an individual's development. This indicates that the regulation of emotions and compensation for excesses of the limbic system occur relatively late in an individual's development. Chapter 7, page 172.

6. Guiding Principle: Physical conditions under which we learn best include aspects of sleep, exercise, and nutrition, and may encompass certain sensitive periods, or times during brain development that are particularly well suited to learning certain types of skills and knowledge.

Big Ideas

a. Like any other part of the human body, the brain functions best with healthy living, including proper nutrition and exercise. Also, environmental factors such as noise and ventilation can influence learning—for instance, by leading to encoding information less efficiently than might be done otherwise and by depriving the brain of needed oxygen. Chapter 6, page 143.

b. Sleep is a key aspect of brain function. During sleep, some of the processes involved in plasticity and consolidation of knowledge take place, consequently playing a pivotal role in learning, memory, retention, and effective knowledge integration. Chapter 6, page 144.

c. Stress interacts with both health and emotion. This occurs in complex ways, important for educators to understand both in terms of working with students, and for maintaining their own healthful functioning on the job. Chapter 8, page 193.

d. Different parts of the brain may be ready to learn at different times. Although often called "critical periods," a more accurate description may be "sensitive periods."

Scientists are verifying that certain periods in an individual's development seem particularly well-suited to learning certain skills. During these key times, the brain uses certain types of stimulations in order to establish and maintain long-term development of the structures and functions involved. At these stages, the individual's experience may become an overriding factor, responsible for profound changes. Chapter 10, page 234.

  e. The paring down of neural connections occurs extensively during some periods in postnatal life. After such a period, connections diminish in number and are less subject to change. The connections remaining are stronger, more reliable, and more precise. Chapter 10, page 236.

  f. If sensitive period learning does not occur during these "windows of opportunity," it does not always mean it cannot occur, but it may take more time and greater cognitive resources, and will often be less effective. Chapter 10, page 235.

  g. Examples of critical periods have been found in vision, sensory enrichment, as well as language, motor, and emotional development. It is expected that more areas may be discovered. A better understanding of these periods and when learning occurs is considered a crucial avenue for future brain research. Differing opinions currently exist on the readiness of sensitive period research to be used by educators. Consensus generally exists that teachers at least should be aware of this aspect of human learning. Chapter 10, page 236.

  h. Substantial brain development continues throughout the school-age years and into the early 20s. Synaptic pruning and myelination in adolescence are surprising new examples from neuroscience about the extent of important brain change for teens. Chapter 10, page 242.

  i. Brain injury or deprivation may have different effects at different periods of life. Severe declines in brain function are of interest to educators. These declines can occur through disease, injury, and disruption of healthy conditions. For adult educators working with older populations, aging is considered a normal process during which the brain can remain relatively healthy and full functioning. Neuroscientists currently believe most severe declines throughout the age span reflect disease, impaired development, or injury processes, and are not a normal part of aging. Chapter 10, page 244.

7. Guiding Principle: The brain is a remarkable pattern-capturing mechanism that regulates the learning process through feedback, including what teachers provide in a variety of forms to effectively support metacognition, the learner's ability to regulate, or shape, his or her own learning.

Big Ideas

  a. Human brains use stored memories to constantly make predictions about what we see, feel, and hear. Some scientists believe that prediction may be a primary function of the neocortex, and a foundation of intelligence. Chapter 9, page 216.

b. Feedback from a variety of sources is therefore a key component contributing to how our brains develop, and what learning gets reinforced. The brain treats feedback as a form of evidence. This is an important principle for teachers to understand as they go about instructional design and working with students. Chapter 9, page 216.

c. When a pattern comes into the brain that it had not associated in that context, a prediction is violated and attention is drawn to the error, or difference. Chapter 9, page 224.

d. Scientists have hypothesized that the brain makes low-level sensory predictions about what it expects to see, hear, and feel at every given moment, and it does so in parallel with many regions of the neocortex trying to predict what the next experience will be. Chapter 9, page 225.

e. Recognizing the limits of one's current knowledge and then taking steps to remedy the situation is extremely important for learners at all ages. This involves metacognition, the ability to monitor self-knowledge. Chapter 9, page 225.

f. Statistical techniques help us explore how the brain is borrowing information from past experiences to make new decisions, through prediction and feedback mechanisms. Chapter 9, page 226.

g. Imaging techniques such as magnetic resonance imaging (MRI) and positron emission tomography (PET scans) are a type of evidence that document how brain networks function, including providing information on how we focus attention, remember, feel, and learn. Imaging is often accomplished by detecting blood flow increases during brain activity. This shows where a function is occurring. Such imaging is done without surgery or other invasive techniques. Chapter 9, page 228.

h. Many brain predictions occur outside of our awareness. It isn't immediately apparent to us how pervasive and near continuous these unconscious predictions can be. Also, our brain can "smooth" and complete incoming data based on prior understanding (representations). Such unconscious operations of the brain potentially have substantial influence of which teachers should be aware. Chapter 9, page 227.

i. Neuromyths are ideas founded on misunderstandings, bad interpretations, or distortions of research results about the brain. Educators can avoid and correct popular yet erroneous ideas about the brain by having sufficient knowledge to understand new ideas. Post-secondary programs have a responsibility through preparing pre-service and in-service teachers for this rapidly emerging area of neuroethics. Chapter 9, page 213.

j. Examples of neuromyths including left and right hemispheres of the brain need to be instructed separately; this includes the neuromyth that people use only a small fraction of their brains. Chapter 9, page 214.

k. One way to address neuromyths is to highlight neuroscience research questions that may interest educators. This could be an important step toward defining an interdisciplinary area of collaborative research among fields of the learning sciences, such as education, psychology, and neuroscience, to the benefit of all. Chapter 9, page 215.

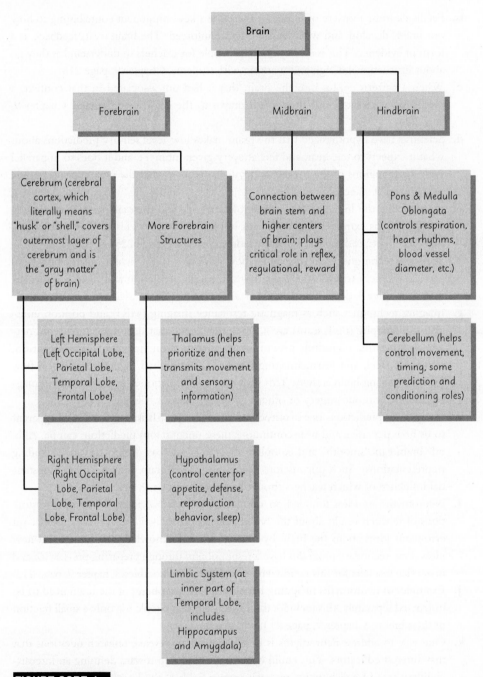

The Brain's Three Basic Units

Frontal lobe
regulates decision making, reasoning,
and planning; contributes to emotions,
problem solving, behaviors, and movement.

Parietal lobe
processes sensory
information such as taste,
touch, and heat or cold.

Occipital lobe
processes information
such as related to vision.

Temporal lobe
contributes to hearing,
language and speech,
and memory.

Cerebellum
contributes to movement,
balance, and coordination.

FIGURE CORE-2

The Brain

The frontal lobe regulates decision making, reasoning, and planning; contributes to emotions,
problem solving, behaviors, and movement.
The parietal lobe processes sensory information such as taste, touch, and heat or cold.
The occipital lobe processes information such as related to vision.
The temporal lobe contributes to hearing, language and speech, and memory.
The cerebellum contributes to movement, balance, and coordination.

Neural Plasticity

CORE Guiding Principle 1 is introduced in this chapter: Teachers play a large role for students in school experiences that literally help shape the brain. The chapter also presents concepts in Guiding Principle 2: Mastering the learning sciences helps empower teachers to identify, advocate for, and support decisions that impact their professional lives and success for students.

Learning Points

1. The brain is a dynamic system physically shaped by what it experiences. Change occurs over a lifetime and is not solely the unfolding of pre-programmed patterns. This is valuable information for teachers, directly related to the relevance of their work.

2. Learning imposes news patterns in the brain. The brain organizes and reorganizes, building on what is most useful. This encodes learning, making it possible to act on what we have learned.

3. Plasticity is the capacity of the nervous system to change substantially in structure and function. After birth, it is believed to be most active in a child's early and school-age years. Neuroscientists believe its purpose is to allow the brain to cope with new circumstances.

4. A common mechanism of plasticity is a process called *rewiring*. Rewiring has at least two overall types of elements aimed at reorganizing the brain into an efficient system. One, it strengthens the neural pathways that are most active and thus found to be most useful and, two, it prunes away unused or unneeded neural circuitry.

5. Changes involve long-lasting and often permanent rearrangement of the brain, thus each brain is unique.

6. The brain is comprised of distinct regions, each with its own primary functions but interconnected in important ways to create a highly dynamic system.

7. The human cerebral cortex plays a central role in learning. It and other areas of the brain govern such capacities as thinking, perceiving, focusing, and many of the higher-order information-processing functions of the brain.

8. Neurons are signaling cells in the brain. Each neuron is a single cell snaking out long thread-like fibers called *dendrites.* Dendrites detect signals sent by other neurons, via chemicals passing through synapses, which are small gaps between some types of brain cells.

9. Neural circuitry and its attendant support form interconnecting systems that accumulate information, relay signals, and guide processes and behaviors. This provides the foundation of brain functions such as cognition, language, and memory.

10. Biology is not destiny; genetic tendencies interact with experience to determine brain structure. The final fate of any one brain connection may be based on whether it is being used, or its "functional validation." This is described as "what gets fired gets wired."

Short Course:
Circuitry

A

Axon—part of a nerve cell, it consists of a narrow tube-like structure that transmits signals between cells.

C

Central nervous system (CNS)—the collection of nerves and nerve signal processors in the body, including (for humans) the brain and spinal cord.
Cerebral cortex—area of brain central to processing higher-order thinking.

D

Dendrite—thread-like fibers that snake out from some neurons (nerve cells) to detect signals.

G

Glial cell—a cell that provides support services to the neuron and insulates between neurons.

M

Myelin—a substance that insulates and protects the electrical signal from getting dissipated in the nervous system.

N

Nerve cell—*See* Neuron.
Neuron—a cell, sometimes also called a nerve cell, such as what is found in the brain and other parts of the central nervous system, that transmits signals. Typically consists of a main cell body with dendrites and an axon attached.

P

Peripheral nervous system (PNS)—bodywide sensory nerves that collect information and motor nerves that send

Short Course:
Circuitry

motor commands. It works together with central nervous system of brain and spine.

S

Spike train—a series of electrical signals from a single neuron that provide a sequence of "code" to which the brain responds.

Synapse—tiny gaps between neurons where chemicals cross, ferrying signals from one cell to another.

Introduction

William James, the distinguished father of American psychology, suffered from serious depression. Near suicidal at times, he once wrote to his younger brother, the famous author Henry James, that he found himself alternating between uncontrollable fits of extreme depression and those of great exhilaration.

As if determined to transform his pain into medical knowledge, he set out to document everything then known about how the brain works—plus some. In 1890, James released his book *The Principles of Psychology*, a forward-looking text in two enormous volumes. It was here that James first identified a fundamental aspect of the brain and coined the word *plasticity* to describe it. Plasticity, the topic of this chapter, has become one of the most important concepts of modern neuroscience and has direct and positive implications for teaching.

In immortal words that foreshadowed what was only dimly imagined then but has been firmly established since, James wrote that nerve tissue, such as that in the brain, "seems endowed with a very extraordinary degree of plasticity" (James, 1950, 1890). The brain, he believed, could mold and reshape to new purpose in the body.

Speaking specifically to educators in his text *Talks to Teachers*, James beautifully illustrated the early coming together of the fields of psychology, education, and neuroscience when he described how he believed plasticity might be involved in teacher work (James, 2005, 1892): "The plasticity of the living matter of our nervous system, in short, is the reason why we do a thing with difficulty the first time, but soon do it more and more easily, and finally, with sufficient practice, do it semi-mechanically, or with hardly any consciousness at all. Our nervous systems have . . . grown to the way in which they have been exercised, just as a sheet of paper or a coat, once creased or folded, tends to fall forever afterward into the same identical folds."

James's prophetic words largely fell by the wayside for decades—not surprising, given the limited state of knowledge at the time. Brain sciences of any sort, including modern psychology, were new fields. Instructors such as James, on the faculty of Harvard University, were scarce. In fact, he described the first psychology lecture that he ever heard as the first he ever taught. This newness of the field was a source of distressing thoughts to James. Sometimes he mentioned feeling he was inventing his teachings on the fly, and he worried what real value he was offering.

Detractors referred to the *Principles* text in which James introduced plasticity as "a work of imagination" and "surest where specialists and experts in his field are most in doubt." But he had impressive support as well. The famous educational reformer and philosopher John Dewey, who insisted that experience and not just rote learning was essential for effective education, rushed to

James's defense. He satirically summed up the criticism, calling the *Principles* "a good book, but too lively to make a good corpse, and every scientific book ought to be a corpse." Dewey's view offered a daunting critique of the state of scientific thinking at the time.

Science moves slowly and James did not live to see his ideas of plasticity verified. Today, neuroscience shows plasticity lies at the center of modern beliefs about how the brain works. This chapter introduces CORE Guiding Principle 1: *Teachers play a large role in school experiences that literally shape the brain in the school-age years, through the biological properties of neural plasticity.* The chapter also presents concepts in CORE Guiding Principle 2: *Mastering the learning sciences empowers teachers to identify, advocate for, and support decisions that impact their professional lives and success for students.*

Plasticity Defined

Formally defined, *plasticity* is the capacity of the nervous system to change substantially in structure and function over a lifetime. It is the first major topic being discussed because of its role in supporting all learning. The mechanisms of plasticity underlie our ability to learn.

The use of the word *plastic* to refer to the property of being able to change and then hold a new configuration existed long before the modern-day synthetic plastics of polyethylene garbage bags and polypropylene ketchup bottles. The word *plasticity* comes from the Greek *plastikos,* meaning "to mold or shape." In the language of artisans, sculptors, and masons, it described malleable substances that could bend to their will and reflect the creator's imagination. In the 19th century, ivory from animal tusks represented the crème de la crème of "plastic" material because it was possible to shape, and so its appeal resulted in widespread hunting and the near extinction of some species of walrus and elephants.

Made of cells and living tissue, the plastic brain does not bend to will or imagination but it does change through what it experiences. In the ancient Greek sense, the brain shows the manner or property of plasticity. It has the capability of remolding or reshaping, and then holding the new configuration. For better or for worse, these changes involve long-lasting and often permanent rearrangement of the brain.

Importance of Plasticity

A spongy, 3-pound mass of fatty tissue, the brain was once considered of so little importance that ancient Egyptians preparing their kin for the afterlife tossed it aside while most other organs were retained and carefully mummified. They didn't know what it did and thought it wouldn't be needed in the afterlife they sought to support.

Now, of course, we know the brain ought not to be so casually dismissed. And although it is correct to describe the brain as a single organ, it is comprised of distinct regions, each with its own primary functions but interconnected in important ways to create a highly dynamic system. To better understand the system as a whole, a team composed of physicists, biologists, chemists, bioengineers, and psychologists from the University of California, San Diego, in 2012, for example, began conducting innovative basic research to investigate how, through collective action, the brain learns, including how as a system it produces coherent functional activity.

At a fundamental level, it is well established that the part of the brain called the cerebral cortex (see the diagram in CORE Figure 2) plays a central role in learning. The **cerebral cortex** is believed to be the most highly developed part of the human brain for higher-order thinking. As a center for cognition, it and other areas of the forebrain govern such capacities as thinking, perceiving, focus, and many of the information-processing functions of the brain. The cortex is divided into regions associated with such functions as vision, hearing, movement, and speech. Some regions are associated with more than one function. In human evolutionary terms, the cerebral cortex is believed to be the most recent structure in the process of brain development. **(See CORE 2b.)**

 RESOURCE

K–12 teachers can use with students: Gopnik, 2010. (See the Citations list at the end of this chapter.)

The cerebral cortex in humans takes a relatively long time to fully mature compared with animal brain development. Some evidence indicates it may take humans well into their 20s before the wiring is fully complete for adult capacities. Furthermore, youth with attention deficit hyperactivity disorder (ADHD) tend to mature in similar patterns but with an average delay of three or more years, according to research done by scientists at the U.S. National Institutes of Health and their colleagues (National Institute of Mental Health, 2007). This means such maturing may continue into the 30s.

What is not as widely understood is that what the brain experiences—what it learns—plays a central role in the shaping of it. Educational research describes how learning is more than a static cataloging of memories, and the brain is more than a library holding volumes of information. Neuroscience indicates learning actually alters the physical structure of the brain, continually modifying its function and behavior. This is brought about through localized changes in brain areas appropriate to a given task. Thus, trainee taxi drivers navigating the myriad streets of London show an increase in brain capacity linked to memory (Woollett & Maguire, 2011), whereas scans of violin players reveal brain parts involved with the left hand, which does the fingering, are enhanced (Elber, Pantev, Wienbruch, Rockstroh, & Taub, 1995).

As a result, learning imposes new patterns in the brain. It becomes organized and reorganized, illustrating what cognitive psychologists find in our developing capabilities over time. Change in the brain occurs potentially at a variety of levels, from minute aspects of cellular change and connectivity (discussed later) to larger-scale changes involved with injury or developmental processes. **(See CORE 1b.)** Reorganization encodes learning, making it more possible to act on what we have learned. **(See CORE 1c.)**

Without the structural changes described in this idea, we humans would not be able to understand the world around us or to reason in the ways that humans do—in short, we could not grasp what teachers teach.

One primary purpose of plasticity is believed to be that it allows change to better cope with new circumstances. **(See CORE 1d.)** Teachers often ask what is meant by this. From a developmental biology perspective, each generation of human beings is born in a somewhat different world. Our environment changes over time and place. To survive and thrive, it helps if the brain has some capacity to adjust to its surroundings. Also, over time, the demands on the brain may change.

Teachers play a role in this as they help students learn. And teachers are not the only actors in playing this role. Others who play significant roles in a child's life shape the child's brain—parents, siblings, caregivers, grandparents, the warm aunt and the witty uncle, all can have a lasting influence.

Since teachers often have more opportunities to formally learn how the brain functions, they sometimes play a role sharing knowledge with parents and the larger community. So, in that way they teach more than just the children and young adults with whom they work; they are endowed with a broader range of outreach.

One point that teachers can share is that research has found brain change occurs throughout life and is not solely the unfolding of preprogrammed patterns. Rather, the brain is a dynamic organ shaped to an extent by experience. **(See CORE 1e.)** This is valuable information for teachers, directly related to the relevance of their work. Research has also shown that understanding this concept can be a great benefit to students. When they learn that the brain can form stronger connections through the process of learning something, say a difficult mathematical concept, students can become more motivated to persevere, as described in research that is addressed in Chapter 5.

Building on What Is Useful

Neuroscience research confirms the important role that experience plays in building the structure of the brain. Harvard brain researcher and professor of pediatrics Charles Nelson, who chaired the John D. and Catherine T. MacArthur Foundation Research Network on Early Experience and Brain Development, elegantly describes neural plasticity as an orchestrated dance between brain and environment (Nelson, 1999). The brain is shaped by experience and, in turn, the newly remolded brain embraces new experiences that lead to more neural changes. And on it goes, *ad infinitum*, says Nelson.

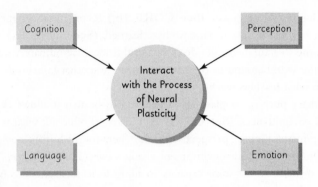

FIGURE 2.1

Some Elements That Drive Neural Plasticity

Nelson also believes that most behavioral phenomena of interest to psychologists (and we would add to teachers)—such as cognition, perception, language, and emotion—are established through the process of neural plasticity (see Figure 2.1). So what is the mechanism of this dance of cognition we call plasticity and how does it occur?

In the human brain, the vast majority of cells that transmit information appear to be in place very early in life. However, considerable important changes do occur, and much of these changes are happening through what connects to what—the *neural circuitry*. This is a type of brain reorganization called *rewiring*. Rewiring shapes the brain at a molecular level in such ways as enhancing particular neural pathways.

A Tale of Two Signaling Systems

The fact that even basic workings of the brain remained mysterious for so long is not surprising. After all, when your heart is working harder, you can feel it. When your skin is colder, you can sense it. When your muscles are in action, you can even see them sometimes. But when the mind thinks, you can't feel the brain at work. It is like a silent haunting presence, furiously working but not visibly so, at least to all outward appearances without special equipment.

Also, it is not just one master "ghost" acting in the brain but many. The brain contains an unimaginably large number of brain cells working together. Neuroscience reveals brain cells are primarily of two types: **nerve cells**, also called **neurons**, which conduct signals to send and receive information, and **glial cells**, which provide support services and insulate between neurons. There are more glial cells than neurons in the brain but the neuron is the primary focus for teachers. Each neuron has its own unique but simple job: detect a signal and pass it along. **(See CORE 2c.)**

To visualize the purpose of brain signaling and what cells are doing, consider the role of a tall castle of stone that sits on a narrow sand spur in southern Italy near the eastern coastal town of Crotone. The castle has been there for millennia; myths link it to Homer's account of the entrapment of *Ulysses*. Today, you can see the structure beautifully restored, a World Heritage site called "Le Castella," or translated, "The Castle." At night it stands immense and hulking in a golden glow of lanterns overlooking the magnificent Ionic Sea.

Le Castella purportedly served as one in a ring of such castles near where battles of Rome and Carthage were waged. If a fleet of invaders appeared, Le Castella, as legend has it, was used to light warning lanterns and the message would be passed along one sentinel to another across a vast area. Its light would beam as far as it could reach and the message would be ferried across countless small bays and inlets, perhaps by people standing at the ready to serve, paid by rich purses intent on protecting their homeland in one of the earliest colonies of Greece, an area much invaded though known for its famous Olympian champions and warlords.

As the message spiraled out in a ring up and down the coast and into the depths of the inland, it may even have reached into the start of the mountains and forest of the beautiful Sila region nearby, an area from which Dante allegedly modeled his dark forest—*selva oscura*—in the opening of *The Divine Comedy*. All in all, it was a simple messaging system used at Le Castella, primitive at best, only light or no light, a sighting or none. But the result was action, motion, movement, an entire region mobilized, each part knowing what it was to do next.

So it is with neurons in the brain. As part of a giant signaling system, the job of the neuron is to collect and accumulate messages. If enough are received to warrant an alert, then the neuron will trigger an electrical signal and pass it along to all its neighbors.

Some neurons collect and send sensory information such as pain when a finger is pricked by a thorn. Others accumulate information that drives still other cells to signal actions such as speech (a verbal "Ouch") and movement (the pulling of that finger away from the offending thorn). Whatever the input, the cells gather information and then mobilize action, such as behaviors.

Each neuron is a single cell (see Figure 2.2) snaking out long thread-like fibers, called **dendrites**, from the main cell body itself. These dendrites detect signals sent by other cells. They branch and billow into copious fragile extensions, getting close enough to the next neuron to lie in a stream of chemical messages that are ferried or spewed across small gaps that often exist between any two brain cells. These are called **synapses**. When chemicals indicate a signal has been sent, a message is received. It is then transmitted down the axon, if the conditions are right. In summary, then, an electrical signal is propagated within a neuron and a chemical process usually transmits information from one neuron to the next. **(See CORE 2d.)**

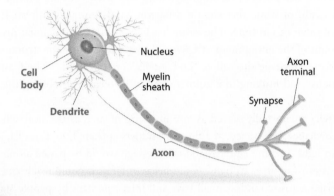

FIGURE 2.2

Example of a Single Neuron, with Axon, Dendrites, and Synapses

Once the signal is sent, it passes along an often lengthy tube-like structure called the **axon**. When the message is received, the axon needs to do its work quickly and get it to the right location. The axon can be hugely long compared to the tiny cell body from which it originates. For instance, from the spine to the foot, axons can extend more than a yard. This is quite a fantastic feat for a single cell far too tiny even for the eye to see.

Like Le Castella, the neuron uses a simple, almost primal signaling system, believed to be mostly capable of only a single note—"Yes, detection has been triggered"—or quiescence, silence, nothing. A series of messages like this from a single neuron become a **spike train**, or a sequence of electrical code. This is the language for which our brains listen.

The spike train could be an urgent beaming of "yes, yes, yes" beating out a strong detection triggered repeatedly, which perhaps could be visualized as triggered by an attack of wolves, or capturing some aspect of a glorious sunset too overwhelming to ignore. Yet again, another spike train may be more languid, "yes," quiet, "yes" again a while later, perhaps detecting a first patter of raindrops on a late autumn day.

The electrical signal involves opening and closing small channels through which charged substances move. When a signal is sent, or "fired," positively charged materials rush across the membrane. This produces tiny voltage changes, temporarily switching local internal conditions from negative to positive. The result is an "action potential"—the signal—swiftly passing along the membrane. Signal speeds of several hundred miles per hour can be reached. **(See CORE 2e.)**

But unlike Le Castella, it is not a small ring of sentinels that send the messages of the brain's spike trains. Rather, new research shows that, on average, about 86 billion neurons in the adult human brain are available to go into action (Azevedo et al., 2009), along with perhaps three times as many supporting cells.

Cells of the central nervous system comprised of the brain and the spinal cord and of the bodywide peripheral nervous system participate in the signaling system. Together, a vast terrain is covered and surveyed. Thus, neural circuitry and all its attendant support form interconnecting systems that relay and process information in the form of electrical signals fired from one neural structure to another across the synapse endpoints.

This process is the foundation of the brain's many functions, including cognition, language, and memory. Like Le Castella, the brain relies on a signaling system that arises from an antiquated landscape. It is ancient, at least in legacy, because parts of the human brain are descended from bygone eras. The basic neuron in primitive creatures works much the same as it does in humans. Much of what makes human brains different is believed to be not the neuron cell unit itself but how the neurons are organized in the network and brain regions.

The neuron consists of four main parts. These need not be memorized by educators but the overall flow should be understood (National Research Council, 2000). Research has shown that for many neurons:

1. Dendrites are branching tree-like structures that detect signals.
2. They connect to the main cell body that accumulates signal information.
3. A cord-like axon extends away from the cell to deliver the accumulated signal.
4. The axon ends in an area releasing chemicals to the next neuron. **(See CORE 2f.)**

To facilitate this process, an importance substance called **myelin** often insulates and protects the electrical signal from getting dissipated, or washed out along the way. **(See CORE 2g.)** Decay of myelin is proving key in some human diseases affecting function of the nervous system.

Staying Thoroughly Modern

Plasticity is what keeps the brain thoroughly modern. For example, plasticity alters the network of how the neurons connect to each other. What will signal, how often, and under what conditions is made anew, to a limited degree, for each person through plasticity. Scientists have begun to uncover the molecular basis of this process, providing growing insight into how learning and memory occur, and helping to unpack "the psychology" of how we learn.

Although each individual brain retains some common characteristics of how information will flow, what neuroscience has learned is that the neural system also substantially modifies in the individual brain over time. It uses clues it encounters in early development and the school-age years to optimize the brain personally for life. For instance, through plasticity, pathways that are triggered frequently by spike trains are reinforced and well maintained. **(See CORE 2h.)**

"Well-traveled" brain pathways are reinforced to make the thinking more efficient. It can make it easier, for instance, for a person to calculate a sum or read a book. In contrast, "sentinels" of the brain that fall into disuse, like the lonely Le Castella on its narrow spur of sand, are allowed to, metaphorically, collapse into the sea. The neurons die or are redirected to other uses. Connections can lapse or move.

Thus, biology is not destiny and genetic tendencies interact with experience to determine brain structure. Examples for educators from the National Institutes of Health shown in Figure 2.3 include such varied experiences as effects of poverty and teaching practices that enhance memory. So every brain is unique. Scientists believe that stating whether nature or nurture is responsible for the process of brain development is overly simplistic, since it is a continuous interaction. For example, most major diseases that have a genetic basis are strongly influenced by the environment. Studies of twins show that although identical siblings have higher risks of getting the same disease,

Working memory capacity is key to learning and was thought relatively fixed. Recent imaging studies suggest training can increase brain activity related to working memory, an example of learning-induced plasticity.

Neuroimaging revealed poor readers have regions of cerebral white matter with decreased organization. Intensive instruction resulted in significantly improved organization, brain plasticity at work for striving readers.

Animal studies reveal impoverished environments are associated with reduced cortical gray matter. For human children, cognitive and imaging studies are beginning to suggest which brain networks may be most influenced by poverty, and why.

- Training of working memory
- http://www.ncbi.nlm.nih.gov/pubmed/14699419

- Reading and literacy change brain structure
- http://www.ncbi.nlm.nih.gov/pubmed/20005820
- http://www.ncbi.nlm.nih.gov/pubmed/20395549
- http://www.ncbi.nlm.nih.gov/pubmed/21071632

- Roles of poverty in plasticity
- http://www.ncbi.nlm.nih.gov/pmc/articles/PMC3421156/
- http://www.ncbi.nlm.nih.gov/pmc/articles/PMC2950073/

FIGURE 2.3

Some U.S. National Institutes of Health Plasticity Examples for Educators research has also shown that the probability is often not absolute and may often be only 30 to 60%. **(See CORE 1f.)**

Exploring the Capacity to Change

Nobelist Eric Kandel, a distinguished Columbia University professor who shared the prize for medicine in 2000 for his work on learning and memory, showed that learning often produces changes by modifying the strength of connections between nerve cells, rather than by altering the brain's basic circuitry (Pittenger & Kandel, 2003).

The mechanisms of plasticity continue to excite researchers as they explore and sometimes disagree on the capacity of the
brain to change. Awareness has also begun to enter more popular
accounts, too. A National Geographic report explained that if
there is a single theme dominating the past decade of neurological research, it is the brain's plasticity—its exciting ability to
reshape and reorganize itself.

 RESOURCE

K–12 teachers can use with students: Shreeve, 2005. (See the Citations list at the end of this chapter.)

Regarding the adult brain, research findings vary about
evidence for the degree of natural plasticity, or how much it
changes. Neuroscientist Michael Merzenich, who provided a
TED Talk on rewiring the brain, has made some of the most
optimistic claims. These include the notion that certain brain
exercises can be as effective as drugs in treating serious mental
health problems in adults, that brain information processing

 RESOURCE

K–12 teachers can use with students: TED, 2004. (See the Citations list at the end of this chapter.)

can be substantially retrained for the elderly, and that adults can reach fluency in a new languages without tedious memorization by using certain brain techniques. At whatever age, such types of training are a topic of much controversy about which teachers should be aware. According to a study published recently in *Nature,* the central question is not whether performance on assessments can be improved by training in cognitive tasks such as planning, spatial skills, and attention, but whether the benefits transfer to improvement on other, related tasks or lead to general improvement (Owen et al., 2010). The *Nature* study reported little transfer and generalizability in their subjects given the study techniques employed by the scientists. Of course, supporting transfer is notoriously challenging in all types of learning, which will be discussed in the next chapter.

Those working with adult learners are especially cautious when making claims, such as University of California, Davis, Professor Hwai-Jong Cheng and coauthor Lawrence K. Low, who published their work with the Royal Society's *Philosophical Transaction*, the old-est continuously running scientific journal in the world. Lessons learned from early develop-ment, the researchers reported, show that the immature brain contains an environment conducive for large-scale change (Low & Cheng, 2006). In the adult brain, they say, the story often appears to be very different.

Whatever the range of shaping might eventually turn out to be, the "hardening down" of plasticity processes in the adult brain is already the target of medical research efforts to turn them back on. Some hope that success in this area might one day offer cures and remedies for a variety of problems. Whether we can make adult brains turn some of the plasticity "pathways" evident in a child's brain back on again to make them more flexible—and whether we even want to do so—are big questions.

That there are disagreements and varying conclusions to brain research is not surprising. Getting a handle on understanding how the brain works is tough, according to work by Jay Giedd, who, in 2011, was chief of the Brain Imaging unit in the child psychiatry branch for the National Institute of Mental Health in Maryland (Giedd, 2008). The brain is wrapped in a tough membrane, surrounded by protective fluid, and encased in bone. This makes it nicely protected from falls, attacks, and the curiosity of scientists, Giedd reports, with humor but also a great deal of truth regarding the challenges of brain research (Giedd, 2008). Whether from the perspective of biology, psychology, or educational research, understanding the brain and how it works is tough. "I hate the brain," one neuroscience doctoral student declared after a stretch of hard work studying the delicate organ.

So it has been a long road leading to understanding how brain plasticity may work in neural systems. It has been known for some time that the brain and the spinal cord compose the **central nervous system (CNS)** (Society for Neuroscience, 2008), and that this connects to the **peripheral nervous system (PNS)** that sends and receives signals in the rest of the body. In the mid-1960s, brain research pioneer Marian Diamond and colleagues at the University of California, Berkeley, published research in the journal *Science* that helped lead scientists down the path of understanding neural plasticity (Bennett, Diamond, Krech, & Rosenzweig, 1964).

The Berkeley team found that research on rats demonstrated differences in brain structure related to what the animals experienced. They described how the brain is responsive to environmental pressure. Their findings on physiological theories of learning and memory showed this conclusion, the researchers said. This was a powerful assertion at the time, generating serious controversy. Although it was the early days in modern brain research, the Berkeley researchers conjectured that when the final story of the brain in learning and memory was written, it would be told in terms of chemistry and anatomy.

Since then, numerous research studies undertaken with tools unavailable to early researchers have revealed that reorganization of the brain is not limited to rats (Nelson, 1999). Research on a variety of organisms shows connections in the brain are being substantially fine-tuned. Limitation of overabundance and strengthening of relevant connections due to

Why Rats?

Why Do So Many Brain Studies Use Mice and Rats?

For one thing, the brains of mice and rats are comparatively easy to observe from a physical standpoint. Both rats and mice offer a relatively smooth cortex in which changes can be measured. In contrast, in the brains of mammals, the human brain especially, the cortices are so folded and marked by fissures and crests that it can be hard to measure changes in surface area. For another, mice and rats are strikingly similar to humans in their anatomy, physiology, and genetics (95 percent of the mouse genome is similar to that of humans.) And finally, mice and rats age much more rapidly than humans do (one mouse year equals about 30 human years), making it possible for researchers to assess life span changes.

Still, we are decidedly not the same. Few describe the similarities and differences between mice and man more astutely than Michael Gazzaniga, one of the world's leading cognitive neuroscientists and the author of several books, including *Human: The Science Behind What Makes Us Unique* (Gazzaniga, 2008). He says it is obvious that humans are physically unique, but we also differ from other animals in more complex ways. We create art, make pasta Bolognese, and dream up complex machines, he quips. Some of us even understand quantum physics—or brain science. A neuroscientist isn't needed for us to know our brains are calling the shots, but is needed if we want to explain how and why we are so unique, he says in a 2008 interview with Edge.org.

 RESOURCE

K–12 teachers can use with students: Edge Foundation, 2014. (See the Citations list at the end of this chapter.)

development and experience have been found (Kandel, Schwartz, Jessell, Siegelbaum, & Hudspeth, 2013).

Brain Growth Pioneer and Legendary Teacher

Today, about the only brain that neuroscientist Marian Diamond will acknowledge cannot grow, no matter how enriched the environment, is the human brain she famously carries to lectures in a cheery hatbox.

Diamond, who is also an author as well as a celebrated teacher, says research done in her lab and elsewhere shows that the brain can grow at any age. What it needs, she maintains, are these five features: proper diet, exercise, proper challenges, new and novel things, and love. Those five characteristics, she explains during an interview in her University of California, Berkeley, office, have all been proven in the laboratory. *Proven in the laboratory* are key words to this celebrated scientist.

Still teaching and actively engaged in brain research as she nears age 90, Professor Diamond is legendary at Berkeley. Tall and elegant, a broad smile setting off the sweep of white hair immaculately styled into her trademark French twist, she's been instantly recognizable to generations of students and is among the most sought-after teacher at the university.

To be in the lecture hall when she places her hatbox on the podium, ceremoniously reaches in with gloved hands, holds up a human brain and declares, "This mass only weighs 3 pounds and yet it has the capacity to conceive of a universe a billion light-years across. Isn't that phenomenal?" is to have one of the signature UC Berkeley experiences. Her human anatomy lectures on the university's YouTube channel turned her into a rock star in the online learning community where learners of all ages and from across the globe have flocked to videos of her anatomy lessons since 2007 (Diamond, 2007).

As noted earlier in this chapter, it is in the research realm as a leading neuroanatomist, however, where she has made a lasting impact in awareness of the brain's capacity to grow and change. Berkeley research scientists David Krech, Mark Rosenzweig, and Edward Bennett were studying the brain chemistry of rats in the laboratory when they found that rats raised in a deliberately enriched environment—notable for larger cages that were stocked with toys and shared with ample companion rats—performed better in mazes than did those raised in comparatively impoverished environments.

Could that mean that their brains were also different? The next step was to look for physical changes in the rats' cerebral cortex, a center of its reasoning power. Using these laboratory rats, Dr. Diamond's pioneering work revealed the potential for the mammalian brain to grow as measured by the thickness of the cerebral cortex when exposed to an enriched environment, and—equally important—to shrink when subjected to an impoverished environment. In 1964, Diamond and her Berkeley colleagues published the results of their study in a paper titled "The Effects of Enriched Environments on the Histology of the Rat Cerebral Cortex." Later work by other scientists demonstrated that the growth in the cortex was due to the branching of the neurons' dendrites and growth of its associated structures.

The continuing work of Diamond and other scientists has greatly expanded enrichment science. When asked, "If you were teaching children today, what would you be sure to teach them about the brain?" she answers that she would teach them that the brain can grow at any age, and that it can grow for them and for their grandparents. Diamond adds that research in the laboratory shows that when exposed to enriching and stimulating experiences, every part of the nerve cell can change.

The understanding of what constitutes an enriched environment has grown to include proper diet and exercise, elements of newness or variety, and the need for regular challenge. In the lab, she explains, without new toys, the rats get bored, so toys are rotated a little at a time. Furthermore, Diamond explains, you need a challenge for the brain to grow; you can't just do the same kind of crossword puzzle over and over. However, Diamond cautions, it is important to build the challenges so they don't overwhelm the brain. Start with the easy questions, she advises.

In 2012, Diamond added the notion of love to the mix of what constitutes an enriched environment. She acknowledges that it was a daring thing to do, especially at a scientific meeting. When asked, as everyone does, "How do you show love to a rat?" Diamond replies that you hold them up to your lab coat and pet them. Every day, while the cages were being cleaned the rats got a little petting and they loved it, she says, adding that the lab rats that had been shown love lived longer and the longer-lived rats' brains grew larger.

Pruning's Surprising Role

In humans, the period from very early childhood into the teen years is all about the brain selecting the most useful components such as particular neurons, synapses, and dendrites to preserve for the adult brain.

In contrast to reorganizing the brain by strengthening neural circuitry, which seems quite logical, is the somewhat surprising but equally important brain-shaping mechanism called *pruning*. In pruning, existing brain cells are rather dramatically pared back. Brain connections that are active and generating electrical currents are more likely to survive, whereas those with little or no activity are more likely to be lost. The brain, then, is sculpted, building on that which is most useful and paring away that which is of little value to create a more efficient system.

When we are born, each neuron in the cerebral cortex is flush with an abundance of synapses. Indeed, a human infant has perhaps as many as 2,500 synapses per nerve cell. By age 2 or 3, this can amplify about sixfold. Pruning cuts away starkly and substantially at the little used or unneeded neural circuitry. By adulthood, it is believed that our brains contain on the order of one-half of the synapses that existed in our toddler brains.

The idea that eliminating brain cells is a good thing often seems counterintuitive, so much so that some teachers, when learning about the process, find it shocking. Young students find it perplexing, as well. They immediately ask why their brains are building connections and then destroying them. To them, it is like a block tower constructed and then toppled over—what would be the purpose? And yet, this is exactly what occurs in early development and in school-age years. And it has an important—indeed, critical—role.

Pruning, in essence, culls the fruit, reducing the overproliferation of synapses in order to concentrate on fewer, higher-quality connections so that what remains can better serve its purpose. **(See CORE 1g.)** This focuses brain capacity on the most important processes and pathways it seems to need, at least based on experiences by the critical dates of pruning. The eliminations seem to be targeted at unused or lesser used brain capacity. Scientists are beginning to find that many areas of the brain are basically being tailored for—and to—what the brain experiences. Importantly, many cuts and changes are permanent, in the sense that the brain becomes a new entity for any further changes. So quite literally, experience and development are shaping the brain.

Brain cell death itself is part of pruning. A variety of new brain-imaging techniques and other approaches are providing information on what is happening in *apoptosis,* or cell death. Brain researchers have found that approximately 50 percent of our brain cells past the stage of undergoing cell division do not survive until adulthood (Low & Cheng, 2006). Some ways the brain changes through plasticity are shown in Figure 2.4.

In pruning, the selection process continues intensively, especially around age 2 and in the early teen years. Presumably, when all goes well, the pruning in the school years is accomplished wisely. This would mean that connections and capacity key for survival and supporting optimal function persist while less useful connections may not.

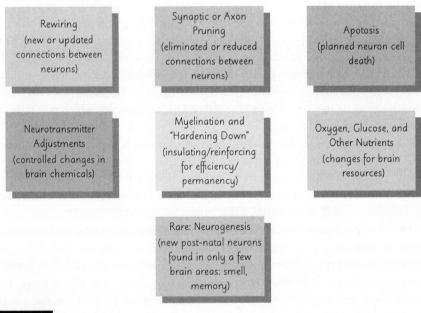

Rewiring (new or updated connections between neurons)	Synaptic or Axon Pruning (eliminated or reduced connections between neurons)	Apotosis (planned neuron cell death)
Neurotransmitter Adjustments (controlled changes in brain chemicals)	Myelination and "Hardening Down" (insulating/reinforcing for efficiency/ permanency)	Oxygen, Glucose, and Other Nutrients (changes for brain resources)
	Rare: Neurogenesis (new post-natal neurons found in only a few brain areas: smell, memory)	

FIGURE 2.4

Plasticity: Some Ways the Brain Changes

Sometimes little-needed neural capacity in one region can be recycled somewhere else, such as where the brain is finding its circuits traversed more often. For example, are there new circumstances facing this child? In such a case, neural capacity may be shifted to the area facing new demand. In a manner of speaking, it builds a brain to suit the demand and then firms it up, more or less for a lifetime.

This makes the human mind highly adaptable to each generation. Cognitive psychology directs us to think of this as a form of fluid intelligence, or a capacity in our makeup to optimize our cognition to the situations in which it needs to be applied. Many educational researchers have adopted the idea of *fluid intelligence*—applying our knowledge in highly adaptable ways—and *crystallized intelligence*, such as facts, ideas, and skills mastered in school or other settings.

Along with pruning, new connections can also form. *Synaptogenesis,* which means the formation of new synapses between neurons, can take place at any time but occurs especially rapidly in some stages of life, often called "sensitive" or "critical" periods (Howard-Jones et al., 2007). This is addressed in detail in Chapter 10. **(See CORE 6d–6i.)**

The basic idea of both pruning and synaptogenesis is this: After the brain is done proliferating cells and new connections at a furious rate in the very early stages of development, it works to concentrate on fewer, higher-quality connections. Through pruning, the brain optimizes capacity to focus on the most important processes and pathways it seems to need.

Point-Counterpoint

The Question of Brain Regeneration

One Question That Neuroscientists Ask Is, When Did We Get Our Brain Cells? Scientists Need to Know If, When, and in What Ways the Brain Regenerates.

Does the brain's cortex create a substantial number of new neurons at any time after early development? To answer this question, let's take a short journey back in time, as neuroscientists do when they study this topic (Purves et al., 2008). Shift your thinking over to the environmental movement, and specifically, to nuclear bombs and atomic waste of the last century.

Research reported in 2011 by the U.S. National Academy of Sciences (Bhardwaj et al., 2011) shows that the Cold War stand-off of the 20th century enters into the story of brain research in an eerie way. The historic rise and fall of atomic dust last century affected the air we breathe, making possible the carbon-14 dating of brains. It has "marked" things about us and about our bodies. Between the mid-1950s and the early 1960s, radioactive carbon-14 levels shot up nearly doubling its atmospheric concentration, before falling when open-air testing dropped off after bans in much of the world (Purves et al., 2008).

For brain researchers, this has provided a kind of time clock, like radioactive carbon dating of artifacts, but for the very tissue of our bodies. Since the vast majority of the new radiation released into the atmosphere came after 1955, those born before then serve as a marker for brain research. Chances are if you were born in the mid-1950s, the only way to have elevated carbon-14 in your cortical neurons would be if you were gaining new brain cells after birth.

To paint the scene, it was already known that in certain small parts of the brain, such as in the olfactory areas where smells are processed, new or "baby" neurons are generated (Veyrac et al., 2009). The list of smells that noses are exposed to in such studies sounds like a grandmother's kitchen: pepper, star anise, fennel, cinnamon, garlic, onion, ginger, juniper berries, clove, nutmeg, lemon, celery, cumin, chocolate, cardamom, thyme, tarragon, capsicum, lavender, and orange.

However, despite what may happen in smells, for humans there was little evidence that much of the cortex, the rippling outer brain that gives us unique powers, could regenerate itself.

So researchers devised an experiment to find out. What if, they asked, they took advantage of the way the Earth's atmosphere had been dramatically altered for a brief period?

Everything from child mummies to Jesus's supposed grave cloth, the Shroud of Turin, have been dated using carbon-14 techniques. So the researchers decided to look at autopsy samples from before and after the key dates for atomic contamination. They settled on the selection of seven people born between 1933 and 1973 (Bhardwaj et al., 2011) who had passed away and for whom suitable brain samples were available. The oldest, at age 72, would have been about 20 years old when the atmospheric radioactive carbon levels started to rise.

The verdict: The people born before 1955 had no significant number of cortical neurons showing elevated carbon-14. This argued strongly against substantial brain cell generation in the adult cerebral cortex, researchers concluded. The implications are that after injury or disease, reorganization of existing neurons and connections happens, but new creation, naturally occurring at a large scale, is unlikely in the adult brain.

However, neuron regeneration found in a few small parts of the brain such as the olfactory areas, where smell is processed, and again in the hippocampus (Eriksson et al., 1998), where some memories are forged (Gibb, 2007), is intriguing. It opens the possibility of artificial or medical means to trigger proliferation. Some researchers have recently claimed other brain cells might be artificially induced to "awaken" and regenerate (Jiao & Chen, 2008). If so, this might dramatically help with Alzheimer's, Parkinson's, and other degenerative brain diseases.

Does the Brain Make Value Judgments?

Neuroscientists use interesting language for what happens in the brain prior to pruning, such as describing "overly exuberant" or "misguided" connections. It sounds like they are making value judgments. Who is to say what is a misguided connection in someone else's brain?

But the value judgment being made in this case is the brain's own. Terms such as *exuberant* and *misguided* just mean that the connections aren't servicing what the brain is encountering—the circuits exist but are not often tapped. So, slowly, over time, they may be eliminated.

Educationally, this can work for or against us. An example is the work of researcher Gary Small, director of UCLA's Memory and Aging Research Center. In a national televised interview known to many teachers, he noted that the average young person spent more than 9 hours each day with her or his technology. What will happen, Small asks, with these "digital natives"—the 8- to 18-year-olds who are spending so much time with digital

RESOURCE

K–12 teachers can use with students: Frontline, 2009. (See the Citations list at the end of this chapter.)

media? And, he asks, What will they be like in 20 or 30 years? Such questions, he believes, are important to consider, given what is known about brain development.

The specific role that technology plays in children's development is an extensive research topic outside the scope of the CORE. Small's work with technology, however, provides an example of the type of questions about which teachers are interested. Small (cited in Frontline, 2009) describes how the effect of technology is much more profound on young, developing brains than on older, more established brains because of pruning. He says that how young people spend their time, what they expose their brains to, will have a profound effect on what their brains will be like for the rest of their lives. This is because from early life through adolescence, as he tallies it, about 60 percent of synaptic connections are pruned away. When asked by the interviewer if this capacity is pruned away forever, Small nods his head. He agreed with the statement. In a sense, the brain doesn't look back, only ahead.

Research shows adults often can create new connections at any age, though it may take longer or be more difficult (Society for Neuroscience, 2008). However, the point is that capacity, once pruned away, if it can be restored at all, would need to be entirely rebuilt. In this way, development moves forward, not back.

To Reason Like Einstein

To reason like Einstein, intelligence researcher Dennis Garlick reported, would require a neural system that possesses the correct connections (Garlick, 2003). But, researchers ask, How does one get such a connected brain?

Basically, for teachers, the message is that how our brains change as we go along matters. Experience helps build a foundation on which subsequent learning rests. Depending on what happens to us, we can never get back to exactly the same brain, even if we wanted to. Therefore, how the connections develop is important for *what we will be able to do.*

For those who take a broad philosophical view of the mind, talk of plasticity sometimes induces a shrug. Like the butterfly effect of chaos theory, it could go one way or it could go another. Who can know where such brain building might lead? We may not be able to know for sure, but there are clues.

Apparently it is the act of being used that tells the brain something is useful, and therefore important or "wise" to keep. Neuroscience indicates that what the brain is called on to do and what it experiences helps to establish what it becomes.

When teachers understand and accept that the brain reorganizes itself and may prune those pathways not being utilized, what they want to know is specific solutions. How, for instance, as one educator described it, can teachers help keep the "pathways for math active" when a student in block scheduling may have algebra I in the fall of sophomore year but not take algebra II until spring of senior year?

Clearly, there is no magic bullet. Needing knowledge to be useful and used means just that. Such large gaps in time without integration or use of the knowledge are not conducive to learning. Teachers already know this; now using the knowledge and backing it with evidence is important. What can they do? Teachers are influential change agents in their school settings. Not only can they bring about change in their own classrooms but they can also advocate for better circumstances for their students, explain the needs and why, and step into leadership positions to influence decisions as their careers move along.

For teachers, these findings may cause a long pause. Does that mean that their work in educating students and having them work in certain areas and not others does more than build knowledge? Does it actually form brains differently? The full story on that is still out. But Garlick (2003), who integrates intelligence research with neuroscience, believes that if people are to acquire various intellectual abilities, they need to be exposed to appropriate stimulation, especially during childhood, at times when the neural circuits are sufficiently malleable and less reorganization has already taken place. Whether this is creativity, musical exposure, scientific thinking, mathematical inquiry, problem solving, critical thinking, or the ability to compose an expressive thought, it may substantially matter how we use our minds when we are young, says Garlick.

What Gets Fired Gets Wired

Whereas genes provide the blueprint for a brain, research has found that experience helps sculpt the brain to match the needs of the environment (Brenhouse & Andersen, 2011). This is true at the most minute levels. The final fate of any one brain connection is based on how

TABLE 2.1 Examples of How Brain Activation Interacts with the Development and Strengthening of Brain Circuitry

What Gets Wired Gets Fired

Element/Function	What It Is	Why It Matters
Neural Circuitry	A network of interconnecting systems that relay and process information in the form of electrical signals.	It is the foundation of the brain's many functions, including cognition, language, and memory.
Plasticity	The capacity of the nervous system to change substantially in structure and function by reshaping and reorganizing the brain at the molecular level.	Change allows the brain to adapt to its surroundings and experiences, making every brain unique and thoroughly modern.
Pruning	The process of trimming away unneeded or poorly executed circuitry.	It creates a more efficient system.
Experience	A key factor in imposing new patterns in the brain.	Neuroscience indicates the act of learning alters the physical structure of the brain, continually modifying its function and behavior.

> This reshaping of the brain is especially active from around ages 3 to 16—the very heart of the school years.

and whether it is being used. This is called *functional validation*, or more commonly described as "what gets fired gets wired." **(See CORE 2h.)** Examples are shown in Table 2.1.

Teachers often ask why our brains are reorganizing like this. What, they want to know, is directing the way the brain forms and how it works, especially in the school-age years?

Brain research suggests selective activity changes the brain through plasticity (Society for Neuroscience, 2008). For instance, brain regions that respond only to visually presented faces are unlikely to be enhanced by something entirely different, such as algebra problems or phonics reinforcement. One activity does not fit all for brain development. This is in contrast to some early learning theories of last century. So-called general "mental muscle exercises," where any kind of thought or brain activity was thought to support every kind of thought and brain activity, are no longer generally accepted (Schunk, 2012).

Teachers also notice that much of the literature on brain plasticity primarily pertains to what can happen when things go wrong: disease, addiction, and a host of other problems. What goes right, the functionality you want to build into the brain, gets far less attention. For teachers, this seems backwards. They want to understand how to best support what goes right. For instance, they ask, is general mental exercise of any kind sufficient for total brain development? The answer is *no;* specific brain regions and networks respond to specific uses (National Research Council, 2000).

Conclusion

What William James, the noted early psychologist, saw was fundamental. Through his sometimes challenging fog of despondency he advanced the fundamental notion of brain plasticity not only for scientists but educators with his work, *Talks to Teachers.* Some 15 chapters encompassed his lectures for Cambridge teachers, and they underscored how important he felt this audience was (James, 2005, 1892):

> I have found by experience that what my hearers seem least to relish is analytical technicality, and what they most care for is concrete practical application. . . . Teachers, of course, will miss the minute divisions, subdivisions, and definitions, the lettered and numbered headings, the variations of type, and all the other mechanical artifices on which they are accustomed to prop their minds. But my main desire has been to make them conceive, and, if possible, reproduce sympathetically in their imagination, the mental life of their pupil.

More than a century later, some things haven't changed with regard to what teachers would like to know. The next chapter continues Guiding Principle 2, and then takes up some concepts of instructional design, within an exploration of cognition, in Guiding Principle 3.

Closing Scenario

Putting New Knowledge to Use

Neural Plasticity

You have decided to try out the suggestion that students can become inspired by knowing more about how their brains function, especially how the brain can get "rewired" and physically reshaped based on what it learns or experiences. You've never taught this before so now you need to put together a lesson plan.

1. The first concept you want to raise is the issue of plasticity, but kids only know of plastic in bottles and toys. How will you help them understand what you mean by the brain being "plastic"?

2. Because relevance matters to all learners, how will you convey why having a brain that can remold and reshape itself is important to them as students?

3. You tell your students that brains are built to change. That's what makes human brains so good at learning. But, why, some students will want to know, does the brain have to keep changing. What will you tell them?

4. Now it is time to provide students with some basics of brain anatomy such as in CORE Figure 2. What activities might be helpful to get students involved in visual modes of learning?

5. It is important to get across the idea of the brain as very active even though students can't feel or watch their brain working like they might with a hand or a foot. How would you help students understand the role of neurons in signaling information?

6. How would you describe how the brain learns?

7. How would you help students to understand the function of pruning?

Citations

Online, Media, and Print Resources for Teachers

Edge Foundation. (2014). *Edge*. http://dev.edge.org/conversation/are-human-brains-unique

Frontline. (2009). *Rewiring young brains*. Retrieved October 30, 2011, from Digital nation: Life on the virtual frontier, Public Broadcasting System (PBS) http://www.pbs.org/wgbh/pages/frontline/digitalnation/living-faster/digital-natives/rewiring-young-brains.html

Gopnik, A. (2010, July). How babies think. *Scientific American, 303*, 76–81.

Shreeve, J. (2005). Beyond the brain. *National Geographic, 207*(3), 1–12.

TED (Producer). (2004). Michael Merzenich on re-wiring the brain. Retrieved from http://www.ted.com/talks/michael_merzenich_on_the_elastic_brain.html

References

Azevedo, F. A., Carvalho, L. R., Grinberg, L. T., Farfel, J. M., Ferretti, R. E., Leite, R. E., . . . Herculano-Houzel, S. (2009). Equal numbers of neuronal and nonneuronal cells make the human brain an isometrically scaled-up primate brain. *The Journal of Comparative Neurology, 513*(5), 532–541.

Bennett, E., Diamond, M., Krech, D., & Rosenzweig, M. (1964). Chemical and anatomical plasticity of brain. *Science,* New Series, *146*(3644), 610–619.

Bhardwaj, R. D., Curtis, M. A., Spalding, K. L., Buchholz, B. A., Fink, D., Björk-Eriksson, T., . . . Frisén, J. (2011). Neocortical neurogenesis in humans is restricted to development. *Proceedings of the National Academy of Sciences of the United States of America, 103*(33), 12564–12568.

Brenhouse, H., & Andersen, S. (2011). Developmental trajectories during adolescence in males and females: A cross-species understanding of underlying brain changes. *Neuroscience and Biobehavioral Reviews, 35.*

Diamond, M. (Producer). (2007, October 17, 2015). Integrative Biology 131–Lecture 01: Organization of Body. Retrieved from https://youtube/S9WtBRNydso

Diamond, M. C., Krech, D., & Rosenzweig, M. (1964). The effects of an enriched environment on the histology of the rat cerebral cortex. *Journal of Comparatiave Neurology, 123,* 111–120.

Elber, T., Pantev, C., Wienbruch, C., Rockstroh, B., & Taub, E. (1995). Increased cortical representation of the fingers of the left hand in string players. *Science, 270*(5234), 305–309.

Eriksson, P. S., Perfilieva, E., Björk-Eriksson, T., Alborn, A., Nordborg, C., Peterson, D. A., & Gage, F. H. (1998). Neurogenesis in the adult human hippocampus. *Nature Medicine, 4,* 1313–1317.

Garlick, D. (2003). Integrating brain science research with intelligence research. *Current Directions in Psychological Science, 12*(5), 185–189.

Gazzaniga, M. S. (2008). Is anybody there? *Human: The science behind what makes us unique* (pp. 276–321). New York: HarperCollins.

Gibb, B. J. (2007). Chemical control: How legal and illegal drugs affect the brain. *The rough guide to the brain* (pp. 171–202). London: Rough Guides Ltd.

Giedd, J. (2008). The teen brain: Insights from neuroimaging. *Journal of Adolescent Health, 42*(4), 335–343.

Howard-Jones, P., Pollard, A., Blakemore, S.-J., Rogers, P., Goswami, U., Butterworth, B., . . . Kaufmann, L. (2007). Neuroscience and education: Issues and opportunities: A TLRP Commentary. http://www.tlrp.org/pub/documents/Neuroscience Commentary FINAL.pdf

James, W. (1950, 1890). *The principles of psychology.* New York: Dover.

James, W. (2005, 1892). *Talks to teachers on psychology; and to students on some of life's ideals.* Retrieved from http://www.gutenberg.org/files/16287/16287-h/16287-h.htm

Jiao, J., & Chen, D. F. (2008). Niche strocytes stimulate neurogenesis from dormant neural progenitors in non-conventional neurogenic regions of the adult CNS. *Stem Cells, 26*(5), 1221–1230.

Kandel, E. R., Schwartz, J. H., Jessell, T. M., Siegelbaum, S. A., & Hudspeth, A. J. (2013). *Principles of neural science* (5th ed.). New York: McGraw Hill Medical.

Low, L., & Cheng, H. (2006). Axon pruning: An essential step underlying the developmental plasticity of neuronal connections. *Philosophical Transactions: Biological Sciences, 361*(1473), 1531–1544.

National Institute of Mental Health. (2007). Brain matures a few years late in ADHD, but follows normal pattern. http://www.nimh.nih.gov/news/science-news/2007/brain-matures-a-few-years-late-in-adhd-but-follows-normal-pattern.shtml

National Research Council. (2000). Mind and brain. *How people learn: Brain, mind, experience, and school: Expanded edition* (pp. 114–128). Washington, DC: The National Academies Press.

Nelson, C. (1999). Neural plasticity and human development. *Current Directions in Psychological Science, 8*(2), 42–45.

Owen, A. M., Hampshire, A., Grahn, J. A., Stenton, R., Dajani, S., Burns, A. S., . . . Ballard, C. G. (2010). Putting brain training to the test. *Nature, 465*(7299), 775–778.

Pittenger, C., & Kandel, E. R. (2003). In search of general mechanisms for long-lasting plasticity: Aplysia and the hippocampus. *Long-term potentiation: Enhancing neuroscience for 30 years, philosophical transactions: Biological sciences, 358*(1432), 757–763.

Purves, D., Augustine, G. J., Fitzpatrick, D., Hall, W. C., LaMantia, A.-S., McNamara, J. O., & White, L. E. (2008). *Neuroscience.* Sunderland, MA: Sinauer Associates.

Schunk, D. H. (2012). Cognition and instruction. *Learning theories: An educational perspective* (pp. 278–323). Boston: Pearson.

Society for Neuroscience. (2008). *Brain facts: A primer on the brain and nervous system*. Washington, DC: Author.

Veyrac, A., Sacquet, J., Nguyen, V., Marien, M., Jourdan, F., & Didier, A. (2009). Novelty determines the effects of olfactory enrichment on memory and neurogenesis through noradrenergic mechanisms. *Neuropsychopharmacology, 34*, 786–795.

Woollett, K., & Maguire, E. A. (2011). Acquiring "the knowledge" of London's layout drives structural brain changes. *Current Biology, 21*(24-2), 2109–2114.

3

Cognition and **Instructional Design**

This chapter will introduce CORE Guiding Principle 3: How we learn dramatically affects what knowledge we can actually use. Instructional approaches such as priming, elaboration, extension, and knowledge integration are keys to learning outcomes. In teacher talk, this is about changing instructional design.

Learning Points

1. Combining knowledge gained from neuroscience, cognitive psychology, and educational research is providing teachers useful insights into instructional design, enhancing the learning experiences they can deliver in their classrooms.

2. Through meta-analysis research, educators can see how the human cognitive system plays out in on-the-ground learning. Because results are compiled from studies in many classrooms and widely varying settings, *best practices* can be identified.

3. As an example among many important bodies of work in educational meta-analysis, education researcher Robert Marzano used meta-analysis to identify nine categories of instructional strategies that appear to bear strongly on learning outcomes in the classroom, including the importance of helping students generate mental pictures — virtual snapshots in the brain.

4. Four instructional design concepts that specifically support comprehension and the ability to use what is learned are *priming, elaboration, extension,* and *knowledge integration*.

5. The human brain develops best in complex environments with sufficient stimulation. Enrichment improves brain function and expands both the weight and thickness of the cerebral cortex.

6. Enrichment is more than visual complexity. Rich use of vocabulary in the classroom, as well as opportunities to visualize, manipulate ideas, solve problems, and receive feedback, are important aspects for instructional design.

7. Effective cognition involves being able to draw on previously learned understanding—or patterns of thinking and behavior—and reapplying them.

8. The brain thrives on discovering and using patterns it finds. Patterns mean the arrangements, configurations, and relationships we can see in what we are learning.

9. One reason that mathematics is often a challenge for students is because of the layering of important patterns. One level of abstraction on another increases the brain processing required, especially for novices who may not have well captured the pattern yet. This general issue can be true in other subject matter areas as well.

10. From a cognitive view, it is useful for teachers to consider that intelligence sometimes can be thought of as the capacity to usefully remember, predict, apply, and extend patterns in the brain.

Introduction

A young teacher described how surprised she was when she first encountered the idea of brain plasticity. She thought it was a thrilling concept

Short Course: Cognitive Connections I

A

Agency—the sense of being responsible for and able to be in control of one's own learning, thoughts, and actions, as an active builder of our own knowledge.

C

Cognitive activation—two meanings: Teachers often use it to describe a student meaningfully engaging with the learning materials. In cognitive psychology and neuroscience, it involves the triggering or probability of triggering a circuit or network in an organism's cognitive system. **Cognitive psychology**—the scientific study of the acquisition, retention, and use of knowledge through the use of psychological approaches and methods. **Cognitive neuroscience**—the study of the biological basis for cognitive functioning, using the tools and methods of neuroscience.

E

Elaboration—restructuring, connecting, and identifying relations in our understandings, as well as linking in new elements of information. **Executive function**—a way in which we control our cognitive processes; includes planning and attention, along with selection, rehearsal, and monitoring of information retrieved from memory. **Extension**—the portion of elaboration (see above) that involves the gaining and interconnecting of new knowledge; since not all definitions of elaboration in the past have included this, an additional term is often found in instructional design and cognition literature.

Short Course:
Cognitive Connections I

I

Instructional design—from a cognitive perspective, the design of external events used to support internal processes involved with learning.

K

Knowledge integration—combining understanding from multiple approaches, mental models, or representations into a useful knowledge base that extends grasp or interpretation.

M

Meaningful consolidation—new material is successfully integrated into understanding by a student such that he or she makes connections to it and finds it meaningful; generally requires not only successful knowledge integration (see above) but conditionalizing the knowledge appropriately and satisfying brain conditions of relevance (see below) to utilize understanding.

N

Neural basis of arousal—not a concept generally in teacher vocabulary at this time but a key idea in neuroscience; brain arousal systems are responsible for maintaining vigilance for monitoring and reacting to important stimuli, such as detecting situations of reward and of novelty.

O

Orienting attention—attention is not a property of the whole brain but rather of specific networks of areas, such as in alerting, orienting, and executive attention; key for teachers is such networks may be successfully trained, sometimes even at young ages, potentially leading to improvements in schooling outcomes.

and wondered if it was as new to others as it had been to her. Why had it not been included in her teacher preparation program? she asked herself. Could it be that her university instructors had a hard time connecting the new knowledge to what teachers did every day in the classroom?

For many instructors, the connection comes through basic concepts of successful instructional design and cognition. In this chapter, we begin to explore Guiding Principle 3: *How we learn dramatically affects what knowledge we can actually use. Instructional approaches such as priming, elaboration, extension, and knowledge integration are key to learning outcomes. In teacher talk, this is about changing instructional design.* A base is built here in fundamental concepts. Then most of the specific examples are supplied in the follow-up Chapter 5, after some necessary implications of memory are introduced. This chapter and Chapter 5 also highlight approaches and topics teachers find helpful to make instructional design work well. In upcoming chapters, we continue to illustrate and connect the fundamentals of the CORE—what the brain is up to—as they might apply to the nuts and bolts of teaching.

Approaching Instructional Design

In teacher preparation programs, instructional design is taught as a process, as described in more detail in Chapter 5. In the instructional phase of the process (see Figure 3.3, shown later in the chapter), teachers learn instructional strategies, also called *pedagogy, instructional methods,* or *message design principles.* Such strategies have emerged over the years from areas such as teacher best practices and from research in education and cognitive psychology. They are incorporated into the instructional design process, which may begin with educational standards and curricular materials, as teachers decide which teaching methods and pedagogical approaches to use to bring the curriculum alive in the classroom. Thus, **instructional design** is a distinct and elaborated process, of which instructional strategies are an important component.

Four important instructional design concepts—priming, elaboration, extension, and knowledge integration—are introduced in this chapter and tied to what we know about how the brain learns. They are:

1. **Priming** communicates to learners what they should bring to the fore about what they already know as they commence learning new material.

2. **Elaboration** prompts deeper thought and reorganization of these initial ideas.

3. **Extension** asks learners to put into practice these emerging ideas, and in doing so to extend what they know and can do with them.

4. **Knowledge integration**, which the brain employs throughout the process, is the ongoing attempt to bring our ideas together and connect emerging thinking and actions with the larger framework of everything else we have mastered or experienced. **(See CORE 3e.)**

> ## Short Course:
> # Cognitive Connections I
>
> **P**
> **Pattern**—a distinct regularity perceived by the brain from which it draws information believed to be useful, including to make an inference, assign causality, or predict events; the brain may be more or may be less correct in any pattern, and is using perceived regularity to establish a type of "best guess."
> **Priming**—exposure to a stimulus that influences or helps trigger a later response; teachers often use priming to activate prior knowledge before new learning, as through a question, image, discussion, or other means that retrieves memories.
>
> **S**
> **Subgoaling**—when the human cognitive system is willing to suspend direct pursuit of a goal, and take a step that reduces barriers to the goal by analyzing and completing a precondition.

When these four aspects of learning come into play, the brain is better supported in developing knowledge and understandings of what it can actually use. This is true whether students are working with literature, mathematics, lyrics of a song, or any other aspect of the curriculum.

According to learning scientists, what all aspects of learning share in common is bringing information into an active form of memory, then engaging a type of **cognitive activation** that requires exploring, reorganizing, and reinforcing learning (Organisation for Economic Co-operation and Development [OECD], 2007). These four important examples are by no means exhaustive of all that might be considered. Later in the chapter, some additional instructional strategies will be discussed and research shared. At that point, teachers are encouraged to consider how their own strategies support learning.

An important theme of this chapter is that few of the instructional strategies to be mentioned will be new to veteran teachers. Why should they be, since they are intended to be examples of best practices established in instructional theory and learning theory? Rather, the point is to interpret such instructional strategies in light of what is known about the developing understanding of the brain and cognitive science. Can we learn something more about the utility of approaches such as examples and nonexamples, prototype formation, visualization, inert knowledge, school learning, situated cognition, and transfer through the lens of the three learning sciences? The goal is to glean information that may underscore understanding best practices.

This chapter focuses strongly on cognitive psychology, as the prior chapter did and the next chapter does on neuroscience. A major connection between chapters as the lens moves among the learning sciences is to appreciate how basic neuroscience underpinnings, such as the growing awareness of brain plasticity, inform what we are learning in other fields. The backdrop of plasticity in the last chapter, or a basic understanding of memory built in the next chapter, inform our understanding.

A number of important instructional design concepts will be mentioned in this chapter. For easy reference, they are summarized in the "Short Course: Cognitive Connections I" box shown earlier in the chapter. Especially noneducators and new teachers are encouraged to review these concepts, which may be more new to them than to in-service teachers.

When instructional design concepts appear in our discussion, as with the four just introduced, it is important for teachers to visualize them to make them "real" in their own brains. So a challenge to the reader at this point is to ask yourself as each strategy is introduced to visualize an example from your own professional practice.

▌▌| Priming, Elaboration, Extension, Knowledge Integration: An Example

Derek, a teacher of 7th-grade English language arts, creates graphic mini-novels in his classroom. Similar to comic books in appearance, they have more depth and often follow the plot characteristics of a short novel.

Derek believes the mini-graphic genre engages students through a literature form not traditionally taught by teachers. He knows that it doesn't matter whether he uses innovative passages or a more tried-and-true classical literature form—so long as it supports student thinking. As a veteran teacher, he has found that some approaches work better than others. In middle school, English language arts approaches and strategies may go by many names, but Derek finds he can illustrate his thinking with the four powerful instruction design ideas: priming, elaboration, extension, and knowledge integration. He finds that other teachers understand these concepts regardless of subject matter or grade-level areas. They can follow his thinking when he describes what he does.

In his graphic novel lesson, Derek begins by *priming*, or exposing students to a stimulus that influences or helps trigger a later response. This will guide their thinking throughout the activity. In his case, he often presents a few "frames," or parts, of a short comic strip, from the once-syndicated *Calvin and Hobbes* creator, Bill Watterson. Although Watterson unexpectedly halted his tumultuous strip nearly 20 years ago, Derek finds that it lives on, delighting young adults even today.

Derek believes the mini-novel experience gives students the chance to explore expression and creativity in a new way. Of course, this requires enough depth in the goals and objectives of learning to tap diverse literature in the classroom. Derek frets school and state leaders will lose sight of this but is hopeful as a professional that the way he can show he supports learning will carry the day.

Next, Derek provides the tools to create visuals. If he has access to the school set of tablets that day, he issues the digital devices. If not, the students get colored markers and butcher paper. Students are instructed to tell a story from their own life entirely in visuals. They start with outlined squares that form a blank comic strip. Then they draw in pictures to form a sequence. About 30 minutes later, Derek sees stories launched all over the room.

Elaboration comes next. Here, students draw arrows and lines, and begin to think through the flow of their stories, such as rising action, conflict, and resolution. Irony and exposition are considered, all with a specific purpose. The intent is to restructure, connect, and identify relationships *that are already nascent, or beginning to appear, through the mental imagery of the strip*. Elaboration literally means restructuring, connecting, and identifying relations in our understandings, as well as linking in new elements of information.

Through reorganization and extending ideas, elaboration allows the brain to make very real connections that are mental, of course, but also physical in nature. A miniature example of plasticity in action, the brain changes itself, or learns to think of the concepts in new ways.

Our veteran teacher goes about helping students elaborate in a variety of ways, such as through prompting for ideas or asking essential questions. He inquires, for instance, whether the students believe their readership would better understand the story if it was written out fully in text. Or do they think the new picture-based approach they've created is better. He asks why?

Using 7th-grade language, such as *glitter graphics* and *emo* and *posting*, students make compelling arguments on both sides. Derek uses their answers to discuss the power of non-linguistic representations in a way students understand. A goal is to share with students findings about effective communication.

Derek isn't surprised when some students talk about animating in digital imaging tools, such as Animoto, or programing apps that "fly" their photo albums together. But he wants to help students take it to a deeper level. As they post their tales in social media, he crafts experiences that bring educational standards to life: He asks students if they prefer to be readers or viewers, and whether they would choose to create words or art.

When the answer is both, Derek uses this as an opportunity for a teachable moment. An *extension* exercise takes place. Here, students gain new associated knowledge. For the first time, the teacher pairs up students to finish the last step: filling in the dialogue bubbles that verbally express the story. The original author talks through his or her ideas and the partner records, creating the strip text through a type of creative summarizing and note taking that annotates the story.

In the end, *knowledge integration* is the goal. This means combining understanding from multiple approaches, mental models, or representations into a useful base that extends grasp or interpretation. Expecting this, the brain is prepared for readiness to learn in the setting, but also for independence in completing tasks.

▓|| The Benefits of Using Your Own Experiences

In trying to connect our experiences with portraits of teachers presented in this chapter, we can ask ourselves what strategy we might use that taps the brain. Veteran teachers and school leaders may find this straightforward, because they have a great deal of experience in the classroom. They will be able to picture many situations from real-life recollections, so their "stretch goal" may be to think of how these relate to the principles and ideas here. New teachers, on the other hand, may not yet have a wealth of experience with their own classrooms. However, we all have a great deal of experience with learning. First-time teachers are encouraged to draw on internships, practicum, and tutoring experiences, as well as their own experiences in the classroom as students. These are all powerful sources of prior knowledge about how people learn. Some readers also may find their experiences as parents, grandparents, relatives, or caregivers for children provide ample opportunities to visualize. The important idea here is to picture each idea in your context.

By placing ideas and examples in the context of your own experience, you will benefit in at least two areas, based on brain-related principles. The first is you will be connecting and associating ideas in memory, which greatly facilitates acquisition, recall, and retention (see Chapter 4 on memory). This means you will have something effective to use later in your career, as your learning persistence and application improves. Second, when you are able to establish both clarity and relevance for the brain, your learning time is better spent—a key idea we will more fully explore in upcoming chapters.

Priming means exposure to a stimulus that influences or helps trigger a later response. Psychologists use the term to describe driving our thinking in guided directions by an initial reminder at the start. Teachers often use another term—*activating prior knowledge*—to carry the same or a similar meaning. For instance, cognitive psychologist Daniel Reisberg (2010b), who has written extensively on the science of the mind, showed how our understanding of stories, or even ordinary conversations in everyday life, depends on extracting key bits of information from an extensive storehouse of knowledge we all have. Otherwise, every story would require all information to be supplied. When telling a youngster a story about saving money in a piggybank, for instance, there would be no understanding of what a piggybank is or why it exists. It would have to be explained. If it rattles when it is shaken, the child would need to be told about metal coins that clink together—but first, you would have to tell the child what a coin is and the role money serves in society. This would be a long story to be sure.

The use of different phrases such as *priming* and *activating prior knowledge* are an example of how cross-talk among "mind" fields introduces new words. The discourse language, or words used to move the conversation forward, may differ between fields. Bringing them together requires discipline. They may also employ different methods or techniques. For teachers, activating prior knowledge, or priming, often takes place through a question, picture, discussion, or other means that retrieves, or triggers, memories. For a cognitive psychologist in a research laboratory, it may be a single word or simple image, kept standardized to trace the reaction of the patient or respondent.

In summary, priming prepares the brain by accessing information it already has. Prior knowledge is brought to bear. The brain also cues signals for what associations might be made for higher-order reasoning, problem solving, and new learning.

Turning to the Classroom with Meta-Analysis

A classroom teacher for 25 years, one veteran instructor described how he has seen many trends in education come and go. Often, nothing lasts because it is replaced by the "latest" idea or fad. This teacher described how he liked findings from educational meta-analysis, or the compilation of many educational research studies together. He called understanding the findings of meta-analysis "a must" for all serious educators and invaluable for the instruction of students.

He is not alone in his tributes. Some of the top best-selling books among educators today are, believe it or not, meta-analysis reports. Hiding behind colorful covers, they help teachers translate research into action by pulling together years and often decades of educational research. The goal, as the veteran teacher points out, is to identify methods of instruction actually proven to increase student achievement.

Meta-analyses are routinely carried out in many disciplines, including education, psychology, and cognitive science. They are even present in neuroscience, such as when bringing together imaging data.

In education, meta-analysis synthesis studies can be found in many areas. Probably the most well-known to teachers today are several large meta-analysis reports from Robert Marzano in the United States, John Hattie working originally in Australia and New Zealand, and early studies from James A. and Chen-Lin Kulik and others on feedback and instructional design in the classroom.

Seen in a larger light, these teaching and learning studies connect to their sister fields in brain science and cognitive psychology in an interesting way: They are basically all working with the human cognitive system. Thus, emerging brain mechanisms underpin neuroscience, and developing views of mind and learning intrigue cognitive psychologists. In meta-analysis, educators see how the human cognitive system plays out through another "lens"—actual on-the-ground learning, compiled over many classrooms.

As an example to introduce how educators such as the veteran teacher described earlier benefit from meta-analysis, we will consider in this chapter some findings from Robert Marzano, with other scholars introduced in future chapters. Author of *Classroom Instruction That Works* and numerous other guides based on meta-analysis (Marzano, 1998, p. 4; Marzano, 2003; Marzano, 2009), Marzano originally taught English in the New York public schools and became interested in studies about what makes teaching successful. New studies always seemed to be coming out, he noticed, but he felt important research would be more useful if it were collected together and analyzed in one spot. Perhaps it would paint a more informative picture. So Marzano went back to school and earned his Ph.D., studying how to bring the field together. His goal was to help students learn and to help instructors teach. The Marzano investigations involved harvesting what was already known from research-based evidence. He asked questions about how the field of education could accumulate findings across many studies to see what they really said, collectively. In order to have an impact on the field, it should be done, Marzano believed, in a way that was helpful for teachers.

 RESOURCE

K–12 teachers can use with students: Dessoff, 2012. (See the Citations list at the end of this chapter.)

Marzano's classroom instruction book identified nine categories of instructional strategies that seemed to bear strongly on learning outcomes in the classroom. Based on the research literature, all nine approaches made important differences in how students learn. He then ranked the strategies in order of what made the most difference. Because the results were from accumulated studies with different protocols and research approaches, they offer a rough estimate of strategy effect and might not reflect identical findings for every classroom. But by giving teachers a synthesis of the results, it seeded ideas and offered results teachers might find useful in their own classrooms. Using the studies, Marzano explained to teachers the impact of the approaches.

To take an example, one teaching strategy on the Marzano list is "nonlinguistic representation." This refers to creating and using pictures, graphics, and visual displays to build understanding and mental imagery during learning. Marzano found it is especially important for students to generate mental pictures while learning. In teaching and learning research, such imagery is called *representation*. So, *nonlinguistic representation* simply means imagery accomplished in ways other than through written text or spoken language. It is a simple concept, but ask yourself this: In a typical classroom of any level, how much of an hour's teaching is taken up by talk or text and how much through visual presentation?

Like a virtual snapshot in the brain, through mental imagery, the brain builds a picture of what we are learning. We knit together relationships into a meaningful whole that makes sense to us. In doing so, we identify discrepancies and build understanding.

Nonlinguistic representation can take place in reading, writing, social studies, math, science, the fine or applied arts, movement, health studies—just about any area. Approaches include drawing our ideas, creating graphs, generating mental pictures, and even making physical models.

Teachers use these approaches often in the classroom, but some more than others. Marzano asked, How much does it matter when teachers help students visualize during learning? It turned out that for teachers who emphasized this approach, it made a significant difference. Across 246 studies, students who were more exposed to these techniques to consolidate their understanding gained, on average, 27 percentile points above those who were not similarly exposed. Such a gain represents, on average, for instance, moving a typical student to the top quarter of the class, or, at the state level, moving an average state into the top five states of the U.S.

Thinking about . . . Cognition

A funny story swept across the Internet a while back. A man who had signed up for a gym membership during the New Year season wanted his money back. "I was supposed to get fit in just two months with this membership," said the man, who had a saggy belly and double chin. "But it's way past two months and just look at me!"

Studying the member's records, a gym representative looked puzzled. She replied, "But sir, you never actually *used* your gym membership."

We laugh at a mental disconnect like this, but it is a simple, albeit humorous, example of human cognition, or how we go about thinking. Cognition has many different definitions but we will define it here as a set of processes for acquiring, retaining, integrating, and applying knowledge (OECD, 2007). As the New Year's joke illustrates, cognition relies on thinking and reasoning, which in turn is founded on brain function. In other words, brain activity is necessary for the information-processing functions and knowledge development we know as cognition. **(See CORE 3a.)**

The gym story amuses us because we identify with the wishful thinking of the pudgy guy while at the same time we recognize the error in his cognitive process: Buying a membership doesn't create the fitness. How nice it might be in our busy lives if we could get fit with just a fee. The whimsical humor emerges through perceiving and identifying with the outraged man's error in *cognition*.

Such examples of cognition, or thought, surround us all the time; indeed, we are constantly engaged in processing understanding of the world around us. As Reisberg (2010b) explains, many human activities don't appear on the surface to be intellectual, yet they would utterly collapse without our cognitive functioning. He describes the method by which many cognitive psychologists work to examine these behaviors as, roughly, beginning with a particular performance or behavior, then hypothesizing a series of unseen mental events leading to it. Not stopping there, they consider what explanations might be plausible, and design new studies to test the new ideas.

In this way, **cognitive psychology** is the scientific study of the acquisition, retention, and use of knowledge through the use of psychological approaches and methods (Reisberg, 2010b). In some traditional approaches, enriched environments might be explored by providing choices to an animal, such as a monkey or a mouse, and then rewarding or reinforcing choices for one pattern of behavior over another. This might lead to a model of decision making that the animal appears to employ, its speed or reliability of response, or another psychological attribute of interest for the research.

By contrast, **cognitive neuroscience**, which is the study of the biological basis for cognitive functioning using the tools and methods of neuroscience (Reisberg, 2010b), might explore the same scenario but with different tools and to answer different questions. Work might focus, for instance, on what neurons, circuits, and networks are activated during the behavioral process. The neuroscience lens might ask what brain structures are involved in the executive functions deployed, **orienting attention**, cognitive activation and arousal, memory formation, and so forth. It also might investigate how the brain physically changes following any learning that takes place.

These approaches of understanding are different ways of knowing, yet they inform each other. Increasingly they are blended or brought together in modern research practices, as has been done in enriched environments.

Who's in Charge: The Mind or the Brain?

Cognition is a cross-over word in the psychology lexicon. Not only is it associated with the brain but it is also deeply related to the concept of mind. So what is *mind* and how does it differ from *brain?*

Here we will define *mind* as the *conscious* thought processes of the brain. Many scientists and psychologists believe that minds are simply what brains do, as Professor Marvin Minsky describes in his Society of Mind course at the Massachusetts Institute of Technology (MIT). In other words, when specific neural pathways are activated, they generate the visual imagery, conscious ideas, thoughts, and reasoning that we have come to know as *mind*.

In this chapter, many of the topics involve conscious cognitive processes of the brain. Often the terms *brain* and *mind* could be used interchangeably. In this text, *brain* is used unless *mind* is specifically required as a distinction. This is not to suggest a knowledge hierarchy, such as the preference of *brain* over *mind*, but so as not to confuse our teacher readers, who may be searching for a specific reason when terms change.

Others go so far as to suggest the term *brain* should not be used unless specifically discussing neurobiological evidence. However, a more nuanced approach for teachers may be to consider *mind* as a verb—the conscious activities resulting from a set of processes in which the brain engages. Cornell University Psychology Professor Shimon Edelman, author of *The Happiness of Pursuit*, for instance, serves up a fairly cut-and-dried case for how the brain gives rise to mind: The *mind* is described as essentially a bundle of ongoing computations, while the *brain* supports them (Edelman, 2012).

Even happiness—which in Edelman's work involves everything from perception, motivation, and emotions to action, memory, thinking, social cognition, and language—is built, he says, on a toolbox of computations (Edelman, 2012).

This concept remains a controversial topic across the "mind" sciences. Even whether it *is* controversial is controversial. The field called "philosophy of mind" is a complex area of study. Over the ages, plenty of twisty ins-and-outs emerged century by century. People have pondered the human mind and come to many different conclusions. Sometimes conceptions of soul and spirit enter in. Other eras focused on the unknowability of ourselves, or inquiry into limits *about* knowledge of the mind, *by* the mind.

In every era, however, mind is strongly associated with the nature of what it means to be human. Therefore, whether mind is purely a biological concept or not has been intriguing and perplexing. In the past, it was more possible for us to self-examine our own conscious thoughts than to inspect or even know about such mechanisms as neural pathways. So understandings about the biological mechanisms of mind have waited to emerge. Today, one perspective in the field describes virtually all psychologists and neuroscientists as agreeing about a purely physical basis in the brain for mind and consciousness (Cherry, 2010). Other stances retain a more metaphysical view, especially for human consciousness. In other words, to be aware of the images and associations—or ideas—our brains generate is one thing. To be aware of what they mean or how we arrived at them may be another.

For teachers, the debate clarifies and becomes holistic rather than broken up into bits, because goals of effective instructional design aim to enhance *both* brain and mind. If brain and mind do not differ but are simply different points of view for the same thing, then teachers draw on both views. If brain and mind retain a physical and metaphysical presence, that works, too—teachers engage with the whole child, or the whole person, as they work together with learners.

It is important for teachers to remember, however, that reinforcing neural pathways facilitates learning, which is the job of teachers and students. At the same time, however, from another vantage point, teachers deeply consider the ideas that students ponder, so this involves the conceptions we form in mind.

Executive Functions: A CEO of the Brain

Touch your forehead. Resting right behind your fingertips is the so-called "CEO of the brain"—your frontal lobe. One of the four major lobes of the cerebrum, the frontal lobe has some major responsibilities for many ways in which we control our cognitive processes (see Figure 3.1). It runs much of our brain's **executive function** (Society for Neuroscience, 2008). Other brain regions are involved too, including the parietal lobe. Damage to the frontal lobe brings on a wide range of symptoms, which can range from poor coordination and slurred speech to personality changes and decision-making issues.

Executive function manages the brain's goal achievement as described in Chapter 1. When teachers consider effective approaches to instructional design, they are often unknowingly wrestling with this very entity. So getting to know the brain's CEO is similar to learning about the leader of any other organization in which we have an interest. If we know a leader's capacities and tendencies, it greatly helps in understanding with what we are dealing.

For instance, do teachers have to work through executive function to capture student attention and hold it? If so, what is known about how the brain monitors incoming streams of information for understanding? And crucially, can executive function itself be trained and improved upon—in other words, can we increase the talent of our CEO?

Executive function isn't a single function in the brain; rather, it describes a disparate group of activities that includes brain processes we use for planning and attention. Also included are the ways in which we direct the selection of information retrieved from memory. The executive rehearses and monitors information as we use it to achieve what we have planned. **(See CORE 3b.)** Thus, executive function is an "umbrella term," or a catchall for high-level abilities that draw on and coordinate more basic work.

Cognitive scientists often group executive functions into three core areas (Diamond, 2012):

- *Inhibition,* including establishing self-control, interference control, and the ability to focus selective attention. Inhibition extinguishes behaviors and promotes cognitive resource use for plans and goals.
- *Cognitive flexibility,* which is our ability to shift brain processing effectively, including exhibiting mental flexibility. This executive function is believed to be closely linked to creativity.
- *Allocation and management of working memory,* which allows us to manage information stored briefly. This topic is discussed more in the next chapter.

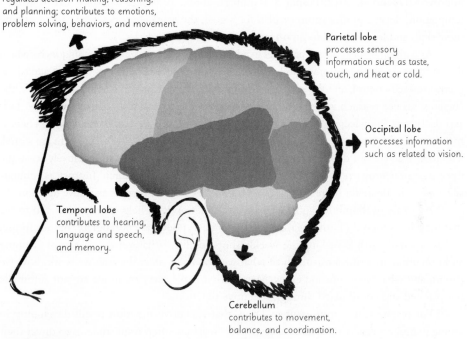

Frontal lobe
regulates decision making, reasoning, and planning; contributes to emotions, problem solving, behaviors, and movement.

Parietal lobe
processes sensory information such as taste, touch, and heat or cold.

Occipital lobe
processes information such as related to vision.

Temporal lobe
contributes to hearing, language and speech, and memory.

Cerebellum
contributes to movement, balance, and coordination.

FIGURE 3.1

The Brain

The brain has three units, the forebrain, the midbrain, and the hindbrain:
- The *forebrain* is the largest part of the human brain. It consists of the cerebrum and numerous structures hidden beneath it.
- The *cerebrum* is split into two halves, each with four lobes: occipital, parietal, temporal, and frontal.
- The surface layers of these lobes comprise the *cerebral cortex*, believed to be critical to our higher-level thought processes. The cortex is extensively wrinkled in humans, giving the characteristic look of the brain. Wrinkling makes it possible for unusually large sheets of cortex to be packed into the human skull.

The other two units of the brain are the hindbrain and midbrain. These include a ball of tissue in the lower brain called the *cerebellum* and the *brain stem* connecting to the spine. These are critical for movement and reflex. The lower and more ancient parts of the human brain are often involved in more automated or unconscious brain functioning, although other parts of the brain can be too.

These core executive functions come together to build higher-order executive functions, such as reasoning, problem solving, and planning (Collins & Koechlin, 2012; Lunt et al., 2012).

Researchers point out that our executive functions are essential for our mental and physical health; success in school and in life; and our cognitive, social, and psychological development. The good news for teachers and one of the most exciting developments in cognitive science research is clear indication that executive function can be trained or improved (Diamond, 2012; Posner & Rothbart, 2000). Although it takes effort to avoid a temptation, delay a gratification, or plan for a goal, the researchers describe that practicing these skills and learning not to go on auto-pilot pays dividends.

As with other areas of best practices in education, teachers have many techniques by which they support developing planning and goal-oriented processes of children and young adults, the exertion of self-control, and the encouragement of attention, effort, and focus. For schools, the cognitive science research is a clear reminder that not only educational content standards—facts and declarative knowledge—but our executive processes need development as well. There is more discussion on this subject in Chapter 11, where insights across the curriculum are shared. This topic is an area for directing research questions that might be asked collaboratively across the three areas of neuroscience, cognitive psychology, and educational research. Instructors continually express the desire for more information on how teachers can support executive function.

As a rule of thumb, the goal of executive function is to help specify goals and to see that they are achieved (Tamminga, 2004). It can be as poetic as choreographing our future, and as down to earth as making the weekly shopping list. Whatever the case, goal planning and execution are critical for much of what we do. They affect the way we work, how we parent, and what we create and enjoy. Many activities we carry on in life are not automatic but planned and coordinated through executive function.

For teachers, it is important to know that executive function is still developing in young brains, especially the brains of teenagers. Teachers often want students to direct their attention to specific aims, to plan future tasks, and to inhibit inappropriate behavior (Howard-Jones et al., 2007). Although these may seem like simple requests to make of students, they all involve complex behaviors that make big demands on executive function.

All in all, the requirements of executive function are a tall order that fortunately our brains are designed to meet. For instance, during the maturation process called "frontalization" of our thinking, the prefrontal cortex in the school-age child is gradually becoming more and more able to take over these capabilities successfully (see Chapter 5).

Ultimately by about age 25, the prefrontal cortex is likely to regulate behavioral responses more fully, which is after the time that even many college-educated students leave formal education behind. Young adults are typically not working with the full maturity of the human cognitive system. Therefore instruction must be designed to support these skills for the developing brain. In this way, teachers are helping to lay down the foundations for our mental success by helping us put the executive function of the brain into practice (U.S. Department of Health and Human Services, 2013).

Executive function plays out not only in intellectual activities but in a variety of socially oriented pursuits. Socializing may seem like fun, but it takes powerful planning to intuit what others are thinking, relate our actions to theirs, and generally to get along and thrive in human society. Whether at work or play, we need our brain power to plan, direct our attention, and bring ideas and concepts quickly into memory. So, to be social taxes our minds as well as expands them.

Also included in executive function is our ability to multitask. This is where we turn our attention from one goal to another, or task switch, often in less than a few seconds. Recent research shows that, at least for simple tasks, the brain may have the ability to keep two separate goals running concurrently in the brain, allocated separately to each frontal lobe (Charron & Koechlin, 2010). Splitting attention comes at a cost, though, and additional goals are handled sequentially but at such a rapid pace that it may appear to be simultaneous to the casual observer. A student may appear to be watching the teacher, turning pages in a book, paying attention to how a classmate is behaving, and feeling the vibrations of a pocketed cell phone text all at once. But in reality, a good deal of task switching and distraction is going on (Harmon, 2010).

In terms of instructional design (see the box "The Standards-based Instructional Cycle"), this leaves teachers facing a modern-day dilemma. To what degree do they select approaches that reduce distraction and clear the path for students to focus very selectively in the classroom? And to what extent do teachers help students learn to thrive in an environment of multitasking?

From the brain perspective, costs come in shifting information in and out of memory to attend to the rapidly changing focal points. During multitasking, when information turns up that the executive portion of the brain doesn't need at the moment but will work with soon, or when information cycles in and out of processing, handy helpers come into play. It turns out the executive has a number of low-level assistants (Reisberg, 2010a). They are used to store information for brief periods of time. Like a piece of scratch paper you scribble on, or as if asking your friend to remember a phone number for you while you dial it, these "assistants" apparently don't do much more than serve as a pending zone. Memory plays a big role in this process. It will be discussed in Chapter 4.

The Standards-based Instructional Cycle

This chapter looks at one aspect of instructional design through a particular lens: what contributions the three learning sciences can make. To step back to give an example of the larger picture in instructional design, in the advanced learning theory course at the University of Oregon (see Preface), we think of instructional design in terms of a "Standards-based Instructional Cycle" (see Figure 3.2). Here, standards refer to educational standards, usually specified for particular subject matter and grade level areas by states or localities in the United States.

The large picture on instructional design for teachers and schools involves not only standards but also the components shown in the cycle:

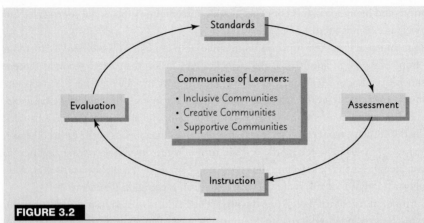

FIGURE 3.2

Standards-based Instructional Cycle

A simple example of an instructional design cycle emphasizes combining components of theory (standards-based theory and instructional theory/learning theory) with components of evidence (classroom-based pre-assessment and follow-up formative, summative, and reflective program evaluation).

- The goals and objectives of the learning (here represented as *educational standards*) need to be specified and understood.
- In the classroom, pre-*assessment* is used to understand where learners stand on the goals, as well as to incorporate processes such as content analysis to unpack the goals relative to the needs of the students.
- *Instructional interventions* are designed and implemented to address the goals and needs. This can include media selection, identifying learning outcomes, scope and sequence, message design, and prototype development, and may be done as a larger process in professional learning communities, and adjusted by teachers for their students.
- *Evaluation* of how the approaches have worked reflects on continuous improvement in schools, and needs to include addressing effective professional development and support of teachers.

The cycle shown here has two components of theory (standards-based theory and instructional theory/learning theory) tied together by two components of evidence (classroom-based pre-assessment and follow-up formative, summative, and reflective evaluation for continuous improvement). Teachers are encouraged to work together to create a supportive learning environment and a "stretch culture" where all students can learn and grow (DuFour, DuFour, Eaker, & Many, 2010).

Brain Power to Spare? No Way

One "neuromyth," or false idea about the brain, that persists widely and that many teachers believe involves brain capacity. Many educators have bought into the notion that we use only about 10 percent, or some other small percentage, of our brains. If only students would use the rest of their brains, the thinking goes, they would do much better in the classroom.

The idea does not, however, come from neuroscience research, and is just plain wrong. Much to the disappointment of many, we don't have a brain "spare tire" waiting around if we would only use it, as the late Dr. Barry Beyerstein of the Brain Behavior Laboratory at Simon Fraser University in Vancouver explains, described in a frequently cited *Scientific American* interview.

It is not known exactly where the 10% myth originated. Some suggest it may be a misinterpretation of early work by American psychologist and author William James, who wrote in *The Energies of Men,* "We are making use of only a small part of our possible mental and physical resources."

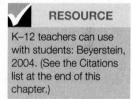

RESOURCE

K–12 teachers can use with students: Beyerstein, 2004. (See the Citations list at the end of this chapter.)

Others suggest it was culled from the early Industrial Age, when factory managers used it to encourage persistence by workers. Certainly the fact that the notion was included in the preface of Dale Carnegie's self-help bible first published in 1936, *How to Win Friends and Influence People,* kept it alive.

Beyerstein (2004) described the 10% myth as the most asked question by audiences following his public lectures about the brain. He debunked the myth by pointing out that brain imaging studies and research on people with traumatic brain injury have revealed that no part of the brain can be seriously damaged without consequences. In other words, the brain uses all of its capacity. Furthermore, cognitive scientists have established that so much information is available in our environments that no single brain has the capacity to attend to it all. Even if we attended to it all day long, the internal and external stimuli available to our senses is too vast. So the result is that we have to make choices about how we use our brains. Contrary to the myth that we have so much to spare, the actual story is that we are constantly engaged in a type of cognitive triage.

Through executive function and other pathways, each individual brain both consciously and unconsciously prioritizes. Responding to the availability of this excess signal, or "too much" information, requires that we filter. Therefore, long before the onslaught of the so-called Information Age, we were already overwhelmed, just by our own senses. This has big implications for educators, which will be taken up more in upcoming chapters.

Environments in Which We Thrive

Ironically, given the idea of cognitive triage, it appears our brains develop best in complex environments, or at least where we have sufficient stimulation around us. **(See CORE 3c.)** Research shows enrichment improves brain function in a variety of ways.

What is enrichment? It can be everything from having adults who respond to us in words we can understand to colorful objects that we enjoy when playing outdoors. Evidence that enrichment builds brains includes prolific animal research (National Research Council, 2000). When raised in a complex environment, animals show:

- Expanded cerebral cortex, including its weight and thickness when exposed to sufficient stimulation
- Increased number of synapses per neuron
- Greater supply of blood and oxygen to the brain
- Provision to the brain of more nutrients and greater capacity for removing waste

By contrast, animal studies reveal that impoverished environments are associated with reduced cortical gray matter. For children, poverty and the effects of a deprived environment are an area of active research (Brito & Noble, 2014; Hackman, Farah, & Meaney, 2010; Lipina & Posner, 2012). Cognitive and imaging studies are beginning to suggest which brain networks may be most influenced by poverty, including those that serve language, executive function, and memory.

An ongoing debate is currently taking place about whether environments really need to be enriched. To get such effects, is it necessary to truly enrich, or simply to avoid neglect—or impoverish—the environment? In other words, how much complexity is enough?

This may seem like a subtle distinction. But scientists point out that much of the research to date has taken place with animals raised in a fairly normal environment—one with companionship, objects such as exercise wheels and toys, and a degree of nurturing—as compared to when these supports are removed. The brain shows better development under the former conditions, establishing that the stimulation is needed. How much more stimulation might help is somewhat of an open question, but one that has a direct impact on schools because it affects resource allocation. How highly enriched do our learning environments need to be to support optimal learning?

So, enrichment is relative. Scientists and other experts in learning debate if there is a baseline for the effect: When is enough enough? Educator and writer Eric Jensen (2006) calls this "the law of contrasts" and describes it as the most important principle for enrichment studies. A complex environment in one setting may be deprived compared to another. For instance, newly designed natural habitats in the world-famous San Diego Zoo Safari Park may be enriched when compared to some municipal zoo settings, yet still remain in less complex surroundings than in an original ecosystem. How do the brains of animals in each environment compare?

Complexity, then, is a matter of degree (Howard-Jones et al., 2007). Scientists agree that severe deprivation results in problems for human learning. The question becomes how much is enough, and can there even be too much? For example, do we need to surround children with blinking computer displays and three-dimensional toys that do every kind of activity? Is this more an appealing gimmick to open the wallets of loving parents and grandparents? What about the people in less advantaged countries and settings? How should they best spend their enrichment capacity?

The international OECD Learning Sciences report sums it up by saying a sufficiently stimulating environment is one that offers each child the possibility to cultivate his or her skills (OECD, 2007). The OECD reminds teachers that cognitive functions undergo important and substantial change for every child in the school-age years, as discussed in Chapter 2. It asks educators to keep in mind that both environmental and emotional factors (see Chapter 9) are in play.

The Organisation for Economic Co-operation and Development also points out that a rich learning environment needs to go beyond what is simply eye-pleasing. Citing neurobiological research on learning, the OECD report specifically mentions supporting not only visual enrichment for students but also so-called verbal, spatial, and problem-solving "enrichment." This means, for instance, during instructional design, providing a rich use of vocabulary in the classroom as well as opportunities to visualize and manipulate ideas, and to solve problems and receive feedback. These are all forms of enrichment, or important stimulation in the learning setting. Instructional designs neglect important opportunities for learning if enrichment is considered visual turf only.

The ideas of enrichment are applicable for teachers across subject matter and grade levels, and in areas as diverse as language, mathematics, physical skills, and social situations. For example, teachers sometimes talk about the "thirty-million word deficit" (Hart & Risley, 2003). In their groundbreaking study published in 2003, researchers Hart and Risley observed the interactions of 42 families from various socioeconomic backgrounds over 2.5 years to assess how interaction between a parent and child shape language and vocabulary acquisition. They found that at age 3, children from privileged families had heard 30 million more words than children from underprivileged families. Follow-up data indicated that the measures of accomplishment at age 3 predicted third-grade school achievement. Thus, the simple act of more speaking and the introduction of additional words is an example of verbal enrichment.

The OECD Learning Sciences report also describes 21st-century views of intelligence as evoking specifically verbal, spatial, and problem-solving skills because this is an era when complex information abounds. Processing it in meaningful ways is a challenge. Understanding and making sense of the moving target of knowledge is key for students. Today's students may hold dozens of different jobs and careers over a lifetime. Learning to learn, and having the capacity to do so, is a crucially important skill.

The concept of enriched environments provides teachers with a good opportunity to consider the research contrasts of cognitive psychology and cognitive neuroscience. Both inform us about patterns in learning but have different approaches and methods.

Allocating Attention: An Example

Jacqueline Gottlieb, associate professor of neuroscience at Columbia University, has described how each of us has millions of things we could attend to every moment. Even just in her own office, distractions include a stack of papers on the desk, technology devices here and there, books and reports on shelves, and a large picture window over the Manhattan scenery.

Gottlieb works with primates to study how the brain learns, reasons, and makes decisions in a changing world. By investigating these functions in the monkey's visual system, she combines brain and behavior focusing on the parietal and the frontal lobes—two key brain areas involved in attention control.

According to Gottlieb, one key concept in attention that teachers should know about is the **neural basis of arousal**. In the brain, this literally means to awaken or wake up. As in arousing us to knowledge or action, when the brain "wakes up" to something around it, we start to really pay attention. And that's when the brain often learns best, neuroscientists suspect.

But Gottlieb asks, When it is time to learn, how do we trigger arousal? This can be a difficult question. Videogame developers and film directors might trigger arousal with fear and violence. But can we trigger it in a more appropriate way?

A certain degree of novelty, or not already knowing, is often necessary, Gottlieb tells educators. A researcher and a scholar, Gottlieb instructs not only budding neuroscientists in her department but teaches courses on the Columbia campus more generally. For the brain, novelty grabs our attention, she tells her audiences. Encountering the unknown, or experiencing uncertainty as Gottlieb puts it, tells us there is something present to be learned, for the primate cognitive system, including for humans.

But Gottlieb points out that there can't be too much uncertainty. Novelty is good, but there have to be patterns there too that the brain identifies. We need to judge that the uncertainty is possible to grapple with, in order to make the effort. Gottlieb describes as an example an electronic screen or computer monitor with nothing on it but a random pattern of white dots, such as the ubiquitous "snow," or static, of the old days of poor broadcast television reception. This qualifies as maximum uncertainty. It is not interesting to the brain, Gottlieb says, because there is nothing for it to decipher. Instead, the brain needs to have a pattern we can access, she describes. She is good at setting up new patterns for monkeys to tackle—objects and activities in their world that draw them in.

Another kind of attention, she explains, is what she calls attention for liking. What is it? Gottlieb explains that if you simply associate any stimulus with a reward, that kind of learning is very, very fast. Just two or three times and you will associate it. Colorful pictures teachers put up in the classroom, a bell for a favorite activity, even the smell of new pencil shavings before we get to tackle something can bring about associations we love in school. A sharp pencil and clean sheet of paper—or the swipe of a finger across a responsive mobile device—and we may find we are ready to tackle the challenge that comes our way.

When the brain judges the association as something important to the world around us and in which we need to engage, that is ice cream on the cake. Gottlieb explains that relevance is a huge topic for the brain.

But for relevance, you need a world model, or a model in your mind of how the world works, according to her research. Without it, the brain cannot gauge what is relevant. But building up our understanding of the world entirely on our own is tough. In fact, Gottlieb says, if humans had to derive everything about how the world works from solely their own experiences, it would take hundreds or thousands of years. Indeed, it would be impossible to do in a single human lifetime, Gottlieb points out.

So this is a major goal of school. Teachers help give us a world model. In fact, Gottlieb states, they give us models we could not learn ourselves otherwise in a lifetime, since they draw on the body of acquired human knowledge, and pass it along.

The Flynn Effect in Cognition

An example of enrichment that fascinates teachers today is the "Flynn effect" in cognition, named after James R. Flynn in the 1980s, a professor of political science in New Zealand. A Flynn effect has come to be known as any major shift in behavior that appears across a population, but happens so rapidly that it cannot be attributed to the slow shaping expected by evolution. James Flynn originally looked at the trend in increasing IQ scores around the world. Today, researchers still ponder whether a dramatic Flynn effect is occurring in human society: Are we all getting smarter?

Much to the surprise of many educators, scores on IQ tests appear to be rising broadly across the population, even when adjusted for ways the tests, respondent population, or score reporting has changed over the years (Flynn, 2009; Rönnlund & Nilsson, 2009). If this is true, the Flynn effect would be a change taking place too rapidly for evolution to be at the root.

Some of the Flynn effect research argues that such a change, if it exists, is coming in large part through how students perform in on-the-spot problem solving without a previously learned exact method (Flynn, 2006). This means figuring out how to do something no one ever specifically taught you.

To do this effectively, the brain often takes patterns of understanding mastered in prior learning, and repurposes them to good effect. When students engage in problem-solving in the absence of an exact memorized method, or algorithm, cognitive activation takes place that engages thought processes with available resources and concepts to help advance a solution.

At the biological level, cognitive activation involves triggering units, circuits, and networks in the brain. At the same time, goals must be established through executive function. **Agency**, or the sense of being responsible for and able to be in control of one's own learning, thoughts, and actions, as an active builder of one's own knowledge, is a key part of effective goal setting and problem solving in novel contexts.

Meaningful consolidation occurs for students when new ideas are successfully integrated into understanding. This means that connections are established in the brain that associate what is new with what was already known, commonly known as *prior knowledge.* Also, the brain must establish the *conditions* under which the new understanding will be useful. Without these conditions, it is not possible for the brain to make strategic choices about what to draw upon in its vast storehouse of knowledge. It must also commit, in a sense, to activating the knowledge under those circumstances—a further attribute of agency.

Of course, problems that are more than trivially complex often cannot be reached directly in a few obvious steps. **Subgoaling** is therefore another important component. Subgoaling means we are willing to suspend direct pursuit of a goal and take a step that may *appear* not to get us any closer to our goal. Yet, if this step reduces key barriers to the goal, it may be an essential planning step.

Elaborate subgoaling is often considered a uniquely human trait. Few other animals show a willingness to move *away* from a goal in order to achieve it. Anyone who has ever walked a dog on a leash and had it wrap around a tree will be able to relate to this idea. It is almost impossible to get the dog to backtrack to unwind the leash if this is in the opposite direction the dog wants to go, yet the goal cannot be obtained otherwise solely by the dog's actions. The unwinding is a simple type of subgoaling (Anderson, 2000).

Research evidence shows such on-the-spot maneuvering requires effective subgoaling and is precisely a skill that needs to be improved in our student population. The quickened pace of modern life makes problem solving without a prior learned solution increasingly important. As humans incorporate more subgoaling in their activities, this skill can be expected to raise the relevance signal and bring about increased support from the allocation of more cognitive resources.

This example provides one illustration of a Flynn effect. But in a sense, if educators decide to emphasize a skill or body of knowledge such as problem solving, and this is also supported as an increasing need in the real world of students and their informal learning experiences, a Flynn trajectory of improvement might be expected. This is an encouraging idea for teachers, who may need to engage students in many new kinds of thinking based on the changing needs of the knowledge economy and directions of the society. We are built for this type of adaptivity, and growing in positive directions does not require a million years for us to accomplish change.

Patterns in the Brain

Effective cognition often involves being able to draw on patterns of thinking and behavior and reapplying them. But what is a pattern? **Patterns** mean the arrangements, configurations, and relationships we can see in what we are learning. Here, we will use the term to describe a set of information from which the brain derives useful associations. Since the brain is a natural pattern-capturing device, it thrives on discovering and using patterns it finds.

A simple pattern a kindergartner might be asked to recognize, for example, is the difference in a set of shapes or colors. For instance, presented with a series of circles and triangles, can a child identify a repeating pattern of circle/circle/triangle or square/circle/square? Or between colors, can the child say, "I have a blue crayon and you have a red crayon"?

Of course, there are more complex patterns. In high school, students may be challenged to describe how results change in a scientific experiment. A pattern might be depicted by changing variables of chemicals or temperatures. To be successful in science education, students need to interpret and understand many patterns, as they engage in scientific inquiry and explanation.

As results are perceived by students, the hope is that they become effectively associated as part of the intended patterns. But sometimes they are not effectively understood; at other times they are understood but not correctly integrated into future knowledge.

From a cognitive view (Hawkins & Blakeslee, 2004), intelligence can be thought of as the capacity to remember, predict, apply, and extend patterns in the brain, all enhanced by an appropriately enriched environment and educational opportunities around us (see Figure 3.3). **(See CORE 3d.)**

The existence of such patterns in human knowledge points out that effective teachers must have extensive *pedagogical content knowledge*. They need expertise that blends subject matter knowledge with understanding effective ways to specifically teach it and support learners. In order to select teaching methods as ways of organizing the curriculum to help students learn, teachers apply their pedagogical expertise around patterns in the curriculum:

- Through content analysis, understanding what patterns are effective in organizing ideas
- Through learner analysis, understanding the range and types of conceptions students tend to construct and how their skills and thinking can be improved

In English language arts or second language acquisition, for example, everything from symbols that represent sounds to quotes in text material are types of patterns that need to be understood. To be effective speakers and readers, we master the patterns of language, both expressive (that we initiate) and receptive (that we perceive and comprehend). Quotation marks, for instance, are a type of pattern in English narrative and expository text. When words are contained in quotation marks, they signify direct dialogue—a character is

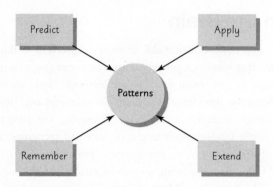

FIGURE 3.3

Some Elements of Pattern Use in Human Cognition

speaking—compared to the narrator's voice. They indicate a useful and important *pattern* through which the brain receptively interprets the written word.

In mathematics, the shape of one mathematical function depicted on a graphing calculator, for instance, denotes a different pattern in the intended quantitative reasoning as compared to another function. Students need to recognize that equations and operations not only suggest algorithms for solution but are most essentially the symbolic abstraction of a pattern. Numbers themselves can be seen as an abstraction for the quantities intended to be involved in the patterns in any given situation.

One reason that mathematics is often a challenge for many students is this layering of important patterns, as discussed in Chapter 11. One level of abstraction on another increases the brain processing required, especially for novices who may not have well captured the pattern yet. Until it is clear in the brain, and until its relevance to knowledge structures and future use is well understood, much may be rote and subject to the vagaries of memory for students. In this way, mathematics turns patterns into a type of universal language. It encapsulates a great deal of power but also places high demands on the brain.

Whatever the subject area or grade level, each new level of pattern making places new demands for decoding the abstraction. For the brain, this means there is a moving target for mastery.

Conclusion

How teachers approach the challenges described in this chapter can affect learning. In the end, students may have much more or much less ability to use the knowledge and skills on which they have been working. Since this is a crucial priority for teachers, frustrating them and their students when learning is inert and cannot serve its purpose, the time spent thinking about the human cognitive system in relation to instructional design is worthwhile, especially as more understanding comes to light.

Learning begins, as we must always begin in every encounter with the outside world, with perception, or how we perceive and collect information on the world around us. But as the Irish poet W. B. Yeats once famously described, our world is full of magic things "patiently waiting for our senses to grow sharper."

Closing Scenario

Putting New Knowledge to Work

Scenario: Instructional Design

In this chapter, we saw how one teacher put key elements of brain-based instructional design to use by having his students create mini-graphic novels. In this scenario, you (or with a small group of colleagues) will create a learning experience that reflects the guiding principle that *how we learn dramatically affects what knowledge we can actually use.*

1. Select a specific, manageably sized unit of the curriculum to teach. What new approach will you take?

2. How are you going to prime your class for this lesson? What specific steps will you take to prepare your students to include the knowledge they already have acquired in this lesson?

3. What elements will you add to ensure an enriched and stimulating learning environment? (Don't worry about budgets, space, or other limitations. Be creative.) Why is this important for the brain?

4. Education research has shown certain practices bear strongly on learning outcomes in the classroom, one of which is helping students to create mental imagery or "nonlinguistic representation." What is meant by such imagery? How will you help students create it for themselves?

5. Elaboration and extension are important aspects of effective instructional design. First describe what they are and then show how to put them to use in this lesson plan.

6. In this final step, we move away from teaching students to focus on their own learning by using knowledge integration. How did you connect the new ideas of instructional design during this exercise with the larger framework of everything else you have mastered or experienced in creating learning experiences?

Citations

Online, Media, and Print Resources for Teachers

Beyerstein, B. L. (2004). Do we really use only 10 percent of our brains? *Scientific American.* http://www.scientificamerican.com/article.cfm?id=do-we-really-use-only-10

Dessoff, A. (2012, March). Education Reformer: Robert J. Marzano. *District Administration.* http://www.districtadministration.com/article/education-reformer-robert-j-marzano

References

Anderson, J. R. (2000). *Learning and memory: An integrated approach.* New York: John Wiley & Sons.

Brito, N. H., & Noble, K. G. (2014). Socioeconomic status and structural brain development. *Frontiers in Neuroscience, 8,* 276.

Charron, S., & Koechlin, E. (2010). Divided representation of concurrent goals in the human frontal lobes. *Science, 328*(360), 360–363.

Cherry, K. (2010). *The everything psychology book: An introductory guide to the science of human behavior* (2nd ed.). Avon, MA: Adamsmedia.

Collins, A., & Koechlin, E. (2012). Reasoning, learning, and creativity: Frontal lobe function and human decision-making. *PLoS Biology.* http://www.plosbiology.org/article/info%3Adoi%2F10.1371%2Fjournal.pbio.1001293

Diamond, A. (2012). *Annual Review of Psychology, 64,* 135–168. http://www.ncbi.nlm.nih.gov/pmc/articles/PMC4084861/

DuFour, R., DuFour, R., Eaker, R., & Many, T. (2010). *Learning by doing: A handbook for professional learning communities at work* (2nd ed.). Bloomington, IN: Solution Tree.

Edelman, S. (2012). *The happiness of pursuit: What neuroscience can teach us about the good life.* New York: Basic Books.

Flynn, J. R. (2006). Beyond the Flynn Effect: Solution to all outstanding problems—except enhancing wisdom. http://www.psychometrics.cam.ac.uk/about-us/directory/beyond-the-flynn-effect

Flynn, J. R. (2009). *What is intelligence: Beyond the Flynn Effect.* Cambridge: Cambridge University Press.

Hackman, D. A., Farah, M. J., & Meaney, M. J. (2010). Socioeconomic status and the brain: Mechanistic insights from human and animal research. *Nature reviews: Neuroscience, 11*(9), 651–658.

Harmon, K. (2010). Motivated multitasking: How the brain keeps tabs on two tasks at once. *Scientific American.* http://www.scientificamerican.com/article/multitasking-two-tasks/

Hart, B., & Risley, T. R. (2003). The early catastrophe: The 30 million word gap. *American Educator, 27*(1), 4–9.

Hawkins, J., & Blakeslee, S. (2004). A new framework of intelligence. *On Intelligence* (pp. 85–105). New York: Times Books.

Howard-Jones, P., Pollard, A., Blakemore, S.-J., Rogers, P., Goswami, U., Butterworth, B., . . . Kaufmann, L. (2007). Neuroscience and education, issues and opportunities: A TLRP commentary. http://www.tlrp.org/pub/documents/Neuroscience Commentary FINAL.pdf

James, W. (1907). The energies of men. *Science, 25*(635), 321–332.

Jensen, E. (2006). The science behind enrichment. *Enriching the Brain* (pp. 47–84). San Francisco, CA: Jossey-Bass.

Lipina, S. J., & Posner, M. I. (2012). The impact of poverty on the development of brain networks. *Frontiers in human neuroscience, 6*, 238. http://www.ncbi.nlm.nih.gov/pmc/articles/PMC3421156/

Lunt, L., Bramham, J., Morris, R. G., Bullock, P. R., Selway, R. P., Xenitidis, K., & David, A. S. (2012). Prefrontal cortex dysfunction and "Jumping to Conclusions": Bias or deficit? *Journal of Neuropsychology, 6*(1), 65–78.

Marzano, R. J. (1998). A theory-based meta-analysis of research on instruction. Aurora, CO: Midcontinent Research for Education and Learning (ERIC Document Reproduction Service No. ED 427087).

Marzano, R. J. (2003). *Classroom instruction that works.* Alexandria, VA: ASCD.

Marzano, R. J. (Producer). (2009). Researched strategies. Marzano Research Laboratory. Retrieved March 11, 2013 from http://www.marzanoresearch.com/research/researched_strategies.aspx

National Research Council. (2000). Mind and Brain. *How people learn: Brain, mind, experience, and school, expanded edition* (pp. 114–128). Washington, DC: The National Academies Press.

Organisation for Economic Co-operation and Development (OECD). (2007). Understanding the brain: The birth of a learning science. doi: 10.1787/9789264029132-en: OECD Publishing.

Posner, M. I., & Rothbart, M. K. (2000). Developing mechanisms of self regulation. *Development and Psychopathology, 12*, 427–441.

Posner, M. I., & Rothbart, M. K. (2005). Influencing brain networks: Implications for education. *Trends in Cognitive Science, 9*, 99–103.

Reisberg, D. (2010a). The neural basis of cognition. *Cognition: Exploring the science of the mind* (pp. 25–5). New York: Norton.

Reisberg, D. (2010b). The science of the mind. *Cognition: Exploring the science of the mind* (pp. 3–23). New York: Norton.

Rönnlund, M., & Nilsson, L. G. (2009). Flynn effects on sub-factors of episodic and semantic memory: Parallel gains over time and the same set of determining factors. *Neuropsychologia, 47*(11), 2174–2180.

Society for Neuroscience. (2008). *Brain facts: A primer on the brain and nervous system.* Washington, DC: Society for Neuroscience.

Tamminga, C. A. (2004). Frontal cortex function. *American Journal of Psychiatry, 161*(12).

U.S. Department of Health and Human Services. (2013). Maturation of the prefrontal cortex. *OAPP self-directed modules.* http://www.hhs.gov/opa/familylife/tech_assistance/etraining/adolescent_brain/Development/prefrontal_cortex/

4

Encoding Strategies and Memory

CORE Guiding Principle 4 is introduced in this chapter: What we learn endures because of memory strongly influenced through persistence practices that reinforce recall of information and experiences.

Learning Points

1. There are at least two kinds of longer-term memory processes. One is declarative memory for facts and events. The second is procedural, or nondeclarative, memory for mastering skills and other performances. The benefits of learning persist because of memory.

2. Encoding information in memory involves physically changing the structure of the brain. Through continued firing together over time, sets of neurons build strengthened neural pathways; "what fires together wires together."

3. Stronger neural pathways result in memory traces. These sustained brain changes are an end result of learning.

4. Three processes must run smoothly to deploy long-term memory: *acquisition,* which is how information is encoded in memory and reinforced for long-term use; *retrieval,* which is the ability to access and use what's learned effectively; and *retention,* which is maintaining knowledge and skills over time.

5. Forgetting is the flip side of remembering and is likely a natural and important feature of the human cognitive system. The brain filters what to remember and maintain based in part on conditions it perceives, consciously or unconsciously, as relevant.

6. How well we remember depends on how well we can generate cues to which the memory is associated. Some researchers suggest we may never truly forget memories; rather, we just lose access to them because we have discarded the cues.

7. To avoid inadvertently preparing students to forget, newly acquired skills and knowledge should be drawn on repeatedly and at times and places not too distant from the original learning (though not identical to the original learning situation.)

8. Within a given learning opportunity, memory can perform differentially. For example, information presented first or last—at the beginning or end of a learning situation—tends to be remembered most vividly.

9. Organizing information in small but meaningful ways, called chunking, improves learning.

10. Learners are limited in how much information they can attend to, rehearse, store in working memory, and transfer to long-term memory at any given time. Educators can address this cognitive load by building connections to what is known rather than presenting isolated facts.

11. When a skill becomes more automatic, the need for certain types of cognitive involvement may be reduced. This jettisons cognitive load and potentially frees up brain processing to do something else.

Introduction

The most renowned story about memory in all world literature is likely a passage about some simple cookies by French novelist Marcel Proust in his book, *Remembrance of Things Past*. No sooner do sweet crumbs of "petites madeleines" touch the narrator's palate than he launches into warm recollections of childhood. That nibble brings forth fond memories of his steadfast aunt, her old gray house, the garden and town beyond, and the roads leading ever away into the rest of his life. A whole world appears, evoked by the ghost of a memory.

We can easily relate to this. A single smell, sound, or image can often trigger exquisitely vivid memories. Today, through the work of brain research, we now have an understanding of the biological foundation of what Proust called a "vast structure of recollection." Memory is built of neurons, synapses, and other brain components, and is the product of brain plasticity reinforced in different ways.

This chapter explores Guiding Principle 4: *What we learn endures because of memory strongly influenced through persistence practices that reinforce recall of information and experiences.*

Why Memory Matters

Teachers and schools depend on the capacity and functions of memory. If we could not remember anything, learning would not do us much good. Only through successfully storing, accessing, and retrieving information and experiences does learning work well on our behalf. This is true for students in every classroom and school, as well as throughout grade levels and subject-matter areas. We all must remember and build on what we know, or it would be like Drew Barrymore's character in *50 First Dates,* perpetually relearning what we once knew. Without memory working effectively for us, we would need to repeat our learning over and over again each time we needed to use it.

Think of memory as the way we navigate through life, basically using a trail of virtual breadcrumbs. Scientists who study memory call these *memory traces.* Crafted from our experiences and learning, memory holds onto key pieces of sensory input. It weaves them together, connecting one thing with another. Through what we remember and think about, we know how to navigate.

In this light, the topic of memory is crucially important for teachers. Instructional approaches that support memory are necessary for best practices in education. So, this chapter on memory connects with important learning strategies presented in our prior instructional design chapters such as scaffolding, fading, priming, and elaboration. Here we ask, In what ways do educational strategies need to support memory for learning to be effective?

▚ Organization of Memory: Two Processes Defined

Memory in humans is organized in two processes. *Working memory* is used for fleeting storage and quick swapping of information. Thus, working memory is transient memory, holding information only for the moment. In contrast, *long-term memory* is arrayed in neural connections for more permanent encoding.

The two systems are constantly working together to meet the needs of tasks at hand and to establish what in working memory is important or useful enough to be kept in long-term memory for later use. In the classroom, knowing how to solve a math problem or write a summary for an English exercise requires accessing long-term memory to recall and manipulate stored ideas and concepts. But to actually calculate the math solution or write the summary, the brain employs working memory to briefly keep track of single words or phrases, or bits of mathematical algorithms, much as we use scratch paper on the way to the solution. If the information is of only fleeting use, the scratch paper is tossed away. If, however, an episode is seen to have value for the future (an example of the brain's executive function at work), it is more likely to be encoded into long-term memory.

■ll Working Memory at Work

Teachers might find it useful to think of working memory as a type of mental "workbench" where the information to be processed is temporarily assembled. We can load up the workbench with new information or we can retrieve thoughts from memory to stock it. But whatever the source, neural activation is the process that manipulates the information.

Working memory is theorized to contain a variety of mechanisms to hold information briefly and to process it. These include a *phonological loop* that holds about 2 seconds of sound or verbal information, and a *visuo-spatial sketch pad* for holding mental images.

To show how working memory helps us navigate the world, consider the brain activity in play when you cross a busy street. Is the light red or green? What cars are in which lane? Are any cars turning into the crosswalk? How much time do you have to make it across the street? Your brain pulls into working memory, or accesses the relevant prior learning and experience. Sensory information and feedback are collected. Your brain updates the scene, moment to moment, and generally acts vigilant on your behalf. All the while, your body executes behavior, such as moving your feet, focusing your eyes, and collecting information through every sense. After a time, the intersection is behind you. Safe once again, you think little of your impressive navigating task as you hurry on your way.

Just as sensory information in visual and auditory transient memory faded quickly, so does working memory for tactile systems—what we feel—and motor systems—what we do. Thus, there are a variety of ways that incoming sensed information is briefly stored. Often we have less than a second to recognize incoming stimuli, analyze it, and decide to accord more attention to it if we feel it is warranted before it is lost to us (Anderson, 2000a). When we navigate a busy intersection, we are busy picking up the important details. We actively discard much more than we retain.

But let's say during your jaunt across the street you notice a new coffee shop at the corner. Or perhaps you spot a friend you haven't seen for ages and stop to have a chat. You might want to remember the location of the coffee shop or the conversation with your friend. Preserving this information requires encoding in more durable, lasting ways. In other words, you must "commit"—bite the bullet—and store the information more permanently. A person acquires a memory when it goes into her or his long-term memory—that is when the individual has altered and updated connections in the brain.

The takeaway for teachers is that a great deal of sensory information is captured and maintained only very briefly by the brain. Temporarily holding sensory information and briefly recalling memories from long-term memory is highly necessary for effective learning in many learning situations (Anderson, 2000a). More formally, working memory denotes the neural mechanisms holding and integrating all information currently being operated on. Figure 4.1 shows an example of how educators view an information-processing model describing the neural basis of working memory.

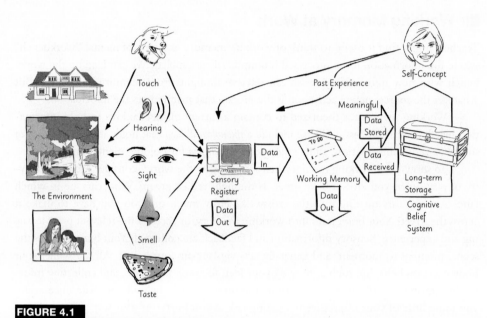

FIGURE 4.1

Example of the Type of Diagram That Educators May Use to Illustrate an Information-Processing Model Describing the Neural Basis of Working Memory

■|| Long-Term Memory Examples and Implications

Successful deployment of long-term memory requires at least three somewhat separate processes to proceed smoothly: memory acquisition, retrieval, and retention (Anderson, 2000a). *Acquisition* is how the relatively permanent representation of the information is encoded and reinforced; *retrieval* involves accessing the information successfully, and *retention* involves maintaining it over time. We will expand on these elements later in this chapter.

When the mental activity of a specific event stops—for instance, when you have finished crossing the street—your transient memory "workbench" clears. Your brain is no longer processing that activity, and its systems are no longer actively working to retain information. Instructors report that the concept of a limited "desktop" on which to hold information while it is briefly used or until it can be processed for memory is a hard one for teachers. The idea that learning experiences can be lost unless encoded in more lasting ways is important to master. Instructors describe that new teachers may find it especially difficult to grasp that not only simple exposure but also repetition, elaboration, and "hard work" are necessary for remembering. As one instructor said, her students came to understand how we humans sense and perceive, and that we have to dump most information that comes in. So, she explains, memory is the product of what we want to work on remembering, or at least for which we invest the cognitive resources toward a more long-lasting commitment, called *memory acquisition*.

Acquisition begins when we store the information into long-term memory systems, so it is available to us over time. This is done through encoding, which means using neurons and neural connections to establish memory traces, or patterns of consistent firing that communicate information to us. We *recall* information through triggering a stored memory trace.

Scientists at Massachusetts Institute of Technology (MIT) have shown that a specific gene in mice controls memory formation (Ramamoorthi et al., 2011). Mice remembered nothing without the newly identified gene. Humans may have a gene that functions similarly, and scientists have already speculated this may have implications for learning.

Because human brains process such information as *what, where,* and *when* about specific events, these encodings become linked together (Society for Neuroscience, 2008, p. 22). Eventually, if retained, the elements compose our recollection of a particular episode in our lives, stored in long-term memory.

As indicated in Figure 4.2, research shows there are at least two basic longer-term memory processes involving encodings: declarative memory and procedural (or nondeclarative) memory. **(See CORE 4j.)** *Declarative memory* involves memory for facts and events; *procedural memory* involves mastering skills and other performances. Coordinating the two processes requires drawing on various brain algorithms and motor routines. Sometimes these are complex, sometimes less so. We may be able to explain the procedures

Sometimes we can *do* but not readily *tell*. Other times we can *tell* but not *do*. Procedural memory and declarative memory are known to draw at least in part on different brain regions.

Declarative Memory vs. Procedural Memory

1. Declarative Memory = You Declare Something

Example: Recalling a fact you know

How It Works: I ask, Can you state who was the first president of the United States? The fact "George Washington" resides in your declarative memory. You give your memory a few cues: *president, first, U.S.* You access (recall) information and find what you are looking for. Now you need to express it back, or "declare" it: George Washington. This answers the question, and the memory quest is complete.

2. Procedural Memory = You Do Something

Examples: Skateboarding, playing a musical instrument, operating your computer

How It Works: Procedural memory is by nature *not* declarative. You don't *declare*; you *do*. As in the previous example, the actions all involve assembling of a set of behaviors and procedures. Coordinating them together requires drawing on various brain algorithms and motor routines. Sometimes these are complex, sometimes less so.

FIGURE 4.2

Two Basic Longer-Term Memory Processes That Involve Encodings

consciously or maybe not. Sometimes we can *do* an activity but not readily *tell* others exactly what we did to be effective or accomplish it. Other times we can *tell* how to do something but not actually be able to *do it ourselves*. Procedural memory is known to draw at least in part on different brain regions from declarative memory.

As we speak of long-term memory, it is good to remind ourselves about brain plasticity, discussed in earlier chapters. With long-term memory, the brain is physically being changed as neural connections are altered, updated, and arrayed for more permanent encoding. Through these physical changes the brain commits to some associations and not others, and the memory will be maintained for some period of time if not forever.

In the absence of anything especially noteworthy, not much specific information is likely to be stored over the long run. We are frugal with our limited cognitive resources. But if we have had a vivid experience such as witnessing the running of a red light, we may remember this for an extended time. We have committed it in some form to long-term memory. Through the use of our executive function, we have it available to draw lessons from or use it to plan a different route next time.

And yet, even with all this intricate processing at work, change is always the name of the game. The state of the brain, as author Shimon Edelman describes it, "is a fleeting, dynamical thing: being simply the activities of all the neurons of which the brain consists, the state changes from one instant to the next, driven by its past history and by external inputs" (Edelman, 2012, p. 28).

Thankfully, our brains know how to encode information automatically. We don't need to think through how to store a memory, nor do we decide consciously everything that will be stored.

Connecting Memory with Instructional Design

With this basic understanding of how memory works in the brain, instructional design ideas from Chapter 3 can now be extended, including understanding the underpinnings of key concepts such as *priming,* which elicits memory from the student before learning proceeds.

From a brain perspective, priming rests on how long-term memory works. Current scientific models describe long-term memory as sets of records activated when we encounter the right cues. These can be either in the environment or prompted by our thinking (Anderson, 2000a). A key premise is that only *some* records connect to each cue. Psychologist John Anderson gives the example of the word *cow* being connected to mostly cow-like things: giving milk, eating grass or hay, having four legs, and so on. Numerous experiments indicate *associative priming* properties of the human brain: The cue makes allied information more available to us, for a brief time.

This concept also applies to higher-level thinking, new learning, and problem solving. In a fascinating series of experiments, one researcher found that when people were stuck on a particular problem, an unrelated phone call that cued them worked wonders (Kaplan, 1989).

Simply bringing up a relevant topic or concept in an entirely different context cascaded solutions to the original problem. In other words, the brain worked double-time—while processing new information, it also sought cues all around to its prior challenge. Researchers found that the allied information could be subtle and that people were unaware of having accessed it (Anderson, 2000a). Yet, decisive evidence revealed the environment remained primed for effective solutions.

Are We Programmed to Forget?

At some level of brain processing, long-term memories exist at least in part because they have been identified as useful or different. But how long do we keep information around? How we go about "forgetting"—or unconsciously dumping information to free up brain capacity—is an interesting and important question for teachers to consider.

Animal research has shown that not only do "remember" cues exist in the environment but so do "forget" cues (Anderson, 2000a). For instance, for pigeons pecking, they can be trained to remember information they master when a light signal is on, but they can *also* be trained to forget information—not retain it—when there is no light signal. This is done by reinforcing information mastered only when the light signal is off; otherwise, the pigeons receive no future reward for employing the information. Consequently, they don't remember it for the long run.

As discussed earlier, a major complaint of teachers is the limited time that learning may persist. Often students forget too quickly, it seems, for all the time invested in learning. When students work hard to understand new information, and then are assessed to gauge that they have gained the understanding, who would believe how quickly they can forget it?

It turns out this is altogether natural. Actually, it is a prized feature of the human cognitive system. Just as humans can show great plasticity to learn new things, humans can also sometimes rapidly forget those they don't seem to need anymore. In fact, some would call it preprogrammed into people everywhere, like our own metaphysical recycling bin. We may simply employ the equivalent of a brain "garbage" system, managing the careful use and recycling of limited cognitive resources, just as the brain is wired to do.

What we forget is not necessarily a conscious decision under our control as learners. If anything, it is quite the reverse. We unconsciously employ triage in recall, just as we do in allocating attention or any other brain resource.

So, the very result that frustrates teachers—forgetting—is actually built into the learning context. If knowledge is not integrated over multiple contexts and reinforced over time, as discussed in Chapters 3 and 5, then there is less reason to retain it.

The problem, of course, is what if the brain decides to jettison what the teacher still thinks is necessary? In what ways might we be inadvertently preparing our students with "forget" signals?

As we've learned, for the human brain, relevant use is a reward. When students in school find they are asked to learn something for a test and then are never asked for the information later, there is no reward for retaining the information. We are, in essence, preparing the human cognitive system to forget. This can happen from time to time in the classroom or on a much larger scale. One common problem of educational standards, for example, is that information is here today and gone tomorrow. Something deemed important to teach fourth-graders one year, for instance, may not ever be aligned into fifth-grade instruction, leaving a yawning chasm for students.

Not only can teachers help students to *not* forget, research shows that teachers can help extend how long memories last. For instance, intriguing brain research in "forgetting functions" helps tell us how long we recall experiences and under what conditions. Different approaches to learning can have different "decay" rates—the lengths of time when the information remains stored and accessible in the brain. Therefore, the way we go about learning may be key to whether we will have knowledge available when the need arises to put our understanding into action.

There are many ways instructors can address this. One important concept teachers need to know is the comparison of people's memories for words with their memories for pictures of the same objects. **(See CORE 4g.)** Humans often show a so-called superiority effect for pictures. Simply put, pictures are retained longer. Due to such findings, teachers should supply multiple ways to access information for all students, with special and specific attention to *visual communication*. If you feel as if you could talk all day to students and the words would flow in one ear and out the other, you may be right. Stop the talking and show some pictures now and again, and the ideas you are trying to convey will have a much better chance of staying in the learner's long-term memory. Regions within the brain that selectively process different categories of information do not seem to be programmed with the same ability to forget quickly. Cognitive scientists find that people may have different "forgetting functions" for how long different types of information sources are managed and retained.

Technology is getting into the action, too. Of course, digital images weren't around in our evolutionary past, so it is hard to claim we're built to process them. But in a way we are, because, as the very name *computer simulations* implies, digital images are intended to be the next thing to real. They move, they speak, and they share dynamic traits just as stimuli in the world around us. High-tech simulations can feed multisensory tracks. Different perceptual subfields gain inputs at the same time.

In this way, memory has more to associate with, and additional ways to make the stimuli meaningful. One international student talks about his experience, underscoring the value of online materials and tools:

> Using multimedia material in teaching methods is very amazing. I am a virtual learner and like to see pictures instead of just text. During my studying in the American English Institute, I found using pictures to memorize English vocabulary is very helpful.

I used [M]indjet, which is an application of mind mapping, to organize the vocabulary words based on their category and support each vocabulary word with relevant pictures. . . . This sort of teaching approach will help learners a lot by letting the information stay longer in their mind[s] and increase their achievement as well.

Other examples of "helping stuff stick," or factors that influence memory acquisition, will be discussed in upcoming chapters. For instance, emotional events often are more likely to be remembered. They remain more vivid with us, and are discussed in Chapter 7, "Emotional Function and Attitude in the Brain." Sleep is also a key factor in memory consolidation, which will be discussed in Chapter 6, "Exercise, Sleep, and Nutrition." Finally, as discussed in Chapter 9, "Feedback and Evidence in the Brain," feedback may influence how memories are acquired, including adjusting our reactions to them along the way.

To summarize, then, from the point of view of teachers, the capabilities of memory are a wonder. We couldn't function as humans without automaticity to both memory function and the clearing of memories. Yet, it might be nice to have more conscious control about what we remember and for how long.

Knowledge Integration

The more a memory trace, or prior neural pathway, is activated, the more "marked" it will become. **(See CORE 4h.)** Less fragile and more frequently reinforced, it is less likely to be forgotten.

In theory, this would be particularly true for information highly connected into our neural networks—the more connected and therefore meaningful to us across multiple aspects of life, the more use and therefore higher priority it might be expected to have for retention. In other words, we are more willing to invest in useful knowledge if we can connect to it and it has meaning for us.

But it is not enough just for teachers to tell us that a certain body of knowledge is useful. From the point of view of cognitive science, it takes more than that to persuade us. Think of it as the brain classifying information it encounters based on a "need-to-know basis." By using analogical reasoning, the brain decides what's worth storing and remembering—a process by which the brain identifies generalizable patterns, or schema, in the world. As your "go-to" place when you encounter new situations, a *schema* is usually defined as involving a set of conditionalized principles or a working model that helps you know what to do.

Schema conceptions go by a variety of names. What they are or how they should be described is hotly debated in cognitive science. From a teacher's viewpoint, whether schema are generalized knowledge structures, mental models, or whatever, is less important to remember than to know that they pertain to multiple ways we function.

Theoretically, then, the brain underscores the relevance of information organized into essential schema. By definition, they are essential, so we need to know. An example of this is the way an award-winning history teacher helped students by having them organize the ideas of social studies into principles, such as the importance of participatory action by citizens in a democracy. They could see the relevance supported not only by lessons of the past but by the impact of their own community-service activities. So, the idea of memory reinforcement is more than building just the strength of a memory trace; it is building a representation or schema in which that trace is involved.

Memory as an Investment and Commitment of Resources

The value—and cost—of memory is interesting for educators to consider. Many teachers think there is no cost to memory, except the heartache if you have to relearn. But the brain is good at finding costs and benefits to everything it does. To educators, it may seem rather simple: Here is what you need to learn. Remember it! But to the brain, this involves investment, among a variety of choices, and there are cost–benefit tradeoffs. Why? Because memories don't come free.

Memories involve physically changing the structure of the brain, which requires an investment and commitment of brain resources. **(See CORE 4i.)** Similar to changing another physical structure we might think of, such as a school, home, or other building, every change comes with a cost: Do you want that bathroom to be remodeled or would you rather have the kitchen upgraded? Here is the price tag. Actually, we're barely making it just keeping the lights on right now, so we'd better not overextend.

The equivalent of the remodel or upgrade in the brain is the small changes of plasticity. We may form new connections, or we may reinforce, downgrade, or restructure others.

Some brain processing becomes easier and faster when we learn, at least for a while. But all this has to be maintained, physically, in the equipment and structure of the brain. This is like keeping the lights on 24 hours a day. Ultimately, brain resources are limited for every individual, so we make some choices.

All this brain processing must be maintained and accessed, which involves a whole cascade of commitments. Myelin insulation of neurons, for instance, makes signals operate faster and more consistently. These protective coverings wrap nerve tissue. The pale, fatty substance and brain tissue enfolded account for as much as 50 percent of the brain, our so-called "white matter" (Fields, 2010). Myelin in poor repair can lead to memory loss and cognitive disability. Other human diseases, such as multiple sclerosis, result from myelin deteriorating as well.

The Three Processes of Memory: Acquiring, Accessing, and Retaining

We have described memory as a cognitive process enabling past experiences through three processes: acquiring new information, retrieving it, and retaining it (Anderson, 2000a). Here, we expand on the three functions.

Acquiring involves building and reinforcing the path of neural activity. Acquiring is the development phase of the neural trace, or forming the "bread trail" pathway of neurons that leads us back to our original thinking.

Retrieval is the reactivation phase of memory; in other words, accessing it once again through the path of the trace in order to recall it. Often this is to bring it back into thought processes for further use.

As shown in Table 4.1, both acquiring and accessing require maintaining and managing memory, or *retention* over shorter and longer time intervals. This includes both remembering, where the trace is strengthened, and forgetting, where associations are weakened due to disuse over time, indicating where memory capacity can be recycled or put to other uses.

For teachers, the fundamental premise to understand is that memory traces, or reinforced neural pathways, are an end result of learning. **(See CORE 4a.)** From a teaching perspective, then, one outcome of effective instructional design, as discussed in Chapters 3 and 5, is establishing a more effective memory trace. Important teaching strategies discussed in those chapters, such as mental visualization and capitalizing on similarity and difference to help create sufficient contrast for students, help support memory—and leave teachers with better long-term learning outcomes for students.

Thus, learning is a biological mechanism, triggering more frequent firing of certain sets of neurons to reinforce the trace. Without use, the trace does not last. So if we think about memory as establishing our "paths through the woods," we find it is easier to get some places than others, partly because of these paths, or memory traces, we have constructed. Like volunteers working on trail restoration projects in the forest, we make some paths robust and maintain them over time; others we let fall away into abandonment.

TABLE 4.1 Memory Acquisition, Retrieval, and Retention

The 3 Key Processes for Long-Term Memory Deployment

Process	Action	Role in Student Learning
Memory Acquisition	Forming permanent representations as information is encoded and reinforced	The essential first step in being able to learn new information.
Memory Retrieval	Accessing information successfully	Provides the ability to use and access learning effectively.
Memory Retention	Maintaining information over time	Determines whether knowledge and skills will have any degree of permanence.

Without all three in place, teachers can experience great frustration in their work, and student learning outcomes can suffer.

Each of these—acquiring, retrieval, and maintaining memory—involve different challenges for the brain, and any can fail for students. In fact, as was seen in prior sections, under certain circumstances, the brain is programmed for encoding, accessing, and maintaining to "fail"—and this is the brain's definition of success. In such situations, teachers can feel the original learning was wasted effort.

So, in order to keep their efforts well aligned with innate biological processes, educators find it helpful to have an understanding of long-term memory. The underlying premise to keep in mind throughout the discussion of long-term memory is that when it fails in any of the three directions of acquiring, retrieval, or maintaining, this can derail school success and frustrate teachers as well as students. As one instructor put it, "I sure felt I taught my students more than they learned." This is a common feeling for teachers.

As noted, specific brain activity associated with the trace, or set of neurons firing, improves over time if we maintain it and invest time and brain resources. Now we get to the heart of a concept we have seen before: "What fires together wires together." Generally speaking, strengthened neural pathways are equal to improved associations, which equals memory building. This "memory trace" is the payoff of learning.

Overall, the takeaway is that benefits of learning persist because of such memory traces. **(See CORE 4b.)** From a brain science perspective, it may be appropriate to say that we have not learned anything new if we have not made any changes in our memory traces.

Let's consider an example that shows an instructional design in which educators *believe* an effective memory trace is being established for the desired goal—when in fact it is not. It involves educators who successfully scaffold, or support, learning but need to learn to fade the support for learners to become independent, as discussed in the last chapter. In a teacher's own words about his experience:

> Examples are broken down so that students can easily interpret them, many times large concepts are divided into many problems as a step-by-step learning model. In class participation and homework, students are able to complete the course work, understand the concept to a high degree, and feel competent in their understanding. However, many times in exam situations students fail. Exams are set up to complete an entire concept with no support, the scaffolding has been removed, but the student does not know how to navigate. I saw this in my statistics classes, and many math classes over the years, where students will be successful on the homework, successful in class participation, and then fail exams. . . . If the scaffolding is held in place too long, or is too comprehensive, then I feel students only learn to a level that they need, and then are unable to produce results without the support.

Parsing this example from the point of view of memory traces, here students are acquiring, accessing, and retaining just what they learned—how to do finely divided step-by-step problems with the teacher pointing out all the steps along the way. What goes wrong is when the teacher asks students to do something entirely different on the tests:

problem solving without hints or guidance on what steps to take. Unguided problem solving of the same type as what was to be assessed should have been practiced in the class exercises and homework. This would establish a memory trace that would trigger the right kinds of skills and knowledge of problem solving, rather than having the students at a loss when no next-step was provided.

Often in situations such as what this teacher describes, the assumption by instructors at the time of the assessment is that memory lapse occurred on the part of their students—that is, forgetting (Wilson & Scalise, 2003, 2006). They could do the task in the classroom and in their homework, but not on the test. Rather, from the point of view of the brain, the goal and objective changed. No memory traces for *independent* problem solving were ever established in the first place. As the old saying goes, You can't forget what you didn't know in the first place. You cannot acquire memories for experiences you have not had. Such wisdom was not taken into account in aligning the instructional design and the assessments.

Luke Skywalker and Accessing Our Memories

Memory researchers can become terrifically imaginative. For instance, Luke Skywalker and the Jedi Knights of *Star Wars* films are at the heart of interesting research by a team from around the world working to understand how neurons activate memories (Quiroga, Fried, & Koch, 2013). Using images of the *Star Wars* heroes, the scientists investigated whether specific brain cell firing occurred when people viewed each of the Hollywood images. First, the researchers wanted to know, would neurons fire for the action figures? Second, if so, would the same ones fire each time the same image appeared?

The answer to both questions was *yes.* When his image was shown, a neuron consistently fired for Luke, the main protagonist of the original *Star Wars* trilogy. This particular brain cell, however, showed no response when test subjects were shown images for other celebrities.

Yet the Luke neuron *did* fire in certain other "non-Luke" situations. It fired, for instance, when a picture of Yoda, the *Star Wars* character known for his legendary wisdom, came on the screen.

Apart from the enduring appeal of *Star Wars,* what was the value of the research? It provided a new understanding of memory networks, showing that related concepts, such as Luke and Yoda, are likely encoded by some but *not all* of the same neurons. In other words, when there is an association in ideas, our networks overlap (Quiroga et al., 2013). In this way, scientists concluded, small groups of neurons "hold" our concepts for us.

Where neural networks overlap, an association is established. The memory traces share some participating neurons but others are different. So the differences frame nuances of a concept for us.

In the end, through the overlapping networks, the whole becomes more than a sum of its parts. The gestalt of the brain brings the entities alive for us. As Proust so ably described, our memories are like "souls," and they are "remembering, waiting, hoping, amid the ruins of all the rest." Proust seems very Jedi-like, doesn't he?

But how many brain cells, exactly, are required to trigger a memory? This has been a large debate in the neuroscience community for some time, with two competing memory theories at play. One argues that it is multitudes of brain cells, on the order of millions or even billions of neurons, while the other says far fewer are needed, perhaps thousands of neurons or even fewer (Quiroga et al., 2013). The full answer is not yet known, but scientists are unpacking some intriguing results as they investigate.

We know now that long-term memory is neither a single entity nor occurring in a single part of the brain; rather, sets of neurons store our recollections. **(See CORE 4c.)** This directly relates to the idea of association and recall for teachers working with students, because the sets are believed to help mark and trigger the associated concepts and ideas.

Memory Retrieval and the Importance of Association

Effective learning approaches, as we now know, help support meaningful consolidation of our ideas. Approaches such as priming and chunking, similarity and difference, elaboration and extension, and ultimately knowledge integration, all deeply organize neural firing. This involves, among other things, building the effective "concept" networks just described.

Consider standardized multiple-choice tests for a moment. Often, they are what cognitive scientists call "recognition memory tests." Correct answers are supplied; we only need to recognize them. Psychologist J. R. Anderson, a key figure in the study of memory and cognitive architectures, describes how people often perform better on these tests than they do generating answers themselves.

One reason is that the activation of a memory trace increases with the number of associated cues provided. In multiple-choice tests, the answers are *all* cues of one type of another. So, on a decently constructed test, we wouldn't be able to select correct answers over and over again if we didn't remember the information in the first place. But we might not have been able to come up with it on our own. So, we get a leg up with all the cues, depending on how we have associated ideas in our memory traces.

The takeaway: How well we remember, Anderson says, depends on how well we can generate cues to which the memory is associated (Anderson, 2000a). He tantalizes us with the possibility that maybe people never truly forget memories; instead, we just lose access to them because we have discarded the cues (Anderson, 2000a). Anderson cites considerable research about how people become disconnected from their memories. The recollections may still be there, but we can't get to them.

How Chunking Builds Useful Memory

Until the correct relationships are made, concepts that should go together can be stranded. Those that should explain each other can be lost. Therefore, we next consider some ways to avoid stranding relationships in memory.

One veteran teacher and administrator describes the biggest difficulty he has seen with schooling: "Decades of teaching adolescents tell me that the single biggest problem kids face with traditional schooling is information overload," he said. "So much random, disorganized, disconnected information is dumped on them they can't come even close to coping with it" (Brady, 2012).

By contrast, schools where a more thoughtful approach can be taken see the payoff. Often, it depends how the planning is approached. For instance, take the experience of one school leader:

> As a high school principal I faced the challenge of helping students meet new math graduation requirements that demanded all students to complete three courses at the algebra I level and beyond. There was a fairly large segment of our student population that struggled in meeting this requirement. As a staff we decided that the most effective approach for many of the struggling students would be to contextualize math in multiple subjects, and by doing so students would associate concepts with more real life situations. We sought for students to put their math knowledge into action. A good example was in our construction course [shop] that became an example at the state level for cooperation between an "academic course" and an "elective" course. We teamed our math teacher with our construction teacher during one period. We brought theories and a whiteboard into the shop. The students put geometry and algebra standards into use completing projects in this course. Nearly all students successfully completed algebra and several were able to also complete the majority of their geometry proficiencies. Students expressed confidence in their math abilities. It was a transformative experience for both the teachers and the students.

Bringing theory and application together in this way is an example of organizing knowledge to make it meaningful for the student—and for the brain. It is also a way of building useful memory by breaking complex ideas into more manageable parts, a teaching practice called *chunking*.

By contrast, some approaches currently in place in curriculum design may make it difficult to organize knowledge meaningfully for the brain. Culprits, according to the U.S. National Research Council (2000), include superficial coverage of facts, disconnected ideas, and too little time allocated to developing important organizing ideas. **(See CORE 4d.)** We can add to this the instructional shortcomings identified in Chapter 3, including lack of integration across subjects, the tendency to strand representations by conditioning them to inadequate situations, and the heartbreaking frustration of teachers: hard-won knowledge that seems to be present but is inert.

From the point of view of memory, organizing information into principles or other strategic chunks is helpful for improving access and retention. This approach supports building the kinds of conditional probabilities the brain needs. Because of the way the brain works, it needs to know where to put things. Then it requires multiple opportunities and spaced practice to reinforce the relationships established.

Effective chunking by teachers supports this and can be used in many contexts. In the following example a principal describes how she uses this approach as she works with her teachers. By co-teaching a brief lesson with her AP Biology teacher, she is modeling the instructional strategy of chunking for the teacher. She hopes to help students build more effective concept networks for reading science expository text:

> Chunking is especially valuable in teaching students how to read complex, difficult text. Students often follow the author-imposed chunks (paragraphs, chapters, bold subtitles, etc.), rather than stopping to make smaller chunks so that they can hold on to their learning. Recently I co-modeled reading strategies with the AP Biology teacher for her AP Biology classes. Before we started the lesson, I asked students to read the first part of a difficult chapter and write a summary of the main ideas. I walked around and noticed that students read straight through without stopping. When I told them to stop reading, I asked, "How many of you remember what you read?" Only a few students raised their hands. When the teacher and I modeled the chunking and then asked students to chunk the reading in a meaningful way, students were able to recall the main ideas at a much higher rate.

Teachers themselves may have to think hard about what meaningfully chunks together. This is an increasingly useful skill for many teachers who are confronting the need to work on literacy and reading objectives across subject matter areas, an approach specified by the U.S. Common Core State Standards, which call out the importance of multiple experiences of concept and skill building across contexts.

The takeaway for teachers regarding memory is that chunking instruction by organizing it in small but meaningful ways is important for improving access and retention.

Repeated Exposure Enhances Memory Making

Scientists ask questions such as, Why do we remember something in the first place? Most fundamentally, scientists ponder how our brains decide when a particular memory applies—how do we know when to use it, and what does it take to actually reinforce a neural trace so that recall works effectively on our behalf?

Just as prior chapters focused on teaching and learning meta-analysis findings regarding instructional design, so too does this chapter bring to the fore those involving memory.

We begin with the work of educational researcher John Hattie, who brought together the findings of many others during his studies at the University of Melbourne and the University of Auckland in Australia. Hattie's findings range from effects involving the instructor and his or her teaching, to the student, school, curricula, and home. It is a wide ranging set of studies, with some aspects of his approaches directly connected to the way the brain remembers and the way teachers teach. Here, we will focus on Hattie's findings related to teaching approaches that have an influence on student achievement.

When considering teaching, Hattie found, as a general rule, that what teachers get *students to do themselves* make the most difference in learning outcomes (Hattie, 2008, p. 35). Student cognitive activation as discussed in Chapter 3—priming, elaboration, extension, and knowledge integration—forms the kernel of many of these activities. This is as compared to what *the teacher* specifically does himself or herself, such as focusing on teaching test taking or using ability grouping.

Regarding memory, the way the teacher structured these student opportunities for learning made a big difference. So, for instance, of the five largest effects for teaching that he reported in his influential book, *Visible Learning*, the one directly involving memory pertained to spaced versus mass practice—in other words, the frequency of different opportunities to learn rather than simply spending more time on task (Hattie, 2008).

The U.S. National Research Council says that convergence of many kinds of research establishes rules governing learning. One of the simplest: Practice increases learning.

In Hattie's work, the best outcomes often depend on repeat exposures. Depending on the complexity of the learning, three or four spaced opportunities to practice usually over several days or more were desirable, and then were revisited in different ways at regular intervals. Under these conditions, both acquisition and retention were improved.

This is likely to relate directly to brain encoding and retrieval because with *spaced practice,* memory traces are underscored repeatedly at regular and frequent intervals, improving their reinforcement. Additionally, in the presence of the necessity for frequent use, forgetting is deprioritized and retention is prioritized. There are likely other effects as well, such as the ability of the brain to better consolidate information given in shorter stretches, and with sleep, relaxation, and other physical supports in between, although these associations are not yet well investigated.

An example of spaced practice is working at math homework for a focused 20 minutes every day after school in an online homework club, as compared to spending the same 100 minutes a week all on one afternoon cramming before a test. Especially when massed practice is "one-and-done"—or only needed for one continuous chunk of time, after which it is assessed and essentially abandoned—brain filtering and storage mechanisms may realize or come to anticipate they can dispense with retaining the knowledge.

Spaced practice pays off, raising reported outcomes such that, on average, a student at the 50th percentile might be expected to achieve more than 10 percentile points higher when incorporated into teaching approaches. The findings about spaced learning have actually been known as a general principle by scientists studying memory for some time. Even as far back as 100 years ago, learning effects from multiple opportunities over time were known to exceed results of extended one-session efforts (Restak & Kim, 2010).

By "practice," Hattie (2008) does not directly mean "drill and kill," or simple memorization repeated many times in a rote way. That, he says, is often dull and repetitive for students, does not provide multiple and different experiences, lacks sufficient context to facilitate transfer, and is often aimed at building less important surface knowledge. Although rote memorization has some advantages and can reinforce memory traces especially for short-term memory, if left without more meaningful associations, it may fade. Instead, Hattie uses the concept of *deliberative practice*. The focus is on multiple opportunities to use what you know and can do, with feedback, context, and meaning. Hattie calls these "motivating experiences." As discussed in Chapter 5, this is an example of using socially augmented cognition in instructional designs.

Practice (of the Right Kind) Makes Perfect

The length of ideal spacing of learning opportunities depends on the intricacy and challenge of the task. Simpler tasks can have relatively brief breaks. Rising complexity requires longer rest periods, often of approximately 24 hours, so learning sessions need to be divided between days, according to the research on which Hattie and others report.

Deliberate practice reinforces memory traces, lowering the difficulty of triggering associations that are meaningful for the learner. In fact, learning, as memory expert J. R. Anderson (2000a) describes, often involves changes in the effectiveness of synaptic connections among neurons so that it becomes easier to pass signals. This can be seen by a variety of measures, such as how much can be remembered about a given subject or set of information, how long the memory lasts, and how long it takes to refresh the memory to bring it back to full understanding when engaged in relearning.

During forgetting, we relearn faster for memory traces that were previously more extensively reinforced. This is important because it means that information that is forgotten is more easily relearned when the memory traces were reinforced when they originally were laid down. So, essentially, if we have established some body of knowledge and skills in the past, even if we don't access it very well at a subsequent time period, we can much more quickly relearn to use it. Something altogether new to us generally takes longer.

As teachers elaborate their instructional designs—as they articulate them, map them, and explain thinking to themselves and others—they can think about whether they are providing opportunities for spaced practice. How are their designs supporting deep and long-lasting memory, or are they?

If instruction is defined not as what teachers do but the interactions in the learning environment among teachers, students, and content (Cohen & Ball, 2000), then Hattie's

(2008) findings over the numerous studies accumulated from other researchers are about how these interactions and effective spaced practice proceed. In his compilation of research on this topic, Robert Marzano (2003) came to some similar conclusions as Hattie, and helped to spell out the characteristics associated with effective practice. His meta-analysis work found that when homework is appropriately designed as a type of practice, it had a large learning effect for students. For instance, practice opportunities that included homework not only assigned but also commented on in helpful ways by the teacher was associated with a nearly 30 percentile gain in the studies Marzano examined.

So, when used in good ways, homework is an example of *spaced* practice. It introduces more opportunities to get away from the original learning context, in space and time, and to come at it again in a different light. There is a natural break in the learning as well. Since at least some time passes between learning opportunities, this is often well-suited to human cognition. Working in different ways and in different contexts is helpful too, as this can support how our memory systems work, building associations across settings.

Making Homework Memorable

Teachers often groan when they see the Marzano (2003) discussion on homework. After keeping children in school for many hours each day, and all too aware of research findings implicating a lack of physical activity for rising rates of childhood obesity, teachers often would like to see *less* homework assigned. Homework can also be a challenge from the point of view of providing a level playing field. Not all children have equal support at home, and this tends to fall hardest on the poorest students.

Books such as *The Homework Myth* (Cohen, 2006) point all this out. But there are different types of homework, and different ways it can be implemented. If what is being done in school is inadequate for learning, such as missing its key alignments with the brain principles described in these chapters, then more of the same at home isn't going to do the trick.

Just as what teachers have students *do* has the largest effect in teaching designs, so too is it the student *activity* in homework that is important. Therefore, the purpose of homework should be clearly identified. Each teacher should ensure his or her assignments are not just placeholders and time wasters, but rather make a meaningful difference in learning outcomes. Teachers should ask themselves, Is this really necessary for students?

If a teacher's answer is *yes,* then a follow-up element is necessary. *Effective feedback* on homework needs to be provided by teachers. The two go hand-in-hand. One does not come without the other, to achieve spaced practice effects.

Not all homework is alike. As noted above, Marzano (2003) found take-home assignments followed by teacher feedback in the form of comments had a large effect size of about .83 standard deviations, associated with, on average, a 30-percentile gain for students. By contrast, this slips to just an 11-percentile gain when neither feedback nor teacher grades are provided.

Feedback can be arranged through a variety of appropriate avenues. Depending on the instructional design, this could include in-class reflection, parent volunteers or aides when available, peer-to-peer learning designs, or even technology products that are designed to include feedback mechanisms.

Marzano (2003) recommends, for instance, that parental involvement be kept at a minimum *during* home assignments. But this does not preclude parents from participating in volunteer training programs and assisting the teacher in appropriate ways. Thus, any of these feedback mechanisms might have a role, along with the teacher.

What *shouldn't* be allowed to take place for students is practicing failure. This means allowing students to perform incorrectly or inadequately on homework without shaping or feedback to rectify the incorrect work. This is not helpful for students. Since the brain encodes and reinforces what it does, practicing failure means encoding and reinforcing the wrong message. This will be discussed in more detail in Chapter 9.

Time spent on homework likely has an increasingly larger payoff as we advance in school, with post-secondary education having the largest component of independent learning. Therefore, time on task and frequency of practice should be adjusted accordingly, with a bearing on age and the schedule available to engage in spaced opportunities to learn.

Primacy, Timing, and Memory

Scientists are learning that within a given learning opportunity, one's memory can perform differentially. For instance, information presented first or last—at the beginning or end of a learning situation—sometimes tends to be remembered most vividly (Anderson, 2000a).

As used by teachers, learning near the start of a lesson has come to be called "prime," from the Latin word *primus,* meaning first or foremost. By contrast, learning at or near the end is "recent," describing its positioning as the instructional material most recently made available for learning. Originally, the language was taken from recall studies employing word lists (Anderson, 2000a), where recall was better for words at the beginning and the end of the list.

Theories for why primacy/recency effects are sometimes seen with the human cognitive system vary. Early ideas had to do with primacy capitalizing on the opportunity to capture and commit early ideas to long-term memory, while recency interacted with information bumping in working memory such as rehearsal systems. Studies are ongoing. Cognitive scientist Michael Posner (2007), for instance, describes how it is now possible to examine physically in the brain brief periods of learning. After short stints of practice with word lists, for instance, activation of frontal circuits generating word associations drops. There is increased activity seen in the more automatic routes. So what happened as the practice took place? Even within the time span of a brief school lesson, brain circuits adapt. Shared research among neuroscientists, cognitive psychologists, and educators may one day help better understand this story.

From a teacher's perspective, short *primacy/recency (P/R) cycles* are intentionally used in instructional design as a type of chunking, built on spaced learning. Like most chunking designs, P/R is intended for meaningful consolidation and memory support. It specifically offers spaced learning with bursts of consolidation activities in between. The P/R segments themselves usually last no more than 20 minutes each in a typical classroom, even for young adult and adult learners. The intent is to keep all new learning brief enough that primacy/recency effects occur throughout the instruction. Consolidation activities between are usually focused to specifically reinforce the P/R segments, and do not last too long. Soon, the next P/R cycle reinforces learning.

By bringing the beginning and end of new learning closer together into primacy/recency cycles, the brain has less middle ground to navigate. Chunking by placing hard-to-learn material at the beginning and end of short segments, followed by the consolidation activities, means more is prime or recent. Shorter and more frequent new learning is featured. The briefer chunks are intentionally connected with activities to master and consolidate, such as discussion and problem solving. Such approaches as small group reflection or hands-on learning help connect primacy and recency cycles.

How Much Can We Remember?

Is seven a magic number for memory? Many teachers believe so. As far back as the 1950s, researchers studying memory found that most people could usually remember a sequence of about seven random numbers or digits (Miller, 1956). When asked to recall information (words or digits, it depends on the study) in psychological studies, a range of five to nine was typical, with seven as the average. The relatively small number surprised scientists and underscored the limits of human working memory. More recent memory studies have revealed seven isn't such a magic number after all. A better estimate may be *four or fewer*, if the digits or words are truly random.

Although the "memory size" research has impressed teachers for generations, the real curiosity turns out to be what comes with it. Investigators in the field soon realized people could recall more if they went about it in a different way—that is, putting the same pieces of information together to form larger chunks. For instance, Americans might perceive the six-letter sequence "FBICIA" as two chunks: FBI and CIA (Dingfelder, 2005). When this happened, subjects could remember it better. One theory for this is that each chunk, whether a single element or multiple, often up to three elements, connected by some algorithm or relationship, take up an available "slot" in working memory (Driscoll, 2000).

For the purposes of instructional design, thinking of crafting larger chunks together rather than their individual elements is a key takeaway. So how much can our memory soak up? Forget about a lesson plan that focuses on seven, or any other particular number. Think instead about connections. The connections between the small bits of information have to be put into place so the information triggers a larger clump. So we can have small bits or larger chunks, but we can get more into working memory if pulled into larger chunks, so we can remember more. We associate ideas together.

In educational research, such meaningful consolidation has proven important for successful teaching and learning outcomes. Expertise comes about through acquisition of relevant patterns encountered during prolonged experience in a specific area, explains psychologist Anderson (2000b). Meaning comes about by the student perceiving a relevant pattern. Elegantly, educational psychologist Dale Schunk (2012) describes learning as meaningful when "new material bears a systematic relation to relevant concepts in long term memory," and leads to expansion or modification of the information in memory. Schunk describes how making meaning thus interacts with our personal aspects, such as how old we are, what experiences we have had in the past, what resources are available to us, and what were our prior educational opportunities.

One teacher described relevant patterns in terms colleagues appreciated. She explained how it is like organizing a clothes closet. If we have hangers on which to place items, we can organize outfits that go together. We then know where everything goes and how a new purchase fits right in. But if our wardrobes consist of stray bits—odds and ends selected without much thought—we may open up a full closet and find clothes jammed helter-skelter. We close it just as quickly, and wonder why we have nothing to wear.

Managing Cognitive Load

Learning puts demands on working memory. So, teachers' plans for instructional designs must allow for the eventuality that learners will be limited in how much information they can attend to, rehearse, store in working memory, and transfer to long-term memory at any given time. Educators call this the *cognitive load* of the learning task (See CORE 4f; Schunk, 2012).

Part of how the load issue is addressed involves how new information is organized for learners (Driscoll, 2000). Because humans, in general, are not terribly good at storing isolated facts, teachers need to focus on other routes. Learners are better at storing relationships and connected ideas. Therefore, teachers should work on building relationships into knowledge—connecting to what is known, what is needed the next time, and what can be used to meaningfully chunk and access information. Approaches also include integrating across subjects and grade levels, as well as revisiting information so that forgetting functions are refreshed and their importance reinforced. In short, it is important to establish for learners not just the *what* and the *how* but sometimes, most importantly, the *why* of knowledge.

Bloom's Taxonomy is one learning framework embraced by many teacher preparation programs and schools (Bloom, Engelhart, Furst, Hill, & Krathwohl, 1956). This well-known cognitive taxonomy traditionally conceived of progressively richer ways of processing understanding as our knowledge, skills, and abilities grew. We begin with a simple type of "knowing" that implies static remembering of a fact or idea and not much more. We then can move to more deeply comprehend its meaning and be able to apply it, analyze its application, synthesize the results, and ultimately evaluate our understanding, or even use it to create something altogether new.

Given the opportunity to learn, learners are moving up Bloom's Taxonomy, for a given core concept. One way of thinking of this is in terms of meaningful consolidation and chunking. As the brain is able to better fuse understanding around a given set of ideas, it essentially can do more with what it has. Likely, it can better perceive and generate effective patterns. Initial ideas extend and elaborate. The brain brings more information into working memory because of effective associations. All in all, this allows students to show more about what they know and can do.

A Word about Skill Acquisition and Memory

Skill acquisition is a very large topic involving memory and learning. Once again, whole books are available on this important topic, which is complex and vast. Here, only a few elements will be taken up that interact with key ideas in CORE.

First, what is *skill acquisition?* Using Anderson's (2006b) definition, skill acquisition is acquiring fluency in the use of knowledge. When an individual becomes highly proficient at something, then the nature of the brain's behavior can change radically. The secret: After a skill becomes more automatic, the need for cognitive involvement is reduced. This jettisons cognitive load and frees up the brain to do something else. Maybe a person will still work on a problematic aspect of the skill to get even better at it, or maybe in tandem the individual will be able to do something else entirely different, if he or she so chooses. Whatever the case, brain activity changes (Anderson, 2000b).

As skills become more well practiced, brain processing often moves from the attention-orienting and problem-solving elements of executive function, which are more frontal in the brain, to automatic operations involving retrieval and memory maps of various kinds. These generally are more posterior in the brain. This brain science process of the autonomous stage is captured by the meme, or idea in teacher culture, of "frontal to posterior."

Anderson talks about stages of skill acquisition, culminating in the autonomous stage. Here, fluency grows automated and rapid. Experts, for instance, may no longer even be consciously aware of what they are doing in the skill. They may be unable to verbally describe the skill or how to do it, or know consciously what the component parts are. This is sometimes called *encapsulated knowledge* and helps explain why sometimes top experts may not be the best teachers, if it means having to explain what they do rather than exhibit it and shape what others do.

In the end, the ability to "start frontal and go posterior" is a means by which humans can take great leaps in their information processing. We can learn in complex realms, then convert to automation sufficiently to go on and learn even more. Our flexibility in doing this may be a major part of what makes us human. As we acquire skill, cognitive load for doing a task or activity also can be reduced, because we have successfully consolidated more patterns together—we can swing the golf club and keep our head in position without having to so carefully monitor each.

In this way, our brains are wired to "create a stretch culture" for us. However, as educators work on helping *all* students learn, an important takeaway of frontalization to posterior findings is that students not there—who haven't achieved the autonomous stage yet—will still be taxing executive function. Building on learning at this point may not be successful. Feedback and evidence of learning, which experts call "feed forward," is not only important but is critical when it is going to the teacher for instructional design decisions. Assessment in this case isn't about a value judgment—good/bad, A/F, plus/minus—but whether the brain is ready to learn. What would best serve student learning outcomes needs to be measured.

Having multiple associations for an experience, concept, or skill increases the brain's ability to more *automatically* remember and access information, said one test developer. The claim also makes common sense, he said. A good way to support accessing memory is to learn something in multiple ways and in multiple contexts. This brings the conversation to the idea of "conditionalizing" knowledge (which will be discussed further in Chapter 5): It triggers memory. "This would mean that my shop teacher," the test developer said, "should have taught me how to change a tire not only in shop where I had a hydraulic scissor jack and pneumatic power tools, but also where it might be more relevant and useful for me—out on the highway with a little bottle jack and a four-way tool."

Reluctant to Give Up Our Associations

The better we are at something or the more we know about it, the more reluctant we may be to give up our ideas or change them even when it becomes clear this is necessary. Why would this be so?

As we know, the brain lets experience shape its dynamics (Edelman, 2012). During learning, memory processes make relational links to other information. Repeatedly activating a set of neurons strengthens these relationships. This becomes the brain's "representation," or set of beliefs it holds about the world. Individuals gradually build on the basis of their own experience a set of "representations," or personal viewpoints, that translate the outside world cognitively into an individual perception. **(See CORE 4e.)**

We constantly use our personal viewpoints to shape our world. In any given moment, for instance, if we see the first element in a representation come to pass and then swiftly the second element, we're expecting the third and so forth—just as we buy a ticket, then enter the theater, then wait for the show to start. In fact, when a series of events are presented in a random fashion, such as when the show starts before we buy a ticket, people reorder them into sequences that make sense when they try to recall them. This is an example of reorganizing or "meaningfully chunking" information.

Researchers consider this kind of dependent situation—when something may at least in part depend on something else—*conditional probability*. This major feature of the brain has important implications for teachers and will be discussed more in Chapter 9, where feedback and evidence are covered. For the moment, it is enough to keep in mind the general idea. Taking place so fast over so many millions of neurons, we can't track the specifics of the neuronal relationship building going on for us. But our brain does. We are so smart, we have our own individual maps of the world around us.

Conclusion

With a fuller understanding of the three big elements of memory function—acquisition, retrieval, and retention—teachers are better able to consider whether students will be able to learn in the first place (acquisition). Teachers will also have a better understanding of whether their students will be able to use and access their learning effectively (retrieval), and whether their knowledge and skills will have any degree of permanence (retention). Without all three in place, teachers can experience great frustration in their work, and student learning outcomes can suffer.

As this chapter points out, the brain's memory systems have a great deal of capacity. But still, we can't do everything. A stunning finding of brain science is that for almost *any* routine task we undertake, large and broadly distributed sets of neural networks are employ. (See CORE 2j.) This means the brain is collecting and evaluating a great deal of evidence all the time. We are hard at work.

The good news is that as we learn more about how memory works in the brain—for instance, that some information is ultimately directed to long-term memory for more permanent encoding in our neural networks and some is not—it becomes possible to design instruction to work with, rather than against, the brain's own function.

At the same time, much of whether we experience success in memory acquisition, retrieval, and retention of learning may be driven by more basic forces at work within us. Consider this intriguing idea: Our brains engage constantly, both consciously and unconsciously, in making decisions about *where* and *whether* to invest intellectual resources.

Closing Scenario

Putting New Knowledge to Use

Encoding Strategies and Memory

Since the benefits of learning persist because of memory, it is useful for teachers to design instruction and deploy practices that work in concert with the way the brain builds strong neural pathways. Using this as a focus, how would you use what you have learned to promote deep and long-lasting memory in a lesson you teach? How will you use effective strategies, from planning the lesson through a classroom session and finally for a related homework assignment?

1. Identify a lesson appropriate to your grade level and/or subject matter.
2. To start, you need to identify the three processes needed to deploy long-term memory. What are they?
3. Within a given learning opportunity, memory can perform differentially. How will you organize your lesson to make use of "primacy" and "recency"? What are the important factors to take into account?
4. Since repeated exposure appears to play an important role in encoding memory, how will you incorporate effective practice into your learning plan?
5. Organizing information in small but meaningful ways, called "chunking," improves learning. As you organize your lesson plan to incorporate chunking, explain why your selected organization is more likely to benefit memory and recall.
6. Until the correct relationships are made, concepts that should go together can be stranded. Those that should explain each other can be lost. What example in this chapter addressed this issue? In your own lesson, how will you avoid stranding relationships in memory?
7. What other instructional strategies that focus on encoding and memory can be used?
8. Finally, how will you design a homework assignment in the most beneficial way? What elements of your assignment will make a meaningful difference in the learning outcome and why?

References

Anderson, J. R. (2000a). *Learning and memory: An integrated approach*. New York: Wiley & Sons.

Anderson, J. R. (2000b). Skill acquisition. *Learning and memory: An integrated approach* (pp. 304–337). New York: Wiley & Sons.

Bloom, B. S., Engelhart, M. D., Furst, E. J., Hill, W. H., & Krathwohl, D. R. (1956). *Taxonomy of educational objectives, Handbook I: Cognitive domain*. New York: McKay.

Brady, M. (2012). The biggest problem with traditional schooling. *Fireside Learning: Conversations about Education.* http://firesidelearning.ning.com/forum/topics/marion-brady-the-biggest-problem-with-traditional-schooling

Cohen, A. (2006). *The homework myth: Why our kids get too much of a bad thing.* Philadelphia: Da Capo Books, Perseus Book Group.

Cohen, D. K., & Ball, D. L. (2000). Instructional innovation: Reconsidering the story. *The Study of Instructional Improvement: Working Paper.* Ann Arbor: University of Michigan.

Dingfelder, S. F. (2005). A workout for working memory: New research suggests that mental exercises might enhance one of the brain's central components for reasoning and problem-solving. *Monitor on Psychology, American Psychological Association, 36*(8), 48. http://www.apa.org/monitor/sep05/workout.aspx

Driscoll, M. (2000). *Psychology of learning for instruction.* Boston: Allyn & Bacon.

Edelman, S. (2012). *The happiness of pursuit: What neuroscience can teach us about the good life.* New York: Basic Books.

Fields, R. D. (2010). Change in the brain's white matter. *Science, 330*(6005), 768–769.

Hattie, J. (2008). *Visible learning: A synthesis of over 800 meta-analyses relating to achievement.* New York: Routledge.

Kaplan, C. A. (1989). *Hatching a theory of incubation: Does putting a problem aside really help? If so, why?* Unpublished doctoral dissertation, Carnegie Mellon University. Pittsburgh, PA.

Marzano, R. J. (2003). *Classroom instruction that works.* Alexandria, VA: ASCD.

Miller, G. A. (1956). The magical number, seven, plus or minus two: Some limits on our capacity for processing information. *Psychological Review, 63*, 81–97.

National Research Council. (2000). *How people learn: Brain, mind, experience, and school: Expanded edition.* Washington, DC: The National Academies Press.

Posner, M. I., & Rothbart, M. K., (2007). *Educating the human brain* (pp. 173–187). Washington, DC: American Psychological Association.

Quiroga, R. Q., Fried, I., & Koch, C. (2013, February). Brain cells for grandmother. *Scientific American, 308*(2).

Ramamoorthi, K., Fropf, R., Belfort, G. M., Fitzmaurice, H. L., McKinney, R. M., Neve, R. L., . . . Lin, Y. (2011). Npas4 regulates a transcriptional program in CA3 required for contextual memory formation. *Science, 334*(6063), 1669–1675.

Restak, R., & Kim, S. (2010). Long-term memory: Imagining the future by remembering the past. *The playful brain: The surprising science of how puzzles improve the mind* (pp. 57–86). New York: Riverhead Books.

Schunk, D. H. (2012). Cognition and instruction. *Learning theories: An educational perspective* (pp. 278–323). Boston: Pearson.

Society for Neuroscience. (2008). *Brainfacts: A primer on the brain and nervous system.* Washington, DC: Society for Neuroscience.

Wilson, M., & Scalise, K. (2003). *Assessment to improve learning in higher education: The BEAR Assessment System.* Paper presented at the American Association for Higher Education (AAHE), Assessment Conference, Opening Plenary Session.

Wilson, M., & Scalise, K. (2006). Assessment to improve learning in higher education: The BEAR Assessment System. *Higher Education, 52*, 635–663.

5

Elaborating on **Instructional Design**

CORE Guiding Principle 3 is continued in this chapter: reinforcing knowledge, raising the relevance signal in the brain, and making effective connections so that learning persists. Knowledge must be associated with the conditions in which it is useful—and used. From generalizing across multiple contexts to incorporating social interaction, the brain elaborates on what it already knows.

Learning Points

1. Learning in the human brain kicks into gear under some conditions more so than others. Instructional design that connects classroom teaching with ways the brain naturally learns can help teachers, school leaders, and policy makers support more effective, lasting learning.

2. The human cognitive system works by gathering evidence to make sense of ideas and distinguish concepts. The brain is constantly forming links and connections between ideas. In this way, relationships are discovered, information is reorganized, and ideas become more useful.

3. By using teaching strategies based on elaboration and extension, teachers help the brain connect and integrate new information to existing knowledge and structures. Supporting the brain in this way increases the likelihood that information and acquired skills can be triggered and put to use when needed.

4. In brain terms, the perceptual field is all the sensory information of which the brain is aware, consciously or unconsciously, at any given moment. From these stimuli, the brain, in a sense, prioritizes what will be processed more deeply.

5. After information is gathered, we may organize thinking with comparisons to categories deemed important. Finding distinctions that matter is called categorical perception. In this way, the brain is making sense of the world around it. In a nutshell, the processes of your brain are asking what matters and what doesn't based on what you already know.

6. The learning brain thrives on detecting and analyzing patterns. Effective instructional designs provide students with experiences to recognize meaningful patterns and distinctions.

7. Teachers can reinforce distinctions by offering contrasts. Showing students what is right as well as what is wrong in their attempts to learn points out the distinguishing features.

8. Teaching approaches that attempt to clearly and consistently point out comparisons and contrasts for students have been found to be an especially effective way for learners to connect learning with prior knowledge. If similarities and differences do not end up clearly captured by student thinking, learning outcomes may suffer.

9. Teachers can reduce complexities and lower cognitive load by employing supportive structures and tools (a practice called scaffolding) that help novice learners master new knowledge and skills.

10. For knowledge to go beyond the classroom and into life's actions or later use, however, teaching supports must be systematically removed (faded) to ensure that the brain can appropriately cue the knowledge and bring it into play independently when it is needed.

Introduction

Even top teachers can struggle with their choice of profession at times. For 2010–2011 Oregon Teacher of the Year Colleen Works, such a period hit when her teenage son was diagnosed with an illness. Like others who have encountered a medical situation in the family and yearned for more ways to help, the teacher wondered if she should have trained as a doctor instead of a teacher—then perhaps she could do more to help.

Her son restored her perspective with a single question: "If all the teachers were doctors," he asked his mother, "who would teach the doctors?"

Teachers in elementary, middle, and high school might not think of themselves as educating doctors, lawyers, and engineers. But indeed they do. They prepare children and young adults for all walks of life, from librarians and shopkeepers to moms and dads, aunts and uncles, to athletes, artists, and astronauts—all the roles in society.

Short Course:
Cognitive Connections II

C

Chunking, Clustering, and Chaining—organizing learning tasks to connect with prior knowledge by presenting material in meaningful "chunks" or patterns. Clustering arranges ideas topically. Chaining builds on one simple idea upon another.

Cognitive load—the amount of information or interaction that must be processed nearly simultaneously during a learning task involving executive control of working memory. Can also be used to identify any cognitive demand placed on executive guidance, including for information retrieval, knowledge integration, and long-term memory.

Conditionalized knowledge—skills, abilities, and knowledge established under particular circumstances, or conditions. When relevant conditions are experienced again, acquired knowledge and skills may be activated again.

F

Fading—the gradual removal of instructional cues, or scaffolds, used to support student learning or to establish a desired behavior.

L

Locus of control—when learners perceive they have some control over their own learning outcomes, compared to the belief that their learning is dependent on factors outside their control, such as genetics or other people.

P

Perceptual field—all the sensory information of which the brain is aware,

Viewed from this perspective, it is helpful to think about what builds a strong base for students and their many possible futures. One thing is certain, what students learn in school needs to persist for them so that they can use it in productive ways over a lifetime.

It isn't enough, for instance, that a student can answer a question in class or on a test. Immediately forgetting the salient point or churning out an adequate or even exceptional score on a state assessment is wasted effort if the student can't apply that understanding later and in other contexts.

To make the investment of schooling worthwhile for the society that provides the education and for the students and teachers who invest their time and effort, we need to care about how knowledge translates outside the classroom. We need to be able to apply knowledge, solve problems, evaluate the outcomes, and adjust our approaches accordingly. This involves what educators call *transfer*, the use of knowledge and understanding learned in one setting applied to another. This chapter elaborates on the essential brain ideas introduced in Chapter 3 regarding instructional design. It will address how neuroscience can combine with teaching practices to deliver the *cognitive flexibility* that real-world situations demand.

Approaching Instructional Design

The idea of using cognitively oriented instructional strategy in educational design was captured into a model by psychologist Richard Gagné. In his 1985 book, *Conditions of Learning,* he described a series of actions such as gaining the attention of students, stimulating recall, and assessing performance that support internal mental processes in learning. Gagne's work contributed to the development of instructional design as a process, describing needs assessment, learner analysis, task analysis, media selection, identifying learning outcomes, scope and sequence, message design, prototype development, and formative and summative evaluation. He encouraged the development of instructional theory to mirror learning theory.

A portion of Gagne's work involved pedagogy, or teaching strategies and methods. He made the point that for best practices in teaching, learning outcomes should be examined, and instructors should reflect on how different elements can be included in the instruction to achieve the intended outcomes. To put this in terms of topics covered in prior chapters, if you are teaching a new concept, a good approach may be to use examples and nonexamples so that students can begin to identify the concept. However, when teaching for memory acquisition, instructors may focus on emphasizing the relevance of the material to establish priority and longer-term recall.

More recently, educational research on how associations in the brain trigger what's been learned is extending our understanding. For example, research by Marcia Linn, a professor of development and cognition at the University of California, Berkeley, suggests we would do well to think of student learning

Short Course: Cognitive Connections II

consciously or unconsciously, at any moment; the brain can prioritize what to pay attention to from many different perceptual subfields, such as the visual field.

S

Scaffolding—providing supportive structure and tools to help learners master new knowledge and skills. These include glossaries for new words, graphic organizers, and simulation and visualization tools.

Spiraling—introducing an instructional idea repeatedly and returning to it for reinforcement by varying the instruction to close gaps in understanding.

Spiraling to nowhere—a problematic use of spiraling that lacks presenting ideas in a new way to stretch understanding over time.

T

Transfer—applying knowledge or skills previously grasped that are relevant or useful to a new context; requires the brain to perceive or successfully recognize the applicability of the prior learning and establish utility in the new setting.

beyond the day's lesson. Think of learning as gathering evidence to make sense of ideas and distinguish concepts, advises Linn and her coauthors in their book on knowledge integration (Linn, Lee, Tinker, Husic, & Chiu, 2006, p. xii). The brain is constantly forming links and connections. Ultimately, by consolidating and integrating ideas, we create a synthesis of knowledge for "life readiness" that serves us well.

Our brains are built for this process but there are many ways it can go wrong. Without sufficient opportunities to integrate knowledge, and without adequate time or attention to consolidate it, a student may have participated and may even be able to show some artifacts of learning, but actualization of the knowledge and persistence over time disappears, leaving student and teacher dismayed.

The approach to instruction that makes Colleen Works, the Oregon Teacher of the Year, so notable, says her superintendent, is that she "moves students from discovery and learning to application and problem solving so seamlessly." Her instructional design is about *practicing* civics engagement, not just learning about it, the superintendent adds.

All teachers engage in components of instructional design. Typically, this takes the form of formal processes such as lesson plans and learning goals. At other times, teachers design less formally through the basic organization of materials and sequencing of ideas to be explored. Both approaches are valuable.

No matter how capable a teacher is, learning is unlikely to be enthralling at every moment. Research is providing insights into what makes the human brain kick into gear under some conditions more so than others. In this chapter, a variety of formal and informal approaches to instructional design will be considered through a series of examples with connections made to current research.

Defining instructional design as the process of translating general principles of learning into specific plans or ideas for instructional materials and approaches was proposed by University of Michigan Professor Carl Berger and Rosalind Kam (1996). The conceptualization of instructional design in this simple but principled definition has proved valuable to education and we will use it here.

The instructional design terms and ideas presented earlier in a box titled "Short Course: Cognitive Connections II" are broad concepts that sweep across many areas and age levels of instruction but are not intended to be an exhaustive list of strategies. Rather, the examples were selected because they are useful in exploring how the brain learns. Instructional approaches are complex and varied, and educators are encouraged to consider their own knowledge and practices in the light of new cognitive science and neuroscience findings. For those outside of education and for undergraduates, some of the instructional concepts may be very new, such as scaffolding and fading. As concepts are discussed, students can look to their own experiences in education as learners to help understand the instructional strategies that are presented.

Approaches to Not Lose Learning

A single new idea can cascade a wealth of prior knowledge. When we anchor a new idea to a context about which we already know something, we more firmly establish it. We encourage the brain to trigger a whole array of understanding. **(See CORE 3e.)** Such anchoring of ideas is believed to help build the cognitive structure of the brain, through establishing or reinforcing brain connections (Driscoll, 2000)—a key concept for teachers. Since we can't "see" inside any one person's brain, teachers wrestle with this idea. How can they know for sure what might effectively anchor an idea for any particular student?

The answer is that teachers make good predictions by thinking about what specific entry points and prior knowledge might be most useful depending on what they are teaching and how students have been learning, in school and out of school. For instance, in second-language acquisition (SLA), if students have learned that socially constructing language and negotiating meaning is more important than having the exact word for every situation they encounter, an anchoring idea might be to strive for *communication* in their new language.

Early on, students may learn it is okay to use four or five often convoluted attempts to get across an idea—"You know that thing you use for writing in math class, that you can erase with if you make a mistake, that you put into a machine to make it sharper? Oh, it's a pencil!" They are encouraged to follow up each attempt by identifying a better word or phrase to use next time. So this idea of a second-language goal as *communication* becomes an anchoring idea for students. Language learners return to it again and again in their work.

Via such elaboration and extension, links are made in the brain between ideas. Information being received is connected to existing knowledge (Anderson, 2000). As the brain sees how it helps achieve success repeatedly in multiple conversation attempts, this triggers "wiring" to prioritize it as a solution. We then organize more ideas around it. In this way, through effective prior experience, anchoring ideas becomes a "go to" for the brain.

Our "Original" Thinking

When learning about elaboration and extension mechanisms such as anchoring, teachers often ask, Where does *original* learning fit into the equation? If, during elaboration and extension, we discover relationships, reorganize, and add to our ideas, where has the original knowledge come from in the first place? Clearly, we must first have assembled some original knowledge, or the starting point for our new thinking.

It is well established that beginning in very early life, infants learn in informal ways. They explore their environments, learn about their bodies and selves, and interact with others. All these moments build knowledge. Children add to these associations and relationships as they go along, connecting, eliminating, extending, reinforcing, and generally engaging in a great deal of new learning over time. This underscores the essential principles of brain plasticity.

From the point of view of school-age children, the first encodings in the brain have long since taken place. In fact, it may be underway in the womb. New research is exploring the placenta's role (specifically the release of the hormone serotonin) in influencing the fetus's forebrain wiring.

RESOURCE

K–12 teachers can use with students: Kalb, 2012. (See the Citations list at the end of this chapter.)

Among scholars, there is substantial debate about exactly when and how early encodings take place, what unfolds naturally or is in place already in the early brain, and what form humans take to organize and build what researchers call developing their "knowledge structures" in the brain, or ways they store information.

The learning abilities of babies and young children have been the focus of more than a decade of influential research by Alison Gopnik, a professor of psychology at the University of California, Berkeley, and author of many books, including coauthoring *The Scientist in the Crib: Minds, Brains, and How Children Learn*. Gopnik states that compared with other animals, human babies take a long time to mature, but that doesn't mean they are not learning and shaping their brains for future cognitive capacity.

RESOURCE

K–12 teachers can use with students: Gopnik, 2010. (See the Citations list at the end of this chapter.)

Pointing to the work of neuroscientists that shows the vast amount of neural pruning underway in very young brains, combined with a high level of chemicals that enhance changes to brain connections, Gopnik says this allows babies' brains to be wonderfully flexible centers of complex learning and creativity. In fact, she suggests, the slow developing prefrontal cortex, a main center of focus and planning in an adult brain, may be an evolutionary compromise that allows babies and children a unique freedom to learn and experiment. Based on her on own research and studies by others, Gopnik has concluded that babies and young children learn very much like scientists: They learn by conducting experiments, their brains innately use complex statistical analysis, and they can grasp cause and effect. In sum, she says, even the youngest children know more than we would have ever thought possible.

Tapping into the Perceptual Field

Influential documentary photographer Diane Arbus, who helped found the New York School of artists in the 1940s and 50s, once said she really believed there were things in this world that nobody else would see unless she photographed them (Arbus, 1972). Novelty caught her eye. She won recognition for her photographs capturing a giant man huddling in a tiny Bronx apartment, a boy maniacally clutching a toy hand grenade, three identical girls sitting primly among three identical beds.

Arbus, it could be said, tapped into a one-of-a-kind perceptual field. **(See CORE 3f.)** Whether it was unusual subjects in common conditions, or common subjects in unusual conditions, she compelled viewers to take her view and look long and deeply. She taught her audience to learn to see what they might have otherwise missed.

In brain terms, one's **perceptual field** is all the sensory information of which the brain is aware, consciously or unconsciously, at any given moment. From this, one's brain prioritizes what will be processed more deeply.

Recognizing relevant features of a situation is one important dimension of learning. For instance, another person at the scene may not have seen the same elements as Diane Arbus did—perhaps other aspects of the surroundings seemed more relevant. The brain must recognize what applies for many different situations in order to go about the needed processing (Bransford, Brown, & Cocking, 2000b).

Sights, sounds, and other sensory input stream toward us nearly continuously. We easily recognize the smiling face among glowering ones, or the voice in the din of a loved one calling our name. In fact, we seamlessly navigate among these types of associations. Generally, we don't find them overtly taxing, which is quite a feat for a cognitive system.

How does information from the outside world register in our minds? Sensory information such as sound and light arrives at our ears and eyes and other biological "sensors" of the body. This is relayed to specific perceptual systems in the brain, such as the auditory or visual system (Anderson, 2000). These systems process and store the information sufficiently for us to identify what is being sensed and act on it if we choose.

Moment by moment, although we hardly notice the effort, our brains are hard at work. To perceive, prioritize, and categorize the incoming cascade of information we must divide—or *segment*—what comes into us. We don't treat everything equally. This selective perceiving is called *segmenting the brain's perceptual field.*

Sometimes in classrooms teachers help students identify what is most important, such as through scaffolds, as discussed in Chapter 4. But many other times we are on our own to pick up clues for focus. Once gathered, we then make comparisons to categories we deem important. Finding distinctions that matter is called *categorical perception,* and it is crucial to the brain's ability to make sense of the world around it.

Intuitively, we might believe that thinking follows perception. This is often correct. Cornell University cognitive scientist Shimon Edelman, author of *The Happiness of Pursuit: What Neuroscience Can Teach Us About the Good Life* (2012), describes how this works. First, we size up the situation we're in, then we act, or "do something about it"—this is our behavior.

Neuroscientists also are beginning to find many circuits in the brain that stumble in ways we may not have expected, unpacking some interesting twists in our behavior. Survival strategies of the human brain sometimes intentionally bypass rational thinking and route vivid emotional experiences directly to automated behaviors. In a heated moment, this allows the fastest of reactions under what the brain may perceive as potentially dangerous conditions, but it also makes us vulnerable to rash actions. Chapter 7 discusses this topic more thoroughly.

Seeing Patterns of Importance

Who has not had the experience of screening out background sound to which we have grown accustomed, such as the hum of equipment or the rattle of a vehicle in which we are riding, but when it is pointed out to us, suddenly we hear it. Sometimes, we suddenly can't stand it. Grating on us though we didn't even hear it before, the brain has segmented the sound information and selectively draws on it. Previously, the sound familiar to us no longer entered into our decision-making process. But now, the brain ranks it high. It becomes

A Brief Example from the Field

Educators who use teaching methods that clearly present patterns in ways that intrigue and engage the mind capitalize on the brain's natural way of learning. Unfortunately, it is not always an easy thing to do, as one perceptive mathematics teacher points out.

Learning math is a difficult process for some students. The teacher described how it ranked among the least enjoyable activities in a school day for some students. Although the teacher loves his subject, he finds it hard to argue with these students.

Instructional materials too often are missing the heart and soul of what math should be, the teacher says. Especially problematic, he finds, is when the materials involve simply memorizing steps to solve a particular problem. As a result, important patterns and relations are never seen. What gets lost, he says, is a real understanding of both the concept behind the problem and understanding the steps to solve it.

To rectify this and help his students focus on what is important—to "train their perceptual fields"—this teacher adopts learning simulations from the Internet. By using the computer's dynamic display capabilities rather the static renderings of textbooks, students are able to manipulate values and see how when values change, the line, curve, or other function changes, too. They can see how numbers and equations have real impacts in the physical world. With the instructional design modified to help students recognize meaningful patterns, they become more engaged and successful, says their teacher.

a priority: We have to fix that squeak NOW! This shows that if we need to—and sometimes even when we don't—we can readily reassess the importance of a segment of our perceptual field. That sound was not lost to us. Our brains just set it aside for the moment.

The ability to segment information goes far beyond screening simple sounds and the like. There's so much information coming to us that our brains have to constantly prioritize the incoming data. We are always actively engaged. We are deciding what to keep and what to throw away. After deciding what to keep, we then move to processes and use it. To make these constant decisions, cognitive scientists say we infer a model of the world against which we need to relate our "sense" data and check our hypotheses, or ideas, on an ongoing basis. In a nutshell, we are asking what matters and what doesn't matter based what we already know.

Flexibility is a key aspect of human cognition. We regulate our decisions in part based on feedback, which will be explored in depth in Chapter 9. This allows us to revisit the prior decisions of segmenting, or splitting up and prioritizing. We might decide to make some changes in the future; we may update, even in small ways, our worldview for decision making.

Segmenting by the brain happens in split instants; it is not necessarily something we consciously control. Given this tendency of the brain to occasionally run on automatic, it is all the more important that our brains effectively "learn to see" the patterns of importance.

This holds true in schooling as well, and has important implications for teachers. Effective instructional designs provide students with experiences to recognize meaningful patterns, as noted in Chapter 3, where the idea of patterns from kindergarten forward was introduced. Making meaning allows us to better recognize what is important (Bransford, Brown, & Cocking, 2000a).

In the end, it is up to each person to recognize among the vast barrage of information, or "learn to see," what is important. Metaphorically speaking, learning to see means that our brains are making wise choices in what we segment as we learn, and how our categories are organized and prioritized.

Similarity and Difference: The SAD Effect

For learning to take place, teachers must clearly understand patterns of similarity and difference (SAD). When these meaningful patterns are made clear to students during learning, it has the largest effect of any of the examined instructional design facets according to Marzano's (2003) collection of findings. Some teachers, for instance, explicitly show patterns through direct instruction or implicitly through having students discover them in project-based or inquiry learning. In either case, students must learn to see for themselves, without help from the teacher, what is similar and different every time, because teachers won't be there all the time. The key takeaway here is: However approached, if similarities and differences do not end up clearly captured by student thinking, learning outcomes suffer.

As described in Chapter 3, "Cognition and Instructional Design," a pattern here means arrangements, configurations, and relationships we can see in what we are learning. The large similarity and difference effect makes sense from a cognitive perspective because the brain thrives on distinct *regularities* from which it can draw useful information. In effect, the human brain takes advantage of trends to form associations, linking ideas in purposeful ways. So, pattern recognition is essential for information processing to go beyond attention (Driscoll, 2000).

Marzano (2003) found that teachers see an average effect size, or result, of 1.61 standard deviation *improvement* in outcomes. In education research, an effect size of 1.61 SD is quite large. It indicates a correspondingly large 45 percentile gain—for instance, moving a student at the 50th percentile, on average, to the 95th.

At its simplest level, the effect of similarity and difference is easy to comprehend—the brain itself is a highly developed pattern-capturing device. Patterns it perceives well can be more ably processed for understanding, and integrated into our knowledge, skills, and abilities. However, if similarities and differences are harder to pick out when faced with a novel situation, learning is harder and can stall.

Part of the human brain's day-to-day job naturally includes going about collecting and assembling patterns it finds in the world around us. The brain systematically collects similarities and differences. So, educators who clearly provide patterns in ways that intrigue and engage the mind feed our capabilities.

A "Training Set" for the Brain

One veteran teacher told a group of colleagues how he loved to teach writing. He described that writing is a summative skill in the education system, because it can support and incorporate everything that students have experienced and digested previously.

What was his most successful strategy from his years of teaching writing?

He said it was to use real student examples and show subsequent classes what their style of writing looked like. That it was written by someone just like them was important to make clear.

He explained that whether it was expository writing, creative writing, or persuasive writing, he found that when he provided these samples from peers, the student writing skills and fluency really took off.

Examples and nonexamples, good illustrations and weak ones, tap into the strength of the similarity and difference effect for the brain. From the point of view of brain science, the writing instructor used similarities and differences to train the perceptual field. He taught students, in a highly effective way, to recognize important relevant features of what successful writing looked like. The specific approach was via the use of examples and nonexamples: "This is what good writing from a fifth-grader looks like and here's why it is good. This is what ineffective writing from a fifth-grader looks like and here's why it doesn't work as well." Teachers reinforce distinctions by offering contrasts. Showing students what is right *as well as what is wrong* points out the distinguishing features.

Writing is a complex process to learn. Usually there are many productive avenues to achieve a final product in any given composing task. This introduces a vast degree of student choice. Often the brain must perceive a great deal of nuance.

The Council of Writing Program Administrators, for instance, describes that writing must take place with informed guidance, both individual and social. By sharing the work products of peers, the veteran teacher provided students with an important kind of informed guidance. The numerous examples and nonexamples were a "training set" for the brain: This is what worked; this is what didn't. They provided an opportunity for pattern capturing.

By using real student work rather than the made-up teacher or adult conceptions, the teacher made a critically important decision. He took advantage of a brain principle that the materials were pitched right at the students' own level of understanding. Examples written by teachers are often too expert. It is difficult for adults who are at a very different stage of writing to effectively exemplify the work of students. They don't offer up examples of the exact tips and traps the student will encounter. By seeing what other students struggled with and how they overcame their challenges, the brain learns to take some roads and not others.

The similarity and difference effect takeaway for teachers is that we must "learn to see" what is important. Teaching can often lose effect if students are unable to identify what teachers want them to learn. Much ongoing work is elucidating the neural mechanisms of such segmenting effects across other senses as well, recently explored even in social behavior (Doreen, 2011; Giardina, Caltagirone, Cipolotti, & Oliveri, 2012; Yovel, Levy, Grabowecky, & Paller, 2003).

To summarize, to be effective, the brain has to capture many detailed and nuanced patterns. A generalized overarching goal often is not enough. Sometimes, as in writing, these patterns are hard to identify even for teachers, must less for students. Therefore, effective instructional designs establish student ability to recognize what is valuable.

Putting Similarities and Differences to Work

Although there are many approaches to SAD, at heart they encompass a simple concept. Similarity and difference approaches attempt to clearly and consistently point out for students the comparisons and contrasts in what they are learning. Much like the brain, coherence requires organizing concepts.

For instance, teachers do this when they ask students what is the same and what is clearly different in a new math concept they are learning as compared to what was studied previously. They do this when they ask students to consider events in history by useful categories. In fact, historian William H. McNeill (1986) famously argued that without organizing concepts, history becomes unintelligible. Historians need to know what to exclude from history, he said, because so much happens simultaneously.

Similarities and differences can be useful in every subject and every grade. One interesting example taught third-grade children about their community. In this curriculum, students learned about organizations that help people with disabilities. The young children explored what it would mean if one of their senses was missing and how they might then interact with the world in new ways. By actually experiencing similarities and differences in their own lives, the children reached a deeper understanding.

It can be useful for teachers to review their own curriculum to identify how effectively similarity and difference components are used. One teacher identified an especially useful approach by assessing what worked best for his fourth- and fifth-grade students as they completed a unit on the solar system.

He described how he put a lot of effort into the unit and created many ways to engage all learning styles. He employed videos, lectures, art, cooperative activities, model making, and reading. To his surprise, however, one approach in particular stood out in producing learning gains. He found activities done with Venn Diagrams had a greater impact than he had anticipated. Even though the approach was only used one day, he described how it had more "stickiness" than all the other types of summaries and notes put together.

Another teacher has experienced much the same effect. She described how she came to the conclusion that there *is* something about Venn Diagrams. She believed there is something so simple and elegant in the circle overlap that really appeals to human brains. The teacher described how children had "a blast" drawing Venn Diagrams of just about anything you asked them to analyze. Particularly amusing was getting no overlap and drawing just two separate circles. When this occurred, the children would then search harder for any connection they could make, so that they could get at least a little overlap. The teacher described how this made her think about the Marzano work that showed compare and contrast activities get a big bang for the instructional buck. Understanding what something is or is not is key.

How Representations Diagram Our Thinking

Graphically, a Venn Diagram (see Figure 5.1) is one way of showing very clearly for students what is similar and what is different in two separate contexts or situations. In academic language, a Venn Diagram is a *representation*. But what is a representation? Some consider it to be an image or likeness, something that "represents" the real thing but is not actually it. In this sense, the Venn Diagram as a graphic organizer represents, or shows, SAD relationships.

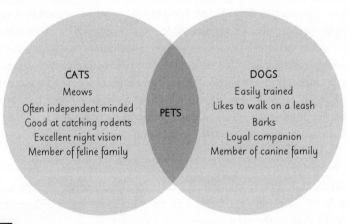

FIGURE 5.1

Venn Diagram Organizes Information Visually

Teachers find Venn Diagrams are a simple and effective teaching tool to illustrate similarities (the shaded middle area) and differences (the outside areas of the circles). Even the youngest students soon catch on and enjoy creating their own. One might even correct the diagram, "My dog is good at catching mice too."

Psychologist Jerome Bruner, who made notable contributions to cognitive learning theory and educational psychology in the last century, described representations as a progression of increasingly abstract ways of saying the same thing. Starting with action-based activity such as physically copying the actions of another, which Bruner calls *enactive*, we proceed to *iconic*, or image-based representations, such as a picture or graph. The most abstract representation, Bruner described, is *symbolic*, such as a mathematical equation or a reading passage. Here, visual or physical clues that directly paint a vivid picture of the pattern are erased, and we have the most summarized version, which we have to decode for meaning.

On the brain side, cognitive scientists speak of a *representation space* (Edelman, 2012). Very simply, when the brain experiences incoming sensory information, it activates a series of neurons. They become associated with each other. Repeatedly traversing them, or activating them over and over again, consolidates them into a memory trace.

Putting all of these examples together, they illustrate that when it comes to the brain and learning, we thrive on patterns. The clearer the pattern becomes to us, the better.

Making Connections "Conditionalizes" Knowledge

Here is an important term for teachers to know: **conditionalized knowledge**. It is knowledge we encounter under the same or similar conditions frequently enough to use it over and over again. Such knowledge development in schools specifically aims to develop, of course, ideas, skills, and abilities that teachers, educators, policy makers, parents, and others involved with schools and school education believe are important.

When learning this kind of knowledge, the brain needs to see it applied in multiple contexts of use. Learning scientists say knowledge must be well "conditionalized" in the brain to be fully useful to us. **(See CORE 3g.)** By making something *real* to the brain, this triggers use of the knowledge later.

In the absence of an appropriate trigger, students are less able to apply knowledge. It becomes inert. Early in the last century, famous educator and philosopher John Dewey described what he saw as the trouble with schooling, recognized even back then: unconnected knowledge in "watertight compartments."

Watertight, to Dewey, meant that each bit of learning in school was carefully sealed away from the next. With no connection to their actual lives, students built "school" knowledge. He was shocked to find that although students might often recall school knowledge when specifically prompted for it, it was not available to them to use in productive ways outside of school. Except when very similar conditions recurred as those that had happened at the time of learning, students gained very little use of the knowledge.

Dewey was ahead of his time. Learning scientists say useful elaboration is essential for meaningful learning because students then organize understanding into a coherent structure. Without this, knowledge may be unavailable for use when it is needed.

So, for effective learning to take place, we now know from science the key importance of establishing connections in the brain. Some of the most critical connections, it turns out, include the *conditions* under which the knowledge is useful, which is the topic of this section.

As Dewey foreshadowed, no matter how thoroughly ingrained at the time, learning without knowing when to use it does not provide genuine preparation for students. Our brains don't draw on the memories in the right situations. Since we do not activate the understanding, it is "inert" to us—we cannot bring our knowledge into play successfully. Long before basic brain understanding was established, Alfred North Whitehead (1929) described inert knowledge as information we can express but not use. Now we know that knowledge not properly "conditionalized" in the brain is often inert because it may not be activated in neural processing, even though it is relevant. The brain does not understand its relevance—has not experienced it as such in a given context—and so has not made the key associations.

Teachers find inert knowledge one of the most frustrating challenges in their profession. When they see their students understand an idea, at least at some level, and can employ it when prompted by some very specific questions, teachers often believe students should be able to work with these ideas or concepts more generally, indicating their ability to use them in other contexts. But to better achieve this often requires extensively engaging with elaboration and extension of the knowledge, which teachers do not always do. Supporting the brain to successfully integrate new information with existing knowledge structures is vital. The likelihood of triggering and employing the information or skills under the right conditions then rises (Kalyuga, 2009).

Making It "Real" for the Brain

Many effective instructional designs render learning operational through real applications. The "cognitive apprenticeship" school of thought, for instance, encourages not just showing but doing in schools. Having students work side-by-side embodies the idea of teacher as journeyman, student as apprentice. Such project-based learning combines traditional apprenticeship ideas of learning through watching and working with others who have mastered the practice. By making thinking visible in schooling, scholars show we can learn even intellectual skills from others through working alongside them and their ideas (Collins, Brown, & Newman, 1990; Collins, Seely Brown, & Holum, 1991).

Yet what constitutes "real" and "authentic" has been a topic of much strident debate in education for many years. In part, this is because schools can find it difficult to facilitate these kinds of educational experiences in some cases. Sometimes, they cannot easily re-create truly "real" situations for large number of students, such as through apprenticeship in workplaces or instructional designs that include community service in the correct setting for understanding the concepts being taught.

So there is limited agreement on what the terms mean and even less on how they would be most appropriately enacted or invoked within the resources and contexts of many schools. The very fact of encountering stimuli and the resulting thoughts and behaviors in many contexts and repeatedly over time makes it "real" to the brain. It is reinforced, prioritized, and underscored at the very molecular level of the brain—generalizing makes it real.

To take another example from elementary science education, along with a nonexample, consider the following account from a parent who is an experienced school administrator herself. She talks about the importance of learning knowledge in multiple contexts and integrated across subjects.

The parent described how her son's third-grade class walked to a park and spent time writing about what they noticed in the pond. Soon they began collecting data on the ducks in the pond and how people behaved around the ducks. This led to a science investigation where the students measured the algae and read about the impact of algae on the pond. Later, the students began an education campaign for people to stop feeding the ducks. They even put their findings in a report and attended a City Hall meeting to talk to the mayor. The unit included math, civics, writing, reading, speaking, listening, and it was authentic. She said her son three years later still remembered and talked about the learning from the project.

In contrast, our parent, the veteran administrator, described a conversation she had at another time with the district science "coach." This coach was a highly experienced science teacher hired to go throughout the district and help other teachers improve their instruction in an ongoing way. The coach talked about her frustration of working with a group of elementary school teachers on integrating science in their curriculum. When the suggestion came up that students could write a reflection after a science-based activity, a teacher commented that science writing didn't come until the May writing unit. The teachers, the coach commented, had trouble adapting the schedule to incorporate ongoing integration of knowledge. Rather, the "watertight" compartment reared its ugly head: Science writing could happen in May and *only* in May and was a lesson unto itself.

Multiple opportunities to see the concept or skill play out in different conditions makes it possible for the brain to generalize. A key takeaway: Knowledge should not be taught in isolation. Rather, prompted by a set of conditions, these should be specifically designed into instruction. They should also appropriately vary, to represent teaching the brain a variety of triggering contexts and resulting actions that are appropriate. Later conditions, then, are more likely to successfully activate the knowledge when needed.

Transfer Is Introduced

Transfer means applying knowledge or skills previously grasped to a new context. This is a very large topic in education, but just one aspect of it will be introduced here. Transfer requires the brain to perceive or successfully recognize the applicability of the prior learning and to plan a route for utility in the new setting.

Educational psychologist Dale Schunk (2012) describes phases for transfer of learning that include *cueing retrieval,* when the brain receives cues signaling previous knowledge as applicable, and *generalizability,* or going beyond the original context. For knowledge to go beyond the classroom and into later use, the brain must be able to appropriately cue the knowledge. It has to bring it into play when it applies. This must happen without all the sustaining influences of the classroom. As such, transfer walks hand-in-hand with the brain-related ideas of "learning to see" and "conditionalizing" knowledge.

Lack of transfer in schools is pervasive and consistent, reports Robert E. Haskell, author of *Transfer of Learning* (2001), and many others agree (Rothman, 2012; Royer, Mestre, & Dufresne, 2005). Haskell, however, puts the dilemma a bit differently: Effective learning and transfer take place all the time, just not so much in school sometimes. Moment to moment in our lives, most everyone engages in transfer constantly, bringing into play their prior experiences to navigate the next situation. Yet transfer from instructional settings occurs less often.

Haskell makes the point, however, that practically all education is built on the premise that knowledge will be transferred. As he describes it, nobody really cares if a learner can exhibit understanding only in the exact moment of the original learning context and never again. Learning this shallow is too ephemeral.

One field of learning research involves how students apply existing knowledge to new but closely related problems and situations (Gholson, Morgan, Dattel, & Pierce, 1990). Broadly, a relevant "analog," or similar situation, is first accessed in memory (Mestre, 2005). Then it is mapped to the problem to be solved. Systematic conditions are identified by the brain—similarities and differences—to see what might be used. Research has identified an important principle: *multiplicity of use.* In other words, transfer is enhanced by the opportunity to practice and form analogs with different content and under a range of circumstances (Schunk, 2012).

Even a little multiplicity of use is quite helpful. For instance, psychologists Mary Gick and Keith Holyoak (1983) found that by just giving two different examples instead of one, a big jump in learning outcomes and transfer occurred for the learners they studied. They described how the brain builds a *schema,* or mapping of relationships, to form a model or rule. The more different examples that apply, the better the schema, and the more likely transfer will occur.

Scaffolding and Fading

For the brain, the relationship between knowledge and when to use it must be clear. From an instructional design perspective, teachers often acknowledge this by providing supports of learning, or, in teacher talk, "scaffolds." **Scaffolding** orients student thinking in helpful directions while learning. But from a brain perspective, the supports can backfire when teachers do not **fade**, or systematically reduce the need for them over time. **(See CORE 3h.)** Thus, impacts of both scaffolding and fading are important for educators to clearly understand.

Scaffolding is any means by which teachers provide supportive structure and tools that help learners master new knowledge and skills. This can include vocabulary lists or glossaries for new words, graphic organizers for students to arrange ideas visually, or simulation and graphing tools that students can replay repeatedly as needed to understand mathematical functions. Scaffolding supports the novice learner by reducing complexities and often lowering **cognitive load**, which is the amount of information that must be processed almost simultaneously during a learning task involving working memory.

Examples of scaffolds are numerous and include:

- Classroom environmental cues; in other words, anything teachers have provided for students to focus on in the classroom, such as bulletin board displays, and timelines showing important events in history
- Specific code words that trigger particular behaviors in the classroom but have no relevant meaning by themselves
- A variety of external motivators, which can be anything from grades and tests to verbal prompting to praise and rewards, with the key premise being that the motivators will not be present in the actual real-life use of the knowledge or skills
- "Hard steps" broken down by teachers into fine pieces that won't be so structured when the information needs to be used

Fading, by contrast, is the gradual reduction of scaffolds. In this context, fading means gradually removing the supports. As the U.S. National Academy report *How People Learn* describes, when scaffolds are seen as helpful in initial learning, instruction should employ a process of fading, or purposefully reducing and eliminating assistance (National Research Council, 2000). As students begin to successfully operate without the extra supports, they gradually come to ask self-regulatory questions themselves, the report describes. In essence, the teacher fades out. So, by the end of the instructional segment, students are more independent with their new learning and may avoid inert knowledge.

Many teachers are not aware of the concept of fading or do not employ successful practices of fading. This interferes with their students becoming able to be independent with their knowledge. Unfortunately, teachers often "conditionalize" knowledge to the wrong condition—*wrong* being defined as association to conditions that will *not* be present in the transfer, or use, situation. This can lead to "inert" understanding, or knowledge structures in the brain that exist but do not activate properly.

One coach who worked with student athletes described his experience when fading didn't occur. Working on a new pole-vault drill, he had his athletes begin by practicing an initial skill of correctly placing the pole. They did this off to the side of the run. They did not have to finish the jump because no actual height barrier was in place. Once the drill was mastered, the athletes tried the whole action for real, but the coach found that the planting-the-pole skill had been somewhat lost between the trial and real conditions. He described how as long as he cued the skill, it continued to be present, but, at least at initial stages, transfer did not happen until the skill had been practiced sufficiently in the real conditions.

To show how fading works, a primary school teacher described removing the scaffolding for one student in a behavior program. She had been fading some of the supports to see if the student could generalize some of his skills learned without prompting. The teacher

Making Connections Work

Spiraling is a technique used by teachers when they are introducing an instructional idea, repeating it and returning to it for reinforcement by varying the instruction. One mistake that teachers often make within their own classrooms is engaging in a process called **spiraling to nowhere**. This is when the same idea is repeated and returned to for reinforcement, but without any attempts to elaborate and extend. Literally, the teacher does the same thing twice, three times, and maybe more.

This does not help pose thinking in additional contexts. It does not help the brain more optimally restructure knowledge, and it does not point out misunderstandings that may mean the original memory trace is reinforcing somewhat incorrectly.

Essentially, spiraling to nowhere is a wasted opportunity. It also demotivates students who understood the first time and see no avenues for novelty or new thinking with the ideas.

The same revisiting can be done much more profitably when teachers keep an eye out for elaboration and extension opportunities while also restating and supporting the learning for all students.

To avoid the trap of going nowhere be sure always *to go somewhere*. In other words, with each turn, spiral to a valuable destination of elaboration and extension.

found the boy had made good progress to transfer skills. He had not only learned norms from the teacher and specialist who worked with him, but he had begun to value being in school with his peers. The boy described how he wanted to be in school to make friends and learn new things. He could transfer from workstation to workstation rapidly, without losing focus or moving off task, and his social skills awareness had increased. The teacher stated that she saw intrinsic motivation prevalent in the student's development, as the supports were intentionally faded. The child was ready for more self-direction.

Sometimes scaffolds need to be entirely faded. Other situations call for students to learn to self-activate the scaffolds. For example, in writing, the strategy for students to organize their thoughts into an outline may be something teachers want students to use. Therefore, teachers may choose never to fade this—but they want it to eventually take place independently, without teacher direction. Getting learners to the point where they re-create this scaffolding themselves is the goal.

Assessment of independence by the teacher who introduces the scaffold is a critical responsibility. Ensuring fading has succeeded should be assessed for *all* students, not just for some.

Content Analysis to Support Identifying Relationships

Teachers often employ a process of content analysis in their subject matter and grade-level areas. A content analysis identifies relationships in the content that can allow the teacher to prepare a sequence in instruction that spirals to reinforce memory traces. Many studies in instructional design have compared different types of media with little or no significant results for teachers, but have found this outcome changes when teachers take on task/content analysis in depth. As one instructor described it, this type of analysis contributes to memory in several different ways that parallel what is covered in this chapter. For example, a good analysis can identify potential patterns of **chunking** for the instructor to use with students. Approaches to chunking, such as clustering and chaining, organize learning tasks to connect with prior knowledge by presenting material in meaningful "chunks" or patterns. **Clustering** arranges ideas topically; **chaining** builds simple ideas, one upon another. These are all examples of pedagogical approaches that help support reducing cognitive load by building successful and meaningful patterns of thinking.

The Social Nature of Cognitive Engagement

Collaboration and social negotiation are a key part of how our brain works. **(See CORE 3i.)** As we elaborate and extend our knowledge about the brain, we soon encounter the idea that no brain stands alone. This is the paradox of cognition. For each of us, social interaction is a constituent component both for early development of cerebral structures and for normal development of cognitive functions and learning (OECD, 2007). The rapidly emerging field of social neuroscience deals with social processes and behaviors.

Sociality, or how we interact with self and others, plays out extensively in instructional designs. Many schools are getting more and more social these days, and it is not just about social media, technology, and the Internet. Rather, the idea of *social acquisition* means that we actively elaborate, extend, and integrate knowledge by working with others.

For instance, as described in Chapter 3, *self-agency* is the sense of being responsible for and able to be in control of our own learning, thoughts, and actions, as an active builder of our own knowledge. Agency and the self-reflection it generates echo throughout the successful process of fading. We become independent in our knowledge and can allow supports to fade as we amp up our own self-reflection and ability to be conscious agents of our own learning success. We learn how to seek feedback from others when we need it, rather than having it automatically provided for us. Effective self-regulation also helps us judge the credibility of our various sources, and array them beside each other for better understanding.

Self-agency is especially important in our reflective practice. Beliefs about ourselves interact with our views about our internal and external control on our learning, or **locus of control**. *Metacognition* is the learner's ability to regulate, and shape, his or her own learning, and will be discussed further in Chapter 9, "Feedback and Evidence in the Brain." As information becomes more accessible at our fingertips, instructors describe how students need less information and more self-regulation strategies and metacognitive awareness.

Our beliefs about the degree to which we can control success in our own learning impacts areas as diverse as our motivation for schooling in the first place (see Chapter 7, "Emotional Function and Attitude in the Brain") or how we "learn to learn," which is an essential aspect of our fast-paced society, as discussed in Chapter 11, "Insights across the Curriculum."

Do Mirror Neurons Capture Social Patterns?

A type of brain cell called a *mirror neuron* fires both when an animal performs an action and when the animal watches the same action performed by someone else. Since the neuron "mirrors" behavior, instructors in education often combine sociocultural/sociohistoric learning theories (see Chapter 7), such as Bandura's social cognitive learning theory, and teach them in parallel with the brain and modeling through the mirror neurons.

One prominent aspect of "socio" learning theories are the ways in which we take note of others and model our behaviors based on what we see others do. Mirror neurons seem to be one way that primates may capture and imitate social patterns of behavior that they observe.

Mary Helen Immordino-Yang, a neuroscientist and human development psychologist at the University of Southern California, describes it this way: Learning involves cycles of perception and action. From a neurobiological stance, neural activity involved with action and perception converge in the brain in mirror neuron areas. She suggests a model in which learners employ their own thinking and preferences to internalize and construct representations of what they see (Immordino-Yang, 2008). Immordino-Yang calls this a process organized by the "smoke around the mirrors"—smoke being the sociocultural and emotional factors we employ in our thinking (see Chapter 7).

Many so-called 21st-century skills today—such as critical thinking, creativity, problem solving, and communication—involve becoming proficient learners on an ongoing or nearly continuous basis. We need to navigate with a successful degree of autonomy as well as draw on social and intellectual capital of groups around us.

We often are more successful at being able to learn ourselves, or "learning to learn," when we gain access to multiple perspectives and different points of view. This includes, as the OECD (2007) learning sciences report described, not only in our "material" environment but also in our "human" environment. These complex environments enrich us.

By becoming agents and advocates for improving our own understanding, we learn to engage in a process of "interrogating" for knowledge. We ask everything from the resources around us to the people we encounter for their knowledge, Are we on the right track? Mastering these approaches can make a huge difference in student learning outcomes, which will be discussed more thoroughly in Chapter 9.

Conclusion

Our brains are built for learning by constantly forming links and connections. By way of these associations, we synthesize knowledge and trigger learning to come into play when needed.

Through effective instructional design, teachers provide students with experiences to help their brains recognize meaningful patterns and distinctions. As we have learned, a number of strategies have proven useful. For example, teachers can reinforce distinctions by offering contrasts and by showing students what is right as well as what is wrong. Pointing out comparisons and contrasts can also be an effective way for students to connect learning with prior knowledge.

If synthesis fails to take place, knowledge effectively becomes of less use. For both the teacher and the student, the goal of learning, of course, is for it to be useful and for it to persist. By designing their practices to draw on what is known about the human cognitive system, teachers can employ strategies that make a difference.

Closing Scenario

Putting New Knowledge to Use

Instructional Design

This chapter illustrated how the brain is constantly forming links and connections between ideas. By integrating knowledge across subjects and across grades, teachers can help the brain connect and integrate new learning so that information and acquired skills can be triggered and put to use when needed. How might you integrate a lesson you teach with that of another subject area or to another grade?

1. In what way do you think your subject area might seem isolated and thus have little "real-world" application for students? In what ways is it relevant to your students?

2. You can connect your subject to another lesson or, if you wish, to something students have already learned in an earlier grade. What will you choose and why?

3. You've learned that teaching approaches that point out comparisons and contrasts are an especially effective way for learners to connect learning with prior knowledge. What comparisons and contrasts will you point out?

4. Similarities and differences, too, must be clearly captured by student thinking, so how will you include this fact in the design of your instruction? And how will you make them "real" to students?

5. Another important aspect of effective instruction is "conditionalizing" knowledge by using it in multiple contexts. Remember, for example, the third-grade class that walked to a local park and spent time writing about what they noticed in the pond and then began collecting data on the ducks in the pond and the behaviors of people who interacted with the ducks? If you had the time, what new context could you bring into the lesson to "conditionalize" the new information you are presenting?

6. An important aspect of the use of elaboration and extension is that it takes time; information has to be reintroduced in contexts that are close enough (but not identical) to the original learning that the brain catches the clue to make connections. How will you build this key point into your instructional design?

Citations

Online, Media, and Print Resources for Teachers

Gopnik, A. (2010, July). How babies think. *Scientific American, 303*, 76–81.
Kalb, C. (2012). Fetal armor: How the placenta shapes brain development. *Scientific American.* http://www.scientificamerican.com/article.cfm?id=fetal-armor

References

Anderson, J. R. (2000). *Learning and memory: An integrated approach.* New York: Wiley & Sons.
Arbus, D. (1972). *Diane Arbus.* Millerton, NY: Aperture.
Berger, C. & Kam, R. (1996). Definitions of instructional design. http//:www.umich.edu/~ed626/define.html

Bransford, J. D., Brown, A. L., & Cocking, R. R. (2000a). *How people learn: Brain, mind, experience, and school.* Washington, DC.: National Academies Press.

Bransford, J. D., Brown, A. L., & Cocking, R. R. (2000b). Mind and brain. *How people learn: Brain, mind, experience, and school* (pp. 114–127). Washington, DC: National Academies Press.

Collins, A., Brown, J. S., & Newman, S. E. (1990). Cognitive apprenticeship: Teaching the crafts of reading, writing, and mathematics. In L. B. Resnick (Ed.), *Knowing, learning, and instruction: Essays in honor of Robert Glaser* (pp. 453–494). Hillsdale, NJ: Erlbaum.

Collins, A., Seely Brown, J., & Holum, A. (1991). Cognitive apprenticeship: Making thinking visible. *American Educator, 6*(46).

Doreen, K. (2011). From ear to brain. *Brain and Cognition, 76*(2), 214–217.

Driscoll, M. (2000). *Psychology of learning for instruction.* Boston: Allyn & Bacon.

Edelman, S. (2012). *The happiness of pursuit: What neuroscience can teach us about the good life.* New York: Basic Books.

Gagné, R. M. (1985). *Conditions of learning* (4th ed.). New York: Holt, Rinehart and Winston.

Gholson, B., Morgan, D., Dattel, A. R., & Pierce, K. A. (1990). The development of analogical problem solving: Strategic processes in schema acquisition and transfer. In D. F. Bjorklund (Ed.), *Children's strategies: Contemporary views of cognitive development.* Hillsdale, NJ: Erlbaum.

Giardina, A., Caltagirone, C., Cipolotti, L., & Oliveri, M. (2012). The role of right and left posterior parietal cortex in the modulation of spatial attentional biases by self and non-self face stimuli. *Social Neuroscience, 7*(4), 359–368.

Gick, M., & Holyoak, K. (1983). Schema induction and analogical transfer. *Cognitive Psychology, 15*, 1–38.

Haskell, R. E. (2001). *Transfer of learning: Cognition, instruction, and reasoning.* San Diego, CA: Academic Press.

Immordino-Yang, M. H. (2008). The smoke around mirror neurons: Goals as sociocultural and emotional organizers of perception and action in learning. *Mind, Brain, and Education, 2*, 67–73.

Kalyuga, S. (2009). Knowledge elaboration: A cognitive load perspective. *Learning and Instruction, 19*, 402–410.

Linn, M. C., Lee, H.-S., Tinker, R., Husic, F., & Chiu, J. L. (2006). Teaching and assessing knowledge integration in science. *Science, 313*, 1049–1050.

Marzano, R. J. (2003). *Classroom instruction that works.* Alexandria, VA: ASCD.

McNeill, W. H. (1986). Organizing concepts for world history. *Review, 10*(2), 211–229.

Mestre, J. (Ed.). (2005). *Transfer of learning from a modern multidisciplinary perspective.* Greenwich, CT: Information Age.

National Research Council. (2000). *How people learn: Brain, mind, experience, and school: Expanded edition.* Washington, DC: National Academies Press.

OECD. (2007). Understanding the brain: The birth of a learning science. Paris: Author. doi: 10. 1787/9789264029132-en.

Rothman, R. (2012). A common core of readiness. *Educational Leadership, 69*(7), 10–15.

Royer, J. M., Mestre, J., & Dufresne, R. J. (2005). Introduction: Framing the transfer problem. In J. Mestre (Ed.), *Transfer of learning from a modern multidisciplinary perspective.* Greenwich, CT: Information Age.

Schunk, D. H. (2012). Cognition and instruction. *Learning theories: An educational perspective* (pp. 278–323). Boston: Pearson.

Whitehead, A. N. (1929). *The aims of education and other essays.* New York: The Free Press.

Yovel, G., Levy, J., Grabowecky, M., & Paller, K. A. (2003). Neural correlates of the left-visual-field superiority in face perception appear at multiple stages of face processing. *Journal of Cognitive Neuroscience, 15*(3), 462–474.

6

Sleep, Exercise, and Nutrition

This chapter introduces CORE Guiding Principle 6: Physical conditions—including aspects of sleep, exercise, and nutrition—can greatly affect brain functions and are directly related to how we learn.

Learning Points

1. Sleep-dependent memory processing is comprised of memory encoding, consolidation, and integration—all of which are required for effective learning.

2. Image studies of the brain have shown that sleep deprivation impairs the prefrontal function of the brain, the area that is necessary for the initial formation of memory.

3. New experience replayed during dream sleep has been shown to enhance memories beyond simply thinking about them when awake. In several studies, sleep following learning has been shown to lead to superior memory performance at later tests.

4. Exercise goes hand in hand with a variety of brain health agents, such as oxygenation, fueling, and cell proliferation to support and protect neurons.

5. Increases in aerobic fitness have been shown to be related to improvements in the integrity of brain structure and function that underlie academic performance.

6. In a school setting, regular participation in physical activity appears particularly beneficial to tasks that require working memory and problem solving, and shows up notably in academic performance in mathematics and reading.

7. A healthy diet rich in protein, carbohydrates, and beneficial kinds of fats has been shown to be vital to the body's ability to develop a healthy brain, to power cognition, and to support other brain functions.

8. The brain has a high energy demand. In young infants, nearly 75% of their energy goes to supporting their brain's function and rapid growth. By adulthood, 25% of the body's energy is used by the brain.

9. New research has shown that cognitive demand can deplete glucose in the region of the brain being taxed, and as glucose levels fall, that lack of fuel affects the ability to think, learn, and remember.

10. Babies and young children suffering from malnutrition can experience learning-related problems that have long-lasting impacts.

Introduction

Recess, lunch hour, and kindergarten nap time. Who could imagine a school day without them? Educators have always known these activities are important, but today research is showing that sleep, exercise, and nutrition have a much more profound role in learning than probably ever imagined. Sleep, for example, appears so vital to human learning that leading sleep researchers suggest that it may be the very reason we sleep for as much as a third of our lives and why babies and young children, who have so much to learn, sleep so much.

New research with school-age children is also showing that it is beneficial to encourage kids to be physically active for the sake of their brains. Exercise may be one simple and important method of enhancing children's mental functioning central to cognitive development, concluded a U.S. National Institutes of Health report, "Exercise and Children's Intelligence, Cognition, and Academic Achievement" (Tomporowski et al., 2008). Also, while students coming to class hungry on a particularly important test day are certainly getting shortchanged from a cognitive standpoint, far worse are those who from a young age have not been provided the proper vitamins, micronutrients, protein, and other components necessary to grow and maintain a healthy brain.

In this chapter, we begin to explore the role of physical conditions in the first part of Guiding Principle 6: *Physical conditions under which we learn best include aspects of sleep, exercise, and nutrition.* Like any other part of the human body, the brain functions best with healthy living, including proper nutrition, rest, and exercise. **(See CORE 6a.)** Health and well-being are important contributors to brain function for ourselves and our students.

Expecting teachers to understand the role of physical functioning and the brain elicits very different reactions from some who are not involved in K–12 education as compared to the teachers themselves. Some noneducators ask, What is the connection between physical activity and education? Aren't these topics more relevant to parents and policy makers—after all, what can teachers really do about these issues? Is it really necessary to include a chapter about the role of physical conditions in a book aimed for educators?

Teachers respond with a resounding *yes*. From beginning teachers to veteran educators and school leaders, teacher educators at universities report that their students absolutely love and understand this content, and that well-being resonates with them strongly. Furthermore, teachers feel there is a great deal they can do with this type of information. After all, part of an educator's role is to educate the community. This includes the students, the parents, and the schools. Teachers ask, What better topic for reaching out to those we care about than sharing fascinating new knowledge on physical well-being and how it supports learning?

Some educators even wanted this to be the first chapter in the book. However, we encourage educators to build the base of knowledge provided in Chapters 1 through 5 before tackling the content here. Although many of the studies seem accessible on their own, being able to visualize the workings of the brain as described in prior chapters will make these studies much more meaningful. Teachers can better establish long-lasting knowledge that transfers to educational practice if they build a base.

Sleep

▮▮ Sleep to Learn Better

Consider this fill-in-the-blank question:

"To sleep, perchance to _____"
A. Dream
B. Boost the brain's learning capacity
C. Improve memory
D. All of the above

Neuroscience findings suggest the best answer is *D: All of the above.* Moving from the poetry of Shakespeare to the findings of new research, sleep is proving to play such an important role in memory and learning, that "To sleep, perchance to learn" may be an apt—and accurate—rewrite of the famous line.

Sleep is a key aspect of brain function. During sleep, some of the processes involved in plasticity and consolidation of knowledge take place, consequently playing a pivotal role in learning, memory, retention, and effective knowledge integration. **(See CORE 6b.)**

A growing body of recent research in the United States and abroad is finding a direct link between sleep and the brain's ability to remember things and learn new tasks. Pull an all-nighter to cram for a test? It's been shown to do more harm than good. On the other hand, taking a short afternoon nap has been found to trigger a neurochemical process that markedly boosts the brain's learning capacity.

The sleeping brain is biologically different from the awake brain. During sleep, the brain is at its most recuperative, but it is not taking a break. Even when asleep, the brain is highly active, running through a set of complex and systematic mental activities (Walker & Stickgold, 2006). Rapid advances in neuroscience are showing compelling evidence that during sleep we:

- Encode memory.
- Stabilize and consolidate memory.

- Integrate new information with what has been previously stored.
- And even reorganize brain activity (in children and young adults) by pruning away excess neural connections (Feinberg & Campbell, 2012).

In the language of neuroscientists and psychologists who study the relationship between sleep and cognition, this is called *sleep-dependent memory processing* and *sleep-dependent plasticity.*

Robert Stickgold, a leading sleep researcher who has served as the director of the Center for Sleep and Cognition at Harvard Medical School, has described how during sleep we process information in a way that enhances meaning by fitting it into a larger context. He believes that such processing seems most likely to have driven sleep's evolution. Of all the functions of sleep, this information processing is the only one that explains why, instead of merely restorative breaks, we go through what has been described as a dangerous phenomenon of losing consciousness.

RESOURCE

K–12 teachers can use with students: Whitfield, 2008. (See the Citations list at the end of this chapter.)

Sleep Happens Where in the Brain?

In identifying the process of how information flows in the brain from wakeful acquisition to memory consolidation during sleep, researchers have found that fact-based memories are stored first but only temporarily in the hippocampus before being sent to the prefrontal cortex for more lasting, useful storage.

University of California, Berkeley, sleep researcher Matthew Walker describes the interaction between the two areas of the brain in terms we can all recognize. He says it is as though the hippocampus is your email inbox with limited storage capacity. When it gets full, new messages are bounced until the inbox is cleared out. Fortunately, the hippocampus doesn't just hit the "delete all" button when it gets full. Instead, during sleep, newly acquired information is transferred from the hippocampus into the "hard drive" of the prefrontal cortex, which appears to have more storage space. The hippocampus, then, is ready for the next delivery of information.

During sleep, new memory is consolidated in the prefrontal area. This consolidation makes it less subject to interference from competing or disrupting factors. The prefrontal cortex is also where the retained information is enhanced through added meaning and context.

▓|| Research Moves Rapidly Ahead

The idea that sleep, and specifically dreaming, helps strengthen memory was first proposed by British psychologist David Hartley in 1801. It wasn't until 1924 in a classic study by Jenkins and Dallenbach that evidence was presented to show that memory is enhanced by sleep. In their study, college students were taught nonsense syllables right before going to bed and in the morning when they were awake. It turned out that the students remembered more following a night's sleep than they did after the same number of hours awake. The researchers attributed this benefit to a lack of mental interference during the hours asleep, rather than any specific function of sleep.

Now we know that the contribution of sleep to learning is not at all a passive undertaking. It is directly related to memory development that occurs through a number of orderly physiological actions of the sleeping brain. These actions are most notably related to different stages of sleep described broadly as *Rapid Eye Movement (REM) sleep* and deeper *non-REM (NREM) sleep* (see Figure 6.1).

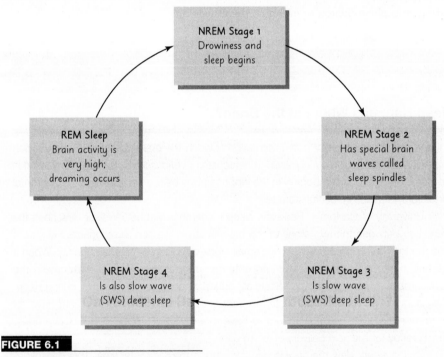

FIGURE 6.1

States and Stages of Sleep

There are two basic states of sleep: rapid eye movement (REM) sleep and non–rapid eye movement (NREM), which is divided into four stages. People experience repeated cycles of REM and NREM sleep, beginning with an NREM phase. This cycle lasts approximately 90 to 110 minutes and is repeated four to six times per night. As the night progresses, the amount of deep NREM sleep decreases and the amount of REM sleep increases.

Research has shown that during all stages of sleep, the mind and brain are working to process new memories, but in unique ways depending on the sleep stage. Research has also demonstrated that sleep provides benefits when we are awake for memory performance across a variety of tasks, including verbal learning, procedural skill learning, emotional memory, and spatial navigation. For students and educators, it's particularly noteworthy that accumulating data now also strongly demonstrates that, relative to wakefulness, sleep following learning leads to superior memory performance at later tests.

When we "replay" new experiences during dream sleep, research shows that we are enhancing our memories significantly beyond what we remember when we are awake and merely think about the same experience. More than just recalling facts, scientists are finding that in processing and transforming fragile, newly acquired memories into more stable, permanent and useful forms, brain processes that occur during sleep appear to give memories both context and permanence (Wamsley & Stickgold, 2011). In fact, in a 2010 online TED Talk, Harvard University's Stickgold says that sleep-dependent memory processing "creates the meaning of our lives" by extracting the "rules" and "gist" of the information and experiences we take in when awake.

Scientists note, however, that the precise function of sleep in memory processing and the exploration of sleep-driven brain plasticity remain active fields of investigation, with researchers integrating approaches that combine behavioral and neurophysiological measurements as they bring more insight into the process (Frank & Benington, 2006).

In fact, some recent research by Giulio Tononi and Chiara Cirelli at the University of Wisconsin-Madison is questioning the common and long-held belief that memories form because important neural links are consolidated and strengthened during sleep. Their research suggests, paradoxically, that during sleep, memory is aided by the brain weakening or removing unimportant nerve cell links. The researchers hypothesize that weakening certain synapses frees the brain from using too much energy on storing daily experiences that don't need to be remembered (Tononi & Cirelli, 2013).

Whatever the precise mechanism, there is little question that during sleep a true and lasting learning process is underway—one that is quite apart from our learning efforts when awake.

Learning While You Are Snoozing?

Knowledge obtained when awake that gets consolidated while asleep is an important part of learning, but what about learning entirely new information while you sleep? It may well be possible. In a demonstration of entirely new information being learned by humans during slumber, a research team at the Weizmann Institute of Science in Israel showed that people were able to learn—and remember—new associations between scents and sounds in their sleep (Arzi et al., 2012). "Our results reveal learning of novel information during natural human sleep and implementation of this new learning in sleep and ensuing wake," the researchers concluded.

RESOURCE

K–12 teachers can use with students: Yandell, 2012. (See the Citations list at the end of this chapter.)

The team leader, Anat Arzi, told the *New York Times* that there may be practical uses for such sleep-time learning, such as conditioning people to change bad habits. As Arzi tells it, we will need to better understand the border between what learning can and cannot take place during sleep.

In the 2012 study, the researchers exposed dozens of participants to the pleasant odors of deodorant and shampoo and to unpleasant smells, such as rotten fish, while they slept. The pleasant smells provoked deep sniffs; the bad smells shallow inhaling. The smells were then paired with specific auditory tones. Eventually (while still asleep) they responded to the tones with deep or shallow breaths whether or not the odors were present, thus showing that they had learned the smell and sound associations.

The learned associations were still in evidence in the morning when they were awake, even though the participants had no memory of smelling or hearing anything when they had been asleep.

One interesting finding was that although the learning of tone and scent pairings occurred during both REM and non-REM sleep, only the pairing learned during NREM sleep persisted into wakefulness the next day.

▉❚❚ Say "Yes" to Naps

Research into how sleep enhances learning has looked at the impact both of short naps and college students' all-night cramming for exams—two activities of particular interest to educators.

Given the findings, nap-time may be worth expanding beyond kindergarten. A 90-minute nap can dramatically boost and restore the capacity to learn and recall information, according to a study at the University of California, Berkeley. The research team, led by Berkeley psychology professor and sleep researcher Matthew Walker, compared the performance of two test groups of young adults. At noon, both groups were subjected to a rigorous learning task intended to tax the hippocampus. At 2:00 p.m., one group took a 90-minute nap; the other group stayed awake. At 6:00 p.m., the participants were given a new round of learning exercises. Those who napped did better on the tasks and actually improved their capacity to learn. The learning abilities of those who stayed awake during the day declined, according to the study.

How long a nap is needed to refresh the brain has not been determined. The Berkeley study used a 90-minute period, but a study at the University of Dusseldorf in Germany found that falling asleep for as little as 6 minutes was enough to enhance memory, although it raised questions among others about how much of the improvement could be attributed to sleep, given the short period (Lahl, Wispel, Willigens, & Pietrowsky, 2008).

■ll The Curse of Too Little Sleep

If sleep is so beneficial to learning, what happens to a person's ability to learn when she or he is deprived of sleep?

Teachers' observational evidence is probably more than enough to convince them that when students come to class without adequate sleep, learning suffers. Image studies of the brain have shown that sleep deprivation impairs the prefrontal function of the brain, the area that is necessary for the initial formation of memory—the encoding of fact-based information. Studies in animals have highlighted specific cellular changes to neurons when animals are deprived of sleep (Walker & Stickgold, 2006).

Behavioral studies have demonstrated impaired learning when sleep is in too short supply. A University of California, Berkeley, study reported that subjects deprived of sleep over 36 hours who were then allowed to sleep normally for 2 days showed a 40% decline in declarative memory retention compared with a non-sleep–deprived group.

In other words, the more hours spent awake, the more sluggish students' brains were. This is an important finding for high school and college students who rely on all-night cram sessions to prepare for big tests. Instead of cramming more information into their brains by staying up all night, they are actually shutting down important brain regions.

Tononi and Cirelli (2013), the psychiatry professors and sleep researchers at the University of Wisconsin, have studied a phenomenon in animals and humans called *local sleep,* in which parts of the brain essentially sign off while most of the brain is still awake. According to the researchers, this occurs to certain groups of neurons when they are subjected to prolonged or intense periods of use. Tononi and Cirelli found that this phenomenon also occurs in sleep-deprived humans and becomes more frequent after intense learning. The latter situation would appear to represent the classic midnight cram session. At such times, the researchers say, people are wide awake but "small chunks of the brain may take quick naps without giving notice." How many errors in judgment or silly mistakes, these authors wonder, result from such local sleep in the brain?

■ll Not All Sleep Is the Same

In general, sleep is composed of predictable 90-minute cycles comprised of distinct stages with specific neurological and physiological functions that may contribute in a distinct way to memory consolidation. In addition to the REM stage, there are four stages of NREM sleep, including two particularly deep stages known as SWS, for "slow wave sleep" (Walker & Stickgold, 2006).

In an experiment at the University of Tubingen's Institute for Medical Psychology and Behavioral Neurobiology, a Swiss and German team found that children's brains, more effectively than adults' brains, transformed subconsciously learned material into active knowledge while they slept. By measuring brain activity while the participants slept, it turned out that the children had much more "slow wave sleep." "The formation of explicit knowledge appears to be a very specific ability of childhood sleep," said Dr. Ines Wilhelm, a study leader (Wilhelm et al., 2013).

Equally interesting, in the University of California, Berkeley, nap research, the learning benefits came during the sleep stage that occurs between deep sleep and dream sleep, known as *Stage 2 NREM sleep*. The Berkeley researchers found compelling evidence that bursts of brain waves known as "sleep spindles" may be networking between key regions of the brain to clear a path to learning. These spindles of electricity are generated during non-REM sleep and they can occur up to 1,000 times a night. People who experience more spindles have been shown to retain memories better.

Bryce Mander, lead author of the study, described that most spindle-rich sleep comes during the second half of the night. So sleeping 6 or fewer hours leaves people shortchanged. Students will have fewer spindles and might not be able to learn as much (Mander et al., 2011). Mander explained in a university news release that late bedtimes, especially when combined with early school start times, prevent adequate sleep amounts for children and young adults. Mander's work highlights the importance of sleep for educational populations, where the need for learning is great.

▮‖ What Information Gets Remembered?

Researchers have also explored the factors that influence what information acquired while awake will be best remembered during sleep. Although there is still a great deal to be learned, the good news is that it is not a haphazard progress.

Learning followed quickly by sleeping is important. In two experiments with high school students that examined their ability to remember vocabulary, a German team of researchers reported that declarative memory is enhanced when sleep follows within a few hours of learning. The time of day didn't matter—only that the learning was fairly quickly followed by sleep (Gais, Lucas, & Born, 2006).

Getting experience into dreams might also help. "When we replay a recent experience in a dream we enhance our memory," said researchers Robert Stickgold and Erin Wamsley (2011). In their lab, they asked people to play a video game that required navigating a 3-D maze. Following the video, for the next 90 minutes, some participants napped while others stayed awake. Those who reported dreaming about the game as they napped were 10 times better at it the next time they played. Those who stayed awake and said they were thinking about the game improved very little.

Of course, the research on sleep is far from conclusive yet. Educators who stay tuned will find many studies in progress.

▪ll Sleep and Brain Plasticity

A key question for scientists is the role of sleep in contributing to long-lasting remodeling of brain structures, the plasticity of the brain discussed in Chapter 2. A 10-year longitudinal sleep study by researchers at the University of California, Davis, Sleep Laboratory has shed important new light on the activity of neural pruning during sleep, providing insight into the brain as it grows from childhood into adulthood.

Using electroencephalograms (EEGs) during periods of slow wave (deep) sleep, the research team was able to follow levels of brain activity as the children aged. Based on this, the researchers determined that synaptic densities in the cortex reach a peak at age 8 and then the connections are slowly pruned away over the next 4½ years. By the time the children reached puberty, said the researchers, their brain activity indicated that the rate of pruning had declined significantly, indicating that their brain functioning had been streamlined to undertake the executive decision making and thinking process of an adult. **(See CORE 6b.)**

By measuring brain activity in the same children as they aged over a 10-year period and collecting more than 3,500 all-night EEG recordings, the study provided the first description of the developmental changes that take place in the brains of children as they sleep, said Irwin Feinberg, director of the University of California, Davis, Sleep Laboratory (Feinberg & Campbell, 2012).

The data aids the search for unknown genetic and hormonal biomarkers that may be involved, said Feinberg, professor emeritus of psychiatry and behavioral sciences, in a university news release. He described how the data provides a baseline for seeking errors in brain development that could signify the onset of diseases such as schizophrenia. This severe brain disorder typically first becomes apparent during adolescence and is believed to affect about 1% of the population. If underlying processes can be identified, it may become possible to influence adolescent brain changes in ways that promote normal development and correct emerging abnormalities.

Exercise
▪ll More Than Child's Play

Six-year-old Wyatt had just started first grade. His aunt asked him what he liked best about school. Without hesitation, he replied, "Recess!" Although he didn't know it, his high level of physical activity during recess was doing more than improving his tetherball game—it was likely stimulating the growth of new neurons and improving his relational memory, speeding up his cognitive processing, and contributing to enhanced academic performance.

An abundance of research since the 1990s suggests that physically active school-age children fare better in the classroom and generally have superior cognitive abilities than their sedentary counterparts. Sufficient physical activity is believed central not only to controlling obesity and strengthening the body but also to children's cognitive development. Exercise goes hand in hand with a variety of brain health promoters, such as oxygenation, fueling, cell proliferation to support and protect neurons, and production of important brain chemicals, say researchers (Tomporowski et al., 2008).

Much of what we know about exercise has come from research on mice and rats. More recently, however, research includes the use of advanced imaging and other tools of brain science conducted in carefully developed experiments with school-age children. Results of such research are showing a clear relationship between vigorous and moderate-intensity physical activity and the structure and functioning of the brain.

■ll Fitness Matters to the Brain

In 2013, the National Research Council published a report titled *Educating the Student Body: Taking Physical Activity and Physical Education to School*. In that report, a panel of Institute of Medicine/U.S. National Academies of Science experts reviewed an abundance of mostly recent research to explore the relationship of physical activity and levels of physical fitness to cognitive and brain health and to academic performance.

Citing what it called ample scientific evidence, the report said that physically active and aerobically fit children consistently outperform their inactive and unfit peers academically on both a short- and long-term basis. "The findings across the body of literature in this area suggest that increases in aerobic fitness, derived from physical activity, are related to improvements in the integrity of brain structure and function that underlie academic performance," it reported (National Research Council, 2013).

For children in a school setting, the research cited showed regular participation in physical activity is particularly beneficial with respect to tasks that require working memory and problem solving. The strongest relationships, the report noted, have been found between aerobic fitness and performance in mathematics, reading, and English, all of which rely on efficient and effective executive function.

After reviewing the research literature, the expert panel concluded that "physical activity is related not only to a healthier body but also to enriched cognitive development and lifelong brain health" (National Research Council, 2013, p. 4).

■ll Run, Mice, Run

Early findings concluding that exercise had a positive effect on the brain arose in the late 1990s when scientists at the Salk Institute for Biological Studies first discovered that mice given access to running wheels produced new cells, many of them neurons, specifically only in the hippocampus, an area of the brain controlling memory creation. The mice that exercised performed better on memory tests than did sedentary mice.

This raised the question: Did the additional neurons improve brain function? A 1999 Salk study by Henriette van Praag and colleagues, again using mice, sought to find out. The research showed that physical exercise (running on treadmills) triggered chemical changes in the brain that regulate neurogenesis (the formation and development of nerve cells) in the hippocampus, synaptic plasticity, and learning (van Praag et al., 1999).

"As expected from the previous work, we saw abundant production of new cells, and importantly, this time we showed that many of those cells are neurons, the class specialized to transmit messages throughout the brain," Salk Professor Fred H. Gage, senior author of the study, said in an institute news release.

As with much brain research related to exercise, the findings are based on correlations, or relationships, between activity and learning. More recently, research is finding direct physical evidence.

A University of California, Los Angeles, study led by neurosurgery professor Fernando Gomez-Pinilla found evidence of a direct biological link between exercise and improved cognitive function. Using laboratory rats, the experiment showed that physical exercise boosted levels of the brain chemical BDNF (brain-derived neurotrophic factor), which is known to stimulate and control the growth of new neurons specifically in the hippocampus.

"The more exercise, the more changes in the brain; we found almost a linear relationship," Gomez-Pinilla reported. "If we block the BDNF gene, we block this capacity of exercise to help learning and memory" (Vaynman, Ying, & Gomez-Pinilla, 2004).

RESOURCE

K–12 teachers can use with students: Ballantyne, 2009. (See the Citations list at the end of this chapter.)

Through such research we now know that exercise increases the production of chemicals that promote growth, survival, and repair of brain cells, and that exercise increases levels of some molecules in the brain that are important for learning and enhances neural connections and synapse flexibility.

Juggling Brain Connections

Juggling may not be the most vigorous aerobic activity, but learning how to keep three balls in the air at once has been shown to have brain benefits. Combining the physical coordination needed to juggle with the cognitive demands of learning something entirely new appears to improve connections in the brain associated with the new activity.

At the Oxford Centre for Functional Magnetic Resonance Imaging of the Brain, researchers set out to see if changes in the white matter of the brain could be seen in healthy adults set to learning a new task or skill. White matter consists of the bundles of long nerve fibers that conduct electrical signals between nerve cells and connect different parts of the brain together. Change in gray matter has been associated with learning, but growth in white matter had not previously been demonstrated.

For the study, a group of young healthy adults, none of whom could juggle, was divided into two groups each of 24 people. One of the groups was given weekly training in juggling for 6 weeks and asked to practice 30 minutes every day. Both groups were scanned using diffusion MRI before and after the 6-week period, according to the study paper published in the journal *Nature Neuroscience* in 2009 (Scholz, Klein, Behrens, & Johansen-Berg, 2009).

After 6 weeks, scans showed changes in the white matter of the jugglers compared to the others who had received no training. The changes were in regions of the brain that are involved in reaching and grasping in the periphery of vision.

After the training, some volunteers were significantly better jugglers than others. But it didn't matter. All showed changes in white matter, no matter what their talent level was. Just making the effort to learn the new activity seemed to be the key.

■∥ Looking Specifically at Children

Much of the research on the human brain and exercise has focused on adult cognition and memory loss in aging brains, and has provided a useful base of knowledge. As mentioned earlier, a growing number of studies today are focusing specifically on children's mental performance.

Recent work at two research centers associated with the University of Illinois, for example, is examining the relationship between physical activity and neurocognitive function of children. Cognitive testing has shown learning improvement and imaging studies have shown change in brain structure of physically fit children.

At the university's Neurocognitive Kinesiology Laboratory, a team led by Charles H. Hillman investigated the relationship between aerobic fitness, learning, and memory in school-age children. They recruited 48 9- and 10-year-olds, half who showed a high degree of fitness and half with a low degree of fitness, and had them learn the names of specific regions on a map. The research team had the students learn in two situations, one in which they were quizzed as the learning occurred, and in a more challenging session when there was no quizzing to reinforce the learning.

The researchers found no difference when quizzing was used to reinforce the learning. However, in the more challenging situation, they reported that the physically fit children absorbed and retained the new information more effectively than children who were less fit. The physically fit kids remembered about 40% of the regions' names accurately, compared with barely 25% accuracy for the lower-fit students. "We interpret these novel data to suggest that fitness can boost learning and memory of children and that these fitness-associated performance benefits are largest in conditions in which initial learning is the most challenging. Such data have important implications for both educational practice and policy," said the published research (Raine et al., 2013).

In a somewhat related study, researchers at the university's associated Beckman Institute for Advanced Science and Technology put the tools of their trade to work to look at differences in the hippocampus between 9- and 10 year-olds. The children were put into two groups, higher-fit children and lower-fit children, as shown by treadmill tests. When the researchers analyzed the MRI data, they found that the physically fit children tended to have bigger hippocampal volume—about 12% bigger relative to total brain size—than their out-of-shape peers (National Research Council, 2013).

The children who were in better physical condition also did better on tests of *relational memory*—the ability to remember and integrate various types of information—than their less-fit peers. Researchers found that higher-fit children had higher performance relational memory tasks, along with larger hippocampal volumes. Laura Chaddock, a graduate student who co-led the study with psychology professor and Beckman Institute director Art Kramer, said in a university news report that, in general, children with larger hippocampal volumes were found to have better relational memory. Furthermore, stated Chaddock, if hippocampal volume is removed from the equation, the relationship between fitness and memory decreases, she said.

◼❙❙ How Much and What Kind?

Whereas these two studies looked at overall physical fitness, other research has examined the relationship between cognition and actual physical activity. It turns out that learning benefits accrue from both a one-time burst of activity, the kind you might associate with recess or P.E. class, and from long-term participation in physical activity.

After such single bouts of exercise, children perform notably better on academic achievement tests, the University of Illinois' Charles Hillman told *Good Morning America* in describing the results of his study, "Cognition Following Acute Aerobic Exercise" (Hillman et al., 2009). Using treadmills, brain monitors, and other equipment, Hillman and his colleagues measured cognition before and after exercise. They found that moderate exercise—30 minutes for adults and 20 minutes for children—results in a 5 to 10% improvement in cognition.

RESOURCE

K–12 teachers can use with students: Shipman, Evans, & Clarke, 2009. (See the Citations list at the end of this chapter.)

Similar findings by other researchers, comparing children who participated in 30 minutes of aerobic physical activity with children who watched television for the same amount of time, showed the active children cognitively outperformed their TV-watching counterparts (Ellemberg & St-Louis-Deschênes, 2010).

Most of the exercise and brain function research has been done using cardiovascular exercise, which has been found to have the greatest impact on academic achievement. However, a U.S. 2011 meta-analysis report, *Educating the Student Body,* found that all types of physical activity, except those involving flexibility alone, contribute to enhanced academic performance (Fedewa & Ahn, 2011).

Teachers respond that they have no problem with any of these concepts. What they struggle with is how to get school administrators and parents to see the value in exercise and the need for it in the school day. For instance, some teachers still keep children in from recess to finish homework. They probably know it isn't the best thing for the children in light of the research, but might say they have no other time to help children who haven't completed class assignments or homework. If other arrangements could be made, they wouldn't keep the children in.

Here, teachers have the opportunity to engage in dialogue in their schools and their professional learning communities. How can support for movement be offered? Discussion drawing on the research can help with planning how to establish more activity into the school day. Elementary schools use movement games in learning. Middle schools take math lessons up and down hallways and climb the stairs to measure slope and estimate angles. High schools engage in hands-on environmental education, eating up miles of terrain. It may not be simple to plan or agree on, and the difficulty and challenges of this should not be underestimated, but learning for both mind and body need not be static.

■|| Walking to School Gets an A

Whatever the ultimate brain-boosting exercise turns out to be, simply riding a bike or walking to school instead of being driven by car or bus appears to increase a child's ability to concentrate in the classroom. The benefit of the morning exercise lasted half the day and outperformed the value of eating breakfast and lunch on sustaining concentration, according to a large Danish study. Almost 20,000 schoolchildren aged 5 to 19 participated in the study called "Mass Experiment 2012," part of an annual Danish Science Week, aimed at examining the link between diet, exercise, and the power of concentration.

The results of the joint study by researchers at the universities in Copenhagen and Aahus surprised even the researchers who reported it. Children who were driven to school, or took the bus, performed less well in a test measuring concentration levels, than those who had walked or cycled.

"The results showed that having breakfast and lunch has an impact, but not very much compared to having exercised," researcher Niels Egelund, a co-author of the report, told the Danish news service AFP. That the benefits of increased concentration lasted for hours was particularly notable. "Most people know the feeling of being refreshed after having exercised, but it is surprising that the effect lasts for so long," Egelund said (cited in Vinther, 2012).

■|| Elite Athletes Excel Off the Court, Too

In a twist on the jock stereotype, elite athletes often excel at cognitive tasks, especially those involving change and distraction. Those who spend years training on specific physical tasks also tend to have enhanced cognitive abilities in these areas.

Using a group of Olympic medalists in volleyball as their test group, researchers found that athletes appear to excel not only in their sport but also in how fast their brains take in and respond to new information off the court. Overall, the athletes were modestly faster at memory tests and at tests of their ability to keep two tasks in mind at once and rapidly switch between tasks. They were quicker to notice things in their peripheral vision and to detect subtle changes in a scene. And, in general, they were better able to accomplish tasks while ignoring confusing or irrelevant information (Alves et al., 2013).

Nutrition

■|| Food for Thought

One pre-service teacher finishing up her training in a classroom found the importance of diet and nutrition in powering the brain to learn was all too clear. She said she noticed how the attention of some students would begin to drift at times and saw how positively they responded to the healthy snacks the teacher made available. Students weren't attentive and learning when they weren't eating properly and for some students that was a frequent problem.

The work of neuroscience, cognitive and behavioral studies, and the results of education research—the "power of three " learning sciences—plus the work of nutritionists are beginning to offer a detailed understanding of the brain's response to nutrition and diet that goes far beyond the accepted (and still essential) need to start the day with a good breakfast. If we start with the simple fact that our brain cells use two times the energy as other cells in the body, then the dynamic role of nutrition and diet in powering the brain becomes clear (Franklin Institute Online, 2004a).

The brain, it turns out, is something of an energy hog. An adult's brain weighs just 3 pounds but uses as much as 25% of the body's energy resources (Purves et al., 2008). The brain's energy needs are even greater in newborn babies. Nearly 75% of a baby's energy goes to supporting learning and the rapid structural growth of its brain (Cunnane & Crawford, 2003).

The brain is powered primarily by energy provided by glucose, the blood sugar produced from simple and complex carbohydrates in the food we eat, and from many substances, even including protein components stored in the liver. Because neurons cannot store glucose, they depend on the bloodstream to deliver a constant supply.

Scientists point out, however, that we should not directly eat sticky, sugary foods such as highly sweetened fruit drinks or candy bars to power the brain, although this is a common neuromyth. As one instructor put it, for teachers, parents, and school lunch and breakfast programs to respond to nutrition needs, it helps to know that money spent on high-carb pizza, high fructose desserts, and heavily sweetened fruit juices is not helping students. Some teachers mistakenly believe that this fuels the brain. By the way, neither does thinking especially hard in school or solving a particularly difficult problem burn up many calories by the brain. Scientists find the effect is small to negligible (Jabr, 2012) and that the baseline rate of one's usual waking activity is demanding enough to trigger the high fuel needs. Think about all the brain does just when we look out a window at a new scene, navigate across a room, or even engage in speaking and listening.

Neurons consume a lot of energy because they're in a constant state of activity; even during sleep, neurons are at work. They are manufacturing enzymes and neurotransmitters that must be transported out to the ends of their axons—some of these nerve branches can be as far as several feet away. But it is the neurons' bioelectric signals, used to communicate throughout the nervous system, that are the most demanding of energy, consuming one-half of all the brain's energy in adults, or nearly 10% of the whole body's energy (Franklin Institute Online, 2004a).

For educators, especially for teachers in the classroom, it is interesting to note that the brain's energy use fluctuates during the day. Different parts of the brain use different amounts of energy. The prefrontal cortex where cognitive control and working memory occur is one of the bigger users of glucose (Howard Hughes Medical Institute, 2012). In general, researchers have found that those neurons that are most active at any given moment use more energy than those that are quieter (Purves et al., 2008).

▋‖ Powering the Brain for Learning

Increasingly, science is providing more and more information to support the notion of what we eat affects our brains. A healthy diet, rich in protein, carbohydrates, and beneficial kinds of fats, has been shown to be vital to the body's ability to develop a healthy brain, to power cognition, and to support other brain functions.

Fats are the essential building material of the brain. About two-thirds of the human brain is composed of amino acids from fats, and different kinds of fats play different roles. The fatty acids DHA (docosahexaenoic acid) and AA (arachidonic acid) are both crucial to the optimal development of the brain and eyes. Omega 3 and Omega 6 fatty acids, also involved in brain cell development, come only from the food you eat; your body cannot manufacture them.

Myelin, the protective sheath that covers communicating neurons, is composed of 70% fat and 30% protein. One of the most common fatty acids in myelin is oleic acid, which is abundant in human milk.

Amino acids from proteins build connective tissue in the brain, produce new nerve cells, and are key components of neurotransmitters. For example, the protein tryptophan helps to make serotonin, the neurotransmitter involved in mood, appetite, and sleep. Dietary protein also has an important function in proper nutrition.

Many minerals and vitamins protect the structure of brain cells and are supplied to the brain continuously for such needs as energy metabolism of neurons and glial cells, neurotransmitter synthesis and action, nerve impulse propagation, and the protection of nerve cells from the effects of oxidation (Drake, 2011).

To illustrate the role of nutrition in the development and function of the brain, the Franklin Institute in Philadelphia has developed a Brain Food Pyramid. To summarize some key points about the brain, the institute says: "Essentially, fats build your brain, and proteins unite it. Carbohydrates fuel your brain, and micronutrients defend it."

RESOURCE

K–12 teachers can use with students: Franklin Institute Online, 2004b. (See the Citations list at the end of this chapter.)

It is important to note that despite what seems to be an endless array of products promising to make us smarter, there's little conclusive scientific evidence to date showing any specific products, supplements, or proscribed diets that directly lead to "brain-boosting" qualities.

▌▍ Nutrition Early in Life Is Key

Although there is still debate over the idea of defined "brain food," there is little doubt that adequate nutrition supplied to babies and young children is vital for proper brain development. Protein in their diet helps children's brains think clearly, concentrate, and learn. Malnutrition, which commonly occurs in children in poor countries, and shockingly so in parts of the United States, has been shown to dramatically affect children's brain function, sometimes well into their teen years.

A study of children between the ages of 5 and 10 in Bangalore, India, found that children with chronic protein malnutrition suffered from lower IQs and test scores in school, behavioral problems, poor memory, and other cognitive deficiencies. The study's authors also reported that the rate of development of attention, executive functions such as cognitive flexibility, working memory, and visuo-spatial functions such as visual construction is more severely affected by protein energy malnutrition in childhood years, when cognitive functions are developing.

The researchers describe that stunting growth results from chronic protein malnutrition. It results not only in physical changes that can sometimes be seen in the body's development but also in cognitive impairments. This includes a slowdown in the rate of the development of cognitive processes. In other words, chronic protein energy malnutrition during childhood years could result in delay in the development of cognitive functions as well as permanent cognitive impairments (Bhoomika, Shobini, & Chandramouli, 2008).

In the United States, the Arkansas Children's Nutrition Center, a federally funded Human Nutrition Research Center, has undertaken research to determine whether obesity is playing a role in learning. The researchers want to see whether interactions between nutrition and cognitive function differ in normal weight and overweight children.

 RESOURCE

K–12 teachers can use with students: Arkansas Children's Nutrition Center, 2010. (See the Citations list at the end of this chapter.)

Despite the high incidence of overweight children in U.S. society, the researchers note, systematic studies of the relationships between nutrition and cognitive function have not been conducted to determine how they may differ from those of normal-weight individuals. The studies hope to provide a basis for dietary recommendations that will enable children with different psychological and physical profiles to optimize learning and performance in school.

▌❙❙ Brain Drain: When You Eat Matters

It used to be thought that, short of starvation, the brain was automatically supplied a stable and ample amount of glucose to keep it functioning properly. But research is showing that cognitive demand can deplete glucose in the region of the brain being taxed, and as glucose levels fall that lack of fuel affects the ability to think and remember. So, coming to class hungry or skipping lunch could directly affect how well students can learn on any given day.

The research suggests the contents and timing of meals may need to be coordinated if we want the most beneficial learning effects, observed University of Illinois Psychology Professor Paul E. Gold, who has studied glucose levels and cognitive demand and is a lead author of a research paper on the topic (McNay, Fries, & Gold, 2000).

The study, using rats and testing their maze-running abilities, showed that as the concentration of glucose in the hippocampus depleted (falling by 30%), their learning and memory declined, indicating that memory processing in the hippocampus may be limited by the availability of glucose. Or, as the study's co-author, behavioral neuroscientist Ewan C. McNay described it in a university news release, insufficient fuel undermines the ability to think and remember.

Changes in glucose usage affect only regions of the brain involved with what the animal is asked to do, Gold continued. The researchers' findings challenged conventional thinking about levels and stability of glucose in the brain. New findings suggest ample glucose is not always present to support learning and memory, described Gold, who also is director of the Medical Scholars Program in the UI College of Medicine at Urbana-Champaign.

◼◫ A Is for Apples

It is heartbreaking for educators when they know that learning is suffering because their students aren't getting the nutrition their brains and bodies need. Apart from making sure that available local and federal food and nutrition support is in place at their schools, what can they do? For one thing, they can teach students the value of eating well.

A pilot study in California's Central Valley (one of the most productive areas in the world to grow fruits and vegetables) suggests that teaching students the value of quality nutrition through a program called EatFit can improve academic performance as measured by standardized achievement tests. For the study, all 6th-graders at a suburban school in which 58% of the students qualify for free or reduce priced lunch were included in the study. Following a nine-session program focused on nutrition education, their test scores on specific mathematics and English education standards increased (Shilts, Lamp, Horowitz, & Townsend, 2008). Students, it seems, may step up to the (more nutritious) plate when they learn what's good for them and their brains.

Such studies about educating students on nutrition and its impact on the brain add a valuable strategy for teachers. Teachers can't go home and prepare meals for students, but they can employ a valuable strategy by educating, illustrating, and modeling for their students. As one teacher educator described, when she discusses this topic, teachers lament that they can't change what the children eat—but such studies show they can have an impact through the tools of the classroom.

Conclusion

Like any other part of the human body, the brain develops and functions best with healthy living. The human need to be properly rested, fueled, and active is vitally important for many reasons tied directly to optimal brain function.

As research is revealing, a great deal of crucial activity is underway in the brain when we are asleep. Sleep-dependent memory processing provides unique functions directly tied to our ability to learn effectively. As Harvard's Robert Stickgold so eloquently puts it, this process "creates the meaning of our lives" by extracting the "rules" and "gist" of the information and experiences we take in when awake.

For children in a school setting, evidence shows that short bouts of moderate physical activity can improve performance on tests, and regular participation in physical activity is particularly beneficial in tasks that require working memory and problem solving. Physical activity is associated with more efficient and effective executive function, with strong relationships shown to performance in mathematics and reading. Even just walking or riding a bike to school has been shown to benefit in-class learning.

Finally, we know that the human brain is a learning machine and that a fully powered, strongly built brain must be optimized to help us learn. Nutritional deficiencies in young children can stunt brain development with lasting results. New findings on glucose depletion in the working brain suggest that even coming to class hungry or skipping lunch could directly affect how well students can learn on any given day.

Closing Scenario

Putting New Knowledge to Use

Physical Conditions: Sleep, Exercise, and Nutrition

Sleep, exercise, and nutrition are critically important to learning, but these elements are often outside the purview of teachers. Parents, of course, play a very important role, but healthy habits are also the personal responsibility of all students. Helping your students understand what they can do to help the brain learn better can be an empowering and valuable step.

1. How will you introduce the special role that sleep has in learning, and why is it more than just the need to feel well rested?
2. What key facts can you use from brain and sleep research to show students how the brain learns when they are asleep?
3. Dreaming and "replaying" new experiences during sleep enhances learning. Ask your students if they remember any of their dreams and if a certain dream helped them remember something. What can you tell them about what science has learned about this?
4. For older students, what can you tell them about all-night cramming that could make a difference to them as they prepare for the SATs or any other exam? What two or three key points will you tell them about how exercise benefits brain health?
5. What can you share with your students that will help them understand changes to the structure of the brain associated with physical activity?
6. Regular participation in physical activity appears particularly beneficial in certain learning tasks. What are these and how do these relate to specific academic areas?
7. Since a healthy diet has been shown to be vital to the body's ability to develop a healthy brain, to power cognition, and to support other brain functions, how will you help your

students see how their own decisions about what to eat will relate to how well their brain works?

8. What will you tell your students about how active the brain is and how much fuel it takes to keep it working?

9. How can you help your students understand why coming to class hungry or skipping lunch could affect how well they can learn or even how well they can do on the afternoon assignment?

Citations

Online, Media, and Print Resources for Teachers

Arkansas Children's Nutrition Center. (2010). Determining nutrition-related factors that optimize learning in school-aged children. *Brain Development and Function Laboratory*. http://acnc.uamsweb .com/research-2/our-laboratories-2/brain-development-lab/

Ballantyne, C. (2009). Does exercise really make you healthier? *Scientific American*. http://www .scientificamerican.com/article.cfm?id=does-exercise-really-make&page=3)

Drake, V. J. (2011). Micronutrients and cognitive function. *Micronutrient Information Center*. http:// lpi.oregonstate.edu/infocenter/cognition.html-executivefunctions

Franklin Institute Online (Producer). (2004b, January 17, 2014). Introducing the brain food pyramid. Retrieved from http://learn.fi.edu/learn/brain/pyramid.html

Shipman, C., Evans, S., & Clarke, S. (2009). Can exercise boost your brainpower? http://kch. illinois.edu/Research/Labs/neurocognitive-kinesiology/files/Articles/Shipman_2009_ CanExerciseBoostYour.pdf

Vinther, D. (2012). Children who walk to school concentrate better. *ScienceNordic*. http:// sciencenordic.com/children-who-walk-to-school-concentrate-better

Whitfield, J. (2008). Naps for better recall. *Scientific American*. http://www.scientificamerican.com/ article.cfm?id=naps-for-better-recall

Yandell, K. (2012, August 27). Learning doesn't stop when you're asleep. *New York Times*. Retrieved from http://www.nytimes.com/2012/08/28/science/study-shows-learning-of-smells-and-sounds-in-sleep.html?_r=0

References

Alves, H., Voss, M. W., Boot, W. R., Deslandes, A., Cossich, V., Salles, J. I., & Kramer, A. F. (2013). Perceptual-cognitive expertise in elite volleyball players. *Frontiers in Psychology, 4*(36).

Arzi, A., Shedlesky, L., Ben-Shaul, M., Nasser, K., Oksenberg, A., Hairston, I. S., & Sobel, N. (2012). Humans can learn new information during sleep. *Nature Neuroscience, 15*, 1460–1465.

Bhoomika, K. R., Shobini, R. L., & Chandramouli, B. A. (2008, July). Cognitive development in children with chronic protein energy malnutrition. *Behavioral and Brain Functions*.

Chaddock, L., Erickson, K. I., Prakash, R. S., Kim, J. S., Voss, M. W., Vanpatter, M., Pontifex, M. B., Raine, L. B., Konkel, A., Hillman, C. H., Cohen, N. J., & Kramer, A. F. (2010). A neuroimaging investigations of the association between aerobic fitness, hippocampal volume, and memory performance in preadolescent children. *Brain Research, 1358,* 172–183.

Cunnane, S. C., & Crawford, M. A. (2003). Survival of the fattest: Fat babies were the key to evolution of the large human brain. *Comp Biochem Physiol A Mol Integr Physiol, 136,* 17–26.

Ellemberg, D., & St-Louis-Deschênes, M. (2010). The effect of acute physical exercise on cognitive function during development. *Psychology of Sport and Exercise, 11*(2), 122–126.

Fedewa, A. L., & Ahn, S. (2011). The effects of physical activity and physical fitness on children's achievement and cognitive outcomes: A meta-analysis. *Research Quarterly for Exercise and Sport, 82*(3), 521–535.

Feinberg, I., & Campbell, I. G. (2012). Longitudinal sleep EEG trajectories indicate complex patterns of adolescent brain maturation. *AJP: Regulatory, Integrative and Comparative Physiology, 304*(4), R296.

Frank, M. G., & Benington, J. H. (2006). The role of sleep in memory consolidation and brain plasticity: Dream or reality? *Neuroscientist, 12*(6), 477–488.

Franklin Institute Online. (2004a). Brain energy demand. *Nourish—Carbohydrates Fuel Your Brain.* http://www.fi.edu/learn/brain/carbs.html

Gais, S., Lucas, B., & Born, J. (2006). Sleep after learning aids memory recall. *Learning and Memory, 13,* 259–262.

Hillman, C. H., Pontifex, M. B., Raine, L. B., Castelli, D. M., Hall, E. E., & Kramer, A. F. (2009). The effect of acute treadmill walking on cognitive control and academic achievement in preadolescent children. *Neuroscience, 159,* 1044–1054.

Howard Hughes Medical Institute. (2012, February). Ask a scientist. *HHMI Bulletin.*

Jabr, F. (2012). Does thinking really hard burn more calories? *Scientific American.* http://www.scientificamerican.com/article/thinking-hard-calories/

Lahl, O., Wispel, C., Willigens, B., & Pietrowsky, R. (2008). An ultra short episode of sleep is sufficient to promote declarative memory performance. *Journal of Sleep Research, 17*(1), 3–10.

Mander, B. A., Santhanam, S., Saletin, J. M., & Walker, M. P. (2011). Wake deterioration and sleep restoration of human learning. *Current Biology, 21*(5).

McNay, E. C., Fries, T. M., & Gold, P. E. (2000). Decreases in rat extracellular hippocampal glucose concentration associated with cognitive demand during a spatial task. *Proc Natl Acad Sci, 97*(6), 2881–2885.

National Research Council. (2013). *Educating the student body: Taking physical activity and physical education to school.* Washington, DC: National Academies.

Purves, D., Augustine, G. J., Fitzpatrick, D., Hall, W. C., LaMantia, A.-S., McNamara, J. O., & White, L. E. (2008). *Neuroscience.* Sunderland, MA: Sinauer.

Raine, L. B., Lee, H. K., Saliba, B. J., Chaddock-Heyman, L., Hillman, C. H., & Kramer, A. F. (2013). The influence of childhood aerobic fitness on learning and memory. *PLOS ONE, 8*(9).

Scholz, J., Klein, M. C., Behrens, T. E. J., & Johansen-Berg, H. (2009). Training induces changes in white matter architecture. *Nature Neuroscience, 12*(11), 1370–1371.

Shilts, M. K., Lamp, C., Horowitz, M., & Townsend, M. S. (2008). Pilot study: EatFit impacts sixth graders' academic performance on achievement of mathematics and English education standards. *J Nutr Educ Behav, 41*(2), 127–131.

Tomporowski, P. D., Davis, C. L., Miller, P. H., & Naglieri, J. A. (2008). Exercise and children's intelligence, cognition, and academic achievement. *Educ. Psychol. Rev., 20*(2), 111–131.

Tononi, G., & Cirelli, C. (2013). Perchance to prune. *Scientific American, 309*(2), 34–39.

van Praag, H., Christie, B. R., Sejnowski, T. J., & Gage, F. H. (1999). Running enhances neurogenesis, learning, and long-term potentiation in mice. *PNAS, 96*(23), 13427–13431.

Vaynman, S., Ying, Z., & Gomez-Pinilla, F. (2004). Exercise induces BDNF and synapsin I to specific hippocampal subfields. *JNeurosci Res., 76*(3), 356–362.

Walker, M. P., & Stickgold, R. (2006). Sleep, memory, and plasticity. *Annu. Rev. Psychol., 57*, 139–166.

Wamsley, E. J., & Stickgold, R. (2011). Memory, sleep and dreaming: Experiencing consolidation. *Sleep Med Clin., 6*(1), 97–108.

Wilhelm, I., Rose, M., Imhof, K. I., Rasch, B., Büchel, C., & Born, J. (2013). The sleeping child outplays the adult's capacity to convert implicit into explicit knowledge. *Nature Neuroscience, 16*, 391–393.

7

Emotional Function and Attitude in the Brain

This chapter introduces CORE Guiding Principle 5: When we effectively learn is influenced by important brain-related factors including emotions and attitude. What we filter out matters as much as what we process.

Learning Points

1. Scientists believe emotion and attitude arise in part through cerebral processes, and are essential for the human brain to function effectively.

2. Emotions are a form of relationship, a brain association on which we operate. They are part of how we represent the world around us.

3. Different emotions employ distinct functional systems in the brain and have their own cerebral circuits. When we are ready to learn, emotional circuitry is likely to have entered into the "green light" that gives us the go-ahead.

4. Emotional information looms large in the brain's decision-making process. It is different from a feeling, say, of love or sadness. It is the highlighting of essential meaning for us.

5. Chemicals called neurotransmitters and neuromodulators may excite or inhibit actions, based on regulating brain processes. Dopamine and serotonin are examples of neurotransmitters.

6. A part of the brain called the amygdala is involved in our emotional processing. It can take control of our actions even before we have time to decide what to do. The same emotional machinery can come into play and block learning for students.

7. Learning resistance is an important phenomenon that likely has biological as well as psychological roots. Mechanisms of resistance are built into the brain's natural learning responsiveness.

8. Retention and recall have been found to be potentially changed by a strong emotional state.

9. As learners, no matter how rational we think we are, identity formation and how we feel about ourselves influence who we are.

10. Establishing relevance and triggering associated emotional attitudes enhances intrinsic motivation.

Introduction

Teachers continually remark on the connections they see between the learning of strategies and skills of students and their emotional response to their own learning. One fourth-grade teacher described how students in her class who come to school eager and ready to absorb, act, question, and learn create positive emotional responses when they are presented with the work of the school day. These positive emotions, she said, seemed to help the whole child adapt and regulate behavior in ways that benefited them.

She is right. This chapter explores our emotional inner life and its connection to the brain. Once again, the power of bringing the three learning sciences together is evident. Educators see the impact of emotions and attitudes on learning in the classroom. Cognitive psychologists see how emotion adds adaptive value to how we function—we change what we do in part based on emotion. And neuroscientists describe how this information helps us achieve needed homeostasis, or a relatively stable state of balance in our lives (Damasio, 2001). Together, these sciences are bringing greater understanding about how emotional functioning plays an important role in reasoning and decision making in the brain.

The Brain Needs Emotional Input

Emotions enter into how the brain functions. Successes, failures, joys, embarrassments, and many more emotions relate to how we think about ourselves. In a learning environment, this is as true for teachers as for their students. For example, a teacher considering whether he is up to incorporating technology in the classroom might feel reluctant if a sense of failure is foremost in his thinking: "Hm-m, last time I tried, it was a disaster." Conversely, a teacher who has enjoyed feeling a sense of success, even when new approaches have proven difficult, might find a sense of resilience come to the fore: "Well, I know how to sail through disasters. I always have a Plan B."

Surprising to many people, teachers included, is the notion that human emotions sit biologically on a bedrock not of heart but of brain and mind. In the context of learning, from establishing your own identity to how you interact with others, emotions arise from cerebral processes (OECD, 2007, p. 25).

As brain researcher Michael Gazzaniga (2011b) describes it, from nothing else but the brain comes our joy, delight, and laughter, as well as our sorrow, grief, and despondency. The basis of our feelings is becoming better understood as neuroscience uncovers the emotional dimensions of the brain (OECD, 2007, p. 25). **(See CORE 5a.)**

Scientists believe emotion and feelings are essential for the human brain to function effectively (Bechara, Damasio, & Damasio, 2000; Dalgleish, 2004; Immordino-Yang, 2007; Panksepp, 1998). Mary Helen Immordino-Yang, a neuroscientist and human development psychologist at the University of Southern California, explains that advances in neuroscience highlight connections between emotion, social functioning, and decision making. She explains that the neurobiological evidence is beginning to show learning, attention, memory, decision making, and social functioning are all profoundly affected by emotions (Immordino-Yang, 2007). She calls this our *emotional thought,* sometimes also called *affective thinking* or the merging of the cognitive (thinking) with the affective domain (emotion/feeling). It is beginning to be evidenced, for instance, in imaging studies of brain networks (Kober et al., 2008).

To begin with an overview on emotion and attitude in the brain, feelings are believed to play an important evolutionary and survival role for humans (Kandel, Schwartz, Jessell, Siegelbaum, & Hudspeth, 2013, p. 1082). Whether it is avoiding danger or seeking advantageous social conditions, we are better able to process complex signals when we color our thinking with how we felt about past experiences. So, emotions are necessary for the adaptation and regulation of human behavior (Kandel et al., 2013, p. 1082).

Just as our brains associate cognitive ideas together and use them to represent the world around us, so too does the brain identify crucial emotions and feelings to some of our incoming stimuli. Sometimes learned and sometimes innate, human emotion modifies our behaviors. Such modifications are the very heart of learning: We have learned to behave differently.

A somewhat startling finding of brain science is that the red flag of emotion—be it warmth and love or rage and anger—is not as free-wheeling as we might think. Our so-called emotional reactions and behaviors, at least to some extent at the level of neurons and circuits, carry the cool calculation of an unconscious appraisal. Emotion adds weight as a driver of what we do. In a sense, emotion is also very rational. Our cool-headed logic is informed by how we feel. Feelings and logic go hand in hand. Although emotional information may not be fully conscious to us and we may not even be aware of how it is entering into our reasoning, emotions are a form of relationship—a brain association on which we operate. They are part of how we represent the world around us.

Teachers describe how they see belief and ownership by students *of their own learning* as a huge factor in both effort and outcomes in their classrooms. Geoff Barrett is a high school teacher who uses alternative programs to work with students at risk.

The number one deficiency Barrett sees is in the development of math skills needed for success at the high school level. He described how his students invariably offer such opinions as "I hate math" and "I suck at math." One student who failed Algebra I twice came to Barrett feeling hopeless about her ability to ever do math. He started her in a program that made use of online resources. The program combined remedial skills with moving forward on more advanced concepts. The student struggled and asked for help almost every day. In the end, however, she passed the state test and was quoted in the local newspaper, saying that she used to be bad at math but had learned that she was actually good at it. Continual positive reinforcement, Barrett said, was the most important factor in that student's success.

Emotion and Feeling Differ

From a brain perspective, *emotion* is a mental state often spontaneously arising hand in hand with physiological changes. These may be measurable in the body, such as changes in blood pressure, heart rate, and sweat production. Or, they may reflect more qualitative forms such as facial expression and body language.

In contrast, *feeling* can be defined as the internal experience we have when engaged in an emotion. It is a subjective experience, it is what we *feel* inside ourselves. Some people enjoy and seek out thrill rides and scary movies; others hate them. The emotion may be fear, but the feelings and sensations about it are highly personal.

Emotion also makes us social creatures. It isn't just about the stirred-up sensations of feelings that the French call *émouvoir,* from which the English word *emotion* comes. We actually use emotional information to navigate in critical ways through life: Emotion looms large in the brain's decision-making process. So, this is a way for teachers to think about emotional function and its relationship to teaching and learning. It is different from a feeling of love or sadness; rather, it is the highlighting of essential meaning for us.

Scientists see emotion as a way we appraise significance. We go through life expending a great deal of energy on, for instance, recognizing faces and associating particular emotional feelings with particular people. By associating detailed responses to often very small differences in details, we gain valuable clues that may serve us well in how we act and what decisions we make. In other words, we *feel* how we should behave.

A leading researcher on emotion and the brain, Antonio Damasio, says that until recently, even neuroscientists have basically neglected emotion as a field of research inquiry.

Subject to what he calls a historical distinction that treated cognition and emotion entirely separately, a lack of agreement existed for a long time on what emotion even was, scientifically (Damasio, 2001).

From the point of view of scientists, now we know that emotions play several major roles in the brain. Very generally speaking, emotions can trigger emergency responses when we don't have sufficient time to think. They also add weight and nuance to our decisions and behaviors more globally. Emotion, then, adds a sense of urgency or "color" to the information we process.

Elements that often differ from one emotion to another include the signal or set of stimuli that brings on an emotion as well as the physiology our body employs in response. The nature of events that trigger emotional responses also vary. But in common is that we tend to experience quick onset across emotions. They often come to us unbidden or not seemingly of our own initiation. Emotions last relatively short durations for any one episode. They also engage somewhat automatic responses by the brain, which coordinates a coherent, or consistent, set of bodily responses (Ekman, 1992). In other words, our brain recognizes emotional response when it comes.

Since specific emotions are often tied to consistent patterns of bodily response, it makes sense that specific brain pathways may be involved. Confirming this, different emotions do seem to employ distinct functional systems in the brain and have their own cerebral circuits (OECD, 2007). While the connection of these circuits to how we learn is still being untangled, one insight is fairly certain. When we are ready to learn effectively in school, emotional circuitry is likely to have entered into the "green light" that gives us the go-ahead.

Scientists debate extensively whether emotions cause body physiology to change or whether bodily characteristics bring on such mental states and feelings. This issue remains unclear, but what is important for educators to understand is that emotions and biology are inextricably linked at deep-seated levels for the human cognitive system. Scientists believe we establish emotional response both innately, presumably encoded in part into our genetic makeup, as well as through experiences that alter the brain physically.

Rather than asking learners to act in the face of feelings and emotions as if they weren't present, students can build emotional resilience and patience in the face of challenge. They can learn to counteract negative self-talk and reduce physiological and behavior impacts (Hayes et al., 2010; Office of Special Education Programs, 2013). Pointing out for teachers that the emotional reaction of a student is not fully under his or her control is important. As one instructor put it from her perspective, this has allowed her to stop trying to change what she can't, and frees her to work on what she can more likely change. She can look for ways to make the students more comfortable with the material and skills. Rather than asking them to deny prior experiences through which they may have attached emotional weight to a particular subject-matter area or type of learning, she can work with them on new, more positive experiences.

Concrete ways to help students overcome fear or other inhibiting emotions and not shut down in class include methods in which teachers provide praise to students (Hawkins

& Heflin, 2011; Kern & Clemens, 2007). Praise that is focused on effort and accomplishment rather than ability helps. Comparing actions to a goal or a set of objectives is important, but feedback on effort is also significant—more so than just praise on the results. (This helps create a growth mindset, as discussed later in this chapter in the section on "The Telling Response to Challenge.")

Momentary time sampling is one useful technique that teachers employ for effective praise. Teachers note in advance on each particular day a small set of students, about four or five, who may not recently have received sufficient praise to support their successful learning behaviors. Then at particular times during that day—for instance, on the hour every hour—teachers scan each of the identified students to see if any of them are engaged in a praiseworthy effort or small accomplishment in their learning.

If so, a *praise statement* is then provided to the student. The characteristics of the praise statement are important. A concrete detail should supply specific feedback from the teacher's observation couched in words of affirmation. Sincere observations that encourage autonomy, positive self-esteem, a willingness to explore, and acceptance of self and others can be especially important:

"Your writing caught my interest and made me want to read the whole story."

"You saw that Sally needed help and you helped her get more organized."

"You tackled that math problem nicely by writing down what you already knew about it."

Momentary time sampling is habit forming. By specifically checking among students several times in the day, and rotating among groups of students, teachers will find opportunities to effectively support every student with praise in the classroom, even on the busiest days. This contributes to a sense of belonging and the ability to succeed for the student, both in the student's mind and for the reaction and support of the peer group. Educational research studies find that praise of this type is both powerful and underutilized in many classrooms.

Other strategies to lower student stress and encourage positive emotions in the classroom are discussed in Chapter 8.

Neurotransmitters' "All Alert"

If we think of surprise as a type of emotional response, what does surprise mean to you?

To neuroscientists, surprise means triggering the release of a cocktail of chemicals that generate an "all-alert" emotional arousal (LeDoux, 2003). During a surprising situation, clues from the context help us interpret threat or enticement.

Some brain chemicals perform types of regulatory and control functions in the brain. Neurotransmitters and neuromodulators may excite or inhibit actions, based on regulating brain processes (OECD, 2007; Society for Neuroscience, 2008). The total number and types of neurotransmitters in the brain remains unknown, but more than 100 already have been identified (Purves et al., 2008). Researchers are gaining insight into the mechanism of molecular neuropharmacology, which provides a new understanding of the mechanisms of addiction and other ways brain function interacts with motivation. **(See CORE 5g.)**

For neurotransmitters (see Figure 7.1), the amount of chemical released and the number of receptors involved can influence our responsiveness. Chemical feedback pathways in the brain control numerous important processes without which we would not be able to survive. Certain molecules may even be responsible for helping to guide and program nervous system development (OECD, 2007). Scientists are gathering clues involving brain chemistry on topics as wide ranging as youth and the aged, and from mood to memory. **(See CORE 5h.)**

In young adults, for instance, the cutback of neural synapses reorganizes the brain, thus preparing it for adult function. Along with laying down insulation and sheathing to better "hard wire" efficient processes into place, the brain matures for more adult thinking.

Such major development takes place often in the third decade of an individual's development. **(See CORE 5i.)** This indicates that the regulation of emotions can occur relatively late in an individual's development (OECD, 2007). In comparison, the brain regions serving motor and sensory functions tend to mature earlier (Gogtay et al., 2004; Sowell et al., 2003). We feel before we can deal, as teachers say.

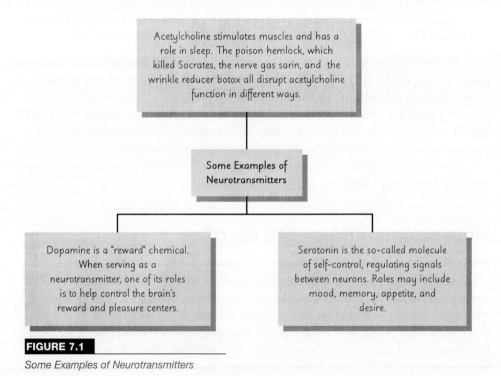

FIGURE 7.1

Some Examples of Neurotransmitters

How Emotion Works in the Brain

As a recent news report so aptly said, the brain gives up information about itself grudgingly. So, not everything is yet known, by any means, about how emotion works in the brain. Of course, the brain is not composed entirely of the cerebral cortex. Many other structures are critical for learning, including the hippocampus, which helps consolidate new memories, and the amygdala, which plays an important role in emotional responses for humans. **(See CORE 5e.)** The amygdala (pronounced uh-MIG-dull-uh) sits deep in the temporal lobe and is roughly almond-shaped. The brain has two amygdalae (plural), sitting left and right toward the side of the head, one on each side of the brain. They are part of the limbic system, known as the "seat of emotions" (see Figure 7.2). Additionally, some cortical structures regulate emotions, mainly the prefrontal cortex as part of its "CEO" role in executive function as described in Chapter 3 (OECD, 2007).

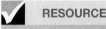

RESOURCE

K–12 teachers can use with students: PBS Newshour, May 20, 2013. (See the Citations list at the end of this chapter.)

Best-selling author, Daniel Goleman, a psychologist who specializes in psychology and brain science, describes how all passion depends on the amygdala (Goleman, 1995). In some cases of severe brain injury, the brain can lose connection to the amygdala. When this happens the consequences are bleak. People without a working amygdala connection are impassive in the face of anguish.

Scientists discovered that without the amygdala, we can no longer judge emotional significance of people and events. In a way, it is like being emotionally blind. We stumble in how we feel about what we encounter. Imagine being unable to feel a sense of joy when we triumph in a difficult task, or of sadness over the death of someone close to us. So, the amygdala is an integral player in the realm of feelings (Howard-Jones et al., 2007, p. 23; Society for Neuroscience, 2008).

The amygdala and hippocampus are adjacent brain structures. They participate together in some of the same neural circuits but serve different functions (Giedd, 2008). The hippocampus is involved in memory acquisition, retrieval, and retention, and the amygdala assesses salience. For a whole range of incoming stimuli, such as sounds and sights and smells, the amygdala determines what is most important to take note of when such information carries emotional significance.

As well, the brain signals action by the endocrine system—our hormones—that may change secretions into the bloodstream. The brain informs the autonomic motor system, such as cardiac or heart, and other visceral organs, including the liver and the kidneys, in case they have a role to play. The musculoskeletal system goes into action at the brain's behest, too. This is the iconic fight-or-flight response, and other motor routines that may apply. It all revs up—or down—when we delight in something, or find it atrocious.

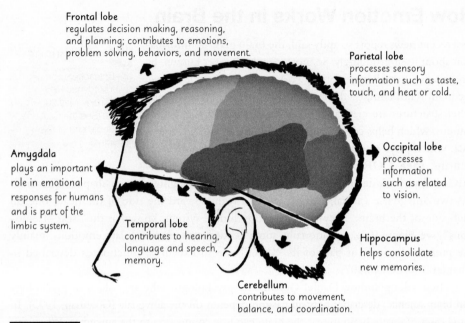

Frontal lobe
regulates decision making, reasoning, and planning; contributes to emotions, problem solving, behaviors, and movement.

Parietal lobe
processes sensory information such as taste, touch, and heat or cold.

Amygdala
plays an important role in emotional responses for humans and is part of the limbic system.

Occipital lobe
processes information such as related to vision.

Temporal lobe
contributes to hearing, language and speech, memory.

Hippocampus
helps consolidate new memories.

Cerebellum
contributes to movement, balance, and coordination.

FIGURE 7.2

The Cerebral Cortex. Besides the cerebral cortex, many other structures are critical for learning. These include the hippocampus and the amygdala.

Of course, establishing emotional significance and being able to remember are intimately connected. This is where the hippocampus and its associated partners come in. Working together, the amygdala trigger and the hippocampus response may enhance memory for certain experiences (Giedd, 2008). That is, joy, love, fear can, by their very nature, tells us essentially "Be sure to remember this; it's important." Or conversely, boredom, apathy, rejection may tell us "Avoid this; it isn't worthy going there."

Researchers at Rutgers University Center for Molecular and Behavioral Neuroscience showed some ways in which emotions generally improve memory (Popescu, Saghyan, & Paré, 2007). For instance, after we get "aroused" emotionally, which is a term neuroscientists use to describe when the brain goes on alert and starts to pay more attention, certain neurons increase their firing rate. This facilitates memory consolidation. For better or for worse, we not only remember more but we connect the knowledge more thoroughly to the circumstances under which the emotion arose. We make associations we later act on.

Emotions biologically consist of three components (OECD, 2007): a particular mental state, often a physiological change associated with that state, and sometimes an associated behavior or impulsion to act. **(See CORE 5f.)** The *mental state* is the brain processing as it responds to incoming data. The *physiological change* includes bodily functions affected, such as blood pressure or sweating. The *impulse to act* is the behavior we may feel compelled to engage in. This might be grand and dramatic, such as lifting a heavy object off a trapped child. Or it may be small and subtle, such as the quick hug of a kindergartner.

Given all these possibilities, one question that can be asked is: What counts as an emotion? Damasio (2001) uses a helpful organizer of primary and secondary emotions. He describes primary emotions as including happiness, sadness, fear, anger, surprise, and disgust. He describes secondary emotions as socially related, such as embarrassment and jealousy.

One principal's experience underscores the range of emotions students may experience and how these lead to beliefs about themselves as learners. He describes how a positively perceived emotion is associated with learning. Students connect it with success. By contrast, a negatively perceived emotion can be associated with failure. The principal explains that understanding these ideas in context with the Marzano meta-analysis (described in Chapter 3) can help teachers focus on this to good effect. In this way, teachers reinforce effort and provide recognition to students. Seeing many students from backgrounds of poverty move toward success when adults believe in them has convinced this principal that this is a critical factor. To put it in his words, the students do not believe in failure because the adult affirms the successful skills the students are building.

Here, the principal points out that beliefs sometimes enter into the school from the outside. They can be generated from the inside as well. Positive emotions may mean happiness, feelings of connectedness and belonging to the school context or culture, and pride or enjoyment in the ability to learn. Negative associations could involve sadness, fear, embarrassment, boredom, feelings of a desire to avoid the learning situation, and even guilt if a student is unable to learn as easily or readily as she or he thinks should be possible, or if the learning is ineffective.

Scientists now know emotions can skip past conscious cognitive processing. Hurtling along, human beings sometimes leap to emotional conclusions long before the brain fully engages its cognitive discourse. This allows us to act quickly when necessary, for instance when fear is provoked. We can engage circuits that allow us to jump away from danger at a fleeting glimpse before fully considering all the aspects of a particular situation. We know what to do when we are afraid.

Unfortunately for schools, the same emotional machinery can come into play and block learning for students. Before a learner even thinks about what he or she is doing, a split second emotional judgment can confront the learner: "I didn't like this before and I'm not going to like it now" or "I wasn't good at this then and I'm not going to be now." And so forth. Our emotional messages whisper to us; sometimes they shout. They help tell us what to do.

Emotional advice that we provide ourselves—"I like this; I don't like that"—is often under our power to redirect, but only to some extent at any given moment.

Damasio describes that while feelings are the conscious embodiment of emotional responses, feelings and emotions we are aware of are not the only ones we act on (Kandel et al., 2013). Largely, in fact, emotions trigger unconscious behavior and cognition, according to Damasio. Many times, we are not aware of the ways our brains react to—or will act on—emotionally charged information.

Cognitive psychologists have long talked about human perception as consisting of attentive and pre-attentive processing stages. In the pre-attentive stage, we process sensory stimuli to filter most out, as discussed in Chapter 3. Then, in the attentive stage, the remaining stimuli get our more active attention. But this is different in scope from what the work of Damasio and others describe. Here, unconscious brain processing operates below the radar for us in many situations, not just initial filtering of some incoming stimuli.

Neuroscientist Mary Helen Immordino-Yang describes how our thinking of which we are less cognitively aware may lead us to allocate more resources or fewer to a given learning situation (Immordino-Yang & Faeth, 2009). Or we may avoid or engage in behavior in association with emotional information (Damasio, 2001; Gazzaniga, 2011a; Kober et al., 2008). But all the while we may not be consciously aware of the decisions we are making. The thinking isn't fully available to us—we don't even know why we are doing it.

This is very important for teachers because they may jump to conclusions about a learner without even being aware of it. For instance, surface characteristics—such as dress, mannerisms, or language—may undermine a teacher's expectations of a student, leading to potentially weakened learning outcomes. For example, research indicates that teachers who are shown pictures of students who are standing in front of high-end playground structures will be judged to be more competent than those students who are pictured with dilapidated equipment. Presumably, the brain is subconsciously assuming the students at wealthier schools are also more accomplished. So, although no bias may be intended, it creeps in due to associations the brain makes and then generalizes. Educators need to be vigilant and aware of this possibility.

Goleman (1995), for instance, describes how in the first few milliseconds of the brain perceiving something (a butterfly appears before us, a person comes on the scene), we decide whether we like it or not. In just fractions of a second what Goleman calls our "cognitive unconscious" gives us an opinion. Our rational thinking may not have access to the thought process. Goleman calls this "emotion having a mind of its own."

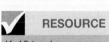
RESOURCE

K–12 teachers can use with students: Gould, 2009. (See the Citations list at the end of this chapter.)

More formally, consciousness is our personal awareness of perceptions, thoughts, feelings, motivations, and self-awareness, or a sense of being "me" as one scholar described. But many mental processes, perhaps the vast majority, are outside of this awareness. We are largely unaware of the computations carried out by the brain for everything from executive function to emotion. These conscious/unconscious brain findings have profound implications for learning, both for students and teacher.

A Framework for Learning Resistance

In education, the term *learning theory* means a conceptual framework to describe how we learn. Some major schools of thought in learning theory include the following:

1. Behaviorist/Empiricist, in which a focus is on sensory organs (eyes, nose, etc.) detecting stimuli in the external world, and the brain responding to customary patterns.
2. Cognitivist/Constructivist, in which knowledge is perceived to have internal structure, signifying that for humans we construct and use meaningful associations in the brain. Higher-order thinking and a whole range of brain processes are made possible by the understandings we gain, build, and infer through the structures of knowledge we construct.
3. Sociocultural/Sociohistoric, emphasizing learning as the creation of a social group, which adapts to and transforms the environment around it.

Chronologically, the theories developed broadly in the order they are listed here. Behaviorist/Empiricist views emerged in the first half of the 20th century. This offered a great deal of new power in educational thinking for directly observable behaviors. Such learning theory gave way to the cognitive revolution in the 1960s as scholars sought to better grasp complex inner processes of the mind and higher-order thinking. Over time, the third general view of Sociocultural/Sociohistoric incorporated the larger culture around us—ways of speaking, belief systems, and how we work together.

Teachers often ask, Don't we have a new family of learning theory for the new century? In a sense, we do. What we have in the current era might be described as bringing together the three families. No longer seen as separate entities, the tradition of one theorist rejecting another is much less pronounced. Rather, the longer view afforded by time is that they all come together.

Schools now often see these theories as nesting different aspects of the human cognitive system—roughly as lower-level brain processing, higher-order thinking, and the social augmentation of cognition. One lies within the other. Together they build to a whole.

One important example of how the three schools of thought are coming together is in the area of resistance in learning. *Resistance theory* looks at what happens when students don't learn. In many cases, students actively seem to resist making the learning progress for which teachers, parents, and school administrators hope.

Learning resistance is an important phenomenon that likely has biological as well as psychological roots, such as emotional well-being. Seen at times in all groups of people, educational research discusses how even teachers sometimes are resistant to learning new ideas. No matter how good a concept or approach might be, learning implies a commitment of cognitive resources. This means not only exerting effort to learn but, physiologically, committing actual brain capacity to what we will build and maintain as knowledge in the brain over time.

Resistance as Part of Our Fundamental Makeup

Critically, to understand resistance, we must remember learning *always* is about *change*. It cannot be avoided. No new learning can take place if we do not change something about ourselves. The principles of plasticity (Chapter 2) guarantee this. At least in some small way, our brains will not be quite the same after we learn.

However, we may not meet change with open arms every time. With adjustments or new learning of any kind come potential barriers of resistance. These can be helpful for the brain, for instance, in ensuring that we do not rush to premature assimilation. Mechanisms of resistance are built into the brain's natural learning responsiveness. Taking things to heart too soon, before we have evidence of how helpful they will be, can be bad news. Some resistance, then, can be a good thing.

Learning theory about resistance draws on a foundation of psychological concepts that involve (1) survival and security, and (2) emotional support, such as loving, belonging, and esteem of ourselves and others, which we will call our *emotional well-being*. Then self-actualization arises. This requires (3) making meaningful and relevant connections to an external reality such that we are comfortable and successful participants in our larger world. We grow confident in ourselves.

These three factors must be considered together, as Abraham Maslow originally described, a humanist who expanded the field of humanistic psychology to include an explanation of how human needs have an impact throughout an individual's life (Maslow, 1943). Looking at this evidence from an educational research perspective, Behavioral/Empiricist schools of thought may look at the observable manifestations and empirical evidence of stimulus and response involved in resistance to change. Cognitivists/Constructivists may focus on the outcomes of higher-order thinking. Sociocultural scholars may see the differential effects of construction established by understandings of the social group. Together, some aspects of a "change theory" for learning and resistance emerge.

Note that we do not necessarily claim the usual interpretation that each of the categories of support described here (survival, emotional well-being, relevance) must be fully achieved before an individual will turn any attention to the next. Instead, we propose an alternative way of considering the relationship. We can treat these factors as "vectors," or priorities along a gradient. We must be able to survive before we are likely to become too worried about nuances of relevance, of course. However, the human cognitive system may not rule out all focus moving from one to the next and back again, as teachers see in students. So, here we discuss these factors more loosely as an array of concerns. We also intentionally back into the topic of motivation from a resistance perspective. Our intention is to provide one of many possible illustrations for teachers—an important example but not exhaustive.

■|| The First Plank: Survival of Body and Mind

From a human standpoint, survival of body and mind is paramount. Yes, the brain is built to learn, but it is also built to keep us alive. Our willingness to learn starts with sheer survival instinct: Will learning a particular new thing reduce our ability to survive? If the answer is *yes,* we resist learning. Resistance to learning is built into brain function.

Recall that the brain reinforces not only the words it hears but especially what it repeatedly experiences. It locks in the information it effectively uses. If we have been successful in the past and have a great deal of evidence that something works well for us, we may cling to these strategies. They work for us; they have well-established "survival" power. (See Chapter 9 for a more formal discussion of the brain and evidence.) Equally, when we've found something that doesn't work for us, or that the struggle is not worth the gain, resistance sets in.

Physical survival needs are one thing; psychological survival needs are another. Resistance to learning shows up in brain function when both physical and psychological challenges confront our well-being. The overload of working memory is an example. Exceeding cognitive load overwhelms some learners, as discussed in Chapters 3 and 5, until they can make meaning of the information without so many moving parts.

"Not now," our brains might tell us, consciously or unconsciously. In coining the phrase, *emotional hijacking,* psychologist Daniel Goleman describes how working memory is swamped when emotions overwhelm concentration. Provoked, enraged, surprised, startled, threatened, even just anxious or worried, all these emotions can override the brain's normal processes. Executive function attempts to establish goals and allocate working memory, but when overloaded we may not think straight, he says (Goleman, 1995). In the throes of too much information—emotional and otherwise—we can become negatively conditioned to learn.

The opposite of this is *flow,* which Goleman describes as a state of concentration so deep that we "self-forget," or set aside what may preoccupy us otherwise (Goleman, 1995). When we are fully engaged, worry, unproductive rumination, success, or failure all take a back seat, emotionally, to what we are learning. We become unconcerned, paradoxically, just as we perform at our peak. Sheer pleasure, is what Goleman calls it. This emotion is one type of *intrinsic motivation*.

Another kind of resistance we may encounter or experience is more personal. We may find it doesn't always pay to change or we may decide we just don't want to change, even in the face of evidence lending support for why it would help.

If we think of this from a more conceptual framework, we see this resistance to learn becomes a tradeoff between potential threats and anticipated benefits: a classic risk/reward set-up. What threats arise if we make the change? And what benefits do we expect to gain? In other words, How relevant is the change to us? This paints a picture of what we might want to do.

From the point of view of learning theory, the term *survival* has an interesting definition that educators need to consider. Not only does it mean survival of our physical persona (nutrition, sleep, and exercise, as described in other chapters) but it also means survival of *ourselves*—of our identities, our commitments, our thoughts and beliefs.

But wait a minute, you may ask, Isn't learning inherently designed to transform? How can we learn without potentially encountering change in our thoughts and beliefs, or remaking our identities in at least some new directions? Change, by its very nature, threatens some types of survival, thrusting emotional response to the fore.

As learners, no matter how rational we think we are, identity formation and how we feel about ourselves influences who we are. We will often protect and defend our identities and beliefs as if there were threats to our very person.

■|| The Second Plank: Emotional Well-Being, the "Hot Button" Lens

If our willingness to learn gets beyond sheer survival of body, mind, *and* identity, then the next need to consider is lowering the barriers to resistance associated with broader support of our emotional well-being. Prior negative experience with schooling or learning is a common barrier that is difficult for teachers to overcome.

Some teachers who champion the need for physical safety may question whether these kinds of emotional threats are within their purview. Psychological aspects of our makeup suggest so. Drawing on the second category of needs, emotional well-being (described earlier), we learn best when emotional information is not interfering with our ability, desire, or motivation to learn. In research that the Organisation for Economic Co-operation and Development Learning Sciences report shares with teachers, retention and recall of an event or information in learning have been found to be potentially changed by a strong emotional state, a special context, heightened motivation, or increased attention (OECD, 2007, p. 27).

For some children and their families, even just arriving at school can be a hot-button emotional issue for learning. Attention to poverty and its impact are discussed in Chapters 3 and 8. One principal who serves a community experiencing generational poverty explained how she attends to the emotional well-being of learners from the get-go. Issues of attendance were always at the forefront for many of her students. She found that these students and their parents had strong, negative emotions tied to school and lack of success from an early age. Not only did the feelings and emotions not lapse but they tended to become more powerful over time, further impacting regular attendance. The principal found that without positive memories to counterbalance the negative ones, this was too overwhelming for some students to overcome.

Her approach was to work extremely hard with both families and students to build relationships with the school and its staff. At the same time, programs were adjusted to provide additional learning supports. These generated more opportunities for success for all students. The principal described how she found the journey to "build the positive" difficult but worth it. The school improved attendance with students, and helped set up a more successful ninth-grade transition for her community.

Examples such as this illustrate how our brains condition themselves. We attach *emotion significance* based on our experiences, making some associations weightier than they might otherwise seem to be. When these associations are in the context of school, they may be good or bad. They could be helpful or distracting to our future learning. But one thing is for sure. Our brains will go about their pattern-seeking business. They will do a good job of bringing up all the associations they can find and at every opportunity—not once, not twice, but on an ongoing basis.

Another principal gave a good example of undergoing similar experiences with his students. He found that negative self-images often created an emotional state that inhibited learners. So he began to ask why students had given up—on coming to school, attending a particular class, participating in a sport, and so forth. The most common answer he found was that the individuals did not feel they had talent: They believed they were not good at it.

Such changes can psychologically and deeply threaten how we see ourselves and the sense of what works well, often based on years of evidence. We may resist premature assimilation. Often, this goes hand-in-hand with lack of clarity in the learning goal by not clearly identifying similarities and differences for students to master. Or students may be undergoing stress from home or other life situations that drag down emotion and cognitive resources. So, if too much intellectual terrain is perceived, or emotions are running high and insufficient guidance is provided, emotional processing may underscore a "danger" zone—the classroom, for instance. And thus, avoidance strategies can result.

New learning or forgetting through long inactivation may weaken or override emotional associations. Generally, though, we retrieve our detailed representational maps very well. This is true especially if thoughts, whether painful or joyful, keep reinforcing, or more deeply engraving the memory traces or encodings.

We "feel" these memories. As successful human beings, we are both honored and cursed by the ability. We have access to emotional information, and we also carry the burden of it. As the OECD Learning Science report states, a positively perceived emotion associated with learning may facilitate success in future situations. By contrast, an emotion negatively perceived ties itself to failure (OECD, 2007, p. 25). **(See CORE 5c.)**

Sometimes students come to recognize this themselves and are able to reinforce their own efforts. This promotes *confidence in learning*, an important attribute of life-long learning. As the elementary and high school educators described, becoming willing to take a risk and getting comfortable with not being expert are important for achieving this confidence.

◼‖ The Third Plank: The Emotional Impact of Relevance

Relevance generates attitudes. When we deem something highly relevant to ourselves or others, we accord it new respect. We may take it more seriously; we give it higher priority. Relevance, then, is a driver of motivation—we have feelings of *caring more about* what is relevant to us.

The idea of relevance and becoming responsible for caring about our own learning is a key concept of the third condition for lowering learning resistance: *self-actualization*. This has been described as the learner making meaningful connections to an external reality. Self-actualization reaches out. It means we seek the knowledge, skills, and abilities to understand ourselves and participate in the larger world. Relevance comes into play here because we are more likely to seek what seems relevant to us.

One important school of thought in psychological research—self-determination theory—describes our most intrinsically motivating conditions, such as autonomy, competence, and relatedness (Deci & Ryan, 2000; Ryan & Deci, 2000). In other words, we are more motivated to learn when we believe it will help us thrive without being overly dependent on others, when we can establish needed competence, and when we can improve our understanding of relationships or our connectedness to the world around us. These are all premises of relevance in learning.

For the human cognitive system, learning to see the relevance or value ascribed to learning has a powerful payoff. We readily become more intrinsically motivated. So the idea of brain satisfaction, an emotion, is directly tied to relevance. From a brain perspective, weighing the emotional information of any given learning situation includes satisfying "relevance" ideas.

A useful point of clarification for some educators is how intrinsic motivation is defined. Intrinsic does not mean immutable. We cannot separate people into two camps of intrinsically motivated and not. On the contrary, we naturally tend to become intrinsically motivated in learning when the brain establishes relevance.

The brain is all about making meaningful connections to the external world. It spends its time gathering data and then it seeks patterns to make meaning. It acts on the information it derives, and marshals the capabilities of the body to make appropriate behaviors relative to the external world.

Based on the brain's own calculus, relevance is therefore important to the learner. And relevance equates, to some degree, with use: connections to other meaningful associations and applications it knows about, and a *perceived need* for the knowledge. What, then, might drive resistance if core needs such as survival and emotion are met? Theoretically, the lack of perceived relevance, consciously or unconsciously, by the learner raises the flag of resistance.

Some teachers recognize the need for this and struggle to find solutions. One teacher working in mathematics described how she believed the hardest part was getting students to truly understand where the instruction was heading. She said it came back to the relevance issue. "Why do I need to know the quadratic formula?" her students would ask.

For other teachers establishing relevance seems obvious. What is relevant is what the teacher—or the parent, school, district, or fill-in-the-blank with the name of the authority— says is relevant.

According to Marcy P. Driscoll, dean and director of University Teacher Education for Florida State University, to be fully invested, the learner must realize some type of personal utility in learning (Driscoll, 2000, p. 328). This might be called the "gain of the brain," or its measure of enhanced relevance. Possibilities include anything from goal attainment to emotional well-being to the intrigue of novelty (discussed in prior chapters). Paradoxically, familiarity can also be a piece of it. If we have at least some way of connecting to the new learning based on our past experiences or current knowledge, this means our brain is associating it to other "important" information it has seen fit to gather along the way. Our brain seeks better understand and amplify its patterns, so this can be a captivating mind factor. The takeaway: All of these are emotional drivers of motivation. They may bring the brain more fully on-board for learning.

From a brain perspective, instructors might turn the relevance question around and ask it this way: Why would *the learner's* brain believe the lesson of the day, whatever it is, has relevance for them to master?

Of course, there is always extrinsic motivation. Holding the learner accountable for knowing a lesson through grades or tests, say, encourages mastery. But even unconsciously, the brain that remains unconvinced to invest is less likely to undertake meaningful learning in the first place. Less tendency will be exhibited to master information, keep it around by investing in maintaining it, or seeking ways to employ it over the long run.

Looking at relevance from the learner's perspective involves considering what elements might enhance or contribute to motivation, from a cognitive perspective. This is no doubt deeply dependent on age, inclination, past experiences, and so forth, and is an area of active research in motivational learning. Some thoughts contributed by teachers on factors that tie attitudes to relevance include:

- Useful and used
- Expressive of ourselves or others
- Readily possible to understand
- Intriguing or novel
- Customized to our interests
- Motivated by past experiences, including successes we have had
- Involving social media and peers, or other social relationship building efforts
- Contributory to society or to a community of interest we have; in other words, involving what is perceived as productive work on behalf of that entity
- *Growing* toward a contributory role by clearly becoming more capable at what *we do that we care about*, through the knowledge, skills, and abilities we are mastering.

Research captures an interesting perspective on this, with a twist. Psychologist Kevin Dutton, who has worked with numerous institutions in the United Kingdom, talks about "supersuasion," or what persuades us to act in a given situation (Dutton, 2010). By combining biology, psychology, and neuroscience, he has built a model for "disabling" what he calls the cognitive security systems, our mental filtering system for relevance and decision making, through five factors: simplicity, perceived self-interest, incongruity, confidence, and empathy.

Many of these factors have parallels in the points teachers make about our emotions and attitudes to learning: Simplicity links to "readily possible for me to understand." Incongruity is about novelty, and empathy maps in part to relationship building. Confidence can be grounded in success and our prior experiences.

The Dutton idea of perceived self-interest spans the gamut: from useful and used to growing toward a contributory role in society. Teachers in their work see students striving for all of these. Community service, for example, has been noted by teachers as a major driver of student interest in high school. Primarily learning experiences, such as volunteering in the emergency room for students on a medical pathway or building rapid co-housing for the homeless for students interested in green design and sustainable housing, there also is a perception of productive work. The work *itself* is meaningful, people noticeably gain by it. Probably because we are a social species, this is something we strive for. Helping others and ourselves underscores the relevance of the learning experience. In this way students, it might be said, are deeply "self-interested." They feel intrinsically motivated to work toward achieving many worthy goals. This regulates what matters.

Educators work toward effective thinking and reasoning. They want to *enable*, or work *with* the brain in effective learning, not against it. The same effective "persuaders," however, can be put to work in either setting.

Novelty, as mentioned in prior chapters, is intrinsically motivating. Babies find things that are new or unexpected so fascinating that novelty is used as a research method. As reported by many researchers, babies often will stare longest at what is new to them. This is an aspect of their preference for examining novelty, most likely as a survival mechanism to learn more about what they need to understand (Gazzaniga, 2011b). As we become older, such curiosity feeds strongly into how our society works, even to how we copy and imitate, says brain researcher Michael Gazzaniga. He describes how most of what humans do originated with somebody's smart idea, copied, and copied again. He uses the example of coffeehouses to make his point. People enjoy coffee and they enjoy social experiences, hence we have similar style cafes all around the world.

Interestingly, Gazzaniga says that although curiosity, invention, and imitation are ubiquitous among humans, who from birth on will gaze longer at something new, this behavior is found to be shockingly rare elsewhere in the animal kingdom. Thus, not only do we have drivers for intrinsic motivation—the brain's security system as Dutton puts it—but some are intrinsically unique to humans and other primates, and the way we work and live.

According to the OECD Learning Sciences report, the benefits of such intrinsic motivation for learning run deep. The expert panel described it as of paramount importance for research to orient efforts toward this domain. **(See CORE 5d.)**

The Telling Response to Challenge

Teachers notice that intrinsic motivation and emotional well-being support several categories identified in the Marzano meta-analysis and in John Hattie's education research. These emotional attitudes are closely tied to concentration, persistence, and engagement. For instance, the willingness to choose more challenging tasks and to stick with them longer may influence everything from homework and practice to how diligently or confidently we approach mental imagery, generating and testing our ideas, organizing our prior knowledge, and even participating in collaborative learning.

Carol Dweck, a leading researcher in learning motivation (C. Dweck, 2006), has identified how learners innately seem to react to challenge. Some children, even in the early grades, consistently seem to rise to the occasion and bring strategies and problem-solving approaches to the fore. Others characteristically seem to retreat in the face of challenge, whether it is attempting to solve a new type of math problem, spell out loud for the teacher, or implement a tough letter combination in cursive penmanship. The group identity—the ways students responded to challenge—tended to stay the same over time, and across numerous areas.

All else being equal, how we decide to meet challenge makes a difference for us. Dweck and colleagues found that when matched for their competency and preparedness at a given age, those students who embraced challenge soon surpassed those who avoided it

(C. S. Dweck & Leggett, 1988). Over time, overall learning differed dramatically between the two groups.

Perhaps even more telling, Dweck identified a link between what students *believed* about themselves and which "challenge" group they fell into. Those who thought of their intelligence as more fixed—an attitude that you have a capability or not, in a given area—tended to avoid challenge. The very fact that something was a challenge to them meant they didn't "have" what it took, so why point it out even more so by trying and failing?

Dweck's theories are about beliefs, and this chapter is on emotion and attitude, so what is the relationship? Psychologists have shown for decades a deep connection between beliefs we have about people or objects and our attitudes toward them. This includes whether we favor them or not and the emotional investments we may make in them (Eagly & Chaiken, 1998; Fazio & Olson, 2003). In Dweck's work, students with a functional attitude based on getting better as they go along through trial, error, and effort tended to embrace challenge. Over time, this becomes a self-fulfilling prophecy, because "embracers" grow good at meeting challenges. The "avoiders," on the other hand, haven't developed the same resilience and self-help skills to persist, nor have they mastered a whole slew of little bits of learning along the way.

Students Motivated by Their Own Brains

Dweck talks about encouraging a growth mindset. It is helpful, she says, for students to understand that humans are not fixed at birth but can build brainpower simply through taking part in learning.

Teachers are finding that part of identifying intellectually as a learner comes from understanding how your own brain works. Specifically, when students understand their brains are made for learning, this is motivating to them. Whether young or old, learners build confidence in the knowledge that the brain knows how to go into action—all by itself. It is not even something we have to do or be especially good at, since we are learning all the time.

Teachers, librarians, school administrators, and other personnel working in schools understand the emotional and confidence issues that learners face at school. Supporting this by simply unpacking the brain for students is highly motivating to them. Understanding that brings learners into the fold is a goal of teachers. And learners like it when it seems not so hard to learn; they are built for it.

The U.S. National Research Council's report on "Engaging Schools" describes a large body of research related to motivating students to learn (National Research Council, 2003). Through engaging emotions that work well on our behalf, it introduces three critical ideas and employs a helpful shorthand to describe them: I Can, I Want To, and I Belong.

To be intrinsically motivated to achieve, students must believe:

- *I Can:* Students need to believe within their own minds they are able to be successful in the learning, that they are capable and *can* do it.
- *I Want:* Learners who find something relevant, based on their own brain-based prioritizing, decide at some level, consciously or less so, that they *want to* do it.
- *I Belong:* Students who identify with and see themselves fitting in with the new demands, without setting off too many alarm bells sacrificing their own ideas or emotions, establish an identity that they *belong* doing it.

Teachers often want to know what they should tell their students about the brain. One group of teachers participating in a materials development project at Rockefeller University worked on creating curriculum materials for use with children and young adults. Teachers examined more than 100 chapters of material related to the brain and selected topics they thought would be best for their students to learn. The end result focused on many of the physical attributes of brain function, such as nutrition, physical exercise, sleep, and stress.

But other teachers wanted to include knowledge that actually motivates children by convincing them they were born to learn. A small study of students ages 4 to 13 first examined what youngsters already know about the brain (Marshall & Comalli, 2012). The results of the study showed the youngest children generally know the brain "thinks," whereas older children know about the brain's involvement in sensory activity such as seeing, hearing, and smelling. In trials in the classroom, the researchers found elementary school teachers even with only very basic and not specialized knowledge of the brain were readily able to enlarge the narrow views of their students with brief classroom lessons and activities. These mostly emphasized the connections between brain and body, as the Rockefeller project teachers described.

However, to transform views of the brain and its role in learning required more than just the biological function connection, the researchers concluded. Learning about the brain's complex role, from knowing to remembering, from emotional regulating and achieving to being "smart," provided important enlightenment.

This is valuable information for teachers, directly related to the relevance of their work. When students learn that the brain can grow stronger connections through the process of learning something, they often become more motivated and more willing to persist through difficult challenges.

■|| Brain Awareness Motivates Her Students

Educator K. Keener, a committed young teacher who worked in the Bronx in New York, teaches students that they can learn effectively by teaching them about neuroscience.

While she is teaching English as her subject matter in high school, Keener doesn't stop there. She teaches her students about the physiology of the brain, and how it works to support them in their learning. Just making her students aware of their brain and how it works makes a difference, she finds.

Keener has become fascinated with the potential influence of neuroscience on classroom practices. She spends her days in the classroom encouraging her students to become active readers and writers. On weekends and evenings she spent her time interning in the neuroscience lab at the Columbia University Department of Psychiatry and New York State Psychiatric Institute. She has worked on studies of so-called socially defeated mice, that, when they encounter struggles, tend to give up sooner than their fellow mice.

According to Keener, doing the research in neuroscience changed how she thinks about her students. If she sees students give up on learning, she asks herself what happened to make them less resilient. She has a couple hypotheses.

Located in the Soundview neighborhood in the Bronx, her school is a so-called transfer school that takes teens who have fallen behind at other schools and tries to get them back on track for graduation. The success is mixed. Graduation rates remain about 4% below the citywide average for all schools, and many students accrue credits slowly. Keener says the school serves a population that misses a lot of class—the teens are in jobs and in court, helping families make it day-to-day by staying home with sick younger siblings, or stepping in to serve as de-facto translator since the teens often have the best English skills in the family.

Faced with such challenges, Keener sees certain students with a special kind of resilience. They use strategies to talk down their negative beliefs or experiences, and know that they can do it successfully. She believes this is especially helpful for students in disadvantaged communities because it creates an alternate model to the authority that says you *must* do it. Rather, they know through understanding how the brain works that they can do it.

Keener wants to know more about how this all works. Her high hopes become high demands for the future of the fields of science and psychology. She says if neuroscience doesn't find a way to leverage the discussion about how people learn, it would be like humans giving up the space program before it even started.

Conclusion

Emotional information is fundamental to making our brains function effectively. We filter stimuli, choosing to act on some and not others, based in part on the emotional weight entering into the equation for us. Teachers, then, need to be attentive to the impact of emotion for classroom learning to be most successful.

As one teacher described, a student may feel a sense of joy when finding the answer to a problem, even if the teacher provides no explicit feedback, as the brain registers satisfaction at the achievement of a goal. Unfortunately, the student could also learn to shut down and not even attempt the problem, especially if the student feels like a failure before she or he has even begun, the teacher stated.

The knowledge that teachers impart isn't always clearly relevant to the brain. Without attention to emotional function, resistance to learning and failure to persist are unfortunately a likely outcome. For students, emotion enters into learning to tag significance—What should I spend my time learning and how will it make me feel? Students are learning not only fact or even process but also how to feel about everything they encounter.

This should come as no surprise to educators. After all, many people become teachers not simply because they find numbers, concepts, or literature interesting. Rather, they have experienced the joy of learning, an emotional response to the act of learning. For them, and to some extent for all students, joy is an emotional footprint of learning.

Emotion arises from many situations. In the next chapter, we look specifically at the impact that stress has on learning. We then move on to the critical topic of how and why the brain reacts to feedback and evidence.

Closing Scenario

Putting New Knowledge to Use

Emotional Functioning and Attitude in the Brain

As this chapter illustrates, students are learning not only fact or even process, but how to feel about everything they encounter. Their brain's emotional response is determined by the relevance of information they encounter and it is one key to their intrinsic motivation. Here, you are asked to consider a recent teaching experience you delivered—or one that you were involved with either as a teacher or a learner—and evaluate it for emotional relevance from a brain perspective.

1. First, identify the experience you will evaluate. Why have you chosen this one? Did you even think about how emotional attitude could come into play?
2. Why would the learner's brain believe this lesson had relevance for them?
3. What elements might enhance or contribute to motivation from a cognitive perspective? In what way, for example, could it useful or used by student?
4. Could it have been tied to a work or volunteer or other experience that might make it meaningful?
5. In what ways did you (or could you) present the learning experience to capitalize on the brain's interest in intriguing or novel experience?
6. Some learners might have had no trouble mastering the lesson, but for those who struggled, how could you use past experiences inside or outside the classroom to generate a sense of confidence that would motivate them to persist? What emotion would be most useful to trigger?

7. Identity formation and how we feel about ourselves influences our emotional response to learning. In your classroom, or among a smaller group of students, can you suggest how their sense of self may have helped or hindered their learning in this situation?

Citations

Online, Media, and Print Resources for Teachers

Gould, J. (2009). Mind-brain problem and consciousness. http://uwf.edu/jgould/documents/mind-brainandconsciousnessproblem_000.pdf

PBS Newshour (Producer). (May 20, 2013). What DSM-5, Updated mental health 'Bible,' means for diagnosing patients.

References

Bechara, A., Damasio, H., & Damasio, A. (2000). Emotion, decision making and the orbitofrontal cortex. *Oxford Journals, 10*(3), 295–307.

Dalgleish, T. (2004). The emotional brain. *Nature Reviews Neuroscience, 5*, 583–589.

Damasio, A. R. (2001). Reflections on the neurobiology of emotion and feeling. In J. Branquinho (Ed.), *The foundations of cognitive science*. Oxford: Clarendon.

Deci, E. L., & Ryan, R. M. (2000). The "what" and "why" of goal pursuits: Human needs and the self-determination of behavior. *Psychological Inquiry, 11*, 227–268.

Driscoll, M. (2000). *Psychology of learning for instruction*. Boston: Allyn & Bacon.

Dutton, K. (2010). The power to persuade. *Scientific American Mind, 21*(1), 24–31.

Dweck, C. (2006). *Mindset: The new psychology of success* (Chapter 1). New York: Random House.

Dweck, C. S., & Leggett, E. L. (1988). A social-cognitive approach to motivation and personality. *Psychological Review, 95*, 256–273.

Eagly, A. H., & Chaiken, S. (Eds.). (1998). *Attitude structure and function* (Vol. Handbook of Social Psychology). New York: McGraw-Hill.

Ekman, P. (1992). An argument for basic emotions. *Cognition and Emotion, 6*(3/4), 169–200.

Fazio, R. H., & Olson, M. A. (2003). Attitudes: Foundations, functions, and consequences. *The Sage handbook of social psychology*. London: Sage.

Gazzaniga, M. S. (2011a). The parallel and distributed brain. *Who's in charge? Free will and the science of the brain* (pp. 43–73). New York: HarperCollins.

Gazzaniga, M. S. (2011b). *Who's in charge? Free will and the science of the brain*. New York: HarperCollins.

Giedd, J. (2008). The teen brain: Insights from neuroimaging. *Journal of Adolescent Health, 42*(4), 335–343.

Gogtay, N., Giedd, J., Lusk, L., Hayashi, K. M., Greenstein, D., Vaituzis, A. C., . . . Thompson, P. M. (2004). Dynamic mapping of the human cortical development during childhood through early adulthood. *Proc Natl Acad Sci, 101*, 8174–8179.

Goleman, D. (1995). *Emotional intelligence: Why it can matter more than IQ*. London: Bloomsbury.

Hawkins, S. M., & Heflin, L. J. (2011). Increasing secondary teachers' behavior-specific praise using a video self-modeling and visual performance feedback intervention. *Journal of Positive Behavior Interventions, 13*(2), 97–108.

Hayes, J. P., Morey, R. A., Petty, C. M., Seth, S., Smoski, M. J., McCarthy, G., & LaBar, K. S. (2010). Staying cool when things get hot: Emotion regulation modulates neural mechanisms of memory encoding. *Frontiers in Human Neuroscience, 4*, 1–10.

Howard-Jones, P., Pollard, A., Blakemore, S.-J., Rogers, P., Goswami, U., Butterworth, B., . . . Kaufmann, L. (2007). Neuroscience and education, issues and opportunities: A TLRP commentary. http://www.tlrp.org/pub/documents/Neuroscience Commentary FINAL.pdf

Immordino-Yang, M. H. (2007). We feel, therefore we learn: The relevance of affective and social neuroscience to education. *Mind, Brain, and Education, 1*(1).

Immordino-Yang, M. H., & Faeth, M. (2009). The role of emotion and skilled intuition in learning. In D. A. Sousa (Ed.), *Mind, brain, and education* (pp. 66–81). Bloomington, IN: Solution Tree.

Kandel, E. R., Schwartz, J. H., Jessell, T. M., Siegelbaum, S. A., & Hudspeth, A. J. (2013). *Principles of neural science* (5th ed.). New York: McGraw-Hill Medical.

Kern, L., & Clemens, N. H. (2007). Antecedent strategies to promote appropriate classroom behavior. *Psychology in the Schools, 44*, 65–75.

Kober, H., Barrett, L. F., Joseph, J., Bliss-Moreau, E., Lindquist, K., & Wager, T. D. (2008). Functional grouping and cortical-subcortical interactions in emotion: A meta-analysis of neuroimaging studies. *NeuroImage, 42*, 998–1031.

LeDoux, J. (2003). *Synaptic self: How our brains become who we are.* New York: Viking Penguin.

Marshall, P. J., & Comalli, C. E. (2012). Young children's changing conceptualizations of brain function: Implications for teaching neuroscience in early elementary settings. *Neuroscience Perspectives on Early Development and Education, 23*(1), 4–23.

Maslow, A. H. (1943). A theory of human motivation. *Psychological Review, 50*(4), 370–396.

National Research Council. (2003). The nature and conditions of engagement. In Committee on Increasing High School Students' Engagement and Motivation to Learn (Ed.), *Engaging schools: Fostering high school students' motivation to learn* (pp. 31–59). Washington, DC: National Academies.

OECD. (2007). Understanding the brain: The birth of a learning science. Paris: OECD Publishing. doi: 10.1787/9789264029132-en

Office of Special Education Programs. (2013). Effective schoolwide interventions. *Technical assistance center on positive behavioral interventions and supports.* http://www.pbis.org

Panksepp, J. (1998). *Affective neuroscience: The foundations of human and animal emotions.* New York: Oxford University Press.

Popescu, A. T., Saghyan, A. A., & Paré, D. (2007). NMDA-dependent facilitation of corticostriatal plasticity by the amygdala. *Proc Natl Acad Sci, 104*(1), 341–346.

Purves, D., Augustine, G. J., Fitzpatrick, D., Hall, W. C., La Mantia, A.-S., McNamara, J. O., & White, L. E. (2008). *Neuroscience.* Sunderland, MA: Sinauer.

Ryan, R. M., & Deci, E. L. (2000). Self-determination theory and the facilitation of intrinsic motivation, social development, and well-being. *American Psychologist, 55*, 68–78.

Society for Neuroscience. (2008). *Brain facts: A primer on the brain and nervous system.* Washington, DC: Society for Neuroscience.

Sowell, E. R., Peterson, B. S., Thompson, P. M., Welcome, S. E., Henkenius, A. L., & Toga, A. W. (2003). Mapping cortical change across the human life span. *Nature Neuroscience, 6*, 309–315.

Stress

CORE Guiding Principle 6, which focuses on the physical conditions under which we learn best, is continued. In this chapter, we explore the complex role of stress. Stress interacts with both health and emotion. This occurs in complex ways—important for educators to understand both in terms of working with students as well as for maintaining their own healthful functioning on the job.

Learning Points

1. Stress is the body's physical mobilizing in response to an event or situation that causes a sense of fear, frustration, anger, or nervousness.

2. Stress is particularly complex because it interacts with both health and emotion.

3. Stress generates an array of physical effects aimed at putting the body and mind into a state of arousal to enable it to cope with the challenge.

4. Acute stress is a short-term response to a specific event, called a stressor. Short bursts of stress can be beneficial to learning.

5. Chronic stress is a result of ongoing stressors such as prolonged environmental, social, or psychological conditions, and it causes many negative health and learning outcomes. Chronic stress appears to impair memory and to suppress the production of new neurons in the hippocampus.

6. When emotional information comes into the brain, the amygdala routes it either to the prefrontal cortex, where learning can move forward, or to a lower part of the brain, where the "fight, flight, or freeze" response is activated and opportunities for learning and memory acquisition are limited.

7. New research is finding that differences in how individuals perform under acute stress and competitive pressure, such as taking tests, may be related to a gene variant that controls the release of stress hormones in the brain.

8. How we perceive pressure-filled events ultimately shapes our physiological response. Controlling perception of events can help individuals avoid the harmful consequences of mild to moderate stressors.

9. To make the most of learning time, teachers are encouraged to adopt strategies that reduce (a) emotional conditions, such as fear, anxiety, boredom, or frustration, and (b) stressors, such as noise and disruption, because these stressors may interfere with successful neural network transmission to the cortex.

Introduction

A little nervousness before a test is normal and may sharpen attention and improve performance. A dose of concern when facing danger focuses the mind and triggers physical survival actions. Even the pressure of an impending deadline can be useful, spurring some procrastinators into action. Such are the beneficial ways in which the brain is wired to respond to short periods of manageable stress. However, too much stress and stress that becomes chronic may harm the body and rattle the brain in ways that have been shown to impair memory and hamper learning.

Stress can be confounding, especially for educators. How much stress is too much stress? It is almost impossible to know because emotional and biological reactions to stress are highly individual. Why do some students thrive when approaching exams while others in the same class, equally prepared and clearly knowledgeable, freeze up at the very idea of a quiz or test? How far should a teacher go in challenging her classroom when some learners will rise to the occasion but others will lose focus, grow bored, or become fearful and retain little of the lesson?

Stress is particularly complex because it interacts with both health and emotion. **(See CORE 6c.)** Science may not be able to provide answers to every individual situation, but research is starting to provide a clearer picture of what's happening in the brain when stress takes hold, why some stress can be beneficial to learning, and how an individual's perception of an event or situation can be meaningful in how he or she responds to stress.

Recently, there has been increasing exploration into the role a specific gene may play in determining why some of us ("warriors") thrive on brief brushes with stress and others ("worriers") suffer from it, particularly when it comes to high-stakes test-taking experiences. The new findings and the classroom-centered work of some influential educators may equip teachers to better understand what's happening when their students, or they themselves, are experiencing stress. These recent discoveries will provide insight on how to approach stress and stressful situations, perhaps even to channel the brain's stress response into positive action. **(See CORE 6c.)**

Stress, Distress, and Anxiety

One difficulty in talking about stress is that the language used to discuss stress is not consistently defined, even by scientists. For learning and the brain, it is useful to distinguish between acute (or short-term) stress from mentally and physically damaging chronic stress. It is also useful to recognize the difference between stress and anxiety.

Stress is the body's physical mobilizing in response to an event or situation that causes a sense of fear, frustration, anger, or nervousness. Scientists who specialize in stress define it as any external stimulus that threatens the normal equilibrium of body function. A stress-inducing event is called a *stressor.* Among the more powerful stressors are those that are psychological and psychosocial. Psychological stress, such as lack or loss of control, can have physiological consequences (Society for Neuroscience, 2008).

Acute stress is a situation in which the body prepares to defend itself. This kind of stress response is generally self-regulating. When the event is over, the stress goes away. Examples of acute stress related to learning outcomes might include facing an important test, being confused by new information, falling behind in lessons, feeling overwhelmed by new demands, or being affected by environmental elements such as loud noise (see Figure 8.1).

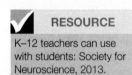

RESOURCE

K–12 teachers can use with students: Society for Neuroscience, 2013. (See the Citations list at the end of this chapter.)

Chronic stress, on the other hand, is caused by chronic or ongoing stressors, be they prolonged environmental, social, or psychological stress. Left unchecked, chronic stress can suppress the production of new neurons in the hippocampus, which will impair memory and contribute to high blood pressure, diabetes, and a host of other health problems, according to the new online primer on the brain and nervous system published by the Society for Neuroscience.

Chronic stress that may come into play in the learning environment for students include the consequences of poverty or troubling home environments. As discussed in Chapter 3, animal studies reveal impoverished environments are associated with reduced cortical gray matter. Studies document, for instance, that stress hormones present in young children from poor families may be higher than those in young children from middle-class and wealthy families (Hackman, Farah, & Meaney, 2010; Lipina & Posner, 2012). Stress hormones increase anxiety and affect school learning.

As one instructor describes it, this finding isn't always easy for teachers to understand. Many are from the middle class, and have most likely enjoyed school and learning their chosen profession. So it can be difficult to imagine that children may have such vastly different experiences that school can be hard or even frightening, the instructor adds. Knowing that the school experience can look different for various individual

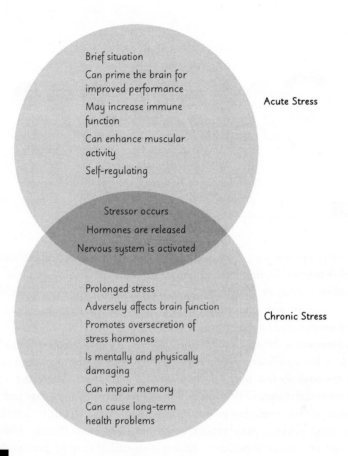

Acute Stress

Brief situation

Can prime the brain for
improved performance

May increase immune
function

Can enhance muscular
activity

Self-regulating

Stressor occurs

Hormones are released

Nervous system is activated

Chronic Stress

Prolonged stress

Adversely affects brain function

Promotes oversecretion of
stress hormones

Is mentally and physically
damaging

Can impair memory

Can cause long-term
health problems

FIGURE 8.1

A Picture of Stress

Acute stress and chronic stress are both triggered by a stressful encounter or event. With both, stress hormones activate the nervous system. With acute stress, when the situation is over, the stress goes away. Chronic stress is ongoing and can have long-term effects.

learners and that this is why we must differentiate is a powerful lesson for teachers as well as school administrators.

Anxiety is defined differently from stress. It is typically described as a feeling of fear, unease, or worry (see Figure 8.2). This feeling continues after the stressor is gone. Sometimes, the source of the anxiety is not known. Anxiety disorders, such as fear that interferes with daily functions, panic attacks, or obsessive-compulsive behavior, are often identified as mental illness (Owens, Stevenson, Hadwin, & Norgate, 2014; University of Maryland Medical Center, 2011).

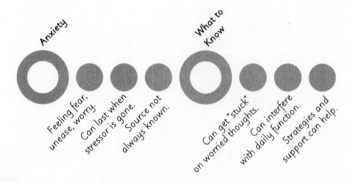

FIGURE 8.2

Thinking about Anxiety

Anxiety symptoms vary, from feeling "on edge" to having trouble separating from adults to exhibiting unfounded fears, obsessive thoughts and actions, or physical symptoms such as trembling, pain, or muscle tension. Many children and young adults experience apprehension at times, and some simple coping skills that teachers can model can be quite helpful; they are described next.

First, however, it should be mentioned that some youth become "stuck" on worried thoughts and require professional intervention. Such anxiety disorders need careful evaluation by professionals so that they can be identified and effectively treated. Disorders can range from generalized anxiety that results in excessive missed school days and avoidance of social activities, to overwhelming preoccupying thoughts and repetitive actions (OCD), to physical and social phobias, panic attacks, or posttraumatic stress disorder from a traumatic or abusive past or current experience. Multiple situations may be present or interact in complex ways, requiring special needs.

For normal types of fluctuating worry that children and teens exhibit, practical recommendations help lower stress and help students manage better. Not all ideas will work in every situation for every learner, but it is helpful for teachers to have some ideas to adapt. Many coping strategies are not new. A genuine understanding of stress will help teachers realize why it is important not only to teach students anxiety strategies but also when to use them.

Lowering stress often starts with simply noticing it. Commenting briefly without the urge to judge, blame, or accuse shows an adult cares and wants to understand. Listening and helping children and teens use words can help strengthen the ability to communicate with language rather than behaviors: "That must have seemed unfair"; "What happened next?"; "How do you think that would work?" Encouraging children to think of a few simple ideas to address a fluctuating concern can help—but then move on. Don't dwell longer than what the conversation deserves.

When lowering stress, teachers and parents should think about the student's use of time. Middle school children and teens, for instance, are expected to exhibit more of their own time management skills as they mature. The students can easily bite off more than they can manage, and not yet know what to do about their own time management. One solution is simply to help identify where all the time is going. Especially young adults can sometimes imagine there are more hours in the day than there really are, particularly when time for eating, sleeping, relaxation, family duties, and even transportation to and from school and other activities are taken into consideration.

Some choices may need to be made by the student about how to allocate his or her time. Teachers can encourage parents and other caregivers to be patient with the student's decision making, and not try to solve every problem for their youngster. Offering guidance to a solution is helpful and, at times, necessary. Also allowing learners to take an active role is part of developing coping skills. Children need some opportunity to come up with solutions in safe, supported ways in order to become good problem-solvers and establish resiliency—learning skills they will use for a lifetime.

To handle the worry that can come with this process of establishing one's own skills, teachers should encourage replacing negative self-talk with positive internal messages: "This is important to me and that's okay—I can give it my best shot and will learn more as I go along." Sometimes learners need ways to keep their worries in perspective, especially in the middle school years while they are just learning about their relationships with others, and even with the outside world. Remarkably, narrative, enjoyment, and gratitude offset stress and ephemeral anxiety. Ways that allow us to refocus and "think differently" about a situation that we are struggling with will help from getting "stuck" in situations of normal worry that come and go for every learner.

Chapter 7 includes ideas and strategies about contributions that emotions make toward learning and how to assist students in the classroom. Chapter 6 describes the needs of physical preparedness, such as sleep, exercise, and nutrition, all of which can quickly undermine our well-being and make us more vulnerable to stress and anxiety. Healthy bodies help support healthy minds, and teachers play a role in helping students become more self-aware about this connection. Chapter 9 discusses the use of feedback and evidence by the brain, including how effective formative assessment helps students feel prepared. This reduces stress, as students show what they know and can do, and builds positive experiences with supportive feedback on their personal growth.

Teachers can offer this information, as well as reassurance and comfort, including how the brain and body work on our behalf to recenter us when needed. Strategies to calm children can include teaching them steps such as eating and sleeping to lower anxiety before a test, and to listen for their own breathing and slow it with counting when they feel anxious. Even young children can engage in other relaxation techniques associated with freeing the brain from stress so that it can work effectively:

- Sit up straight in a chair, press feet firmly against the ground, and stretch your frame to raise the head "as tall as possible" while counting slowly to five. Teach students to think about each muscle in the body from head down and consciously release all muscle tension in a stream of relaxation. Repeat three times and then relax the body. Helping young students learn to do this in discrete and habitual ways will allow them to better persist over time and carry their coping skills into middle school and high school. Students who haven't been taught this early will still benefit enormously, as they can become skilled at whatever age.

- For effective breathing, take a deep breath that fills the diaphragm and teach children to recognize when their diaphragm moves down so the lungs can fully inflate. Feeling with a hand on the upper abdomen at first will help support the internal feelings they can also quickly recognize. Once again, be sure to repeat a few times. Shallow breathing and muscle tension are bodily reactions to stress that are not helpful in learning. They deprive us of oxygen and keep us from experiencing our better states of well-being. They may also lead students to future avoidance behavior if the brain makes unhelpful associations between the feelings of worry and anxiety, and whatever was going on at the moment in the schooling challenges.

- Also teach children that mental visualization is not only for skilled athletes that they see on television. Children, too, can briefly close their eyes, rest their fingertips gently on their forehead and palms on cheeks, and imagine a quiet landscape scene. Teachers will find it effective to offer some pictures of serene locations as examples, and then ask children to think of their own ideas and draw out in pictures. Constructing our own experiences like this builds vivid memories that we can turn to for lifelong support. Connecting the visual with the kinesthetic means we won't get "too cool" for these helpful techniques as our brain discovers and makes the physical associations. Ask any top athlete if he or she would abandon what works for them.

Remember, too, that teaching is a stressful profession. What we do ourselves and as teachers and leaders shows what perspectives we bring to our own communities. Employing these same coping skills puts us in a better place and gives the added advantage of being able to serve as role models. English instructors teach literature passages that help us aspire, such as from the opening of Rudyard Kipling's "If—": "If you can keep your head when all about you/Are losing theirs and blaming it on you. . . . ." When we find ways to cope, this includes advocating for appropriate and effective decisions in schools, we bring about positive climates for teachers and other staff as well as students. This is an important road to well-being of brain and mind.

The Stress Response

In a stressful situation, the body's nervous system is activated in a number of ways. In the brain, neurotransmitters, such as dopamine, signal the adrenal glands to secrete hormones that are released into the bloodstream, producing an array of effects aimed at putting the body and mind into a state of arousal to enable it to cope with the challenge (Society for Neuroscience, 2008).

Key brain regions implicated in mediating the effects of stress are the hippocampus and the prefrontal cortex, both of which, as we have already learned, are critically involved in learning and memory; and the amygdala, which is associated with emotional response (Sandi & Pinelo-Nava, 2007).

Some major stress hormones are *adrenaline* (also called *epinephrine*) and *cortisol* (or *glucocorticoid* in humans). When released in a fight-or-flight situation, they can prime the brain for improved performance, increase immune function, and enhance muscular activity. When the stressful situation is over or more resolved, the nervous system usually attempts to restore the body to its normal state (Society for Neuroscience, 2008).

The Society for Neuroscience goes on to report that studies in rats have shown that too much of these hormones may age the brain, causing impairment in the neural function of the hippocampus, which has long been known to be highly sensitive to stress. Chronic stress, in which the stressful situation does not resolve substantially or reduce over time, appears to promote oversecretion of stress hormones that adversely affect brain function, suppressing the production of new neurons in the hippocampus and impairing memory. Too much stress hormone has also been shown to suppress immune function, contribute to high blood pressure and diabetes, and cause sleep loss and other health problems.

Another way of viewing the stress response that may be particularly helpful to teachers is presented by California teacher educator and author Dr. Judy Willis, a neurologist and former middle school teacher. When she speaks, teachers listen, as evidenced by her presentations at conferences for educators. Willis builds an approach to addressing student stress based on research that shows that emotions, particularly stress and fear, influence the limbic system's filter through which data from the senses must pass before reaching areas where information is consolidated into memories (Willis, 2012b).

The amygdala and the hippocampus are both parts of the limbic system. During stress, Willis describes, researchers report some evidence that sensory input that is not most immediately vital to survival may be blocked by the amygdala from getting to higher cortical processing areas (Pawlak, Magarinos, Melchor, McEwen, & Strickland, 2003).

To help teachers—and students—understand how the stress response works in the brain, Willis describes the amygdala as a "switching station." When new information comes in, the amygdala routes it to either the "higher reflective prefrontal cortex" where conscious thought, logic, and other aspects of cognition can respond to it, or to the "lower reactive brain" where the "fight, flight, or freeze" response is activated and opportunities for learning and memory acquisition are limited (Willis, 2012a).

To make the most of learning time, Willis advocates teaching strategies that reduce students' fear, anxiety, boredom, or frustration—any emotions that will trigger the switch that shunts the flow of new information away from the reflective brain. It is logical, she says, for survival purposes for the amygdala to respond to threats to physical safety by preparing the reactive brain centers for automatic action. Willis goes on to point out for teachers what they already know: This is not the type of response desired for students when they are learning. For example, students who perceive tests or assessments as a threat can generate a strong, chronic emotional stress responses, and this triggers test anxiety. Not the healthiest condition for learning, nor the most adequate circumstance for gaining effective measures, many schools already work to lower test anxiety in students—an important connection among the learning sciences of neuroscience, cognitive psychology, and educational research. For instance, as far back as the 1980s, educational research described aspects of the correlates, causes, effects, and treatments for test anxiety (Hembree, 1988). This is an important issue for schools, since the value of collecting information on student learning is also associated with yielding large learning gains for students. (See Chapter 9, "Feedback and Evidence in the Brain.")

"Resilience Education"

Stress-Busting Strategies for Teachers

Helping students to avoid viewing learning in stressful or fearful ways, whether during classroom learning or in taking tests, is a key component of Judy Willis's approach to what has been called "resilience education" (Willis, 2012b).

Taking risks is a part of learning for most children, she says, but moving out of their comfort zone can make them feel stressed. Test taking is but one stressor. Others include fear of being wrong, feeling too embarrassed in class to ask or answer questions, boredom or frustration caused by lack of mastery of material or lack of personal relevance, or feeling overwhelmed by increasing academic demands, such as moving into a new grade level.

Taking steps that reduce stress at such times is especially important so that students can approach learning with positive affect. Willis described that her goal is neurological in a sense: Help students make that connection from the amygdala to higher cognition in the prefrontal cortex. She tells teachers how she wants to increase the consolidation of ideas, which educators know as *meaning making* (see Chapters 3 and 5 on instructional design). Willis also wants to facilitate managing information in long-term memory so that hard-earned knowledge is active on behalf of students. But she wants it without negative influences from stress. She doesn't want circumstances to interfere with successful neural transmission; rather, she wants to see the brain learning effectively.

Among Willis's recommended strategies is the use of what she cleverly calls "SYN-NAPS." These are breaks where teachers change the learning activity to let the brain chemicals replenish and the amygdala to "cool down." She says 10 minutes of doing the same type of activity depletes neurotransmitters needed for memory and attention (Willis, 2012a).

Although a neuroscientist herself and a stickler for accuracy in review of the science, Willis uses friendly, accessible words and terms with teachers. As an effective and thoughtful communicator with teachers and educators, she exemplifies a new breed of scientists doing outreach to important stakeholders and audiences for their work. She doesn't want her message to get in the way of her meaning.

Willis also tries to find routes that identify types of condition-action pairs (see Chapter 5) that may be directly relevant to teachers. Not complex nor needing a degree in science for teachers to understand them, recommendations from Willis include setting "achievable challenges" to prevent stress by avoiding boredom and frustration. She defines an *achievable challenge* as "one in which the learner has the capacity (or skills to develop the capacity) to meet an ambitious goal. A challenge that is too difficult leads to hopelessness, and a challenge that is too easy can produce boredom. A learning challenge that is within reach, says Willis, will induce the amygdala to allow new information to pass to the prefrontal cortex and move learning and memory acquisition forward.

In addition, Willis is a strong advocate for teaching students about how the brain works to help them develop what she and others (such as the original researcher Carol Dweck) call a "growth mindset" (see Chapter 5 on instructional design). When you teach students about their brains, particularly about neuroplasticity and the influence of stress on higher brain thinking, Willis says, they are more engaged in their own learning and more willing to stick with learning, even if they are faced with setbacks.

 RESOURCE

K–12 teachers can use with students: Willis, 2009. (See the Citations list at the end of this chapter.)

Stress, Up to a Point, Has Benefits

Research into how stress influences cognitive performance goes back to 1908, when two researchers, Robert Yerkes and John Dodson, first found a clear relationship between stress and performance. Their research subjects were dancing mice and their stress test involved confronting a specific task in the laboratory. The researchers found that when the mice were given a simple task, their performance improved with increases in stress (called arousal levels). Even when the task got more difficult and their stress levels rose, their performance continued to improve. But at the highest levels of arousal, the performance of the mice was impaired, as shown in Figure 8.3.

In a nutshell, the Yerkes–Dodson Law established the concept that acute stress is beneficial to cognitive performance, but only up to a point. The researchers work laid the foundation for decades of exploration into the relationship of stress levels to brain function and behavioral performance.

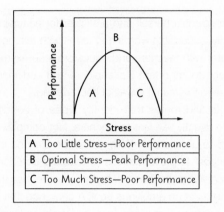

FIGURE 8.3

The Yerkes-Dodson Curve

Today, it is well accepted that stress is a powerful modulator of learning and memory processes. By joining together neurobiology and psychology, researchers are further fine-turning their understanding of the connection. Whether stress is beneficial, detrimental, or incidental to cognitive performance depends on a wide range of variables. Among the factors often studied are the impact of the levels of stress hormones released into the brain, sources of stress, stressor duration, stressor intensity, stressor timing with regard to memory phase, and learning type (Sandi & Pinelo-Nava, 2007). For example, what is the impact on memory when the stress is intrinsic—in other words, directly related to the learning context? This is as compared to extrinsic, or completely outside of the intended learning environment, such as an unexpected loud, shattering noise. These are areas of active research.

Furthermore, does it matter whether the stress occurs at the time of memory consolidation versus the retrieval phase? Some research is showing that a stressor during encoding often appears to be generally helpful to the vividness of a memory. As if the body were saying, "Remember this!" we may cling to memories of moments associated with stress, perhaps as a human survival mechanism. Sometimes when we are trying to access a memory, by contrast, stress just seems to get in the way. As a distraction, generally it impairs memory and recall (Diamond, 2005; Sandi & Pinelo-Nava, 2007).

Brief Stress Primes Neuron Growth

In one important new insight, researchers at the University of California, Berkeley, have uncovered exactly how brief, acute stress primes the brain to perform better. Daniela Kaufer, associate professor of integrative biology, and her team at the university's Helen Wills

Neuroscience Institute found in their study with rats that significant but brief stressful events caused stem cells in the rats' brains to proliferate and as soon as 2 weeks later improve the rats' mental performance.

Intermittent stressful events help keep the brain more alert, Kaufer (cited in Kirby et al., 2013) explained in a university news report, and we perform better when we are alert. Kaufer described how she was especially interested in how both acute and chronic stress affect memory. Much research has demonstrated that chronic stress elevates levels of glucocorticoid stress hormones, which suppresses the production of new neurons in the hippocampus, thus impairing memory. But what effect, she wanted to know, does short-term stress have on neuron production? To find out, the research team subjected rats to acute but short-lived stress by immobilizing them in their cages for a few hours. This led to stress hormone levels as high as those from chronic stress, but limited to only a few hours. The dose of stress doubled the proliferation of new brain cells in the hippocampus, specifically in the dorsal dentate gyrus, one of two areas in the brain that generate new brain cells in adults, which is highly sensitive to glucocorticoid stress hormones.

The researchers discovered that the stressed rats performed better on a memory test 2 weeks after the stressful event, but not 2 days after the event. Using special cell-labeling techniques, the researchers established that the new nerve cells triggered by the acute stress were the same ones involved in learning new tasks 2 weeks later.

In terms of survival, Kaufer explains the nerve cell proliferation doesn't help the subject immediately after the stress. Cells need to become mature, functioning neurons. But in a natural environment, acute stress happens on a regular basis. Kaufer says this keeps the rats more attuned to the environment and to what actually is a threat or not. Her ultimate message is an optimistic one: Stress can be something that makes us better. The question is how much, how long, and how we interpret it.

Test-Taking Warriors and Worriers

Why is it that some students thrive when taking exams while others in the same class, well prepared and clearly knowledgeable, freeze up at the very idea of a quiz or test? How we handle acute stress is a complex interaction of emotion and biology. But performing better under stress and competitive pressure may have something to do with a gene that regulates how quickly the prefrontal cortex is cleared of dopamine, the neural transmitter that signals the release of stress hormones. Adele Diamond, a professor of developmental cognitive neuroscience at the University of British Columbia, explained that when dopamine floods the prefrontal cortex, it can interfere with problem solving and reasoning functions, much as an engine flooded with too much fuel sputters.

 RESOURCE

K–12 teachers can use with students: Bronson & Merryman, 2013. (See the Citations list at the end of this chapter.)

The gene that regulates the clearing of the dopamine is called the COMT gene. It has two variants. With one variant, enzymes slowly remove the dopamine flowing into the brain during stress. With the other, enzymes rapidly clear the dopamine.

Scientists speculate the quick-acting variant may be particularly useful in threatening environments where the greatest possible performance is needed, and thus has become popularly known as the "warrior gene." The variant that removes dopamine more slowly, dubbed the "worrier gene," appears to have evolved more recently and may be particularly useful in complex environments where top performance is required on tasks of memory and attention. The COMT gene is also implicated in impulse, anxiety, and other human behaviors. The persistence of both variants, say some researchers, suggests that both warrior and worrier strategies can potentially be advantageous, depending on the circumstances (Stein et al., 2006).

So, which is better when it comes to learning? It depends on the situation, according to the researchers. In normal situations—that is, when acute stress is absent—studies have shown that individuals with the slow-acting variant have a cognitive advantage in working memory and attention tasks, and the advantages increase as levels of education increase. But when under stress stimuli, such as during test time, the cognitive advantage shifts to those with the fast-acting enzyme, as their abilities to concentrate and solve problems increase. Conversely, exposure to acute stress hampers the performance of those with the worrier gene.

Researchers in Taiwan investigated the impact of the gene in the high-stress environment of students taking that country's Basic Competency Test for Junior High School Students. Until recently, the test determined who among the country's 200,000 middle school students would gain admission to high school, and among those, who would go to the best schools.

Using blood tests of nearly 800 students taking the test to determine who had which variant of the COMT gene, researchers at the Science Education Center at National Taiwan Normal University found that high-performing students with the slow-acting enzymes, on average, scored 8% lower than those with the fast-acting enzymes. Researchers described it to the *New York Times* as if some of the A and B students traded places at test time.

With Taiwan moving to 12-year compulsory education for all students, the national test is now a thing of the past. Still, the pressure to perform on high-stakes standardized tests is growing for students and teachers—as the call for educational accountability proliferates. As this research demonstrates, some students who perform best in normal conditions may not be the same who perform best under the pressure of test taking.

In yet another study, British researchers focused on the role of working memory in test-taking stress. They found that when working memory was poor, increased stress was associated with low test scores. When working memory was good, stress was associated with higher test results.

In the study, 96 school students ages 12 to 14, from several schools, completed measures of stress and working memory using computer tests. The students were then tested for cognitive ability and math performance. The research enhances our understanding of when, specifically, stress can have a negative impact on taking tests. The findings also suggest that there are times when a little bit of stress can actually motivate students to succeed, said Dr. Matthew Owens, a researcher at the University of Cambridge who carried out the study while at the University of Southampton (Owens et al., 2014).

Perception Matters . . . a Lot

Although there is still much to learn about the role of stress and cognition, teachers and parents know that when students feel anxious or fearful, they aren't in the right frame of mind to learn. And, although the role of genes and biology cannot be overlooked, how we perceive pressure-filled events ultimately shapes our physiological response. Controlling your perception of events can determine how you perform when faced with pressure. If an event or situation doesn't seem stressful to you, that outlook can do much to avoid the harmful consequences of many kinds of mild to moderate stressors, states the Society for Neuroscience (2008).

Among the body of research that has shown that a change in mindset helps students cope with stress is work by Jeremy Jamieson at the University of Rochester (Jamieson, Mendes, & Nock, 2013). His studies showed that college students who were told that stress actually improves performance scored an average 6% higher than those in a control group. Jamieson's work focused on the effect of stress perception for students taking the Graduate Record Examination (GRE), but athletic coaches, performers, emergency responders, among others all have found ways to turn what are often stressful situations to their advantage, or at least to not let the stress negatively affect performance.

Conclusion

Stress is so widespread in modern society that it seems unfair, even impossible, to ask teachers to address it in their classrooms. But it can be helpful—and less stressful to teachers themselves—to be aware of *how* stress affects learning by having an understanding of the distinct kinds of stress and why, from the perspective of brain processes, some kinds of stress may be beneficial to learning and some quite negative.

Perhaps the most important point is that although the role of genes and biology are important, often how we perceive pressure-filled events ultimately shapes our body's response to them. A teacher can use his or her knowledge to help students by reducing conditions that may cause stress in the classroom. For teacher and student alike, science is showing that by learning to control our perceptions of events so that they appear less stressful, we can go a long way to avoid many harmful consequences and help the brain make the connections that enhance learning.

Closing Scenario

Putting New Knowledge to Use

Stress

Stress, as this chapter has shown, triggers physical changes that can be directly linked to how the brain responds in a learning situation. Although short bursts of stress may be beneficial at times, the concern is that some kinds of acute and nearly all kinds of chronic stress interfere with learning. In this exercise, educators are asked to identify stressors and, where possible, to suggest actions to remove or reduce them.

1. Identify some likely causes of acute stresses to students, colleagues, or yourself, directly related to the learning environment in which you work.
2. What are some possible causes of chronic or long-term stress that students encounter at your school?
3. For stress caused by the physical environment in which you learn or work, what can you do to remove or lessen the cause?
4. Stress is difficult to define because it affects individuals differently. What signs do you notice (or have seen in the past) that could help you to identify when students feel stressed?
5. Let's suppose that you notice a few students who appear to be particularly distressed when they are called on to read aloud in class. What strategies could a teacher employ to try to reduce this stress?
6. Test taking can be a stressor for many students. In designing a lesson and in preparing to test comprehension, what could a teacher do that is specifically aimed at reducing this stress?
7. Boredom or frustration can also cause the kind of stress that inhibits learning. What actions or approaches can teachers take that will give learners and their brains a useful boost?
8. Judy Willis and other teacher educators have found that students often persist better and are more resilient to setbacks when they understand how learning affects their brain and especially how stress hurts and helps their learning. What three points from this chapter do you think would be helpful for students (or colleagues) to know about stress and why? How would you present this information in class or in a professional group discussion?

Citations

Online, Media, and Print Resources for Teachers

Bronson, P. O., & Merryman, A. (2013, February 6). Why can some kids handle pressure while others fall apart? *New York Times*. Retrieved from http://www.nytimes.com/2013/02/10/magazine/why-can-some-kids-handle-pressure-while-others-fall-apart.html?pagewanted=1&_r=0

Society for Neuroscience. (2013). Brain facts. http://www.brainfacts.org/about-neuroscience/brain-facts-book/

Willis, J. (2009). How to teach students about the brain. *Educational Leadership, 67*(4). http://www.radteach.com/page1/page8/page44/page44.html

References

Diamond, D. M. (2005). Cognitive, endocrine and mechanistic perspectives on non-linear relationships between arousal and brain function. *Nonlinearity Biol Toxicol Med., 3*(1), 1–7.

Hackman, D. A., Farah, M. J., & Meaney, M. J. (2010). Socioeconomic status and the brain: Mechanistic insights from human and animal research. *Nature Reviews: Neuroscience, 11*(9), 651–658.

Hembree, R. (1988). Correlates, causes, effects, and treatment of test anxiety. *Review of Educational Research, 58*(1), 47–77.

Jamieson, J. P., Mendes, W. B., & Nock, M. K. (2013). Improving acute stress responses: The power of reappraisal. *Current Directions in Psychological Science, 22,* 51–56.

Kirby, E. D., Muroy, S. E., Sun, W. G., Covarrubias, D., Leong, M. J., Barchas, L. A., & Kaufer, D. (2013). Acute stress enhances adult rat hippocampal neurogenesis and activation of newborn neurons via secreted astrocytic FGF2. eLIFE. http://www.nebi.nlm.nih.gov/pmc/articles/PMC3628086

Lipina, S. J., & Posner, M. I. (2012). The impact of poverty on the development of brain networks. *Frontiers in Human Neuroscience, 6,* 238. http://www.ncbi.nlm.nih.gov/pmc/articles/PMC3421156/

Owens, M., Stevenson, J., Hadwin, J. A., & Norgate, R. (2014). When does anxiety help or hinder cognitive test performance? The role of working memory capacity. *British Journal of Psychology, 105*(1), 92–101.

Pawlak, R., Magarinos, A. M., Melchor, J., McEwen, B., & Strickland, S. (2003). Tissue plasminogen activator in the amygdala is critical for stress-induced anxiety-like behavior. *Nat. Neurosci., 6,* 168–174.

Sandi, C., & Pinelo-Nava, M. T. (2007). Stress and memory: Behavioral effects and neurobiological mechanisms. *Neural Plasticity, 2007,* 1–20.

Society for Neuroscience. (2008). *Brain facts: A primer on the brain and nervous system.* Washington, DC: Society for Neuroscience.

Stein, D. J., Newman, T. K., Savitz, J., & Ramesar, R. (2006). *CNS Spectr., 11*(10), 745–748.

University of Maryland Medical Center. (2011). Stress and anxiety. *Medical Reference Guide: Medical Encyclopedia.* http://umm.edu/health/medical/ency/articles/stress-and-anxiety

Willis, J. (2012a). *Engaging the whole child: Teaching for cognitive, social and emotional learning.* Paper presented at the Learning and the Brain Conference, San Francisco, CA.

Willis, J. (2012b, February 16–18). *Neurological distressing of test taking.* Paper presented at the Learning and the Brain Conference, San Francisco, CA.

Yerkes, R. M., & Dodson, J. D. (1908). The relation of strength of stimulus to rapidity of habit-formation. *Journal of Comparative Neurology and Psychology, 18,* 459–482.

Feedback
and **Evidence**
in the **Brain**

CORE Guiding Principle 7 is introduced in this chapter: The brain is a remarkable pattern-capturing mechanism that regulates the learning process through feedback, including what teachers provide in a variety of forms to effectively support metacognition, the learner's ability to regulate, or shape, his or her own learning.

Learning Points

1. The brain is a remarkable pattern-capturing mechanism that regulates the learning process through feedback. This occurs at many levels in the brain, from the smallest biological processes to our most complex executive thinking.

2. To think effectively, we rely on brain processes of feedback and evidence that help us explain, predict, and plan what to do next. Some scientists believe that such predicting may be a primary function of the neocortex and a foundation of intelligence.

3. Because few things are ever certain, the brain must work with probabilities. Using what it learns, it constantly makes predictions about what we expect to see, feel, and hear next, and how to interpret it.

4. During learning, when our understanding is still fragile, we need input to help guide us. Teachers who employ effective feedback practices have been shown to generate significant gains in learning.

5. Successful feedback supports the learner's ability to regulate, or shape, her or his own learning.

6. One key concept for teachers is that feedback is instruction.

7. The brain cannot effectively self-regulate unless it knows what the goals of learning are, where the learner stands on the goals, and how close he or she is to them.

8. When feedback is provided, the opportunity to effectively use the feedback needs to be built into learning activities and without too much delay or the value may be lost.

9. Lack of sufficient response information in learning activities can cause students to practice failure, underscoring and reinforcing memory traces for incorrect or less appropriate solutions and behaviors.

10. The brain responds to feedback that is both relevant and surprising. When the mind's prediction of what to expect gets upended, it can be a good thing for learning.

Introduction

"Sometimes the road less traveled is less traveled for a good reason," quipped comedian Jerry Seinfeld when a blizzard shut down his wintery flight into New York during the second season of the long-running TV show.

"I'm not afraid of flying," Seinfeld went on to say, quickly backpedaling with comic bluster. "I think fear of flying is quite rational because human beings cannot fly. Humans have fear of flying [the] same way fish have fear of driving. Put a fish behind the wheel, and they go, 'This isn't right. I shouldn't be doing this. I don't belong here.'"

Seinfeld, of course, does angst like nobody else. But a point well taken behind his humor is that we—our brains—have reasons for what we do. We bring together evidence—winter cold, don't go to Buffalo—and information such as emotional feedback—"I don't belong here [flying]"—and cast our lot in certain directions and not others. This is the road we travel.

At the same time, by gathering a little feedback and seeing how things turn out, we adjust our actions constantly. Especially during the learning process, when our understanding is still fragile, feedback and evidence are essential components of shaping our thinking. We don't know that we are on the right track yet, so we need input to help guide us.

Infusing information, comments, and viewpoints are all part of feedback. Evidence flows to us from events and outcomes, such as what happens after we act, but also from people around us, such as peers, parents, and teachers. When teachers employ effective practices of sharing evidence of learning with students, some of the most significant gains in teaching and learning are found. As we will see, the learning brain thrives on feedback.

Feedback Abounds in the Classroom

Feedback is everywhere in the classroom. Teachers know it can be a powerful learning tool, and its importance in learning is acknowledged generally. Grades and assessments are among the most traditional and valued forms of feedback. But many other responses—an encouraging nod of the head, a word of advice, a tip on an essay, or discussion of a math problem—are all ways learners receive useful feedback (Rabinowitz, 1993).

However, teachers also know that providing feedback demands time, creativity, or both, and often wonder if it is worth the effort. Brain science and education research tells us that it is, and teachers who employ student feedback as a core learning and motivating tool agree.

For instance, in one class as students work together in groups or teams, their teacher provides a common language for effort and achievement. This is delivered through a visual representation of the effort, with a graph, chart, or display. Charting or graphing outcomes, the teacher described, provides a source of instant feedback. This proves to be particularly motivating when students can see a visual representation of their efforts.

Another teacher goes about providing feedback differently. He wants to work with students individually and is highly attuned to the roles they play in the classroom. Will they step up and take leadership? Do they shut down and never feel confident enough to contribute the many worthy ideas they have? In his elementary and middle school classroom, he focuses on preparing students to be active learners. He strolls around the classroom with a clipboard in hand, dashing out notes on sheets of labels printed with student names. When he sees someone contribute, he jots a brief record that describes the tone or pitch of the student's work in the classroom. In a matter of weeks, according to his investment of a few minutes a day, his notes provide students (and parents) with a portrait of what he sees. This teacher affixes the labels to a portfolio chart for each student, and soon collects a set of individual comments—or a comment card—specifically for each learner. Depending on the teacher's plans, this may be shared with parents at a parent–teacher conference, referenced by students as an ongoing record of how they are learning and growing, or used by the teacher more internally to make plans for working with the student and family. The feedback unfolds in a natural way.

Teaching Teachers about Feedback and Evidence as a Brain Concept

Increasingly, college instructors are beginning to be asked to include a unit on feedback and evidence in cognitive science courses. Previously, the topic was likely to be more confined to methods courses, learning theory instruction, and assessment modules for teachers. However, the deep significance of how feedback and evidence are used in the classroom has brought the topic to the fore for the field of cognitive science, just as more is being understood about how the brain uses evidence.

As background, feedback is a highly researched concept in educational learning theory. As discussed in Chapter 7, from behavioral sciences (positive and negative reinforcement), constructivist views and a sociocultural conception, learning theory on evidence complements perspectives. Each adds to our knowledge rather than rejecting a previous theory, although historically the next theory may have developed because of frustration with some inadequacies of the previous theory to address everything in learning.

This complementary view is now taught by many instructors in courses on learning, and extensions are made to cognitive science, as explained in the next section. Connections will be seen to the following:

- Cognitivist/Constructivist perspectives—for instance, when advice is to involve students in authentic problems to apply what they have learned, or when discussing how the brain needs effective feedback in order to elaborate and extend higher-order thinking
- Behaviorist/Empiricist approaches when the discussion involves being concrete about specific feedback that focuses on goals and objectives, the benefits of novelty in reinforcement activities, and how the brain's chemicals mimic behaviorist reward/reinforcement patterns
- Socioculture/Sociohistoric roots when learners and learning communities are invited into the processing of unpacking objectives of feedback in the classroom, and helping assign meaning to the discourse that takes place around evidence

Teachers and educators will be able to make many other connections with prior knowledge throughout this chapter, and are encouraged to do so as they go along.

How Feedback and Evidence Work in the Brain

Feedback, from the point of view of brain functioning, is both an external and an internal process. Externally, a variety of information is received through sensory input—everything from "What did that person just say?" to "Ouch! I collided with the sofa" is part of what we perceive. *Feedback* is defined as coming in direct response to something we have done, said, thought, or believed. *Evidence*, by contrast, is defined more broadly as any type of input or stored information that we may use to evaluate and perform subsequent actions (see Figure 9.1). So, feedback is an important type of evidence. Our brain stores other kinds of evidence, too. It isn't necessarily direct feedback to the outcome of an event or particular happening but might nevertheless prove useful one day: memories, conditions under which a variety of decisions have proven successful for us before, even negative evidence. For example, our brains might signal us "Whatever you do, avoid this" or "Beware! Don't do that."

Internally, our brain exploits a great deal of evidence from the past stored in memory or more immediately passing through our neural networks to influence brain regulation or changes about what is done in the future. We don't usually think of it in this way, but feedback is what keeps critical physiological processes within often narrow limits. Necessary for

> **Feedback**
> Anything coming in direct response to something we have done, said, thought, or believed

- **Examples:**
  - Sensory and environmental: thirst, hunger, temperature, "Ouch, that's sharp."
  - Receiving praise: Recognition in class, confidence-boosting attention
  - Securing rewards: Good grades, gold stars, special opportunities

> **Evidence**
> Any type of input or stored information that we may use to evaluate and perform subsequently

- **Examples:**
  - Information stored in memory
  - Information immediately passing through our neural networks to influence brain regulation

> Feedback provides the brain with evidence for how to behave, make corrections, or take action.

FIGURE 9.1

Feedback and Evidence in the Brain

vital function, neuroscientists cite cell division, energy metabolism, molecular synthesis, and cell signaling as among the many examples of vital functions with feedback loops (Kandel, Schwartz, Jessell, Siegelbaum, & Hudspeth, 2013).

The idea of a regulatory system seems simple but is important to explore to provide some common language used by scientists. Nobel Prize–winning neurologist Eric Kandel and his coauthors provide a nice example of regulation by looking at a simple assembly of water supply pipes (Kandel et al., 2013). Water pours into a tank from the supply pipe and out through a drain pipe. Water, in this case, is the substance to be regulated. A float in the tank provides evidence, or feedback, about what is happening to the water level. If the water is too high, the float evidence provides negative feedback: It slows the entry of water.

Negative simply means an aversive stimulus, one that stems the flow. If the float is too low, positive feedback allows more water to flow in. Positive means a reinforcer; it stimulates the flow. Alternatively, depending on how the regulation system is set up, feedback could act on the drain increasing or decreasing its openings—for instance, through positive or negative feedback on its operation. Habituation is a decrease in a response to a given stimulus. We have already taken it into consideration so we need not keep adjusting for it.

Conceptually, similar types of basic regulation occur in the brain. Whether referring to the neuron, circuit, network, or entire brain region, they all have a role in the evidence/feedback response. Some brain components are in communication with each other, exchanging rapid fire feedback—as if playing the role of the "float"; the other components may receive or interpret feedback, responding in positive and negative directions. At the circuit level, for instance, one circuit, or portion thereof, may provide a feedback signal and influence the functioning of another. This can prompt a feedback loop, or cycle between two parts that affect each other.

Of course, feedback in the brain gets much more complicated than a single loop. In fact, a virtual barrage of feedback is taking place. Sensory, or more internally generated feedback and evidence, inundate the brain constantly. Since the brain regulates many functions, tiny adjustments take place constantly in response to information received. So, in this sense, feedback is like a type of dialogue taking place within the brain, and between the mind and the outside world, modifying processes based on results or effects.

Neuromyths: The Tale of the Wrong Turn

Feedback and Evidence on Neuromyths

The Value of a Fundamental Base of Understanding

Given that this chapter focuses on feedback and evidence, it is time to provide some important feedback from experts in brain science: Sometimes a little knowledge can be a dangerous thing. Yes, there is growing agreement that educators need more formal teaching in the neurobiological basis of learning. On the other hand, there is an equally strong concern about teachers, parents, and policy makers putting into practice notions about the brain founded on misunderstandings, bad interpretations, and distorted or out-of-date research. **(See CORE 7i.)** In short, experts fear the misuse of common but incorrect beliefs about the brain called *neuromyths*.

Here are a few of the common neuromyths addressed by the Society for Neuroscience Brain Facts blog. (We've briefly encountered some of these earlier.)

- Neuromyth: At any given moment, we only use 10% of our brain.

   Facts: Neuroimaging technology has conclusively shown this to be false. We use our entire brains. Although not all of the brain is active all at once, functional magnetic resonance images (fMRI) show several brain areas are at work for any given activity, depending on what function is needed.

- Neuromyth: Unlike other cells in our bodies, our brains can't make new cells.

  Facts: Our brains constantly generate new cells and remain adaptable as we age. Most brain cells, or neurons, are created before we are born. However, throughout adulthood, new neurons are born in a brain region called the *hippocampus,* where new memories are formed. After the cells are created, they integrate into existing brain regions.

- Neuromyth: People are either "right-brained" or "left-brained" and need to be taught in different ways. **(See CORE 7j.)**

  Facts: Regardless of personality or skill set, we use both the right and left hemispheres of the brain to perform everyday tasks. Although it is true that certain functions—such as speech production, handedness, and facial recognition— tend to be dominated by one side of the brain in the great majority of people, most tasks require parallel input from both hemispheres. Integrating input between right and left sides of the brain is handled by the *corpus callosum,* the bundle of neural fibers that connects the two hemispheres of the neocortex.

The right-brain/left-brain myth is a good one to explore to illustrate how valid early research can be misinterpreted and misused when nuance is lost and why it is important to keep up to date on brain research.

The notion of a right brain and a left brain having specific functions that appear to work independently of each other came about from highly specific research based on a handful of epilepsy patients who had undergone a radical kind of brain surgery first undertaken in the 1940s. The surgery attempted to provide relief for patients suffering severe seizures. By slicing through the corpus callosum, the surgery disconnected the two sides of the neocortex, which is the home of language, conscious thought, and movement control.

With brain-scanning technology still decades away, these patients provided neuroscientists a rare opportunity to study brain function. With the cooperation of some of these split-brain individuals, neuroscientists were able to assess the actions of the two hemispheres, learning how each functioned independently and sometimes quiet differently. For example, information, often in the form of pictures or other images, presented to one hemisphere was unnoticed in the other.

The importance of the early split-brain work led to a share of the 1981 Nobel Prize in medicine awarded to neurobiologist and neuropsychologist Roger Sperry. Through later research, neuroscientists found that the left side usually processes speech and language, whereas the right side is important for visual-spatial processing and facial recognition. At the same time, they have generally concluded that connectivity between active brain regions is as important, if not more so, than the operation of the distinct parts.

Unfortunately, the misuse of the early hemispheric brain research generated a whole pop-psychology lingo and questionable notions about personality and cognitive styles that promoted the idea of two kinds of individuals—the "left-brain people" being more logical or methodical and the "right-brained people" as more creative and intuitive.

Today, research using brain imaging technology has shown no evidence that people preferentially use the left or right hemisphere. Some people may think of themselves as "intuitive learners," or others believe that they are "visual" learners, but apart from individuals with certain medical conditions, humans coordinate activity on both sides of their brains almost all the time.

Given the number and durability of neuromyths, it is not surprising that the U.S. National Research Council makes a special point to advise educators to be careful to avoid adopting or promoting faddish concepts not scientifically demonstrated to have value.

In fact, this is a key area of an emerging field called *neuroethics.* It says that having sufficient basic knowledge to combat erroneous ideas about how the brain learns is an ethical responsibility of educators. The Society for Neuroscience further suggests that neuroethics for educators includes comprehending the emerging cognitive basis for ideas related to learning, self-concept, personal responsibility, free will, social behavior, and emotional well-being (National Research Council, 2000a, p. 117). Some university programs in teacher education are already addressing this responsibility through preparing pre-service and in-service teachers for this rapidly emerging area of neuroethics.

One way to help address neuromyths is to highlight neuroscience research questions that may interest educators (Society for Neuroscience, 2008, pp. 34–35). This could be an important step toward defining an interdisciplinary area of collaborative research among fields of the learning sciences, such as education, psychology, and neuroscience, to the benefit of all. **(See CORE 7k.)** One aim of The Mind, Brain, and Education master's program at Harvard Graduate School of Education is to develop educational neuroscientists who are knowledgeable in both fields so that they can help translate research findings for educators as well as communicate education's needs to researchers.

In Europe, Bruno della Chiesa, a senior education analyst at the Organisation for Economic Co-operation and Development (OECD), has recommended that one way to help laypeople become intelligent consumers of neuroscience research is to train teachers to develop critical views of what is reported in the media. One approach, he says, is to invite both researchers and the heads of teacher training programs to share knowledge that could shed new light on their policy decisions and practices.

RESOURCE

K–12 teachers can use with students: della Chiesa, 2009. (See the Citations list at the end of this chapter.)

Feedback and Evidence from the View of Teachers

From a broader point of view, as we move away from neurons to higher degrees of brain coordination shepherded, for instance, by executive function, feedback takes on a face more familiar to teachers.

Still, the principle is the same. Using what it learns, our brains constantly make predictions about what we expect to see, feel, and hear next, and how to interpret it. **(See CORE 7a.)**

A key feature of control in the brain, as Kandel and coauthors (2013) point out, are motivational states, such as hunger, thirst, safety, and emotional well-being. Feedback arriving into the brain includes a vast array of detail to help address the specific informational needs of these states. This includes environmental sensory evidence, of course, but also how well we are fulfilling goals, satisfying intrinsic motivations, receiving praise, and securing rewards. These all serve as types of feedback and evidence. A discussion of effective praise during feedback is presented in Chapter 7.

The takeaway is that by whatever the mechanism, the brain treats feedback as a form of evidence for how to behave and how to take corrective action (OECD, 2007, p. 32). We have expectations based on the prior evidence about what is likely to happen. Our predictions may be met or not in any given situation. This triggers new rounds of updating our beliefs. We potentially adjust our actions, make new often unconscious predictions, and then wait to see what happens next. The brain is very busy. Some emotional and motivational rewards come from making predictions, even if those predictions are somewhat wrong and require updating.

Some scientists believe that such predicting may be a primary function of the neocortex, and a foundation of intelligence (Hawkins & Blakeslee, 2004, p. 86). In fact, feedback from evidence is believed to be a key component influencing what makes each brain different. **(See CORE 7b.)** We don't all do the same things, so we don't get the same feedback. Even if we did, we'd likely interpret it differently, or respond or adjust at different levels. Thus, the diversity of personal experience and the mental imagery we employ implies different brain conditions for every person: Each brain is unique in many ways. Individual feedback we receive helps make it so.

Feedback That Works: What Does the Evidence Say?

Richard Gagné, the influential psychologist and instructional design pioneer discussed in Chapter 5, described goals of instructional design as including learner guidance, assessing performance, and delivering some type of feedback.

Even young children in very informal learning settings, such as at home or at play, receive immediate feedback through their own successes and failures (Haskell, 2001). The feedback is mediated by parents and peers who provide models of how to behave as well as by specific structures and strategies, such as praise, correction, and encouragement. These include making connections to prior knowledge and communicating with children about what to do next. All are forms of valuable evidence for the brain. Psychologist Robert Haskell, author of a text on transfer of learning, describes children as an excellent example of how evidence underpins the culture of learning.

The end result from lack of sufficient feedback really can be undoing the good that teachers and students hope to achieve. As was seen in earlier chapters, practice has a huge impact on memory acquisition and retention. Unfortunately, practicing something the wrong way also forms habits—but the wrong habits. When student thinking goes awry without sufficient shaping, the brain receives a signal. The signal says the learner is good to go, since no error was perceived or no discerned change was needed. Since there is no correction to its internal prediction, the brain builds an ever stronger memory trace that is incorrect.

Feedback in education includes two distinct aspects: (1) helping the learner and (2) improving the profession and the ability of the teacher to teach (see Figure 9.2). Noted education researcher John Hattie (2008) addresses both in his work. He concludes that both, although quite different, improve learning outcomes.

Effective approaches to feedback and evidence have strong impacts on learning outcomes, teaching and learning meta-analysis research finds. This is for both the student and the teacher. In his work, Hattie (2008) found that providing formative evaluation for the instructional design program itself is the top effect in his area of teaching.

Throughout his work, Hattie (2008) argues that a key factor in the power of learning is providing feedback to teachers on what is happening in their classrooms. In effect, this feedback helps teachers to teach better. Sometimes called *feed forward*, it is

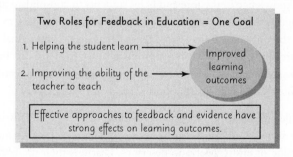

FIGURE 9.2

Two Roles of Feedback

evidence that helps teachers move forward in their instruction. This effect size suggests as much as nearly a full standard deviation in outcomes when the practice of formative evaluation is well employed, as compared to when it is not employed or is much more limited in scope.

Hattie describes that the teachers' judgments, along with data and evidence, including visual representations such as graphs and displays of student learning, had the largest impacts. Perhaps just as important, of Hattie's five top teaching outcomes, three involved leveraging how students themselves use evidence. These are:

- Provide feedback directly to students.
- Employ metacognitive strategies where students learn how to reflect on their own evidence.
- Work through reciprocal teaching approaches, a peer-to-peer instructional design in which students take turns in the teaching role and provide instruction, feedback, and evidence to each other.

Rounding out the top five strategies are:

- Use spaced versus massed practice. This was previously discussed as a supportive brain strategy in Chapter 5.
- Employ comprehensive interventions for students with learning disabilities. (This includes feedback but is not limited to this support alone, so ranges more broadly.)

Direct feedback by teachers often is straightforward for educators to perceive as evidence useful for learning. But the idea of metacognitive strategies—particularly the use of self-reflection—is not always understood as valuable evidence. Providing feedback to oneself is a process of self-reflection. Providing it to fellow learners is a peer-to-peer approach. These may seem less familiar concepts to educators than feedback from teachers directly. After all, are the students themselves or their peers sufficiently expert to provide reliable sources of feedback? Often, as Hattie's results show, simply the process of pondering and discussing brings knowledge to the fore and helps students to consolidate understanding. So, success can be improved for students, even for those with learning gaps to close.

Hattie isn't the only education researcher to focus on the influential role of feedback. Educational researcher Robert Marzano, introduced in Chapter 3 for his work in meta-analysis, also speaks to the power of the feedback approach. His work acknowledges feedback approaches that show strong effects (Marzano, 2003):

- First, consider reinforcing effort and providing recognition. This includes words of affirmation as a type of attitudinally focused evidence. For instance, praise should teach the value of effort, Marzano describes. Learners then understand success as an attainable goal. It is under their control rather than being seen as an endowed characteristic. This keeps the learner focused on task-relevant behavior. Affirmation as feedback often speaks less to specific details on corrective action but instead highlights when appropriate behaviors are taking place.

- Second, employ setting objectives and providing feedback. This is feedback given in more substantive detail relative to the learning targets. Marzano describes how it needs to be directly referenced to well-defined goals. By defining goals, the learner has a clear sense of direction. By providing feedback in reference to the goals, the learner sees where she or he stands and what remains to be achieved.

Moving from the research perspective to an applied example, one special education teacher described her efforts to see how students responded to self-regulation. She related that as she worked with students in writing, which she found was not a preferred activity, she documented results impacting performance. This included praise for effort given frequently—in her case, once every 2 minutes. The teacher found that the students continued to attempt the writing activity throughout the entire 25-minute lesson. However, when praise was provided less frequently, only about every 5 minutes, her students asked for more assistance and finished less work. For the students, otherwise capable of completing the assignment, only half as much was done when they received no positive reinforcement at all. Over time, when students became confident that the writing could be done readily and associated it with positive feelings, the teacher stretched out the praise. Still, students finished. She said this information was critical to how her team redesigned interacting with the students at the start of a difficult subject.

Some teaching strategies combine both affirmation and substantive types of feedback. One approach, called *pause, prompt, and praise,* has the teacher pause a student or group of students engaging in a task. He or she then prompts them to make an improvement or extension. This is a type of corrective feedback focused on the goals of learning—to get farther in their thinking with each attempt. The teacher then follows up with recognition as appropriate for the new attempts. Affirmation instills confidence.

One school counselor described two effective approaches she sees schools use to facilitate success. The first is positive reinforcement utilizing Positive Behavioral Interventions and Supports (PBIS). The second is the use of rubrics and detailed feedback for students. Here, we can see her two strands parallel the Marzano ideas of supports through recognition or affirmation evidence, along with substantive feedback for learning goals. To build self-esteem, one must build relationships with students, the counselor said, and acknowledge their effort and successes. She combines helping students feel successful so they feel encouraged to take more chances with their learning, with clear feedback from use of rubrics and comments to underscore what success looks like. Then, states the counselor, students have a clear picture of what direction they need to take to further their learning.

Feedback and Attention

Getting students to pay attention is related to feedback. Dale Schunk, an expert in information processing, argues that some learning outcomes may be the result of how teachers decide to allocate cognitive resources following feedback and evidence (Schunk, 2012). For instance, Schunk adds, take the idea of allocating attention. Attention is a key cognitive resource, as discussed in Chapter 3, and its allocation by the brain has a wide range of impacts. Through attention, factors such as motivation, prior learning, self-regulation, and even perceived task demands come into play. Yet attention itself is a limited brain resource. It is allocated in part, Schunk describes, based on feedback about the effectiveness of the allocation. Even recognizing mistakes requires paying attention (Reif, 2008).

To become independent with skills, supports ultimately need to be faded, as discussed previously. This is where the art of teaching comes into play. Teachers are responsible for helping students get to the point where they are successful with the knowledge and skills when explicit support such as feedback is removed. Students cannot expect to be told every time they are wrong. They must develop self-regulation and competency skills themselves, or suffer the frustration both teachers and students see when progress is half-mastered but still inert on its own. It is important for teachers to be mindful that fading student support is a significant part of the learning process.

Feedback or Instruction?

Providing feedback takes time, as every teacher will tell you. And unlike parents, who are often working with one or only a few children at a time, a typical U.S. elementary school teacher may encounter as many as 30 to 40 students daily in class, not to mention in the hall, playground, at lunch, and even potentially during after-school duties. For middle school and high school teachers this number can rise to 150 or more students encountered each day. Providing feedback during even a handful of these key interactions requires quite an investment of time.

Some teachers describe this as a tradeoff of providing instruction or using their time to provide feedback. Which should they do, they wonder, and in what combination? But the idea of considering feedback and instruction as opposing tradeoffs competing for teacher time is a red herring. Feedback *is* instruction.

Feedback can involve pointing out a misconception broadly across the class or it can be more individualized. The point is that the instructional design that a teacher selects should include specific forms of feedback and allow sufficient time for this to take place.

Making Formative Assessment Effective

Formative assessment is so named because it helps "form" the learning taking place. It shapes the instructional experience. It does so by allowing the teacher to change approaches and the students to receive the feedback and evidence they need to support the brain in learning.

Meta-analysis work on formative assessment by United Kingdom educational researchers Paul Black and Dylan Wiliam reviewed the results of many classroom assessment approaches (Black, Harrison, Lee, Marshall, & Wiliam, 2002, 2003; Black & Wiliam, 1998). They describe that formative assessment effects are large; based on accumulated studies they predict an average student might move to the top third of the class and an average state might jump to the rank of the top five.

The researchers also found that many different approaches teachers already know how to use are effective. The key often is that the feedback opportunities are missed or skipped in the whirlwind of active school days. Black and Wiliam described three elements that formative assessments need to provide in order to be effective. Students need to know:

- What the learning goals are
- Where they stand on the goals
- How to close the difference

Feedback and evidence that consistently provided these three elements tended to work well, even via a wide variety of approaches. These might range from the newest technology techniques, such as mobile devices and interactive classroom data displays, to more traditional solutions such as effectively eliciting essential questions from students. The method of *how* the feedback was given was less important than the fact that feedback was, indeed, given. What mattered was that it happened, and that it delivered for students on the three elements: identifying the goal, where the student stood, and how to improve.

Teachers often believe helping students know the goals and showing them where they stand on the goals is relatively doable. However, teachers relate that they often have trouble providing feedback that helps students close the gap. This, they say, is a challenge.

Psychologist Robert Haskell helps solve this problem. He describes one of the most effective approaches as comparing student work to model work, or other kinds of work samples (Haskell, 2001). He tells a story about Benjamin Franklin, the learned American publisher, scientist, and statesman. Franklin would often select a well-written passage in a book he admired. Then he would examine the structure and style of the work for why it was effective, and try to reproduce it in his own way. A critical step came in comparing his work to the original. The evidence came in identifying, as Haskell says, the similarities and differences between the two. Franklin claimed he learned to organize his thinking this way, and went on to persuade the world of many important ideas.

In a 2012 National Research Council workshop on assessment, educators called this using *assessment as a verb*. Rather than thinking of a test, quiz, or any other student work product, assessment should be viewed as a process.

■|| When Going Extinct Is Desirable

In contrast to mastering something new, sometimes a process called *extinction* is the desired goal of feedback in learning. Extinction involves forgetting or lessening the use of a particular approach or strategy. Extinction happens all the time on its own as a more-or-less strategic forgetting in which the brain engages. Lack of use weakens the memory traces and habits. When the brain finds repeatedly that a solution does not lead to the intended goal, the weakening occurs.

Examples of some teacher-directed approaches to extinguishing less appropriate behaviors include having time-outs, when a child engaged in an inappropriate behavior must stop what he or she is doing and take a forced break removed somewhat from the group. Other teachers invoke or revoke tokens, rewards, or privileges. As students learn new and more satisfying habits, self-destructive or less appropriate learned patterns can tend to diminish (Driscoll, 2000).

■|| Feedback and Evidence Traps to Avoid

Teachers should ask themselves, "Can my students recognize how to close the gap from corrective feedback, incorporate the information, and apply the knowledge immediately or soon after in a new challenge?" The brain works with such information. The learning activity does not end when the student gets the feedback. The brain needs to fully perceive and soon apply again the evidence it receives. Teachers often instigate this follow-through or breakdown of the feedback cycle by what they do. Here are some common traps to avoid in the use of feedback and evidence:

- One trap for teachers is a belief that research findings on the power of feedback and evidence don't apply to their own students. How so? These teachers accept that feedback and evidence make a difference for students who are especially trying to learn, but they doubt it helps most students. This is, however, not what the studies have found. Broad meta-analytic research studies such as those engaged in by Black and Wiliam do not focus only on a select group of students. They pertain to findings across a wide variety of students, including the ones in our own classrooms. Since the brain is a natural pattern-capturing device, it will tend to grab patterns to which it is exposed. So, use of effective feedback goes a long way to improve learning. A takeaway: Never give up on the human brain.
- Another trap that can be hard to avoid is investing the bulk of educational evidence exclusively on external monitoring of schools. Assessments can be terrifically important

in monitoring school systems and bringing about change over time, but this is not the type of feedback and evidence we are talking about here—it is not the kind of feedback the brain uses in learning. Assessment information exclusively used for monitoring usually is provided too late to schools to be available for immediate feedback or evidence in the classroom. Also, rarely does it contain the types of information Black and Wiliam describe. So it is not the metacognitive, regulatory information the brain seeks.

- A pernicious trap that every teacher has experienced is when not enough time is available to follow student activities with sufficient and effective feedback. It is important for educators to understand that when students perform assignments of all kinds, they are reinforcing memory traces. From a brain perspective, students believe they are learning how to do things right. When the effort spent on this is followed with insufficient correction, students can wind up practicing failure. Scholars call this a kind of *mislearning*—or learning gone wrong. The misconceptions become increasingly stable over time, reinforced by effort and practice in the absence of corrective feedback.

- For a last trap to mention, one of the saddest observations in the classroom is when effective feedback is provided but not used. Consider a teacher who has put considerable effort into providing feedback, such as comments on essays. The student gets his or her paper, glances quickly at the grade, is disappointed or not, and shoves it into a backpack. Hurrying off to the next class, the student never sees, much less processes and applies, all of the carefully provided feedback. Note that when students don't make the most of their feedback opportunity, it is really a failing of the instructional design. The opportunity to effectively use feedback needs to be built directly into the learning activities. To avoid this trap, teachers need to have students work with the information as a follow-up exercise. Regulation of information comes about by feedback in the brain, but to be effective it must be considered and acted on (Hawkins & Blakeslee, 2004).

Here's a Test: Can Quizzing Help You Learn?

There is growing evidence that teachers using low-stakes testing and intermittent quizzing as students are acquiring new information can enhance learning. Some researchers claim that this finding, known as the *testing effect*, shows up in studies from elementary school through college and has been associated with encoding strategies that support better retrieval (Rohrer, Taylor, & Sholar, 2010).

With the testing effect appearing, according to researchers, even when just one quiz is added before a summative test is given, the question has turned to, What kind of tests work best? Overall, the findings suggest that all types of tests and quizzes, including multiple choice, can produce measurable benefits. Testing that engages the brain in ways that have been shown to support learning—such as through the use of visuals, formation of short answers, and in ways that are novel, or even just slightly different from the way in which the material was originally presented, thus requiring a level of transfer—have been shown to be particularly effective (Rohrer et al., 2010).

One study by researchers at Washington University in St. Louis found that quizzing helped improve eighth-grade science and social studies test scores by 13 to 25% when three multiple-choice quizzes with feedback were spaced across the coverage of a unit. In other investigations, the researchers changed the placement of the quizzing, with students being quizzed on some content prior to the lecture, quizzed on some immediately after the lecture, and quizzed on some as a review prior to the unit exam. The researchers found that the review quizzing produced the greatest increases in performance of the exam used for assessment. The benefits of quizzing (relative to not quizzing), they reported, persisted on cumulative semester and end-of-year exams (McDaniel, Agarwal, Huelser, McDermott, & Roediger, 2011).

Despite the suggested benefits from research and its relative ease of use, say researchers, intermittent quizzing to enhance learning is underutilized, especially in courses in which students primarily listen to lectures and read.

On another front, simply the act of preparing for the law school entrance exam, which is associated with reasoning and thinking rather than mastery of facts, has been shown to increase connectivity between parts of the brain (Mackey, Whitaker, & Bunge, 2012). Researchers at the Helen Wills Neuroscience Institute at the University of California, Berkeley, have used diffusion tensor imaging (DTI) scans of the brains of 24 college students and recent graduates. They found that studying for the grueling LSAT can reinforce the brain's circuits involved in thinking and reasoning, appearing to strengthen the connections between the left and right hemispheres of the brain.

Reflections on Goal Setting and Feedback

The brain has been shown to be most attentive to feedback that is both relevant and surprising. When the mind's prediction of what to expect gets upended, it can be a good thing for learning. We pay closer attention. For instance, perhaps certain neurons are expected to be involved in upcoming sensory input based on the brain's predictions of most likely scenarios. But they don't activate, which violates the expectation. This alerts the brain that something unexpected is going on, and so attention is drawn to the error. **(See CORE 7c.)** Eventually, this extra attention leads to investigating the situation and improving our predictions—that is, better learning and understanding of what is going on. This adjusts our thinking (Hawkins & Blakeslee, 2004, p. 86).

As discussed previously, much human behavior is highly goal oriented. The more different something is from what is expected, the more attention gets directed to how to adjust to meet the goal. In fact, we humans are the species famous for intricate layers of goals within goals, called *subgoaling*, like Russian dolls that fit one within another.

Teachers often notice how even minimal feedback reinforces goal setting for students. This can be true for students even most challenged by the schooling system, such as those on individualized education programs, or IEPs, as one teacher described. Her work with goal setting and evidence underscores the Hattie results, that supports for students with special needs can be very effective. The teacher finds that reviewing the students' IEP goals with them weekly and allowing them to track their own progress is strongly connected to getting them motivated to learn and grow toward their goals. She was surprised and amazed by how simply having students graph their own results led them to make growth at a faster rate.

Prediction and Evidence

Some scientists hypothesize that the brain makes low-level predictions constantly at the level of sensory input about what it expects to see, hear, and feel all the time. **(See CORE 7d.)** At any given moment, an individual's brain is trying to predict what the person's next experience will be (Hawkins & Blakeslee, 2004). The individual notices when she or he encounters an odd smell, a novel face, or an unexpected sound.

Teachers notice this, too, and use it to help students learn. One educator described how he saw examples and nonexamples of this nearly every day. Take, for instance, a system he set up to take advantage of expectations. Noticing how students performed very well for him when their efforts were recognized, he also saw they tended to slack off when there was no evidence their efforts would be noticed. So, at the end of each day, he began to sign student planners with a percentage score they had earned for the day. He found that students reacted to this new practice, especially when they received a score that was higher or lower than what they thought they had earned. This opened opportunities where students sought feedback. The expectations were further reinforced when their scores were checked at home.

The teacher found that collaboration with parents made his classroom management system more effective. When student planners were consistently checked each night, student efforts were enhanced. This became a concrete yet simple strategy he could work on with parents to bring them into a culture of learning with their students.

As the U.S. National Research Council points out (National Research Council, 2000b), recognizing the limits of current knowledge and seeking ways to grow is extremely important for learners at every age. **(See CORE 7e.)** This involves metacognition, or the ability to monitor our self-knowledge.

One of the things that surprised another teacher most about her own students was that they did not really think about how to best help themselves learn. She found that in some cases, sadly, they were their own worst enemies because they did not seem to have skills to think about their own learning. This teacher discovered that one of the best ways she could help students was to teach them to think about how they can help themselves.

Many educational approaches do not explicitly teach students skills about how they can "learn to learn," or, in other words, the students are unaware of the self-regulation strategies that make some learners more successful than others.

A school principal described how investing in helping students learn these skills and encouraging self-directed understanding helps not only in class but also in the hallways, the bathrooms, and on the playground. She said it is an important skill set for students, and she strongly supports her teachers when they work with their students on learning these skills for themselves.

Accumulating Evidence to Make Decisions

The brain gathers a great deal of evidence as it works. It takes a lot of processing for human brains to operate. So you may think you don't know how to do statistics, but in a way your brain already does. Because few things are ever certain, the brain must work with probabilities (Hawkins & Blakeslee, 2004, p. 90).

For every action we take, we constantly put a great deal of sensory evidence together, process it, make predictions consciously or less so, and arrive at some conclusions. Often, we are remarkably accurate. Our ability to do this helps make human intelligence possible.

Although it is not yet known exactly how the brain goes about its calculations, to some degree we may use an informal method of learning by trial and error, called *heuristics:* "It worked last time, so I'll try it again," or "I can cross the street now because everyone else is doing so." But we are also likely to be doing a great deal of unconscious calculating. Statistical techniques help us explore ways in which the brain is borrowing information from past experiences to make new decisions through prediction mechanisms. **(See CORE 7f.)**

For instance, consider how a neuron may accumulate information. In most cases, a neuron doesn't act on, or fire, based on a single piece of evidence. Rather, in classic cases a neuron combines information it receives in order to determine if a signal should be sent. For the brain, some information collected may encourage a neuron to fire and some may inhibit it. **(See CORE 2i.)** Like collecting a sample of information rather than relying on a single source, it is akin to what statisticians do in trying to get a representative set of information. To make their analysis valid, they make sure there is an adequate array of voters at the polls, that there is sufficient medical records to monitor an emerging disease, or that there is a useful amount of incoming sensory information. All are sets of potentially valuable evidence that paint a fuller picture of what is going on.

An interesting difference exists between how statisticians approach data and how cognition may work. When handling evidence, there are lots of ways to go wrong with it. Both statisticians and the brain try to avoid making mistakes. Two classic issues are presented by two kinds of errors: a false positive and a false negative. For a *false positive,* we believe something is true when it is not. Statisticians work especially hard to avoid false positives: They don't want to accept a claim unless they are very sure it is true. By contrast, human survival instincts may be more aligned to protect against the *false negative,* or the failure to identify an important risk. For instance, we need to know if a particular plant is poisonous to eat or if an animal is dangerous, and we may err on the safe side if we are not certain.

To make sure we have the best chance of survival, our brains protect against missing something important. One way to protect against such false negatives is by not holding too high a threshold for accepting the evidence. Sometimes described as *superstitious learning,* people and animals can display conditioning when there appears to be a relationship between response and reinforcement—even when there is not, or the link seems weak.

For teachers, this helps explain or interpret some puzzling behaviors they may see in the classroom. Especially for students who may be coming from different backgrounds or experiences than that which the teacher is familiar, contingency planning can take many forms and may be hard to anticipate. Depending on what the student is unconsciously perceiving and interpreting, he or she may develop some less adaptive strategies in schooling that an aware educator can help redirect to better purposes. This explains a lot, one educator said. He had come to understand we are wired to do this for a good reason. He said it is as if when lightning hits in our lives, we better start thinking about why. Thus, we are constantly coming up with "causes" for the patterns we see.

Mindfully Filling Gaps

As introduced in Chapter 7 on emotion, many times when our brains make predictions, we are not aware of them. **(See CORE 7h.)** Pervasive and near continuous (Hawkins & Blakeslee, 2004, pp. 86–87), these unconscious assumptions can exert great influence on us. They let us know what we expect to happen next. We may contrast this with any surprises and consider new learning if necessary. But also our brains will try to "smooth" and complete incoming data, basically filling in blanks with our best guesses, to the extent the brain believes plausible (Hawkins & Blakeslee, 2004, p. 94).

For instance, this concept of unconscious or less aware brain processing may help explain some troubling findings in diversity studies. Studies show that in experiments taking an image of one child and placing it before a play structure set in poorer neighborhood or a richer one often leads to different conclusions by the teachers about the child. Explicit beliefs are not necessarily biased—teachers will describe that all children can learn—rather, the brain takes what it knows from prior experiences and maps the data inadvertently onto the picture. Our brain is engaged in the process of making its prediction. Much like a statistics program examining a data set, we find relationships in the data, based on what we may have seen before.

Additionally, research on teacher expectations has shown that when educators have beliefs about students' initial interactions with them, this can influence outcomes. Early studies showed that teachers who were intentionally given false background facts about students, such as who were the higher-performing and less-successful students in the class, led to these very characteristics emerging over time (Rosenthal & Jacobson, 1968). Since then, studies have found teachers may unintentionally underestimate student abilities in many situations, including low socioeconomic contexts (Ready & Wright, 2011), intercultural contexts (Tapia, 2004), and when working with second language learners (de Courcy, 2007).

All in all, we seem to be more comfortable when we can account for evidence around us. In our eagerness to make meaningful consolidation of our understanding, we can take

Evidence: How Do Scientists See Inside the Brain?

A variety of informative techniques are used by neuroscientists to gather evidence. They can range from brain scans and imaging, which view how the brain works directly or indirectly through producing pictures and graphical displays of the brain, to electrophysiology data, which measures voltage change and electrical current in cells and tissues.

Also included are behavioral studies of organisms and theoretical models of brain function. Often, a number of these techniques are combined. They provide multiple lenses that inform each other and better reveal what is happening.

For imaging techniques, for instance, approaches such as magnetic resonance imaging (MRI) and positron emission tomography (PET scans) document how brain networks function. **(See CORE 7g.)** They can provide information on how we focus attention, process information, remember, feel, decide, and learn (Howard-Jones et al., 2007; National Research Council, 2000b; OECD, 2007). For individual cells, electrical activity of neurons can be detected through electrophysiology techniques.

Imaging is often accomplished by detecting blood flow increases during brain activity. This shows where brain function is occurring. Such imaging is done without surgery or other highly invasive techniques. Many new techniques are rapidly coming into operation in neuroscience, and can be expected to inform the field in upcoming years.

large leaps of invention. So, although prediction is a powerful aspect of the human brain, we need to remain vigilant. Employing our rational and mindful thinking along with the brain's innate prediction mechanism is necessary and important.

The brain can be thought of as employing a type of logic sometimes called "Bayesian," in honor of a scholar named Thomas Bayes who lived in the 1800s. A mathematician and minister, Bayes did not work on the brain or thinking, but rather framed some useful mathematics about probability. In essence, one theorem called Bayes' law states in mathematical terms that if we have prior knowledge about what has happened in the past, this may give us clues about what we could expect to happen in the future. The term *Bayes' law* arises frequently in brain-related articles, so it is useful for teachers to grasp the essence of the idea. The concept of Bayes' law helps teachers understand one set of reasons why some students behave differently from others. Different experiences may be influencing their brain predictions.

Conclusion

Evidence cuts two ways in the brain. We use it to form our goals and set priorities, and we check back in with what happens after we act to see if we are on track. In other words, we seek feedback.

Feedback occurs at many levels in the brain. From the most minute of biological processes to our broad executive thinking, the brain seeks the results of its actions. Used to predict, plan, and regulate future processing, teaching and learning research evidence shows that feedback in myriad avenues has powerful outcomes.

We can learn through feedback from instructors, self-reflection, and peer interactions. A great deal of evidence is garnered just from the moment-to-moment results of what we do.

Lack of sufficient response information in learning activities can cause students to practice failure, or underscore and reinforce memory traces for incorrect or less-appropriate solutions and behaviors. The brain cannot effectively self-regulate unless it knows what the goals of learning are, where the learner stands on the goals, and how to close the difference. Thus, feedback and evidence is as much about forming rich patterns for the brain as for monitoring by teacher or school.

A number of tips and traps for evidence use in learning were discussed in this chapter. Perhaps foremost among them is that feedback must be *used* to be effective. Well-supported opportunities for students to actively process feedback after it has been given should be directly built into the instructional design. Unfortunately, this is missing from many classrooms. Educational research and many teachers' own experience shows that taking steps in this direction reinforces brain processes that support learning.

Closing Scenario

Putting New Knowledge to Use

Feedback and Evidence in the Brain

During learning, when understanding is still fragile, you need useful input to help guide you. Teachers who employ effective feedback practices have been shown to generate significant gains in learning. With the key point that feedback is instruction in mind, you are asked to put what you have just learned to work.

1. First, select a learning opportunity on which to focus your efforts. Identify your goals in using this approach to using feedback. If you have taught this lesson before, how effective were you? Where do you think using feedback in a new way will make the biggest difference? How will you judge how successful you've been? What kind of feedback will let you know how to judge your success?

2. Students will benefit by knowing about how the brain uses feedback to learn. So, start by describing for them why you are going to focus on feedback in this new learning experience. Specifically how will you help them see that the brain thrives on feedback?

3. Identify the three elements research has shown to be key to effective formative assessment. How will you deliver these to your learners?

4. How will you build feedback into your learning activities? How—and when—will you have students use it? And how can you help them transfer it for use in a related but different task?

5. The brain responds especially well to certain kinds of feedback. What are they? How will you incorporate these elements into your efforts?

6. Finally, without sufficient feedback, the brain doesn't have evidence to change its course, so it goes on reinforcing what's incorrect. How will you detect when a student's learning has gone off track? And how will you use feedback and evidence to bring it back on track?

Citations

Online, Media, and Print Resources for Teachers

della Chiesa, B. (2009). Beginning in the brain: Pioneering the field of educational neuroscience. *Usable Knowledge, Harvard University* (March). http://www.uknow.gse.harvard.edu/learning/LD322.html

Eisenberg, A. (2011, December 17). Making science leap from the page. *New York Times*. Retrieved from http://www.nytimes.com/2011/12/18/business/online-textbooks-aim-to-make-science-leap-from-the-page.html

References

Black, P., Harrison, C., Lee, C., Marshall, B., & Wiliam, D. (2002). *Working inside the black box: Assessment for learning in the classroom*. London: King's College.

Black, P., Harrison, C., Lee, C., Marshall, B., & Wiliam, D. (2003). *Assessment for learning: Putting it into practice*. Buckingham: Open University Press.

Black, P., & Wiliam, D. (1998). Inside the black box: Raising standards through classroom assessment. *Phi Delta Kappan, 80*(2), 139–148.

de Courcy, M. (2007). Disrupting preconceptions: Challenges to pre-service teachers' beliefs about ESL children. *Journal of Multilingual and Multicultural Development, 28*(3), 188–2013.

Driscoll, M. (2000). *Psychology of learning for instruction*. Boston: Allyn & Bacon.

Haskell, R. E. (2001). *Transfer of learning: Cognition, instruction, and reasoning*. San Diego: Academic Press.

Hattie, J. (2008). *Visible learning: A synthesis of over 800 meta-analyses relating to achievement*. New York: Routledge.

Hawkins, J., & Blakeslee, S. (2004). A new framework of intelligence. In *On intelligence* (pp. 85–105). New York: Times Books.

Howard-Jones, P., Pollard, A., Blakemore, S.-J., Rogers, P., Goswami, U., Butterworth, B., . . . Kaufmann, L. (2007). Neuroscience and education, issues and opportunities: A TLRP Commentary. http://www.tlrp.org/pub/documents/Neuroscience Commentary FINAL.pdf

Kandel, E. R., Schwartz, J. H., Jessell, T. M., Siegelbaum, S. A., & Hudspeth, A. J. (2013). *Principles of neural science* (5th ed.). New York: McGraw-Hill Medical.

Mackey, A. P., Whitaker, K. J., & Bunge, S. A. (2012, August 22). Experience-dependent plasticity in white matter microstructure: Reasoning training alters structural connectivity. *Front. Neuroanat.*

Marzano, R. J. (2003). *Classroom instruction that works*. Alexandria, VA: ASCD.

McDaniel, M. A., Agarwal, P. K., Huelser, B. J., McDermott, K. B., & Roediger, H. L. (2011). Test-enhanced learning in a middle school science classroom: The effects of quiz frequency and placement. *Journal of Educational Psychology, 103*(2), 399–414.

National Research Council. (2000a). 5. Mind and Brain. *How people learn: Brain, mind, experience, and school: Expanded edition* (pp. 114–128). Washington, DC: The National Academies Press.

National Research Council. (2000b). *How people learn: Brain, mind, experience, and school: Expanded edition*. Washington, DC: The National Academies Press.

OECD. (2007). Understanding the brain: The birth of a learning science. doi: 10.1787/9789264029132-en. Paris: OECD Publishing.

Rabinowitz, M. (Ed.). (1993). *Cognitive science foundations of instruction*. Hillsdale, NJ: Erlbaum.

Ready, D., & Wright, D. (2011). Accuracy and inaccuracy in teachers' perceptions of young children's cognitive abilities: The role of child background and classroom context. *American Educational Research Journal, 48*(2), 335–360.

Reif, F. (2008). *Applying cognitive science to education*. Cambridge, MA: MIT Press.

Rohrer, D., Taylor, K., & Sholar, B. (2010). Tests enhance the transfer of learning. *Journal of Experimental Psychology, 36*(1), 233–239.

Rosenthal, R., & Jacobson, L. (1968). *Pygmalion in the classroom*. New York: Holt, Rinehart and Winston.

Schunk, D. H. (2012). Cognition and instruction. In *Learning theories: An educational perspective* (pp. 278–323). Boston: Pearson.

Society for Neuroscience. (2008). *Brain facts: A primer on the brain and nervous system*. Washington, DC: Society for Neuroscience.

Tapia, J. (2004). Latino households and schooling: Economic and sociocultural factors affecting students' learning and academic performance. *International Journal of Qualitative Studies in Education, 17*(3), 415–436.

Sensitive Periods

CORE Guiding Principle 6 is continued: Sensitive periods are introduced. Scientists find different parts of the brain may be more ready to learn at certain times. We seem particularly able to learn specific types of knowledge, skills, and abilities during such stretches. The brain is making key changes and reorganization of associated components—so what does it all mean?

Learning Points

1. There appear to be at least some sensitive periods during brain development that may be particularly well suited to learning certain types of skills and knowledge.

2. Different parts of the brain may be ready to learn at different times, and these times may be age related.

3. A sensitive period is a time when we seem particularly able to learn certain types of knowledge, skills, and abilities, because the brain seems susceptible to making change and reorganization of associated components.

4. Suspected sensitive periods have been found for many areas, including vision, sensory enrichment, language, motor, and potentially emotional and social development.

5. During these key times, the brain uses certain types of external stimulations to establish and maintain long-term development of brain structures and functions involved in specific kinds of skills.

6. At these stages, the individual's experience and exposure to certain types of external stimulation—for instance, sound, visuals, touch, feel, and smell—may become an overriding factor, responsible for profound changes in how the brain develops.

7. Cognitive flexibility allows the developing brain to uniquely organize for the needs it finds around it. In sensitive periods, learning may happen faster and the shifts in outcomes become more prominent.

8. During sensitive periods, similar patterns are expected to be seen characteristically across many students and cultures, aligning with milestones in human development.

9. The idea of sensitive periods is both attention grabbing and a controversial topic for teachers. It raises important questions about curriculum development and subject-matter timing.

10. However, so little is known about how the human cognitive system responds during sensitive periods, many researchers believe the topic is not yet ready to contribute meaningfully to designing formal curriculum. Educators should be careful not to overinterpret early research, nor to accept claims too readily until more is known and established in the field.

Introduction

Mary, a young administrative assistant in San Francisco, was astonished to learn she had once spoken Swahili with ease. A native of India, her family had migrated to Kenya when she and her sister were young girls. Mary remembered briefly living in Africa but not many details about it. The family had later moved to England, and now she'd been living in the United States for several years. It wasn't until she saw some old home movies her father had made during their short time in Kenya that she heard herself, and her sister, speaking Swahili with local play-mates. As young children they had picked up the new language without any formal training. Mary had not only forgotten the language, she had forgotten she'd ever learned it.

Today, if Mary wanted to learn to speak another new language, it would not be as effort-less as when she was a child. Research has shown that very early exposure to language is particularly beneficial because the developing brain appears especially primed at that period to respond positively to language learning. The result of such early exposure is peak proficiency in learning many formal properties of language, such as grammar, syntax, rhythm, and accent (Newport, 2006; Newport, Bavelier, & Neville, 2001).

Scientists have long theorized the existence of particularly receptive periods during human development—certain windows of opportunity—in which our brains learn best. In 2000, the U.S. National Research Council (NRC) agreed that ample research shows some learning experiences most powerfully influence lasting brain development during specific times of our lives and declared that sensitive periods do exist.

This chapter brings us full circle to the discussion of plasticity that started in Chapter 2, but now with more background to consider it. Neuroscientists describe that when the effect of experience on a particular region or process of the brain is characteristically strong during a limited period for a particular kind of organism, this period is referred to as a *sensitive period*. Although sensitive periods are exhibited through behaviors, researchers say that behaviors actually arise from properties of how our neural circuits develop (Knudsen, 2004). Having times of heightened sensitivity to experience allows neural circuits to be especially malleable. This allows the brain to represent information in a way that is more adaptive for the individual organism.

Sensitive periods, then, represent a particular aspect of brain plasticity. A sensitive period is an age, or a span of time, when we seem particularly able to learn certain types of knowledge, skills, and abilities, because the brain is susceptible to making physical changes and reorganizing itself related to these traits. In this chapter, we explore a highly controversial topic: the role of sensitive periods in brain development. Scientists find different parts of the brain may be more ready to learn at certain times, although little is known definitively about what the implications may be, if any, for educators.

Sensitive periods seem to be a perfect topic for educators, but there are a few issues with introducing them. Much of the research that establishes the exact times and durations of sensitive periods has been completed in other organisms but not in humans. This helps prove the general concept and provides a great deal of information to scientists, but teachers are less interested in the firm evidence we have about how hearing develops in the barn owl or when songbirds learn their tunes. Instead, teachers want to know about the following:

- What are the specifics of sensitive periods discovered in human development?
- What stages are "sensitive" for children and teens, and specifically which behaviors, brain networks, and circuits are being adjusted?
- How much variation is seen across human populations?
- To what degree is this variation associated with a range of identified conditions?

Therefore, this chapter needs to start off by saying, given these questions, educators will be disappointed.

In the same sense that the combination of neuroscience, cognitive psychology, and educational research have informed each other in other parts of the book, research in human development and the yet limited human brain studies of confirmed sensitive periods would be needed here. We believe the research is currently too sparse for detailed answers. So, although some sources for educators may specify definite year spans and appear to make fairly detailed claims, we encourage teachers to establish a more global understanding of sensitive periods—what are they and why all the excitement in neuroscience? (See Figure 10.1.)

Sensitive Periods or Critical Periods?

It is worth a moment here to distinguish between the use of the term *sensitive periods* and that of a similar phrase, *critical periods*. Teachers will see both terms in the literature. These descriptions are sometimes used interchangeably, and sometimes are meant to carry distinct weight about the intensity of the period identified. However, because *critical periods* can imply to educators that if learning doesn't happen in a specific window it may be impossible to develop certain functions at other times, the use of the term *sensitive periods* may more aptly reflect current research indicating that different parts of the brain may be more ready to learn at these times. **(See CORE 6d.)**

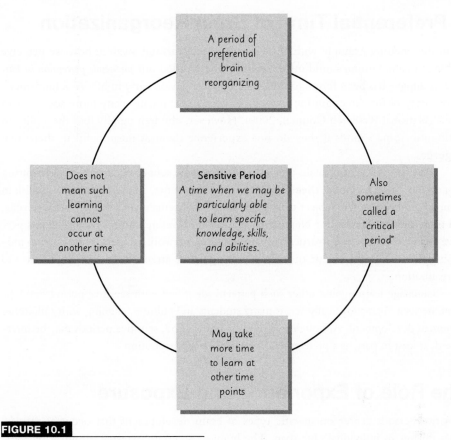

FIGURE 10.1

Aspects of Sensitive Periods

As the Organisation for Economic Co-operation and Development of Learning Sciences report explains (OECD, 2007, p. 30), if sensitive period learning does not occur during these "windows of opportunity," it does not always mean it cannot occur, but it may take more time and cognitive resources, and will often be less effective. **(See CORE 6f.)**

The suggested takeaway for teachers on these two terms then is that although *critical* or *essential* may denote too much, or be too strong a statement for them to employ, the *inclination* to learn in certain areas at certain times is sometimes being seen by scientists. For the purposes of not overstating claims, we will therefore refer in this book for educators to all such windows as *sensitive periods.* But we ask educators to refrain from interpreting this as intending to make a distinction between the two possibilities, or actually from the spectrum of possibilities. Rather, the use of a single term is a recognition that understanding remains limited at this time. So any distinctions, if they emerge as science moves forward, should be interpreted cautiously.

A Preferential Time of Brain Reorganization

As in the opening example with Mary's experience learning Swahili, how we perceive and organize incoming sound information—what's called our *phonemic perception in language learning*—has been found to involve a sensitive period early in life. As a fundamental property of human cognition, young children discriminate many more sounds than adults (National Research Council, 2000). However, children rapidly lose the ability to distinguish some sounds if they do not experience them as meaningful in their own languages.

This paring down of brain processing for language sounds occurs extensively during infancy and early childhood. **(See CORE 6e.)** At such times, connections may diminish in number and become less subject to change. Those that remain are stronger, more reliable, and more precise (Society for Neuroscience, 2008). Therefore, during what scientists perceive as a sensitive period, a particular brain function, network, or area of information processing or motor movement may be receiving extra attention for development and reorganization.

Language learning and other such patterns identified with sensitive period development are seen characteristically across many students and cultures, aligning with milestones in human development. Although not yet fully understood, sensitive periods may be interpreted, at least in part, as a preferential time of brain reorganization.

The Role of Experience and Exposure

Sensitive periods center on specific types of brain development that occur at specific times during an individual's life span. The brain uses certain external stimuli it receives, such as sound, visuals, touch, feel, smell, to establish and maintain long-term development of the structures and functions. At these stages, the individual's experience and exposure may become an overriding factor responsible for profound changes in how the brain develops.

Suspected sensitive periods for the human cognitive system have been suggested for many areas of brain development, most notably vision, auditory sensory enrichment, language, motor, and emotional development. **(See CORE 6g.)** Examples are shown in Table 10.1, which outlines some important examples of potential sensitive periods. As a set of examples, we believe these are useful to describe the general direction of sensitive period research for teachers. We do not go into more depth here because there remains a lack of consensus and limited research to connect the widely distributed neuroscience findings over many parts of the brain and types of learning with the field of human development.

Continuing with the classic example of language acquisition, in the first years of life, infants and toddlers are especially attracted to processing language and forming sounds that are meaningful in the native, or characteristic, communication surrounding them. To picture this example concretely, imagine the "r" sound and the "l" sound in the English language. Both sounds are prevalent in many English words and phrases, but such sound distinctions are not typically encountered by native Japanese children and many other speakers of Asian languages. (National Research Council, 2000, pp. 10–11). By frequently hearing such differences over time, the National Research Council points out, English speakers naturally retain the sound distinctions, but less is retained by Japanese speakers because the sounds are not employed as much in their language. Sensory processing of the sound when not experienced early in life is also less easily recouped later in life.

Similar examples for other sounds and phonemic combinations abound throughout language; this particular example serves merely to illustrate a general principle of the brain: What gets used repeatedly in everyday life and is encountered throughout frequent experience receives investments in cognitive resources. By contrast, what appears less meaningful is downplayed.

Cognitive flexibility allows the developing brain to uniquely organize for the needs it finds around it. Especially in the early childhood and school-age years, this is a key aspect of

TABLE 10.1 Some Examples of Potential Sensitive Periods

Area	Example
Language Acquisition	In the first years of life, infants and toddlers are especially receptive to processing language and forming sounds meaningful in the native communication surrounding them. Somewhat separate development windows may be associated with different types of language processing, including phonic articulation, syntax, grammar, and even vocabulary development.
Auditory Processing and Sensory Enrichment	Sounds in a child's early environment influence the structural development and response of the auditory cortex. For instance, ubiquitous noise can be problematic at early ages, whereas meaningful audio patterns may influence future brain perception, such as becoming increasingly able to perceive fine distinctions following repeated exposure or sensory enrichment.
Vision	Neural development for vision is strongly influenced in early childhood. Babies born with cataracts recover sight better when treated earlier as compared to later, as brain networks form differently in the absence of working vision. More complex processes such as developing skill in 3D visualization and spatial orientation may be associated with experience in later years, such as middle school.

(Continued)

TABLE 10.1 *(Continued)*

Parental Bonding and Imprinting	Emotionally related factors, such as recognition and bonding to parents and siblings, known as *neural imprinting*, is sensitive to early connections.
Orienting Attention	Orienting networks appear in infancy and early childhood, whereas the executive attention network begins to develop later, notably from ages 2 to 7. Both networks function better when exposed to experiences and teaching.
Motor Skills	Cerebellum and motor cortex development for large motor skills—walking, navigating objects, engaging in active play—is a focus of early childhood years. This is often followed by both increased skill acquisition and refinement of fine motor skills. The role of exposure, stimuli, and practice in relation to age for motor skill development is an area of research interest.
Self-Regulation	Self-regulation increases in childhood and is associated with goal attainment and life skills; scholars are studying whether intervention benefits only limited periods or acts more generally.
Social Behavior	Some scholars postulate sensitive periods for social development, with children from about 3 to 6 years closely observing expected behavior of individuals, followed by modeling, consolidation, and practice of observed traits. This is followed in later childhood and early adolescence with observation of larger groups at work and play, such as peers, pairs, and teams, followed by increased interaction and social development in group contexts.
Second-Language Acquisition	Children at pre-puberty ages often have been found to achieve more fluency than older learners during acquisition of a second language, a process especially sensitive for expressive practices such as pronunciation and formation of proper syntax.
Executive Function	Planning, goal formation, and engaging in some other executive processes often matures in adolescent and young adult years; scholars are interested in the role of experience, observation, and opportunity on outcomes at strategic times.
Risk Taking, Moral Development, Empathy, Decision Making	Some developmental aspects may also mediate other human behaviors at key times, including risk assessment, moral development, empathy, and the tendency to feelings and behaviors of social belonging.

our human intellect. Sensitive periods operate to meet brain needs. Brain reorganization through learning attempts to build the "best brain" for its day and time. In sensitive periods, learning may happen faster and the shifts in outcomes become more prominent.

As was stated previously and will be brought up again and again because it is such an important point for teachers to remember, in this book, the term *learning* refers both to informal learning through exposure to experience/stimuli *and* formal school learning, as shown in Figure 10.2. In some cases, human society intentionally tries to structure learning, such as in schools, sports teams, and work situations. But the human cognitive system is also very adept at picking up knowledge from all kinds of experiences that have nothing to do with formal lessons. These informal experiences often come to the fore in the discussion of sensitive periods. It is almost as if our minds may be seeking out what they need, to the best of their ability, to nurture a time of the naturally developing brain.

To continue with examples in Table 10.1, neural development for vision also is strongly influenced in early childhood. Babies born with cataracts, a congenital clouding of the lens present at birth, recover their sight better if treated earlier as compared to later. Although the eye itself responds similarly in both cases, the brain networks form differently when working vision is absent for a longer span of time.

Much as with the language processing example, brain development in part depends on what stimulation is presented to the learner. As shown in Table 10.1, sensitive periods focus not only on sensory and motor skill development but also may potentially involve a wide range of human behaviors. From bonding with parents and siblings to social development with others, some characteristic patterns of learning in response to exposure may take place during specific age spans. Children from about 3 to 6 years, for example, are often seen to closely observe the expected behavior of their friends and

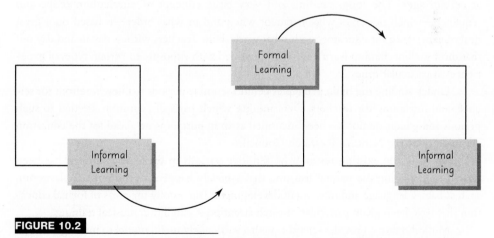

FIGURE 10.2

Two Ways to Learn. Formal learning such as in school lessons and informal learning such as during play, interaction, and conversation at home can contribute to brain reorganization during sensitive periods, as is true at other times.

the older children around them, followed by taking part in modeling—or acting out—what they have seen. They practice the observed traits and consolidate their understanding of individual behavior. Later in childhood and early adolescence, the same young people may spend extensive time observing larger groups at work and play. In pairs, triplets, groups, and teams, they strive to increase interaction and extend social development at these times—the bane of middle school, perhaps, but also the core of social connectedness.

Language, vision, and social development also illustrate another interesting property of some sensitive periods: There may a series of different windows most receptive to varying aspects of skill development. With language, for example, there appears to be somewhat separate windows associated with phonic articulation, syntax, grammar, and even vocabulary development. For vision, more complex processes such as 3D visualization and spatial orientation may be related to exposure in later years, such as during middle school. Opportunities to learn may be suited to mastery as students gain both a larger knowledge base and a better working understanding of the world around them.

Early Musical Training and the Brain: An Example

This idea of sensitive periods existing in learning certainly does not seem surprising to many educators. They have long known that children seem ready to learn certain skills more easily at certain ages. The long-standing and very basic concept of curriculum scope and sequence—which describes what is taught when and in what order—is based on a great deal of experience for educators with what works best. Teachers witness day in and day out that most students tend to learn best when provided with exposure to certain types of experiences at particular times.

Understanding the brain principles behind sensitive periods is a new forefront for science, and intriguing for teachers. Determining which parts of cognition are tied to such periods and which are not has been identified as an important issue ahead for the education community by the National Research Council.

Much of the existing research on sensitive periods in brain development has been related to exploring the natural learning that typically happens outside of the classroom, such as babies' language and movement development. But among the areas of formal education that have been given particular research attention is childhood musical training.

Musical training provides scientists with a particularly useful model to investigate sensitive period effects on brain development. Clearly, young children can learn to play a musical instrument. One important question is whether this early training has greater effects on brain structure than training later in life. In other words, is there a window of opportunity that is especially beneficial to becoming an accomplished musician? A least one study had provided evidence that there is.

A number of studies have shown that early musical training is related to greater amounts of white matter in the brain. White matter is needed for efficient communication within the brain. One key question, however, is: Do highly accomplished musicians—for example, the likes of child musical prodigies such as Yo Yo Ma and Pablo Casals—benefit from such a structural brain change specifically because of early training, or because by beginning training when they were young children lengthened their total training time?

A 2012 study by a Canadian and German team led by researcher Christopher J. Steele sought to examine this issue and concluded that evidence exists to support the claim that early musical training may lead to changes that endure and are long-lasting in both behavior and brain. Using brain imaging, the authors examined the bundle of nerve fibers called the *corpus callosum* that links the two cerebral hemispheres. Playing a musical instrument typically requires the coordinated action of the two hands, an action mediated by this part of the brain. This allowed the researchers to measure not only the amount of white matter in the brain but also whether it was organized differently in musicians who learned to play instruments when they were very young and those whose training came later in the life. By matching for the years of training and experience, they found that the musicians who trained as young children had greater connectivity. The authors proposed that training before the age of 7 years results in changes in white-matter connectivity. This may serve as a scaffold on which subsequent experiences build, concluded the authors (Steele, Bailey, Zatorre, & Penhune, 2013).

Childhood music lessons may also have long-lasting brain benefits even for those who never follow through with their early training. A 2013 study by neuroscientists published in *The Journal of Neuroscience* found that older adults who took music lessons as children could process the sounds of speech faster than older adults who did not. This finding is a key benefit because typical decline in nervous system function with age can result in difficulty understanding speech, especially in challenging listening environments. The researchers suggested that the stage for interaction with sound may be influenced by early musical training. The result is sharpened neural processing in central auditory nuclei. Gains may be sustained well into older age, said the authors. The study group consisted of adults who had some music training (4 to 14 years) early in life, but who had not played an instrument for decades (White-Schwoch, Woodruff Carr, Anderson, Strait, & Kraus, 2013). Not all types of learning have shown such clear relationships with time periods, but as these musical training studies indicate, for those that do, exposure to appropriate stimuli may influence learning outcomes and may permanently help to enhance cognitive or sensory capacity.

Thus, a better understanding of human sensitive periods and when learning occurs is considered a crucial avenue for future brain research, and it is expected that more age-related periods of human cognitive development may be discovered.

Research Frontiers in Sensitive Periods

Already one new research frontier into sensitive periods has been opened up by findings that substantial brain development related to large phases of synaptic pruning continues throughout the school-age years and into the early 20s, as discussed in Chapter 2. Because such pruning depends on similar mechanisms of brain reorganization as are found in the early years during sensitive periods, some scientists suspect sensitive periods may be present in adolescence and later life as well. **(See CORE 6h.)** This may include some types of higher-order reasoning, emotional sense making, and decision making. Goal planning framed in adult terms may fall into this category. So, the concept of sensitive periods in later-age brain development is becoming a topic of active research interest as well as in the early years.

Another example focuses on research into learning algebra. Neuroscience findings indicate many teens learning algebra may draw on, or activate, different areas of the brain than do adults. The reasoning goes that this might imply a stretch of time-specific reorganization, between early adolescence and adulthood (Luna, 2004; Qin et al., 2004). The difference may involve different memory processes, or long-term storage approaches, which may be undergoing a specific time of active reorganization. How the degree to which any brain reorganization taking place is influenced by specific exposure to quantitative reasoning at key times is not yet understood. Someday the prospects of understanding important brain change may be on the horizon, but not yet.

Teachers may hear that fields such as epigenetics also are bringing new ideas to the forefront. Epigenetic research examines the interplay of genes and environment with age. The intriguing notion that environmental exposures may have effects on how our genes actually work is a finding of epigenetics. Researchers in the field point out that there may be age-related phases in sensitivity to the environment. It appears, then, that our very genes themselves may be "sensitive." In some cases, they may swing into operation differently depending on what we are exposed to at key times.

How Early Can Students Begin to Learn about the Brain?

Teachers sometimes wonder if there is a special time when students are particularly receptive to learning about the function of their own brains. Brain research cannot yet answer that question, but inspiring stories abound. Ben Carson, Director of Pediatric Neurosurgery at Johns Hopkins University, reports when he first became enamored of brain science (Carson, 2010).

Raised in poverty, Carson was struggling in elementary school. At about age 10, he learned his brain was made to plan, strategize, and exercise control over his environment. Is that a fact? he pondered. He began to read book after book about science. Not even 2 years later, he rose from the bottom of his class to the top.

"This academic transformation was so dramatic that one might have suspected a brain transplant if such a thing were possible," he joked for a profile in *Parade Magazine*. "The actual change occurred in my self-perception and my expectations. I had gone from victim to master planner."

A Caution on Overinterpreting Findings

As noted previously in this chapter, the concept of sensitive periods can be both tantalizing and somewhat disconcerting for educators and parents alike. Who wouldn't wish to capitalize on potential benefits of sensitive period development? But at the same time, who wouldn't worry about the possibility of missing a learning window associated with a particularly desirable skill or behavior?

The key point to remember is that while scientists in the United States and in a number of other countries are actively working to understand the mechanisms and implications of brain development related to sensitive periods, such research remains in its infancy. With so little known about how the human cognitive system responds during sensitive periods, teachers are broadly cautioned. They may be justifiably interested in the new findings, which are fascinating, but educators should be careful not to overinterpret early research, nor accept claims too readily until much more is known and established in the field.

Jumping to conclusions will not be helpful for students, say policy makers in the United Kingdom Learning Sciences report, some of whom urge extreme caution in addressing sensitive period research at this stage (Howard-Jones et al., 2007). For example, researchers in the field are concerned it may create too great a sense of "now or never" that is incorrect. If learning does not occur during some identified windows of opportunity, scientists say, it does not always mean it cannot occur. It might take more time and employ more cognitive resources, and perhaps be less effective, but too little is known yet to gauge this. Many sensitive periods, the researchers state, may be best thought of as rather subtle differences in the brain's ability to be shaped by the external environment.

 RESOURCE

K–12 teachers can use with students: Howard-Jones et al., 2007, p. 4. (See the Citations list at the end of the chapter.)

Furthermore, the U.K. report describes, sensitive periods may not directly apply to classroom-based learning. To date, windows of opportunity have been primarily identified for basic sensory, movement, or memory function. The U.K. report authors argue these are commonly shaped naturally by the environment in everyday or informal learning—in the home, the playground, with our families and friends, and so on. Thus, they may apply less to school learning and the intentional instruction designed by teachers. However, this distinction between formal and informal learning in regard to sensitive periods is not well understood, and remains a topic of speculation rather than much evidence. The U.K. report describes how research on sensitive periods, although fascinating, is not yet ready to contribute meaningfully to designing formal curriculum (Howard-Jones et al., 2007, p. 4).

Thus, putting into practice the application of knowledge too soon may be problematic—it's not wrong, it's just that we don't know enough yet. Many teacher resources tend to agree that educators should be at least aware of this aspect of human learning. Minimally they should understand at least the fundamental concept and the research trends. Today's teachers must expect to see much more of this research appear over the course of their careers. And, as professionals in their subject matter and grade-level areas, they will be expected to stay current about developmentally appropriate learning, including potentially sensitive periods.

Furthermore, no matter what happens with the research, teachers, curriculum developers, policy makers, and other educators working in teaching and learning undoubtedly will be faced with many new products offered to schools. These may be based more and less soundly on brain findings. Marketing efforts simply adding "neuro" in the name, or including other superficial inclusion, are not enough for school adoption, of course.

Sensitive or Deprived?

The discussion in this chapter has focused on brain functioning under healthy conditions. Development delays, specific language impairment, autism, and other conditions will not be discussed here, although some research has begun to indicate sensitive periods may be involved. For instance, very recent research on the brain region of the cerebellum has suggested that sensitive-period disruption of internal brain communication may contribute to some of autism's key features. In general, scientists have found in the study of many organisms that injury or distraction during sensitive periods can have more significant impacts than the same injury or deprivation at other times. This is believed due to greater plasticity of the circuits being developed at these times (Society for Neuroscience, 2008).

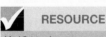

RESOURCE

K–12 teachers can use with students: brainfacts .org, 2012. (See the Citations list at the end of this chapter.)

Finally, disease, injury, or disruption of healthy conditions may influence development by different mechanisms. **(See CORE 6i.)** Any specific injury is not a normal, expected part of human development. Scientists believe that most severe cognitive declines throughout the age span, whether in youngsters or well into old age, reflect disease, impaired development, or injury processes. They are not a normal part of correctly working developmental processes.

Conclusion

To recap, the provocative nature of research findings on sensitive periods is apparent. Teachers wonder if findings on sensitive periods will reveal a better way of teaching, or if they should teach reading, art, math, second language or some other subject or topic earlier or later. Is fifth grade, say, the pivotal time for a particular educational standard to be met, or perhaps not until high school? We can't know what we don't yet know. And we can't know what will change in neuroscience understanding. Such an active area is bound to yield fascinating results, but what we can conclude so far remains sparse but potentially interesting for educators to watch.

As one teacher educator described it, her experience was that most teachers have a hard time not trying to "optimize" on the research they see emerging on sensitive periods of development. She helps teachers understand that findings are rapidly appearing, and need to be couched in sufficient evidence. After all, this is how the human brain works generally. We often weigh what is known and then come to conclusions. With regard to the evidence around sensitive periods, it is growing but it should not be overinterpreted. The human brain has remarkable resilience and capacity to learn.

Closing Scenario

Putting New Knowledge to Use

Sensitive Periods

A district staff meeting has been called in your region to brainstorm improvements to the curriculum. There has recently been a lot of news and discussion about sensitive periods for learning. Your breakout group is asked to consider whether the teaching of various subject-matter areas should be aligned with specific age groups based on the when the brain is more prepared to learn certain subjects.

1. To make sure everyone in the group is on the same page, how would you define a sensitive period in brain development?

2. In what areas have researchers found, or suspect, that sensitive periods for brain development exist?

3. What kinds of stimulation have been shown to trigger the brain at these windows of opportunity?

4. What are some examples of age-related learning that might be associated with sensitive periods for long-lasting brain development?

5. Sensitive periods are intriguing, but should we really try to align what and when we teach something based on what we know now? What cautions should be foremost in your report back to the group?

6. How would you summarize the pros and cons of future discussions on how to address the issue of linking sensitive periods for the brain with curriculum development and subject matter teaching?

Citations

Online, Media, and Print Resources for Teachers

brainfacts.org. (2012). Critical periods in early life. *Brain development.* http://www.brainfacts.org/Brain-Basics/Brain-Development/Articles/2012/Critical-Periods-in-Early-Life

Howard-Jones, P., Pollard, A., Blakemore, S.-J., Rogers, P., Goswami, U., Butterworth, B., . . . Kaufmann, L. (2007). Neuroscience and education, issues and opportunities: A TLRP commentary. http://www.tlrp.org/pub/documents/Neuroscience Commentary FINAL.pdf

References

Carson, B. S., Sr. (2010). *Cerebrum 2010: Emerging ideas in brain science.* New York: Dana Press.

Knudsen, E. (2004). Sensitive periods in the development of the brain and behavior. *Journal of Cognitive Neuroscience, 16*(8), 1412–1425.

Luna, B. (2004). Algebra and the adolescent brain. *Trends in Cognitive Sciences, 8,* 437–439.

National Research Council. (2000). 5. Mind and brain. *How people learn: Brain, mind, experience, and school: Expanded edition* (pp. 114–128). Washington, DC: The National Academies Press.

Newport, E. L. (2006). Critical periods in language development. *Encyclopedia of cognitive science: Wiley Online Library.* Retrieved from http://onlinelibrary.wiley.com/doi/10.1002/0470018860.s00506/full

Newport, E. L., Bavelier, D., & Neville, H. J. (2001). Critical thinking about critical periods: Perspectives on a critical period for language acquisition. In E. Dupoux (Ed.), *Language, brain and cognitive development: Essays in honor of Jacques Mehler.* Cambridge, MA: MIT Press.

OECD. (2007). Understanding the brain: The birth of a learning science. doi: 10.1787/9789264029132-en: OECD Publishing.

Qin, Y., Carter, C. S., Silk, E. M., Stenger, V. A., Fissell, K., Goode, A., & Andersen, J. R. (2004). The change of the brain activation patterns as children learn algebra equation solving. *Proceedings of the National Academy of Sciences of the United States of America, 101*, 5686–5691.

Society for Neuroscience. (2008). *Brain facts: A Primer on the brain and nervous system*. Washington, DC: Society for Neuroscience.

Steele, C. J., Bailey, J. A., Zatorre, R. J., & Penhune, V. B. (2013). Early musical training and white-matter plasticity in the corpus callosum: Evidence for a sensitive period. *The Journal of Neuroscience, 33*(3), 1282–1290.

White-Schwoch, T., Woodruff Carr, K., Anderson, S., Strait, D. L., & Kraus, N. (2013). Older adults benefit from music training early in life: Biological evidence for long-term training-driven plasticity. *The Journal of Neuroscience, 33*(45), 17667–17674.

11

Insights across the Curriculum

The CORE Guiding Principles are applied in specific subject-matter areas. What do we know about the brain in quantitative reasoning? In language and literacy? In reasoning and some aspects of creative expression? This chapter provides quick glances at big topics, preparing teachers to take the next steps.

Learning Points

1. Cognitive neuroscience organizes brain research into specific types of information processing rather than through subject-matter areas, as teachers often do.

2. Scientists are not equipped directly to provide instructions to K–12 teachers in how to apply brain science knowledge. Therefore, educators, cognitive scientists, and others vested in K–12 teaching and learning are called on to work together to understand important fundamental findings and to make the connection to teaching and learning research.

3. Approaching mathematics from the way the brain functions means considering how the brain interprets quantitative information and draws inferences from it.

4. Math, as well as other subject-matter areas, recruits broadly across the brain. Different areas of the brain are activated for different functions. Certain areas tend to be activated for digits, others for when numbers are spelled out as words. Some areas activate for comparison, others for error assessment and correction.

5. Hard-won math facts and important quantitative problem solving fade quickly when meaningful connections are not made, when relevant ways to use the information are not presented, or when emotional and attitudinal barriers get in the way.

6. At least four separate brain areas specialize in parsing language: hearing words, seeing them, speaking them, and generating them. Learning scientists consider these as different "meta-skills" that are now beginning to be reflected in aspects of the way language is taught and assessed.

7. To the brain, writing is in a sense a type of augmented memory system. Story and narrative are seen by the brain as a type of evidence, or "social proof," that reflects on experiences that have been valuable or compelling to others.

8. By using hypothesis generation in science inquiry and other areas, learners are working as their brains do. They acquire concepts and activate cognition by setting forth tentative ideas about attributes involved and then testing them.

9. Social studies education offers an opportunity to help the brain draw effectively on multiple perspectives. By transferring thinking and using it in the real world, learners build knowledge structures that are more nuanced and flexible so they can better represent complex situations.

10. Through creating and appreciating human expression, such as in the arts, students share thoughts and feelings, and perceive those of others, in a variety of sensory experiences for the brain. Among many positive attributes of the arts in education, effective shifting of viewpoint can help us avoid pitfalls of brain habituation.

Introduction

Janet Dubinsky, winner of the 2009 Science Educator Award of the Society for Neuroscience, described how important she finds sharing neuroscience with teachers from kindergarten through 12th grade. Teachers already perceive a need to know how the brain works to become better professionals, she said, and they are making demands to be included in both the background knowledge and the evolving conversation (Dubinsky, 2010). It is a matter of teacher professionalism, she believes.

Dubinsky describes how teacher demand to understand neuroscience has generated an explosion of conferences, educational products, and training opportunities. Although the plethora of options all broadly claim to be based on neuroscience, Dubinsky, a neuroscientist herself, finds a wide range in the mix. Some conferences or presentations share important findings but may overly tweak their work toward marketing unproven or even somewhat dubious products, causing the experience to backfire as educators struggle to discern the chaff from the wheat. Others lecture to spread accepted scientific knowledge and peer-reviewed studies but don't make a connection to teaching. They fail to answer teacher questions, she said, or neglect modeling specific strategies for the classroom. This is unhelpful in a whole different way—teachers tend to dismiss the knowledge as irrelevant. They are thwarted in seeing a connection.

According to Dubinsky, neuroscientists and cognitive psychologists don't know enough about the specifics of kindergarten to high school teaching to create concrete applications of learning science for these ages. Nor do they know enough about this age group to model teaching approaches appropriate much below university level, even when brain science findings are available that might apply or be helpful.

Not surprising, then, providing teachers with practice in applying brain science knowledge in their specific areas often is a key missing element of neuroscience and cognitive science education for many teachers, Dubinsky points out. Thus, educators themselves must provide the missing link, she says. They hold the expertise that is needed to make the connection to teaching and learning research and practice as discussed in Chapter 1.

The term *applying* in this chapter means helping educators think through how fundamental brain research interacts with their grade-level efforts and content-matter areas, as covered in the CORE and described in the preceding chapters. Here, no new guiding principles of the CORE are introduced. Rather, the many Big Ideas of the prior chapters provide a "'thought whiteboard." These explore connections in specific subject-matter areas.

As a recap, Chapter 10 completed the initial presentation of CORE concepts in this book. As of that chapter, all the guiding principles and Big Ideas introduced in Chapter 1 have been explored. Each received some opportunity for context and background in Chapters 2 through 10. This and the next chapter do not introduce any additional "brain facts" or new CORE ideas for teachers to know. Rather, they provide an opportunity for application, consolidation, and reflection of the CORE ideas already presented. This chapter explores some insights across the curriculum. Organized in three sections, it asks: Are there ways to think about CORE ideas that might impact specific subject-matter areas? Chapter 12 continues from this to explore larger actions teachers might take: Are there any sum-up actions that teachers and educators may wish to take together as they ponder deploying more understanding of CORE concepts in their schools and communities?

A common request from instructors is to provide more modeling for many of the strategies mentioned in this chapter, including specific instructions and prototypes that can be applied directly in the classroom. This is not done for two reasons. First, it would turn this chapter into a book all by itself. Second, the point is to illustrate some of many *connections* that can be made between CORE ideas and ways teachers already know that students learn.

Teachers provide these teachable connections. By intention, most, if not all, of the strategies discussed here are already well described in both educational research and in teacher handbooks and professional development materials. The point of assembling some illustrations here across subject-matter areas juxtaposed with the CORE is not to describe novel strategies or offer entirely new components of instructional design. Rather, the intent is to ponder the learning sciences as a way of confirming and enhancing best practice. Of course new findings will point to new directions, and teachers will respond with enthusiasm to new ideas, but this chapter is specifically not about a new tool belt for teachers. Certainly, many other strategies could have been selected and described. That said, noneducators may find additional resources on instructional methodology helpful if they encounter an unfamiliar topic here.

The way in which cognitive neuroscience organizes brain research into specific types of information processing is somewhat different from how teachers think of their subject-matter areas. This causes challenges as the fields of neuroscience, psychology, and education begin to work together more.

The brain, for example, has a visual cortex, not a reading cortex. School learning doesn't always match up neatly with the research agenda. Ways of thinking and knowing (Griffin, McGaw, & Care, 2012) that the brain employs in its work often cut across traditional school subjects. This chapter explores some topics in quantitative thinking, language and literacy, and reasoning across subjects.

Curriculum for the Classroom

Teachers want curriculum they can take into their own classrooms. As more knowledge emerges, teachers can expect more resources to be available in their focal disciplines. Two resources that have proved valuable more generally are:

- The Annenberg Learner online resource, "Neuroscience the Classroom: Making Connections" provides modules that contain a unit that discusses implications of brain science for schools (Annenberg Learner, 2012). "I've found it to be very helpful in discussing neuroscience implications for pre-service teachers," said one instructor who works with new teachers.

  RESOURCE

  K–12 teachers can use with students: Annenberg Learner, 2012. (See the Citations list at the end of this chapter.)

  Modules are created from the work of Mary Helen Immodino-Yang at the University of Southern California's Brain and Creativity Institute and her colleagues Kurt Fischer, director of the Mind, Brain and Education Program at Harvard University, and Matthew H. Schneps of the Smithsonian Institution. Whether it is figuring how to give students more choice to improve the relevance to them of what they are learning, or teaching students positive self-talk to reduce the physiological stress of test anxiety, Immodino-Yang and her colleagues have ideas for teachers.
- BrainU, launched by Professor Janet Dubinsky of the University of Minnesota, shows teachers how to use ideas from neuroscience to enrich their teaching. The project focuses on an inquiry pedagogy for teachers and provides many resources available online. The BrainU website section on neuroscience concepts

RESOURCE

K–12 teachers can use with students: BrainU, 2014. (See the Citations list at the end of this chapter.)

and activities is organized by grades: PreK–3, 4–6, 7–8, and 9–12. BrainU includes a series of teacher professional development workshops, along with associated "Explain Your Brain" resources for exhibit hall and class activities, and a "Brain Trunk" of neuroscience resource materials for the classroom. BrainU also includes a forum for teacher questions, "Ask a Neuroscientist." Overlapping educational experts with neuroscientists, BrainU is a joint project of the University of Minnesota Department of Neuroscience and its Department of Curriculum and Instruction.

Quantitative Thinking in the Brain

To no one's great surprise, the Organisation for Economic Co-operation and Development Learning Sciences report describes mathematics and quantitative thinking as essential learning for every student (OECD, 2007). Many mathematics educators working in K–12 education ask questions such as: How is fluency for two-digit multiplication achieved? and At what ages are children "brain ready" to work with mathematical justification that culminates later in more formal kinds of proof? (Lee, 2005; National Council of Teachers of Mathematics, 2007).

A more fundamental unit is required even to start the conversation: the concept of quantity. Therefore, quantitative thinking—not how to teach arithmetic or geometry—is the topic of this section. As cognitive scientist Michael Posner points out, to think in terms of brain processing, we need to take a step back (Posner & Rothbart, 2007). The question we will ask is: How does the brain interpret quantitative information and draw inferences from it? Inferences then may be used in such areas as number recognition, mathematical operations, and problem solving. Key numeracy ideas include both how the brain learns math and how it uses mathematical concepts and skills.

Harvard Professor Susan Carey, author of *Conceptual Change in Childhood*, describes mathematical computation as a ubiquitous talent across the animal kingdom. Bats interpret mathematical frequencies bounced back by biosonar. Honey bees navigate via rays of polarized light. Electric fish detect the absence or presence of pulses. In fact, Carey says, it would be extremely surprising to find any animal lacking computation in its arsenal. She describes quantity and ways to interpret it as marvelous specializations that illustrate an organism's neural machinery for computational tasks (Carey, 2001, 2008).

Unlike bats and other species, humans get more formal with their math. Bees use innate computation to find their ways back to the hive; human toddlers use it to take steps and not fall. But after those first wobbly steps, humans take more ambitious cognitive strides and use computations to build bridges to span rivers, taking into account the forces of high winds and determining maximum loads. It is all computation.

We can marvel at the astonishing beauty of patterns, proofs, and problem solving. That so much of our world obeys mathematical principles is "stinkin' amazing," as one middle school student put it. We have access not only to tools of mathematical computation in the brain but also to the conscious meaning we make when drawing from it. We can use it—and we can understand it.

Not unlike the honey bees tuning into their polarized coordinates, we also engage naturally and often less than consciously in many quantitative processes in the brain. We may not give them a moment's notice but we engage in mathematical inquiry constantly to draw on number, direction, duration, measures, interval, and order. We employ decision-making calculations and case-based reasoning—even each one of our very movements is composed of detailed math. So, yes, our brain uses math all the time. We could not function without it.

This is a terrific example of teachers using brain science to help students understand how they learn. For the student who says he or she is bad at math, one reply that teachers may make is, "Well, your brain is very good at math, and here's how."

▧ ‖ Following Cognitive Hunches

Human perception and reasoning, in fact, are "shot through" with rules of thumb, short-cuts, confabulations, and less than well-proven assumptions, says philosopher Patricia S. Churchland, emerita professor at University of California, San Diego, and coauthors (Churchland, Farber, & Peterman, 2001). These authors describe how cognitive systems are ill-suited to detect all possibility of error in our thinking. Our brains as machines are not "truth preserving" or fully precise in the formal mathematical sense. We are willing to follow a hunch.

This often makes us well designed for fast and adaptable action based on partial knowledge. Humans use incomplete information remarkably well, considering the challenges. So in this sense, we work naturally with probability and possibility, not certainty.

Humans start on the development of their quantitative thinking early. Even in infancy, we distinguish different numerical values of objects. Babies detect the difference between zero and one, one from two, and two from many. Numerous so-called "habituation" studies, which get us used to something and then note whether we can tell the difference when it changes, reveal that babies show surprise when they have learned to expect one object hidden behind a screen but find two or more. Such studies show at a very early age we have both a concept of object and quantity.

Not all human languages across the world specifically have a counting sequence for numbers. A Brazilian tribe, the Pirahã, does not define numbers above two—after that, it is "many," which no doubt many schoolchildren first learning their numbers could appreciate. Yet scientists find "numerical concept" is

RESOURCE

K–12 teachers can use with students: Biever, 2004. (See the Citations list at the end of this chapter.)

foundational across cultures. In the absence of counting numbers, relative words and sounds stand in and express quantity, such as "one," "another," "few," and, of course, "many" (Carey, 2001, 2008).

The idea of a symbolic number, such as a digit or symbol, being connected to represent a given quantity also arises fairly early. Preschoolers often can begin to make this association. Even monkeys can be trained to relate specific digits to the size of an award— for instance, "asking" for more grapes by plunking a lever with the larger number on it. Even when the levers swap places, monkeys seeking the fruit will continue to choose the largest digit available, say 6 over 4. This shows they can appreciate the concept of quantity and they also can associate a larger or smaller amount with a different symbol (Posner & Rothbart, 2007).

This association of quantity and symbol takes quite a bit of training, whether for monkeys or for human children. A year or more of training may pass before the concept of number, including this idea of order, is established. And even recognizing that a number is more or less than another does not mean we can reel off a whole sequence in order, or that we can make fast and accurate comparisons within the sequence, such as operating on it to generate new quantities. Teachers know that figuring out sums or differences takes time and effort for children to master.

▮▮ Our Mental Number Line

For humans, the idea of sequence or ordering of quantity is believed to employ cognitive representations. We consult what scientists call our mental "number line" when we do our figuring. This is a one-dimensional, analog map of quantity we hold in our heads. Such number lines offer some useful mathematical properties. They are *ordinal*—in other words, they represent an increasing order in one direction and a decreasing in the other. They also are *interval*—which means we interpret there to be a fixed unit along the same distance of the line, no matter where it occurs. In other words, an inch is an inch is an inch. The length of an inch doesn't vary depending on where it occurs in the line.

Number lines of this type are consistent. They give us a quick, visual way to estimate difference by using distance. Our brains work well with this, but the system does have some curious artifacts. For instance, brain studies reveal that the closer two numbers are to each other, the harder it is for youngsters to distinguish if one number is higher or lower than the other. In other words, it may take a child longer to answer whether 5 is above or below 4 as compared to 2.

To a child's mind, 2 is so clearly below 5 that it is easy to place. He or she will have to think a little harder for 4 (see Figure 11.1). Older children and adults may not need to resort to their number line calculators, however. They may have encountered these quantities so often they have memorized them. They don't risk making a mistake in their mental imagery.

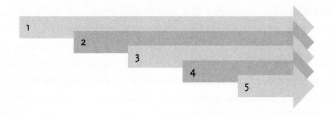

FIGURE 11.1

A Visual Number Line

To a child's mind, 2 is so clearly distant from 5 that it is easy to place. He or she may have to think harder for 4, which is closer to 5.

Even without formal mathematics training, children will convert pattern to a meaningful quantity. They will readily recognize five objects as more than four, for instance, or be able to group dots into consistent groupings.

Given all this math ability of the brain, educators often want to know where exactly in the brain all this simple math is taking place. But it isn't simple at all. Posner describes how first the vision centers are activated when a number is displayed. Interestingly, the area activated for digits is different from the area activated for numbers spelled out as words. Another quite different part of the brain activates for comparison, and yet another for error assessment and correction. So, what we think of as "math" recruits broadly across the brain, and calls for a variety of distinct sets of information processing.

Why does this matter to teachers? For many teachers, especially in elementary school where they are responsible for many subjects and not just mathematics, it helps them understand the need to specifically establish different kinds of quantitative reasoning for the brain.

The syndrome of *dyscalculia* is a learning disability in arithmetic (Howard-Jones et al., 2007). Progress is being made in understanding the brain specifics for young children, but the consequences in school for quantitative reasoning can be similar to dyslexia in reading (Moursund, 2012). Often, less attention is paid to helping these students because schools are just learning about new findings of the brain research. Already enough is known that early strong detection and intervention taking place in reading should also occur in mathematics.

Daniel Ansari, director of the Numerical Cognition Laboratory in the Department of Psychology at the University of Western Ontario, works on pushing back the frontier on understanding atypical or developmental issues in our quantitative processing. His work in developmental dyscalculia points out important findings regarding some students exhibiting divergence between IQ and mathematics performance. Often, these findings result in such students being assigned to special education programs. Ansari describes how students with dyscalculia can work effectively with size comparisons as compared to controls for their age group, but not with number comparisons.

Ansari and his colleagues argue that dyscalculia, for which brain organization is not yet well understood, is atypical brain representation and processing of numerical magnitude (Price, Holloway, Vesterinen, Rasanen, & Ansari, 2007). Teachers should be on the lookout for students who lack the ability to process numerical magnitude. They will have difficulty learning the meaning of number expressions and will struggle to maintain them in memory. Ansari and his students cite a prevalence of dyscalculia in the student population between 3 and 10%, comparable in magnitude to dyslexia but much less understood and supported for students in schools. Research publications on dyscalculia are outnumbered nearly 15 to 1 compared to dyslexia, Ansari says, not surprising due to the relatively recent emergence of understanding in this area.

Ansari also studies students with math phobia, for which a higher representation is shown for developmental dyscalculia. Math anxiety is present, as well, for students who don't exhibit developmental issues. This can be characterized by highly intrusive thoughts and ruminations during mathematical problem solving. These thoughts distract focus from often complex mental processing. One challenge for cognitive load is that numerical comparisons are not the only type of representation that students need to master in mathematics. Making connections between important but decidedly *different* ways of thinking in mathematics is where many children find themselves stranded as they progress to middle school and high school. How to connect this graph with that equation with this word problem? These draw on separate brain processes and students often need help to coordinate the ideas into a cohesive whole.

This is not to suggest math in the brain proceeds in a set of serial or linear steps. On the contrary, Posner points out that the brain is time efficient. It tends to look up many familiar codes in parallel, and performs processing at many levels during a task. Posner strikes a hopeful note when describing how specific training in the use of quantity by young children appears to improve prospects for success in school. Approaches include neurosensory methods, such as using small, physical objects that can be manipulated easily by a child's hand to consider mathematical ideas. Math manipulatives focus attention on quantity and pattern through touch and feel as well as sight.

Virtual tools exist, too. Adaptive computer games are built to give young children more practice with number-line thinking. But it can be even simpler than that to reinforce understanding. Just as reading to children at home helps build literacy, numeracy can be built by thinking together through ideas of quantity and counting.

Posner reports that the basic brain areas involved in comparing such number-line quantities don't change from age 5 to adult, but they do speed up. Response time for tasks drops, on average, by nearly half from age 5 to 9 in the studies Posner reports, and to a third by adulthood. Interestingly, Posner suspects this may have to do with the difficulty young children have in organizing their actions to express their ideas—even understanding the goal and reporting back an answer takes longer for them.

Of course, in formal schooling, mathematical ideas often are taught as coordinated into logical routines. But this is not enough for understanding. We must also make "meaning" of the routines. We may supposedly know "how" to do something and might even exhibit a memorized routine when it is directly demanded. Yet we have little independence with the skill. This frustrates teachers and students alike.

But what about more advanced mathematics? Learning scientists in the United Kingdom report that many math educators may need to take another look at what they mean by "mathematics education" in order to understand it in the brain. Specifically, the interplay between numerical reasoning (quantity and number) and our spatial cognition (location, size, distance, direction, shape, connectivity, overlap, and so forth) has fundamental implications in modern mathematics. The U.K. report describes that a much deeper understanding of space and pattern in the brain is likely to influence teaching methods and even possibly the presentation of mathematics curricula and materials in the future (Howard-Jones et al., 2007).

For example, like other educational areas, visualizing can be helpful to get a new idea across in the brain. But in mathematics, there is something more fundamental at work. Ultimately, concepts such as space, function, frequency, movement, and pattern *are* math. Spatial reasoning is a fundamental concept in mathematics along with number, quantity, operation, and algorithms. The spatial processing systems of the brain are distinctly different, however, and need to be prompted and trained in their own right for mathematical thinking, perhaps like dual phonics and visual word form recognition in reading.

▬‖ Some Approaches to Support Mastery

A body of work in brain science is exploring spatial perception and quantitative memory, as well as how we go about making predictions and manipulations on spatial and visual information. An interesting study, for instance, describes how the brains of London cab drivers structurally change when they must master "The Knowledge"—a test of getting efficiently to any address in the city, a complex spatial challenge.

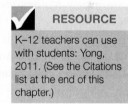

RESOURCE

K–12 teachers can use with students: Yong, 2011. (See the Citations list at the end of this chapter.)

Hard-won math facts and important quantitative problem solving fade quickly when:

- We haven't made meaningful connections that we are likely to access in the brain.
- We fail to encounter frequent opportunities for relevant use.
- Emotional and attitudinal barriers get in the way.

Vinod Menon, director of the Stanford Cognitive and Systems Neuroscience Laboratory, has recently reviewed a tantalizing body of work on how memory systems in the brain play an important role in generalization beyond individual problem attributes (Menon, 2014). Systems anchored in a portion of the temporal cortex are implicated, also involved in long-term memory formation. Meaning making for quantitative thinking comes to the fore with a fascinating potential link to modes of transfer and problem solving that we may employ.

Two U.S. National Academies Press books have a strong focus on mathematics and cognition: *How Students Learn: History, Mathematics, and Science in the Classroom* (Lee, 2005) and *Adding It Up: Helping Children Learn Mathematics* (Kilpatrick, Swafford, & Findell, 2000). Both emphasize how the brain employs metacognition and develops adaptive reasoning for ongoing sense making, reflection, and explanation to oneself and others. "The Neural Foundation for Learning Math" (Peterson, 2012) describes the importance of engaged learning as well as feedback and intrinsic motivation. If students can do the math steps but the brain has no idea of why or what the knowledge is really good for, problems arise. Students do not develop the strategies of reflection and self-feedback. (See Chapter 9 for feedback on which the brain thrives [Lee, 2005].)

For frequency and opportunity of use, integrating math across the subjects is important for the brain. Teachers should be tapping student ability to employ quantitative reasoning in history, economics, English and language arts, health, and the arts. One social studies teacher did just that when he had his students calculate the impressive cost to the royal treasury if France were to have literally followed Marie Antoinette's haughty declaration, "Let them eat cake." All teachers have quantitative reasoning abounding all around them. Or, take the history of Isaac Newton, one of the most famous scientists of all time. How many students know his "other life" as Britain's master of the Royal Mint? He instituted the shift to the gold standard, and made sure every coin added up to its proper weight in the precious metal—banishing coin shaving and building social justice in his society. Mathematics and computer science educator Dave Moursund described in his article, "Cognitive Neuroscience, Computers, and Math Education" (Moursund, 2012), that working with hands-on activities such as computer science allows students to solve math problems in innovative ways, building lasting connections in the brain.

These examples illustrate that just as reading needs to take place outside of reading class, and all teachers are encouraged to support reading across the subjects, so too should this be true with mathematics. Math across the subjects is arguably one of the most neglected needs in schools today.

One emotional hot button for many students in school is experiencing a moment when they are lost in their mathematics and don't know what to do. Interestingly, this often comes about simply because a class or two has been missed along the way, where some seemingly small but actually key concepts have been missed. For teachers, detecting when this has happened and building in ways by which students can recoup the key concept is vital.

Not having a favorable disposition toward quantitative thinking is a huge monkey on the back of students, says the U.S. National Academies publication on how students learn math (Lee, 2005). Simply having an anti-math attitude puts students at a disadvantage, regardless of their actual skills at any given point in their learning. Withdrawing from challenges weakens their mastery strategies.

What can teachers do? As one teacher described, students can be hesitant to take risks when it comes to a difficult math problem or complicated language analysis, partly due to the fear of embarrassment around their friends. He found that teachers offering small successes through reinforcement of effort and positive but informative recognition and feedback lessened what he described as the social challenge. This helps students build identity in mathematics.

Other strategies based on the brain science of the CORE that teachers may wish to employ include:

- *Use worked-out examples (called "worked examples" in mathematics research).* Make use of examples that clearly show the trail of mathematical reasoning in a task, written at a level of informative feedback that makes sense to students and interests them.

- *Teach "math think."* Include formal instruction in techniques of mathematical inquiry for all students and not just some, such as the idea in the 1980s of teaching middle school and high schools students specific skills they can use repeatedly of Entry, Attack, and Review for mathematical inquiry and problem solving (Mason, Burton, & Stacey, 1985). Students learn to conjecture, generate diagrams, practice quantitative thinking in interesting and challenging contexts—basically, they learn how to get ahead in "math think." Interestingly, the strategic approach captivates the brain's problem-solving centers and is intrinsically motivating. This is often seen in Math Olympics and other competitions, as well as at carnivals or fairs. Unfortunately, it is not taught to all children and young adults in school. Especially neglected are students who experience less success in math—the very students who may have the most to gain by pumping up interest level and love of learning.

- *Help students "Friend" math.* Focus on building a professional disposition in math, or on strengthening an affiliation with the field. For instance, one principal speaks of the "high" that students get in school learning that makes them want to experience it more—or conversely, the low or negative experience that leads students to avoid it. She connects this to student attendance, even as early as the middle school level, where experiences in math class especially have a big impact. The principal continues to describe how for the most impacted families, due to an early negative experience and lack of success that they experienced, the feelings linked were overwhelming. When working with families, she also noted that the negative emotions parents recalled were similar to those of their children. When what we know is failure, she described, it is difficult to change beliefs about school.

- *Monitor for flexible thinking.* Realize, as some educators put it, that "you haven't taught until they have learned." Finding ways that impact, transfer, and persist are important. Some math teachers may need to better monitor progress in quantitative thinking, including whether thinking is becoming flexible enough to carry outside the immediate assignment or even the class setting. How can this be done? Surprisingly, there is an important developmental perspective to learning often overlooked in mathematics: Even here there is not a single right and wrong answer from students. Rather, student work, if investigated in enough detail, usually exhibits a whole range of reasoning from partial to more full correctness, or a progression in the emerging learning. For the important brain role of meta–cognition, each student needs to know where he or she stands on the goals, and how he or she can improve and be successful.

Literacy, Reading, and the Representation of Language in the Brain

Dubbed "The Brain on Jane" project, researchers at Stanford University discovered that readers of Jane Austen novels activated very different brain regions when they were instructed to read critically for literary form as compared to when they read for casual enjoyment (Goldman, 2012). The researchers concluded that literary reading provides a valuable exercise of the brain—something many English teachers would agree with, whether focusing on Jane Austen or many other authors whose work is shared in schools.

Research to understand the representation of language in the brain is a big topic for educators. It encompasses the mechanics of fluency such as the symbols, semantics, and syntax of language all the way to the breadth of comprehension and composition, including complex narrative writing and expository text.

Once again, to narrow the scope and help identify some key topics in this section, we will draw on the analysis of the CORE described following Chapter 1. As in the previous section on quantitative thinking, we will not go beyond the fundamentals in the CORE here, but rather use this section to illustrate some new examples of research and ideas for teachers.

Drawing on the OECD Learning Sciences report (OECD, 2007), *language* will be defined here from a brain perspective as (1) a finite number of symbols, (2) a set of semantic principles, and (3) rules of syntax, all combined together to form a system of communication. Full-blown systems for human communication didn't arise all at once. They are believed to have developed over time, through the demands of social cultures and the development of language. The symbols used from one system to another vary, of course, and may represent objects, concepts, emotions, ideas, and thoughts (OECD, 2007).

A rich variety of approaches across languages with which the brain must cope include:

- Phonemes, or sounds, are the smallest meaningful unit of speech sound such as "b" or "p" in *bet* or *pet* (National Research Council, 2000).

- Graphemes, or symbols, are written letters such as "b" or "p" in English, but also other graphic depictions of communication (OECD, 2007).
- Gestures, or actions and movements, are, of course, central to sign language but are also used in many other less formal ways as standardized movements to express or react.
- And now, computerized visuals that go viral on the Internet, animations, sound bytes, and evolving so-called symbol "memes" on the fly are part of language. These culturally recognized artifacts—from happy faces dubbed *emoticons* and *emoji* to phrases like *Google it*—flow ubiquitously and immediately into school settings everyday with the "digital native" children who arrive at school doors.

A general consensus in brain research concludes that young children distinguish many more phonemes than do adults (National Research Council, 2000). Even by early teen years, youngsters begin to lose the ability to distinguish sounds that are not commonly heard in their native languages (see Chapter 10, "Sensitive Periods").

Languages include their own particular set of phonemes, or meaningful sounds. Many sounds overlap, meaning they occur in many languages, but not all. Dr. Robert Sylwester, author of numerous books on the brain, reports that human languages typically employ only about four dozen phonemes, which remarkably equals about the same number of "signal sounds" used by some nonhuman primates. But Sylwester says such animals tend to use each signal as a blockbuster, to mean one thing. One signal may relay "Food on the horizon" or "Watch out for danger." By contrast, in human language single phonemes may be meaningless. For instance a "d" doesn't necessarily convey any particular object or event in English—but when put together with other sounds it forms a word that conveys a clear meaning.

▮❙❙ Words and Parsing Language

Language arts instructors often are delighted to hear that language—not math, not science, not technology—was one of the first functions discovered to have a cerebral basis, a clear connection to how the brain works (OECD, 2007). The foundational research was undertaken with individuals with aphasia, a condition that hampers a person's ability to communicate. With one type of aphasia, people can produce speech but it is riddled with errors. In a second type, the ability to hear speech and comprehend it may be impaired. By investigating the different types of brain damage involved, two European scientists in the 19th century, Pierre-Paul Broca and Carl Wernicke, began to identify the parts of the brain involved in language processing (OECD, 2007).

Just as the brain has systems for processing perceptual subfields such as in vision, hearing, taste, smell, touch, and pain (See CORE 2k; Society for Neuroscience, 2013), so too are there separate brain areas specializing in parsing language itself. When it comes to words, whether we are hearing them, seeing them, speaking them, or generating them makes all the difference to the brain. The OECD learning scientists consider these four different "meta-skills," now reflected to a greater extent in the U.S. Common Core State Standards (Common Core State Standards Initiative, 2010; OECD, 2007).

Whereas these four meta-skills may come together seamlessly for teachers and others, in the brain the skills are dependent on separate types of subprocessing. So, to the extent they are separately represented, stored, and handled in the brain, the U.S. National Research Council reports, teachers need to think about helping students coordinate the skills. They may not be as closely related as teachers think (National Research Council, 2000). We may need to work harder at meaningful hearing or active listening when reading the same message is a breeze, or we might be able to speak eloquently, but generating the words is a difficult chore.

Teachers often draw on alternate modalities—the ways the brain processes information—to support language skills and literacy, such as drama, music, or drawing. One method a veteran teacher described involved a type of scaffolding to help students learn literature by presenting or reviewing information in a song. When teaching the poetry of Emily Dickinson or Arthur Miller's play, *The Crucible,* for instance, this teacher used music to reinforce elements of rhythm or plot details. He also allowed students to compose their own songs, such as to consider a theme of *The Odyssey* or relate the main conflicts of *Beowulf.* By reinforcing meaning in a powerful way, the teacher found the approaches connected with the students and seemed to last.

For humans, the arts of speaking, gestures for communication, and language comprehension are considered innate, or biologically driven. However, it takes humans more conscious effort to master written text—and frankly, the human body isn't all that well suited to it (Sakai, 2005). One little secret of the brain is that although language acquisition is one of the most fundamental of human traits, some of the machinery we deploy, such as for reading and writing, was never intended for the purpose. Scientists believe we harness ancient tools of the brain to undertake new and unexpected purposes.

In his illuminating book, *Reading in the Brain,* psychologist and cognitive neuroscientist Stanislaus Dehaene describes how our eyes aren't all that great as text scanners (Dehaene, 2009). Only the very central part of the retina, which is the light-sensitive layer at the back of the eye, has fine enough resolution for reading. The area is so small as a receptor that we must consequently jerk our eyes around in tight stretches on the page to get the right part in play. About four or five times a second, we refocus, essentially making many tiny snapshots as we read. Then we must knit them all together again.

In reading, we also face something called the *invariance problem:* How can we pick out a sequence of letters when we allow the character shapes to vary so broadly? We have to deal with printed and handwritten letters, upper- and lower-case versions, and various font styles and shapes. It has been said that each of humanity's written characters, no matter the language, is like Shahrazad's Arabian nights, and can take on "a thousand and one" interesting and tortuous shapes.

So, to help the brain learn, it would seem logical that teachers should always be sure to use the simplest, easiest-to-read fonts in written materials with students. Not so, apparently. In yet another example of the complexity of the learning process, researchers from Princeton University and Indiana University found just the opposite to be true, at least up to a point. In two experiments, including one in the field with more than 200 high school students in Cleveland, students were assigned material in easy and difficult fonts across subjects and grades on a randomized basis. Those reviewing material in hard-to-read fonts did better on regular classroom assessment tests than did their randomly selected counterparts reading the same material in easier fonts. By making the typeface more challenging to read, the authors concluded the students concentrated more carefully on learning the harder-to-read material. They said this is consistent with the concept of *disfluency*—the idea that when something is difficult to do it can lead people to process information more deeply. The researchers cautioned that more research is needed and that font styles and typefaces that are too obscure and impossibly difficult to read could backfire or turn away students who were already struggling (Diemand-Yauman, Oppenheimer, & Vaughan, 2011).

Dehaene (2009) points out that the invention of reading is far too recent for evolution to have created it. Language and socializing perhaps have an evolutionary basis because they stretch back far enough. But reading, only a few thousand years old, is just too recent—a mere blink of the eye in biological terms. Thus, scientists suspect the human reading capacity is made up of, in a sense, recycled parts—something that exists for some other use. If that's true, what capacity did we have in the first place that we turned into reading?

To answer the question, scientists turned a keen eye on other primates. Monkeys and apes can't read, but they do have many brain circuits similar to those of humans. So, what are they doing with the capacity we use to read?

Researchers put a variety of images, objects, faces, and other visuals in front of macaque monkeys. The most widespread primates outside of humans, macaques have elaborate social behavior, such as synchronizing dance movements with each other or designating who gets what berries based on their social hierarchy. Researchers found that the brain of the macaque monkey responded to fragments of shapes. A "T" shape, where three edges of a cube came together, triggered neural firing, for instance, as did an "L" shape cast by a tree trunk meeting the ground. This happened with numbers too—a figure eight where the head of an upright cat met its body, and a zero-like silhouette along outside edges of a roundish form. As Dehaene (2009) describes, the scientists had stumbled upon an alphabet in the monkey brain.

Researchers now believe circuits such as these exist in the human brain and are turned into machinery for reading, along with a whole array of other brain accouterments. These include executive function to guide the reading process and close-knit coordination between two reading routes in the brain that involve phonics pathways and sight-memory reading of symbol shapes. Such elements of coordination include:

- From letters to words and their meanings stored in our mental lexicon, which is our dictionary of common terms, or
- For words not yet well known to us, from letters to their sounds, and from there deciphering if we can comprehend the vocabulary meaning of the sound we believe the letters represent.

Then there is comprehension, and our reading brain finds ways to benefit enormously by borrowing information from the context in which it finds a letter, word, sentence, or even entire theme or narrative. Once again, we are good at capitalizing on incomplete information. Where there is context, we have access to more brain coding, or neural connections to the idea, and may make better predictions about the meaning of what we are detecting. This is as true for the monkey brain gazing at the intersection of a tree limb in a complicated forest as for a child puzzling out the letters on a "big book" picture page.

▌▌ Moving on to Meaning

Comprehension, of course, is a large and important story for language and literacy. Many resources are available to teachers to describe the teaching and learning research in this area, but the brain story is just beginning to unfold. So, once again, teachers should expect more to be discovered over the course of their careers, and may wish to keep an eye on the field as it unfolds.

So far, we have focused on what our brains do effectively. Although our eyes are good at many logistics of seeing, like holding lenses in place with the right combination of finely balanced muscles, or keeping the retina supplied with nutrients and oxygen while removing waste products, a lot can easily go wrong. Systems are so complex. For instance, we get a lot of mileage out of monochrome vision in poor light—seeing only in black and white at early dawn or twilight for instance. If you don't believe it, try it out. You will see color only when there is sufficient light; otherwise, red, green, blue, and all the other colors are merely shades of grey.

Because we depend on so many things coming together correctly, conditions easily can go awry in language comprehension. Whether reading, writing, speaking, or any other form of expressive or receptive communication, when we are engaged in this "fragile" process of recycling our brain capacity from very different ancient uses to new modern demands, even the slightest mishaps in circuitry can throw us off, Dehaene (2009) says.

The highest profile and most known of these is dyslexia, where otherwise capable students find reading inordinately difficult (Howard-Jones et al., 2007; Society for Neuroscience, 2013). Dylexia, widespread and prevalent, is neurobiological in origin (OECD, 2007). Most commonly it is characterized by:

- Difficulties with accurate and/or fluent word recognition
- Difficulties with spelling and encoding abilities
- Challenges with the phonological component of language
- Atypical cortical features involved with sound elements of languages
- Open to change with targeted intervention, especially when identified early

Scientists today generally agree that most cases of dyslexia that take this form are linked to problems with processing phonemes, the basic sound units. There is a tendency that dyslexia runs in families, thus, a strong genetic component is suspected (Dehaene, 2009). Anomalies in a handful of genes seem to control where certain neurons migrate in the fetal brain, making the circuitry work differently. Dehaene and others describe how new intervention strategies and reading methods are bringing fresh hope for striving readers (Dehaene, 2009; B. A. Shaywitz et al., 2004; S. Shaywitz, 2003).

Due to the needs of early intervention for strongest results, neuroscience studies are examining whether variations in brain development as early as kindergarten predict individual differences in reading ability by grade 3 (Myers et al., 2014). Volume changes in white matter in a particular area of the brain often implicated in phonological processing were found to be a sensitive marker for later reading abilities and by extension, researchers say, to reading difficulties and the need for early intervention. It may be possible to go even farther back than that. In dyslexia, intergenerational studies are now taking place to compare imaging across generations of families, and some sex-specific transfer patterns have begun to be identified (Hoeft, 2014).

Of course, language literacy includes not only expressive and receptive skills in our first language but it can also be grounded in mediating communication in any additional language we acquire. In signing and in second-language acquisition, literacy strategies harken back to parts of the CORE. For instance, one veteran Spanish teacher described how, in second-language learning, he found it important to use pictures and other visuals to help students learn, retain, recall, and apply what they have learned. The pictures helped trigger prior knowledge for the students and activated prior experiences that they began to relate to the current task, all the while connecting the vocabulary to associations the students already had. The teacher then had students compare and contrast their experiences from looking at visuals, underscoring the sociocultural aspects of coming to a shared understanding.

The work on language in the brain brings us back to a more philosophical question: What is so relevant to the human brain about reading and writing that we bend over backwards to make it work for us? Here, we move from the *what* and *how* of language to the *why*. Spelling, symbols, syntax—it is all quite complex. In this age of YouTube and Instagram video tutorials are everywhere we look. It might be hard to fully appreciate what written communication does for us. But passing down the human transmission of knowledge through the ages often has depended on our ability to record information with written symbols. Writing creates more flow—from one person to another, from one generation to the next.

So, to the brain, writing is a type of augmented memory system. The late Nobelist in Literature, Czelaw Milosz, who lived through repression in Warsaw during World War II and then fled Communist Poland to finally publish freely in the United States, wrote elegantly about how books are much more durable than our thoughts and memories. As they disperse and perish, he writes, books will always be on the shelves.

▮❙❙ Some Approaches to Support Mastery

The literature of Milosz and so many other important writers illustrates another facet of human brain processing: the importance of narrative to us. Story and narrative are a major way in which the brain learns. They are seen by the brain as a type of evidence, or "social proof" that reflects on experiences that have been valuable or compelling to others.

As is typical for the brain, our interest is usually in relationship to how relevant the stories may seem to us, consciously or unconsciously. Narrative delights but also helps the brain frame what to avoid, optimize, or be wary of in future encounters. Without having to perceive and cope with finding solutions to everything alone, the information the brain seeks through narrative delivers a powerful payoff. Whether through storytelling, written word, film, drama, or song, we pay attention. A picture may be worth a thousand words, but a story is worth all the millennia of attention the human race has devoted to it as an art form—and a major mode for transmission for knowledge, principles, and culture.

Often traditionally rooted in literature, language narratives today can be produced in video, audio, and presentation software to support any of the four language-related meta-skills, which are hearing, seeing, speaking, and generating language. They also can be highly effective in supporting the brain-based principle of integration across subjects (Rabinowitz, 1993).

By deploying narrative in one of these four language meta-realms, teachers can have students focus substantively on curriculum-aligned topics drawing on quantitative thinking, scientific or social studies reasoning, or creative expression such as in art, music, or movement classes. Of course, a major drawback that schools must face in integration is the degree to which language arts teachers, for instance, could support teaching a literature passage employing quantitative reasoning.

This is parallel to the problem of mathematics instructors incorporating language arts or social studies to raise the relevance signal in their field. Math teachers may feel they only know about math and will focus on problem solving in areas they feel most comfortable; conversely, language teachers will naturally focus on traditional literature sources and may leave numbers, proof, scientific thought, or social studies reasoning out of their language development and narrative work. "Reading across the subjects" is not yet "subjects across the subjects," but it is no doubt heading in that direction.

There are other broad strategies that teachers may wish to employ that tap into CORE brain ideas but don't always come to mind as supporting brain function in language acquisition. These include:

- Teach and use summarizing and note taking. Marzano and other researchers find summarizing and note taking to be a powerful skill that teachers can directly instruct to good effect (Marzano, 1998, 2003, 2009; Smith & Ragan, 1999; Weinstein & Mayer, 1986). Outlining focuses on overarching ideas and supporting details. In summarization, students who paraphrase in their own words make sense of new material by connecting it with concepts they know (Weinstein & Mayer, 1986). Many schools no longer spend much time teaching students how to take effective notes, but some systems such as AVID Cornell note taking are starting to pick up steam. Teachers report that although such systems can be challenging tools for students at the start, they get better quickly and almost magically become more intrinsically motivated as they see their understanding of the content increase. Grades improve when teachers provide feedback on notes while shaping summarization skills. But once again, don't just teach notes and summary in an English class and then abandon them everywhere else. This leads to inert knowledge and limited future access of the skills. Is it worth it to follow through? Teachers go so far as to say this strategy alone can change the climate of classrooms.
- In language arts and second-language acquisition, often rubrics, decision rules, or other ways of identifying what to look for in student work are helpful. For example, using rubrics for grading and then sharing those rubrics with the students helps learners know what the goals are, where they stand on the goals, and how to close the difference. These are all key aspects of formative assessment that make strong differences in learning outcomes. For the teacher, "common assessments" can be effective. Here, teachers collaborate to score and interpret student work, providing a natural venue to reflect, elaborate, and extend their own knowledge of their profession.
- Make sure feedback is put to use. Teachers providing feedback in written assignments need to make sure the feedback is incorporated into student assignments. It is so terribly disappointing for a teacher to spend time preparing comments for students only to have the students never really implement the feedback or even read through the comments carefully. Without working with feedback, one doesn't often benefit much from it. Effective teachers, therefore, build this into the process.
- Become a "coach" at times. Besides written feedback, on-the-fly "coaching" is effective in primary- and secondary-language acquisition. Take a page from the athletic playbook. Coaching is as big a hit for students learning reading and writing as it is in soccer or volleyball. But this doesn't mean only to give praise (Wilson & Cole, 1996). *Coaching* means observing students as they complete tasks. It means providing guidance

and help as *appropriate for the individual learner*. Good coaches see themselves as monitors, motivators, providers of comments and feedback, and promoters of articulation, elaboration, and extension (Jonassen, 2001).

• Draw on the power of goal setting for students. This can even be a language and literacy exercise itself. One teacher described how during units of study, his class would design and settle on a definition to reflect the meaning of effort and achievement for the task. Then, as students worked together in teams, the teacher could hear the common language arising that the students used to praise and support each other. He saw an increase in the students' effort, motivation, and focus on their combined goal. The teacher added, "Don't forget working in those opportunities for integrating quantitative reasoning." Using the language of the goals and then charting or graphing outcomes became a source of instant feedback (and helped support math across the subjects).

Reasoning in the Brain

At Columbia University's Brain Expo, a neuroscience outreach event for parents, teachers, and kids, the brain coloring booth enraptured a little girl in a red velvet dress, crayon clutched in her fist. The 4-year-old was doing her best to stay within the lines of her brain coloring book as her mother stood with her. "Motor cortex—oh, what a nice green you used," her mother chattered cheerfully, leaning over her daughter, watching her draw. "Pa-ri-e-tal lobe," the mom sounded out, "Wonder what that is? Orange. No, red? Wow, orange *and* red. What a nice brain you are making!"

A few moments later, the mom helped the little girl fold her picture, tape it and plop it on her head—now the 4-year-old had a "brain hat" added to her fancy outfit. The little girl skittered away, her colorful brain schematic bobbling shakily atop her curls like a party hat. "This is probably our most popular brain event," the coloring booth lady said, looking around the room with satisfaction at the full crowd bustling from booth to booth. "Parents love it and kids too. It's a great because everyone is thinking about all the reasoning going on inside our heads."

Reasoning is a big topic in the neuroscience world. Scholars would like to get a better understanding of it because in the end it may be our most human of traits—we can think in some very complex ways. We take in information and experiences, add them all up, and strike; we make our decisions on the basis of . . . what? Wrestling with reasoning proves tricky. First of all, what do we even mean by the term *reasoning?*

If we define *reasoning* as does cognitive scientist Vinod Goel, who wrote a book about the neural basis of logical reasoning, we talk about brain activity as drawing inferences. In other words, the brain comes to conclusions based on some evidence or a premise we have in mind (Goel, 2005).

As we have seen, the brain is endlessly engaged in this kind of reasoning (Fugelsang & Dunbar, 2005; Mercier & Sperber, 2011). At times this reflects a rational undertaking, at other times less so. We may use emotional evidence and a hard-and-fast survival premise to reach conclusions not at all conscious to us (Run! It's a lion!).

▣‖ The Brain as a Reason Machine

Students use their reasoning to devise new and more accurate models of the world, inform their thought processes, enhance skills and ability—even to expand the brain flexibility we call creativity. In subjects from science to social studies, and arts to health and welfare, students can be seen to reason and create, especially when they are encouraged to focus less on memorization and more on putting knowledge to active work.

RESOURCE

K–12 teachers can use with students: Kaufman, 2013. (See the Citations list at the end of this chapter.)

Here, we take up three examples of brain-related reasoning in different school settings: hypothesis generation in science education, drawing on multiple perspectives in social studies, and a brain conception of creativity illustrated in the arts.

The first stop is hypothesis generation. It may sound technical but this just refers to when we think about how the brain asks questions and how it explores those questions with evidence. Marzano and others have found that this approach in instructional design has strong positive effects on student learning outcomes. To use a definition that goes back more than 50 years from psychologist Jerome Bruner and his colleagues regarding *hypothesis testing in education,* learners acquire concepts by setting forth tentative ideas about attributes involved and then testing specific instances against these hypotheses (Bruner, Goodnow, & Austin, 1956).

Formally, we may propose hypotheses and explicitly work with them in our thinking and learning. But more informally, and especially with young children, simply working with modes of thought that involve asking questions and exploring the answers based on evidence offers students an opportunity to refine their working ideas. Students also connect their thinking to concepts and beliefs they already hold. In education, *scientific thinking* refers to both the content of science and the set of reasoning processes fundamental to the scientific method. The U.S. K–12 framework on which the Next Generation Science Standards (NGSS) are based call these "inextricably fused." The framework encourages content and reasoning processes to be blended at all times in science education for U.S. students (National Research Council, 2013).

From the point of view of the brain, this blending brings together cognitive activation. Induction, deduction, abduction, experimental design, causal reasoning, concept formation, and other aspects of reasoning are all involved in hypothesis testing for students.

University of California, Berkeley, Professor Alison Gopnik and coauthors point out in their book, *The Scientist in the Crib: What Early Learning Tells Us about the Mind,* that even as babies (actually, especially as babies), we are all engaged in hypothesis testing as our natural route of learning (Gopnik, Meltzoff, & Kuhl, 2000). Gopnik, whom we first met in Chapter 2, shows this is the way young humans discover their world and that babies' and young children's cognitive abilities are much greater than once thought. Her charming subjects were described by the *Seattle Times* as "flirtatious" babies making us laugh—and think. Gopnik's research, for all its charm, illustrates serious findings about human acquisition of skills and knowledge. In their ongoing research, she and her colleagues have shown that babies and young children are essentially engaged in research and development. They learn in the same way scientists do—through generating hypotheses and working on verifying and updating them. Furthermore, they have shown that even very young humans can imagine another person's experience and grasp cause and effect.

This is particularly impressive because babies aren't easy to work with in that they don't yet communicate with spoken language. Gopnik has found a secret tool, however: broccoli. Give youngsters two bowls of food, one filled with raw broccoli and the other with delicious goldfish crackers, and you can begin to understand what's going on in their minds.

It turns out that even in natural-food–loving Berkeley, Gopnik points out, babies prefer the goldfish crackers to the veggies. In one particularly eye-opening study, she had actors perform skits before 18-month-old children to show that they loved the raw broccoli but hated the crackers. Then the actors asked the children to give them some food from one of the bowls.

It turns out that 18-month-olds will readily offer up the broccoli to the actors who ask for it, but 15-month-old babies won't. The slightly younger children stare in disbelief that anyone would prefer the vegetables. Then they hand over the crackers. At this age, babies are still wrestling with what to value. They haven't established the hypothesis that we don't all prefer the same thing, so they are momentarily stuck at a standstill in their reasoning when they find evidence that suggests there is a difference between us. They show, perhaps not surprising, they prefer their own reasoning.

What is astonishing is that just 3 months later, the children have done a complete flip-flop. They move to the other side of the communication bridge. At this age, they appreciate what someone else wants. This is a huge advance for socialization of a species.

It often doesn't take long for young children to adjust their ideas when they encounter sufficient evidence, as Gopnik's work illustrates. It may take adults longer, however, in part because they may have had more prior evidence to the contrary. As highlighted previously in the CORE, we update our beliefs weighted in the presence of not only one bit of current evidence but a great deal of past experience as well. In science, the ability to ask questions and answer them is a required skill. According to the OECD Learning Sciences report, discovery triggers the processes of using and building knowledge and skills.

A caution in science education is that students also need activities that actually build understanding in science fundamentals, practices, and cross-cutting concepts as well as sufficient feedback to stay on track. Jonathan Osborne, the Shriram Family Professorship in Science Education at Stanford University, said he is not surprised that hands-on science activity isn't always associated with stronger learning gains. Many hands-on activities in science are just busy work, in a sense. If it doesn't engage cognitive activity and provide adequate feedback, he says, it wouldn't be expected to have cognitive outcomes. For instance, impressing students with a demonstration that delivers a loud bang or a high flame is common in many schools, but it doesn't necessarily lead to brain processing for the science behind the flashy activity. If the scientific principles aren't presented clearly and if students aren't allowed time to work through the principles to establish meaningful understanding, there's not a lot of deep thinking going on.

Supporting student thinking through *scaffolding* is important in hypothesis generation. It is easy to go wrong, and in school, there may not be time for endless exploring if we are going to get through all the learning that needs to take place. One veteran teacher said he feels that scaffolding enhances problem-based learning. Useful techniques, he describes, include modeling a task, giving advice, and providing coaching. He believes that the effective use of scaffolding gives his students the impression that they have discovered solutions on their own. Some other strategies that teachers may wish to employ that tap into CORE ideas through hypothesis generation include:

- *Support learning visually.* Move beyond teaching methods that rely solely on words and language. One teacher describes how he supports whatever theme is being studied with videos from Netflix, YouTube, or a science site such as NOVA. To make sure the students understand the important ideas from the video, he prepares an outline with relevant vocabulary, all the "big ideas" they need to master, and a few bonus items he finds interesting. The outline lets students focus on important information and feel confident they don't have to master everything.
- *Provide more than one example.* Take the word of Jim Pellegrino (cited in Committee on the Foundations of Assessment, 2002–2003), one of the lead authors of "Knowing What Students Know" and many other informative publications in education and psychology: If you really want students to get the deep context, you have to give them more than one example. When the hope is that students generalize in their reasoning, once is not enough for the brain to feel a broad sweeping pattern is warranted—even if teachers says so. The human cognitive system has built-in checks to keep us resistant to premature assimilation. So, keep it coming.

Add in some lively social debate where appropriate. When we test our working ideas, appropriate transfer to new contexts is important. To make practice personally meaningful, engaging in a lively social debate can help. Doing so shifts the learning experience from transmission of knowledge to developing meaning around concepts, describes one school counselor. She said she saw how activities became intrinsically more interesting for students as they had the opportunity to articulate their own process of understanding concepts. This is all about making meaning (Restak & Kim, 2010). The idea of making meaning moves us to the topic of how the brain draws effectively on multiple perspectives.

The human brain is all about cognitive flexibility. In social studies, history, and economics, as in other fields, one aspect of this is commonly understood to mean that exposing students to multiple points of view helps them better understand happenings, trends, and events.

If teachers can help students rearrange the information they already have, as well as construct new knowledge, their mental structures hammer it out in neural structure and connections change. In this way, learners effectively elaborate and extend. They may show more ability to transfer their thinking and use it in the real world. In doing so, learners build knowledge structures that are more nuanced and flexible. Thus, they can better represent complex situations.

As shown in previous chapters, students can become caught up in social studies by taking it into the real world. As humans, we exhibit tremendous intrinsic motivation when the ideas are connected with the world around us. If students can mentally leave the school walls behind them, they may better see their learning connected with human goals, raising the important relevance flag in the human brain.

Under such conditions, students—especially those in middle school and high school who are beginning to reach out beyond themselves—may strive in ways that make them "go and go," observed one teacher who connects learning about other cultures with community service for young adults.

▣‖ Toward Intercultural Competence

The consideration of cultural diversity is always an important instructional strategy, of course. Often, students are members of many different cultures. Not only do they come from a variety of ethnic and racial backgrounds but they are also affiliated in various ways with different economic experiences, geographic regions, religions, and parental expectations (Driscoll, 2000). Critically, the types and availability of information sources in the home or online can be quite different from one student to the next, all influencing their perspectives on the world. Consequently, students make sense of their experiences in different ways.

This is similar to the perspective of situated learning theorists: Not only should new knowledge be well-situated (coherent, concrete, and organized to us) to be understandable, but learners themselves should be situated. In other words, especially when it comes to social studies learning, we hold a unique place in the very systems about which we are learning. In instructional design practices, multiple perspectives from others enrich what we know (Driscoll, 2000).

Some students at any given age are better at drawing on multiple perspectives and being able to generalize in a given situation than others—and it may not be the ones that teachers think. For example, those who have excelled when memorization was the goal may not be as proficient when asked to infer, hypothesize, and synthesize.

Here's what making this kind of shift might look like: Instead of asking for simple memory or recall of rote facts or ideas, students work to show their mastery by being able to fluidly use ideas and skills, as described in the instructional design Chapters 3 and 5. A social studies student might not only know of an event from history but be able to value its impact or identify another event he hypothesizes is related. In science, a student might infer a conclusion based on evidence she has collected, or synthesize together two trends and project a probable outcome. Some students who aren't intrigued by simply recalling and memorizing facts may find the school experience turns around for them when they are asked to do critical thinking.

But what is the definition of *critical thinking?* Depending on how one is using it, it can range from the narrow slice of being able to decide if a claim is true or can be supported, to the wide swath of defining it as the whole field of reasoning and everything it encompasses.

Psychologist emeriti Jack Meacham, previously a distinguished teaching professor at the State University of New York in New York, says what is key for teachers to communicate to kids about critical thinking is the need to be able to be critical of their *own* thinking. Many students are good at shooting down the ideas of others. What looms large for education is if students can be as critically reflective of ideas they themselves hold. Can they bring evidence to their beliefs, and can they adjust their thinking and learn when the evidence so warrants?

In developing this type of critical thinking—being critical of our own thinking—we have a role of so-called "agency." We need to see ourselves and our own thinking as susceptible to evidence just as we see that of others.

▪‖ Some Approaches to Support Mastery

Our brain networks should have the ability to self-reflect. If all "our" ideas are closely held and all others are lightly dismissed, we won't be asking the brain to legitimately work with what it has. We short-circuit the brain's ability to reason.

Reasoning through History and Geography

Michael Shenefelt, a New York University master teacher and coauthor of *If A, Then B: How the World Discovered Logic*, asked in a *Chronicle of Higher Education* essay, "Why study the Greeks?" He addresses how the Greeks became so important in early history. Shenefelt's answer: Study the map.

In Greece, notice two things. First, the land terrain is rugged. Mountains and lakes divide the islands into many independent regions. Also, sea routes are ample. The rough terrain divided the land into many small communities. This allowed new thinking to arise. The sea routes let the ideas travel. Using causal reasoning, Shenefelt argues geography helped result in the Greek diaspora, or the spreading of thought from Greece outward.

Causal reasoning like this can be a powerful kind of schema reinforcement for the memory trace (Davidson, 2012). By contrast, disconnected ideas can seem irrelevant to the brain. When focusing on history, Shenefelt argues for trading in a plethora of facts and dates for key organizing ideas.

From Chapter 4, we know also that memory reinforcement in social studies as well as other areas is more than building just the strength of a single neural trace. We are building a larger representation or schema in which that trace is involved. For social studies, economics, and history, this is often what we call *causal*. That is, we are often asking students to reason in a way that involves causality, or what cognitive scientists call a causal model—what caused what and why (Anderson, 2000).

Some effective approaches teachers may find helpful include:

- *Make use of cognitive apprenticeship.* This takes a problem-solving approach to instruction whereby students work with others to reason through multiple, authentic cases (Brown, Collins, & Duguid, 1989; Collins, Brown, & Newman, 1989). This can be hands-on or more through thinking and reflection, but should focus much like the work of actual practitioners. Apprentices "of the mind," as the researchers have described it, build a repertoire of knowledge that may help prepare students to think and reason more like experts (Schunk, 2012). Fading is naturally built in as students strive to work as independent thinkers.
- *Try Socratic dialogue.* This means constructing an argument using a question-and-answer method to anticipate the questions in the lesson of the day, and the challenges that will arise and that need to be addressed. Socratic dialogue approaches in social studies not only honor the great man but are surprisingly aligned with brain CORE principles. It is a type of social augmentation that naturally scaffolds and fades, by turning back on the learners their own questions and asking them to be critical of their own thinking.
- *Reflect, reflect, reflect.* Social studies teachers don't need to be told that reflection requires students to look at what they have done, analyze their performance, and compare it to others, including peers and teacher. It is all about feedback galore and sharing multiple perspectives. Of course, teachers need to make sure students don't spiral to nowhere, or walk away with even more deeply entrenched misconceptions (such as, avoid the brain principle of practicing failure). To end on a positive note, help students effectively reinforce memory traces, especially where meaningful patterns and organizing principles can generate powerful ideas for them.

An Example of Habituation

When it comes to habituation, take the example of American Arash Ghadishah, an Emmy-nominated field producer with *ABC World News.* The Weekly Standard blogger Matt Labash wrote about his first encounter with Ghadishah in 2003 when a hotel siren sounded at their war news field site in Iraq. Incoming missile, the shrieking signal warned. Labash said he sought advice from Ghadishah about what to do, but Ghadishah was blasé. He had experienced so many war sirens he hardly responded. He had become habituated. "Do you mind if I film you while you put on your mask and run to the basement?" Arash asked, only half joking.

Finally, the last illustrative example, in the arts, connects to the brain in a somewhat different way. In the human brain, a number of tensions are at work when multiple perspectives are introduced in reasoning. The human brain has a strong tendency toward habituation. This means a decrease in a response to a stimulus after it has been repeated many times, from the same perspective and approach. We tend to adopt a stance toward it and stop responding. Even if it is something rather dramatic happening around us, the brain has decided it knows what to do about it already. It has formed a type of habit.

So what does habituation have to do with the arts? Expression of human creative skill is powerful. The visual arts, such as painting and photography, bring us new information and perspective to the visual centers of the brain. Film and dance are multimodal; touch is involved in new types of kinesthetic media; smell and taste are nurtured in the culinary arts; and music engages the auditory centers. These are but a few forms of human art and expression. Through creating and appreciating expression, we share thoughts and feelings, and perceive those of others, in a variety of sensory experiences for the brain.

Although there is much to say about the arts and learning, in this one aspect alone a lot is captured for educators. Teachers find it frustrating when they can't get through to kids. However, leaving out everything else aside, just simply the day-in and day-out habituation of school feeds a brain process. There is a tendency for the brain to stop responding.

But when we can perceive and create, when we can both experience and generate novelty, the brain reawakens to the new stimuli. We are *sensitized* to it, to use a term of science. It is as if the brain gets a prod, "Now it is time to sit up and listen." For teachers, simply getting increasingly more emphatic with the same signal doesn't have the same effect—the siren goes off and it is ignored. But through creating and appreciating human expression, such as in the arts, students share thoughts and feelings, and perceive those of others, in a variety of sensory experiences for the brain. Among many positive attributes of the arts in education, effective shifting of viewpoint can help us avoid pitfalls of brain habituation.

Where repetitive experiences put a student in a groove or rut, truly "educative" experiences promise the opposite. They promote growth and desire and they help the brain seek. The arts help cultivate the desire to learn.

The words of a student who had just completed an art class illustrate this. Before taking the class, artwork to him existed only in a museum or big gallery, he said, but in the course he learned to see art with a broader definition. Art was what attracted the mind, he said, and consisted of thoughtful works that interested him.

Some effective approaches in this area that have been suggested for teachers include:

- Incorporate the concepts of sensitization and habituation when thinking about the direction of instructional design in daily lessons. How can creative expression help "reset" some of the brain's tendency to shut down?
- When possible and appropriate to the learning context, incorporate ways to lower the "heard that already" barrier, and stimulate the brain to respond to new stimuli. Whether an educator teaches in the arts directly or not, he or she can draw on the arts as a powerful venue for the classroom.
- Across subjects, consider the brain's conception of creativity illustrated in the arts.
- For the brain, the arts are an example of gaining diversity of perspective. So, as the U.K. Learning Science report describes, there is a contribution to both reasoning and expression when the arts are incorporated in the curriculum (Howard-Jones et al., 2007).
- As with some of the suggestions in other areas, this may mean some teachers need to become more familiar with the arts in a variety of forms. Educators may consider areas in which they have interests. They may wish to supplement their understanding and engagement in the arts in these areas over time.

Conclusion

This chapter provides a glimpse into applying CORE brain principles to some of the subject-matter areas. Just as the chapter opened with neuroscientist Janet Dubinsky describing her award-winning BrainU work with educators, the intention was not to dictate how neuroscience can inform teaching but to let fruitful practices emerge. As highly skilled professionals in their subject-matter and grade-level areas, teachers who are willing to grapple with ideas make the connection with their work.

At the end of each BrainU workshop day, Dubinsky described, teachers discussed how the day's content and activities applied to their profession. In this way, said Dubinsky, teachers made connections regarding how neuroscience knowledge applied to their classrooms. Whether problem solving or role-playing, inquiry learning or direct instruction, avenues of cognitive activation were explored. Dubinsky found this helped strengthen teacher resolve. They made sense of findings, and put their thinking on a fast track. It became real to them.

RESOURCE

K–12 teachers can use with students: Dubinsky, 2013. (See the Citations list at the end of this chapter.)

As more comes to be known about the brain and how we learn, fuller treatment for specific areas and examples is expected to emerge. This can already be seen in some fields, such as reading, where specialized texts go beyond the fundamental CORE provided here. Such advanced materials often interest teachers as a next step in their knowledge base, after gaining a fundamental basis from which to think about the brain. They are ready to know more, but they often want it applied in their area of expertise. Over time, teachers will find more details emerge as knowledge of what the brain is doing grows by leaps and bounds.

The U.K. Learning Sciences report describes how burgeoning knowledge of the brain is producing expectations of new educational insights in many specific areas. Insights are beginning to surface, with much more to come, they say, especially as neuroscientists grow increasingly interested in how the brain functions in complex environments. Classroom, school yard, community, and home all represent centers of learning. Whether in formal or informal learning, a rich array of interesting challenges await cognitive neuroscience.

Closing Scenario

Putting New Knowledge to Use

Insights across the Curriculum

Because many neuroscientists and cognitive psychologists often don't know enough about the specifics of teaching in particular contexts to point out concrete applications of learning science appropriate to educators, teachers are going to have to close the loop themselves. Few teachers can be expected to do this entirely on their own; success will more likely come with teachers working together. So, in this scenario, you are asked to work in small groups, ideally representing expertise in different age levels and/or subject-matter areas to address the integrated questions. Your goal is to model teaching approaches based on fundamental brain science findings such as those represented in the CORE that might apply or be helpful to your practice. *Hint:* Be careful to actively avoid *neuromyths*, such as those discussed in Chapter 9, and to focus on what is known about the brain and human cognition.

1. By transferring thinking and using it in the real world, learners build knowledge structures that are more nuanced and flexible so they can better represent complex situation. How can you apply real-world connections in a social studies unit, a physical education or health lesson, and one other field of your choosing?

2. By generating hypotheses and working on verifying and updating them, student learning is mimicking the way our brains learn. Because this kind of approach has been shown to enhance success but is not always easy to incorporate in some areas, work together to apply this approach to two subject-matter areas. In each case, you must apply it to elementary school learners in a grade or age of your choice and a high school class.

3. The brain sees storytelling and narrative as a type of evidence, or "social proof," that reflects on experiences that have been valuable or compelling to others. Put this finding of brain science to work in a writing or art assignment, and in a mathematics or science lesson.

4. The brain is all about cognitive flexibility. This is commonly understood to mean that exposing students to multiple points of view helps them better understand happenings, trends, and events. Describe how you can use this in an elementary school context, in a middle school history assignment, and in a high school economics lesson.

5. Finally, given your experience in this exercise, what advice would you give to colleagues and others trying to link learning science to classroom work?

Citations

Online, Media, and Print Resources for Teachers

Annenberg Learner (Producer). (2012, February 2, 2014). Unit 6: Implications for schools. *Neuroscience and the classroom: Making connections.* Retrieved from http://www.learner.org/courses/neuroscience/text/text.html?dis=U&num=06&sec=01

Biever, C. (2004, August 19). Language may shape human thought. *New Scientist, Science Express,* pp. 1–10. http://www.newscientist.com/article/dn6303 - .Un1lDGp3vX4

BrainU (Producer). (2014, October 19, 2014). BrainU: The brain. Retrieved from http://brainu.org

Dubinsky, J. M. (2013). BrainU: The neuroscience teacher institute, BRAIN to middle schools, BRAIN to high schools. http://brainu.org/brainu-neuroscience-teacher-institute

Kaufman, S. B. (2013). Reasoning training increases brain connectivity associated with high-level cognition. *Scientific American.* http://blogs.scientificamerican.com/beautiful-minds/2013/03/18/reasoning-training-increases-brain-connectivity-associated-with-high-level-cognition/

Yong, E. (2011). Not exactly rocket science: How acquiring The Knowledge changes the brains of London cab drivers. *Discover Magazine.* http://blogs.discovermagazine.com/notrocketscience/2011/12/08/acquiring-the-knowledge-changes-the-brains-of-london-cab-drivers/ - .UazhXuAhmnk

References

Anderson, J. R. (2000). Acquisition of memories. *Learning and memory: An integrated approach* (pp. 185–225). New York: Wiley & Sons.

Brown, J. S., Collins, A., & Duguid, P. (1989). Situated cognition and the culture of learning. *Educational Researcher, 18*(1), 32–42.

Bruner, J. S., Goodnow, J. J., & Austin, G. A. (1956). *A study of thinking*. London: Chapman & Hall.

Carey, S. (2001). The representation of number in natural language syntax and in the language of thought: A case study of the evolution and development of representational resources. In J. Branquinho (Ed.), *The foundations of cognitive science* (pp. 23–53). Oxford: Clarendon.

Carey, S. (2008). Math schemata and the origins of number representations. *Behavioral and Brain Sciences, 31*(6), 645–646.

Churchland, P. S., Farber, I., & Peterman, W. (2001). The view from here: The nonsymbolic structure of spatial representation. In J. Branquinho (Ed.), *The foundations of cognitive science* (pp. 55–76). Oxford: Clarendon.

Collins, A., Brown, J. S., & Newman, S. E. (1989). Cognitive apprenticeship: Teaching the crafts of reading, writing, and mathematics. In L. B. Resnick (Ed.), *Knowing, learning, and instruction: Essays in honor of Robert Glaser*. Hillsdale, NJ: Erlbaum.

Committee on the Foundations of Assessment. (2002–2003). J. W. Pellegrino, N. Chudowsky, & R. Glase (Eds.), *Knowing what students know*. Washington, DC: National Academy Press.

Common Core State Standards Initiative. (2010). *Common core state standards for mathematics*. Washington DC: National Governors Association Center for Best Practices and the Council of Chief State School Officers.

Davidson, C. N. (2012). *Now you see it: How technology and brain science will transform schools and business for the 21st century*. New York: Penguin.

Dehaene, S. (2009). *Reading in the brain: The new science of how we read*. London: Penguin.

Diemand-Yauman, C., Oppenheimer, D. M., & Vaughan, E. B. (2011). Fortune favors the bold (and the italicized): Effects of disfluency on educational outcomes. *Cognition, 118*, 111–115.

Driscoll, M. (2000). *Psychology of learning for instruction*. Boston: Allyn & Bacon.

Dubinsky, J. M. (2010). Neuroscience education for prekindergarten–12 teachers. *The Journal of Neuroscience, 30*(24), 8057–8060.

Fugelsang, J. A., & Dunbar, K. N. (2005). Brain-based mechanisms underlying complex causal thinking. *Neuropsychologia, 43*, 1204–1213.

Goel, V. (2005). Cognitive neuroscience of deductive reasoning. In K. J. Holyoak & R. G. Morrison (Eds.), *The Cambridge handbook of thinking and reasoning*. Cambridge: Cambridge University Press.

Goldman, C. (2012, September 7). This is your brain on Jane Austen, and Stanford researchers are taking notes. *Stanford Report*. http://news.stanford.edu/news/2012/september/austen-reading-fmri-090712.html

Gopnik, A., Meltzoff, A. N., & Kuhl, P. K. (2000). *The scientist in the crib: What early learning tells us about the mind*. New York: William Morrow.

Griffin, P., McGaw, B., & Care, E. (Eds.). (2012). *Assessment and teaching of 21st century skills*. Dordrecht and New York: Springer.

Hoeft, F. (2014). Intergenerational imaging of reading networks. http://www.bcbl.eu/activities-and-seminars/fumiko-hoeft-intergenerational-imaging-of-reading-networks/

Howard-Jones, P., Pollard, A., Blakemore, S.-J., Rogers, P., Goswami, U., Butterworth, B., . . . Kaufmann, L. (2007). Neuroscience and education, issues and opportunities: A TLRP commentary. http://www.tlrp.org/pub/documents/Neuroscience Commentary FINAL.pdf

Jonassen, D. H. (2001). Handbook of research for educational communications and technology (3rd ed.). Mahwah, NJ: Erlbaum.

Kilpatrick, J., Swafford, J., & Findell, B. (Eds.). (2000). Adding it up. Helping children learn mathematics. Washington, DC: National Academy Press.

Lee, P. J. (2005). Putting principles into practice: Understanding history. In M. S. Donovan & J. Bransford (Eds.), How students learn: History, mathematics, and science in the classroom. Washington, DC: National Academies Press.

Marzano, R. J. (1998). A theory-based meta-analysis of research on instruction. Aurora, CO: Mid-continent Research for Education and Learning (ERIC Document Reproduction Service No. ED 427087).

Marzano, R. J. (2003). Classroom instruction that works. Alexandria, VA: ASCD.

Marzano, R. J. (Producer). (2009, March 11, 2013). Researched strategies. Marzano Research Laboratory. Retrieved from http://www.marzanoresearch.com/research/researched_strategies.aspx

Mason, J., Burton, L., & Stacey, K. (1985). Thinking mathematically. Essex, England: Pearson.

Menon, V. (2014). Arithmetic in the child and adult brain. In R. C. Kadosh & A. Dowker (Eds.), The Oxford handbook of numerical cognition. Oxford, England: Oxford University Press.

Mercier, H., & Sperber, D. (2011). Why do humans reason? Arguments for an argumentative theory. Behavioral and Brain Sciences, 34(2), 57–74.

Moursund, D. (2012). Cognitive neuroscience, computers, and math education. Information Age Education Newsletter (91). http://i-a-e.org/newsletters/IAE-Newsletter-2012-91.html

Myers, C. A., Vandermosten, M., Farris, E. A., Hancock, R., Gimenez, P., Black, J. M., . . . Hoeft, F. (2014). White matter morphometric changes uniquely predict children's reading acquisition. Psychological Science, 10, 1870–1883.

National Council of Teachers of Mathematics. (2007). The learning of mathematics: 69th NCTM yearbook. Reston, VA: National Council of Teachers of Mathematics.

National Research Council. (2000). How people learn: Brain, mind, experience, and school: Expanded edition. Washington, DC: National Academies Press.

National Research Council. (2013). Next generation science standards: For states, by states. Washington, DC: National Academies Press.

OECD. (2007). Understanding the brain: The birth of a learning science. doi: 10.1787/9789264029132-en: OECD Publishing.

Peterson, M. (Producer). (2012, February 2, 2014). The neural foundation for learning math. Retrieved from http://daleadershipinstitute.com/content/neural-foundation-learning-math-0

Posner, M. I., & Rothbart, M. K. (2007). Numeracy. Educating the human brain (pp. 173–187). Washington, DC: American Psychological Association.

Price, G. R., Holloway, I., Vesterinen, M., Rasanen, P., & Ansari, D. (2007). Impaired parietal magnitude processing in developmental dyscalculia. Current Biology, 17(24).

Rabinowitz, M. (Ed.). (1993). Cognitive science foundations of instruction. Hillsdale, NJ: Erlbaum.

Restak, R., & Kim, S. (2010). Long-term memory: Imagining the future by remembering the past. The playful brain: The surprising science of how puzzles improve the mind (pp. 57–86). New York: Riverhead Books.

Sakai, K. L. (2005). Language acquisition and brain development. Science, New Series, 310(5749), 815–819.

Schunk, D. H. (2012). Cognition and instruction. *Learning theories: An educational perspective* (pp. 278–323). Boston: Pearson.

Shaywitz, B. A., Shaywitz, S., Blachman, B., Pugh, K., Fulbright, R., Skudlarski, P., … Gore, J. C. (2004). Development of left occipito-temporal systems for skilled reading in children after a phonologically-based intervention. *Biological Psychiatry*, 926–933.

Shaywitz, S. (2003). *Overcoming dyslexia: A new and complete science-based program for reading problems at any level.* New York: Knopf.

Smith, P., & Ragan, T. (1999). *Instructional design* (2nd ed.). New York: Wiley & Sons.

Society for Neuroscience. (2013). Brain facts. http://www.brainfacts.org/about-neuroscience/brain-facts-book/

Weinstein, C. E., & Mayer, R. E. (1986). The teaching of learning strategies. In M. C. Wittrock (Ed.), *Handbook of research on teaching.* New York: Macmillan.

Wilson, B., & Cole, P. (1996). Cognitive teaching models. In D. H. Jonassen (Ed.), *Handbook of research for educational communications and technology* (pp. 601–621). New York: Macmillan.

12

Action Plan

This final chapter takes a look ahead at the future of learning sciences for educators and brain-based concepts such as those contained in the CORE Guiding Principles. It includes a short reflection on action steps for schools and recommendations for teachers, as well as an invitation to increase dialogue in this important area.

Introduction

When teachers and other educators begin to learn about how the brain works—how making connections strengthens neural pathways, why the way in which information is presented directly affects what's retained in memory, and why feedback is so important—the link between brain science and learning becomes obvious as well as exciting. In short, it becomes "a no-brainer." And yet, this connection is not always seen, even when it matters most by those who care deeply about improving education.

Consider this example: In his February 2013 State of the Union address, President Obama continued to lay out a path for improving education. He made the case for high-quality pre-school and reinforced his "Race to the Top" call for a smarter curricula and higher standards in high schools. Two months later he announced a major new research program designed to revolutionize our understanding of the human brain. The BRAIN Initiative, with $100 million in first-year funding, he said, would give "scientists the tools they need to get a dynamic picture of the brain in action and better understand how we think and how we learn and how we remember" (The U.S. White House, 2013).

President Obama stated that this could lead to treating or even preventing brain disorders, train new generations of scientists, and create businesses and jobs in high technology we can't yet envision. But nowhere did he connect his BRAIN Initiative with his education ideas.

We can't be too hard on the White House. It happens all the time. And that is really the point of this chapter. Educators—be they policy makers, administrators, or teachers—need to be in the conversation regarding improvement in education. In this text, the fields of neuroscience, cognitive psychology, and educational research—our Power of Three—are brought together to show how brain sciences inform educational practices (see Figure 12.1). In whichever way one defines the learning sciences, it is clear that we are just at the beginning of what they can tell us about learning.

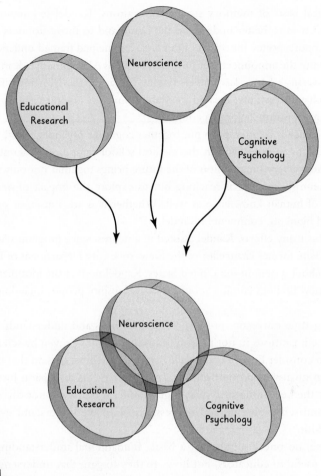

FIGURE 12.1

A Powerful Triad

The Perspective from Scientists

Scientists, who are driven by ideas and excited by the possibilities that discovery can bring, are, as a whole, a cautious group. So, even while they advocate for advances, they evaluate and challenge new findings. This approach is equally well suited to educators and others as they evaluate the value and the limits of the emerging field of learning sciences.

One of the most respected commentators on the neuroscience field is Nobelist Eric Kandel, a recipient of the 2000 Nobel Prize in Physiology or Medicine for his research on the physiological basis of memory storage in neurons. Kandel is known for bringing together perspectives to better understand the brain, and to move frontiers of knowledge forward. He supports policy initiatives in this area, and helped framed understanding across the field following the announcement of the Obama BRAIN Initiative. Kandel is active in Columbia University's ambitious universitywide initiative, the Mortimer B. Zuckerman Mind Brain Behavior Institute, created to establish linkages among virtually all disciplines (http://zuckermaninstitute.columbia.edu).

"Neuroscience is an attempt to put together cognitive psychology and brain science," Kandel remarked in an interview on the medical school campus of Columbia University. He described how a very broad vision of the future brings together not only cognitive psychology and neuroscience but is reaching out to explore the impact of neuroscience on all other areas of human knowledge as well. Whether it is art, music, or economics, the brain and mind figure in, commented Kandel.

Among his many efforts, Kandel assisted in a neuroscience program with educational reformer Joe Klein, former chancellor of the New York City Department of Education, the largest public school system in the United States. Kandel nods at the idea that brain science and the many new findings coming about excite and inspire people, including teachers and their students.

As a long-time university professor, Kandel enjoys and understands teaching. But as a scientist, he is cautious in not making leaps that are not proven by scientific inquiry. When asked to consider how brain science can help teachers, he said that it is important but as of yet an unanswered question. "In fact, we had this discussion just recently," he said. "We're at the beginning of a very large mountain but we're not there yet. . . . We don't understand schizophrenia and depression, [and] we understand even less about how to teach kids."

Of course, no one disputes that a basic, fundamental understanding of how the brain works is useful to educators, but how are they to gain that understanding when so much else is at work in the lives of teachers? So, when told the story about the kindergarten teacher who got excited about the National Research Council "Mind and Brain" report (see Chapter 1), Kandel pondered, half to himself, "But is it going to help her be a better teacher?"

The Perspective from Teachers

Asked that same question, teachers often respond enthusiastically. For them, the answer is *yes*. In their positive response, teachers may be viewing the question differently from the data-driven way a scientist sees it. What teachers are saying is that they see value in understanding how the brain functions and in knowing about its role in learning. Having this understanding, they say, helps make them better teachers.

"I think it is very important, absolutely, even for a younger elementary teacher like myself to learn about the brain," one teacher said. "I feel like I have the same epiphanies as the kindergarten teacher (in Chapter 1) did, that, wow, this is important."

One basic brain concept that teachers have said they find particularly powerful, and the first of the seven CORE Guiding Principles that have comprised this book, is how highly dynamic the brain is. They are impressed by how it is physically and permanently altered, particularly in childhood and teen years, in part by experience. The brain is shaped by what it learns.

"I didn't think about the fact that as teachers we are affecting the way our students' brains are developing and absorbing the information," said another teacher. "We talk about how we shape lives—but that we *really do shape minds*," she said, was a new concept to her. "I wasn't taught this way," she said. "It wasn't the way we learned. But it's very important and it's exciting to me."

Classroom teachers, of course, already know a great deal about how to effectively teach the next generation. Exposing them to a few more ideas from cognitive science, educational research, and neuroscience will not result in a revolution. For one thing, teacher preparation institutions have been holding conferences and building neuroscience into teacher preparation programs for at least several years, and cognitive psychology and educational research have been incorporated for nearly as long as they have existed.

As one teacher educator described it, integrating research and theory from the learning sciences into understanding for teachers' action is a powerful narrative—and has been for some time. Teachers are pragmatists, the educator said, looking for tools for their teaching that work and an understanding of why they work so that they can be multipurposed. The challenges faced by teachers today are daunting; the learning sciences have had and will continue to have the potential to strengthen their arsenal and allow them to increase their effectiveness. The message from this educator is: Teachers are empowered by the early idea of the differences in definitions of learning, from psychology to neuroscience, together with the knowledge that learning physically changes and builds the brain. What can be more important?

The takeaway is to be respectful of what teachers are doing in the classroom. Acknowledging that it is also research-based is important, even as teachers are invited to join in an exploration of what the learning sciences will continue to reveal over time about learning.

A middle school teacher, for instance, discussed how she believes the information presented in the CORE was as useful to her outside the classroom as in it. She described how having this kind of information in parent conferences helped her think about how to better relate and communicate the ideas she intended to share. When providing information on students, she could think of parents as learners too—and even consider her own mindset.

A high school teacher concurred. "I think from the very beginning [of the first guiding principle] where it said we as teachers have a dramatic effect on the development of our students' brains was eye opening," she said. "But then when it went onto the emotions and how our emotions can interfere—for me I know that there are times that I can tune out. To know that this is a natural, normal part of learning, for me this just gives me more compassion. There is reason behind every behavior."

For some educators, brain conversations spark not only thoughts about how they teach but also about how they themselves learn, providing encouragement that they, too, can learn new and sometimes difficult subject matter. Technical information can be challenging to comprehend, especially for those without a science background, but it is possible. As one pre-service English language arts teacher described, learning the basics of brain science at first felt overwhelming to grasp: so much science. But as she went through the ideas of the CORE principles, she said she felt confident that "with an instructor, with discussion, with expertise to guide me, to answer my questions," she could master the material.

A veteran school counselor described how educators need to approach a move toward the learning sciences from two directions: using how the brain works to maximize the learning experience but also teaching in such a manner that actually contributes to the growth of the human brain. As a school counselor, she had always felt that these issues were important—even critical—for students. For her, Guiding Principle 1 reminded her once again of the importance of being aware of student developmental stages and abilities. She saw teachers at her school already fully committed to providing a wide range of experiences so that they could help students develop new pathways and connections in their thinking.

So, as described in this book, all three perspectives of the scientist, psychologist, and educator can be useful. Because the neuroscience of how the human brain learns is still in the early stages, exactly how and to what extent it may ultimately inform teaching is an open question. But by acquiring a base of knowledge that can connect brain function to educational research, teachers and other educators already can gain valuable insight into how we learn—information that may improve how they teach. To recap the research-based fundamentals that comprise this book's CORE knowledge, here again are the Seven Guiding Principles:

- **Guiding Principle 1:** Teachers play a large role in school experiences that literally shape the brain in the school-age years, through the biological properties of neural plasticity.
- **Guiding Principle 2:** Mastering the learning sciences empowers teachers to identify, advocate for, and support decisions that impact their professional lives and success for students.
- **Guiding Principle 3:** How we learn dramatically affects what knowledge we can actually use. Instructional approaches such as priming, elaboration, extension, and knowledge integration are key to learning outcomes. In teacher talk, this is about changing instructional design.
- **Guiding Principle 4:** What we learn endures because of memory strongly influenced through persistence practices that reinforce recall of information and experiences.

- **Guiding Principle 5:** When we effectively learn is influenced by important brain-related factors including emotions. What we filter out matters as much as what we process.
- **Guiding Principle 6:** Physical conditions under which we learn best include aspects of sleep, exercise, and nutrition, and may encompass certain sensitive periods, or times during brain development that are particularly well suited to learning certain types of skills and knowledge.
- **Guiding Principle 7:** The brain is a remarkable pattern-capturing mechanism that regulates the learning process through feedback, including what teachers provide in a variety of forms to effectively support metacognition, the learner's ability to regulate, or shape, his or her own learning.

It Takes a Village: Actions That Schools and Educators Can Take

One teacher who felt confident in his understanding of the fundamentals of the Guiding Principles said, "I could take this with me." He then followed with an important question: "But can I apply it?"

This is a question that raises issues from several perspectives. One is that teachers have a great deal to know and master. This is just one area in a portfolio of teacher knowledge, albeit an influential foundation that touches many others. Another is that this is a rapidly emerging field and staying current will be vital. So, while teachers often will need to decide for themselves how to apply what's been learned, the real key is for a school and district culture to be supportive of brain-related ideas to emerge.

One answer to the teacher's question is this: Work together. Large or small, it is helpful to remember the power of socially augmented cognition. Whether employing professional learning communities, teacher collaboration circles, or other shared efforts, teachers often desire to move in concert with colleagues. This also supports coherence within the school, and allows teachers to serve as important resources for each other.

A second strategy is for teachers to frequently consider the instructional strategies they employ in light of understanding the brain. How do their approaches support human cognition? What small changes might make a large difference to learning outcomes? As a part of ongoing school and classroom efforts, and to instill confidence and expand skills, it may be helpful for teachers and school leaders to ask essential questions such as:

- What am I already doing that achieves one or more of the seven Guiding Principles effectively?
- Is there anything I need to add?
- Do I see anything I should take away?

In this way teachers may deploy their own preferred approaches. For instance, one teacher might like to use prompting questions and reflective discussion, while another employs Socratic dialogues and case studies, or technology-based simulations and social media collaboration.

The point is for teachers to firmly be able to underscore the larger cognitive principles in their instructional designs. The approaches should be purposeful, and then evaluated and assessed, to provide the feedback and evidence the brain needs to update its decisions and move ahead effectively. The most effective teachers are not those who maximally adopt everything new, but who make *strategic* adoptions.

On a broader scale, encouraging a principled culture of the learning sciences requires validation through research. Adopting the latest fads sweeping through schools can be appealing to some, but it leads to pendulum change that burns out teachers and undermines their willingness to engage in change. When teachers see important relevant principles being brought into play in school directions, especially based on making connections with valuable prior knowledge and bringing in new information, then attitudes are entirely different.

Part of this view encourages examining the learning principles behind systems that are being proposed and adopted in schools. A theory of action is needed—how reforms work and why teachers are expected to be successful for the given context. As they consider their decisions, teachers should look for opportunities to put proven ideas based on fundamentals, such as those in the CORE, into play.

Finally, when moving toward encouraging or adopting cognitive science approaches in the instructional program, schools often find it challenging to take on too much change

Preparation Pays Off

Students who are better prepared often experience more success in future tasks and grades. This is an example of what is called an "echo" effect. Students well prepared by teachers in the early grades may evidence even more success as they go along (McCaffrey, Lockwood, Koretz, & Hamilton, 2003). In other words, success builds success.

The extra efforts schools invest in preparing teachers to understand fundamentals of the changing nature of the brain will help underscore the importance of preparation.

Generally, preparation and success in school are some of the most important associations with what students know and can do later in life. Therefore, teachers helping students to achieve improvement early and often is important. The effects of real achievement—when students really do make substantial learning gains—are not only immediate but often experienced over the longer range.

at once. It is more successful to support incremental, steady progress. Schools may phase in such change in a variety of ways—for instance, through selecting a subset of principles to become a center of more focused adoption in a given year. Using this approach, schools can adopt a small set of key ideas to address during a given time period. Teachers and administrators can then examine their current instructional design approaches for how well the principles are met and where gaps exist. When doing so in the context of educational goals and objectives, the change has greater relevance and can become more meaningful.

Moving Ahead in the 21st Century

The oldest known document in history that mentions the human brain is a fragile piece of papyrus nearly 4,000 years old. Artistic red and black characters on a taupe background contain an astonishing ancient treatise on brain surgery—but for all its beauty, the document indicates how woefully little was known about the brain back then. Today, scientific discoveries emerge daily. How will human society react to the new information about its most closely held prize, the brain?

For many years a common way of describing the human brain was to compare it to a computer. Imagine, people would say, if we just could put a new hard drive into our heads, learning would be a snap. But as we move further into the 21st century, the tables have turned. The newest approach to computing is computers that work like our brains and some of the driving force in the development of artificial intelligence is based on the human nervous system. University researchers and commercial technology companies are working on processes to mimic how neurons react to stimuli and connect with other neurons to interpret information.

In this new, biological-based vision to computing, electronic components may be connected in ways that work like synapses. Electrical signals may strengthen and change based on what has been learned. A new kind of computer chip won't come programmed; instead, it might be highly networked to change and alter its actions based on what it experiences, or needs to "learn." Computer scientists describe how a spike that generates a signal will travel to other components and continually change the entire neural network of whatever that is comprised.

Sound familiar? Part of what is holding back progress, say developers, is that scientists still have a long way to go in fully understanding how the brain functions. Yet, it is such an alluring concept that the largest class at Stanford University in Fall 2013 was a graduate-level machine-learning course covering both statistical and biological approaches, with 760 students enrolled.

> ✔️ **RESOURCE**
>
> K–12 teachers can use with students: Markoff, 2013. (See the Citations list at the end of this chapter.)

Can we make a machine that is as fast and as flexible as the human brain, and able to predict, remember, understand, conceptualize, and plan what to do next? In other words, can we replicate the learning mechanisms of the brain? To give you an idea of the task ahead, *The New York Times* reported that in 2013, an IBM supercomputer simulation of the brain that encompassed roughly 10 billion neurons—more than 10% of a human brain—ran about 1,500 times more slowly than an actual brain and required several megawatts of power, compared with just 20 watts of power used by the biological brain (Markoff, 2013). So there is much work ahead. But we live in interesting times when it comes to considering all manners of cognition.

Conclusion

In calling for educators to think critically about how research in neuroscience is important to teaching, the U.S. National Research Council, the International Organisation for Economic Co-operation and Development, and other influential bodies are not suggesting that teachers become brain scientists (Howard-Jones et al., 2007; National Research Council, 2000; OECD, 2007; Society for Neuroscience, 2013). What they are saying is that an active and ongoing dialogue among educators, cognitive psychologists, and scientists can help contribute to understanding how and when humans learn. Already in agreement are teachers who acquire a base of knowledge and see, from a scientific basis, why certain teaching practices work and why others might be less successful in a given situation.

Brain science cannot prescribe what or how teachers should teach. But an awareness of how the brain learns and the findings of new research into brain function and cognition can help equip educators to more effectively draw on their own classroom experience and benefit from insights about learning based on education research.

That teachers may find themselves both intrigued by how they can apply the coming advances in brain science and somewhat daunted by what the future may bring is understandable. At the same time, they have reason to feel both heartened and exhilarated. Unlike computer engineers, teachers already have in their classrooms students equipped with a learning machine that is the envy of the brightest minds in science and technology: the human brain.

Citations

Online, Media, and Print Resources for Teachers

Markoff, J. (2013, December 28). Brainlike computers, learning from experience. *New York Times*, p. A1. Retrieved from http://www.nytimes.com/2013/12/29/science/brainlike-computers-learning-from-experience.html?_r=0

References

Howard-Jones, P., Pollard, A., Blakemore, S.-J., Rogers, P., Goswami, U., Butterworth, B., . . . Kaufmann, L. (2007). Neuroscience and education, issues and opportunities: A TLRP commentary. http://www.tlrp.org/pub/documents/Neuroscience Commentary FINAL.pdf

McCaffrey, D. F., Lockwood, J. R., Koretz, D. M., & Hamilton, L. S. (2003). *Evaluating value-added models for teacher accountability.* Santa Monica, CA: RAND Education for the Carnegie Corporation.

National Research Council. (2000). *How people learn: Brain, mind, experience, and school: Expanded edition.* Washington, DC: National Academies Press.

OECD. (2007). Understanding the brain: The birth of a learning science. doi: 10.1787/9789264029132-en: OECD Publishing.

Society for Neuroscience. (2013). Brain facts. http://www.brainfacts.org/about-neuroscience/brain-facts-book/

The U.S. White House. (2013). Remarks by the President on the BRAIN initiative and American innovation. http://www.whitehouse.gov/the-press-office/2013/04/02/remarks-president-brain-initiative-and-american-innovation

Technical Report on Development of the CORE

(See Chapter 1 for CORE introduction.)

Introduction

What teacher has not stood in front of a classroom at one time or another, gazed out upon the assembled students, and wondered, "What is going on inside their brains?" Today, while that question may yet stump the best of us, thanks to advances in the tools, technology, and discoveries of neuroscientists, we are gaining a clearer insight than ever into how the brain works.

This technical report examines a suggested "core" of knowledge in neuroscience and cognitive psychology for teachers. This appendix has a very specific purpose. The supporting material supplied here provides additional detail on how the documents and ideas of the CORE laid out in the Framework of the CORE were derived. By delving further into the derivation of the CORE, readers can access the original supporting materials of the CORE, as well as understand how to extend and supplement CORE ideas as additional information arises.

For readers interested in this extension to the text, this appendix can be used to (1) explore the methodology of the approach in the Methods section and (2) investigate the results and conclusions in the subsequent sections.

By contrast, readers who prefer instead to focus primarily on the specific principles and ideas presented in the CORE should skip directly to the Framework of the CORE and the outline provided by the Seven Guiding Principles derived from the work that this technical report describes.

For both reader groups, Appendix B provides a full listing of CORE-related resources used in Chapters 2 through 12, including citations for published research studies and analyses.

Insights gleaned from these resources may not only help crystalize a core of understanding for teachers and educators, they may also be used to explore specific topics and delve into related research in more depth. Note that the book bibliography, shown in Appendix B, includes additional citations, including teacher and educator resources of a less technical nature.

Approach to Developing a CORE

Overall, the CORE asks, What should every teacher, educator, and educational leader know to establish a lifetime of learning in this emerging area of brain science? Although much is already established about how the brain functions as compared to what has been known in prior years, considerably more understanding is coming. So here we ask, What do teachers need to know that they can take into the classroom as useful today yet also benefit from as new findings arrive?

This is a big question and probably could be answered effectively in a number of different ways. Here, the approach taken is based on our research that it makes sense to turn to the key resources that teachers are using, or wanting and needing to use, concerning the learning sciences: What skills and knowledge do they require of teachers? Establishing a common base assists in providing materials teachers find useful and relevant, and connecting to prior understanding.

The question asked is, What basis offers a sound footing to get started with key resources in the learning sciences? Those that focus on the brain and human cognition as related in education are the goal. So, in order to explore teaching and learning meta-analysis findings through the lenses of neuroscience and cognitive science as described in Chapter 1, we here consider essential brain science ideas for teachers.

Numerous books, reports, Web resources, and other references put forward their own perspectives, often somewhat differing, about what educators should know about the brain. There is not yet a clear consensus in the field, nor is there a widely accepted summary document about what this "core" knowledge should be, although a number of overview documents are very useful. In this appendix, a suggested core is developed by sampling through a set of these resources. A flexible focus on looking ahead is also maintained, as teachers need a base of knowledge that will serve to build long careers in education. Reflecting on where current brain science materials for teachers establish common ground and, conversely, how they differ can help illuminate information for a suggested core. So, such a study was employed here. The purpose was threefold:

- To use the literature itself to clarify what brain science ideas might shed the most light on teaching and learning, and to build on this in the context of educational meta-analysis research results in subsequent chapters. This provides us with an initial learning science "lens" consistent with the scholarship in neuroscience, cognitive psychology, and educational research—what we have called "the power of three."

- To cast a forward-looking eye by identifying what emerging areas need to be added to these core ideas, such that teachers have a solid career-long foundation for encountering new findings to inform practice on an ongoing basis. This will help situate teachers with the knowledge to build effectively on brain-related ideas over the course of a career.
- To work specifically with neuroscientists and other scientists to explore directly what important gaps, if any, must be bridged in the literature for teachers. We've asked, What has been left out that is important to include for education that is sufficiently well understood to share with the field at this time?

Methods

As in prior work (Scalise et al., 2011), a systematic synthesis of reviewed materials described here was based on the Harris Cooper methodology in the third edition of *Synthesizing Research* (Cooper, 1998). Methods in the Cooper approach are premised on systematic guidelines for evaluating the validity of synthesis outcomes. In this methodology, concepts offered to explain a particular phenomenon are collected together and compared in breadth, internal consistency, and the nature of their predictions, from a selected set of materials. Such reviews can contain descriptions of critical experiments already conducted or suggested, assessments of which theory is most powerful, and reformulations or integrations of abstract notions from different theories. The methodology specifies clear approaches to problem formulation, data collection, data validation stage, data synthesis, and presentation of results. These include five stages of work:

1. Establishing the research question or questions that clearly define the scope of the project for problem formulation
2. Utilizing basic tenets of sound data gathering to produce a sufficiently comprehensive integration of relevant materials in a data collection stage
3. Implementing a data validation stage, where clear methodology is used to assess and compare the quality of evidence in the materials
4. Employing an analysis and interpretation (or synthesis) stage, where the carefully scoped, collected, and evaluated data are triangulated through synthesis techniques as appropriate to the body of work examined
5. Disseminating results designed to share the synthesized research endeavor with policy makers and educators

In this case, the research question was to identify a set of core ideas from neuroscience and cognitive science research described as most important for educators of school-age children to understand. "School age" encompassed children from approximately ages 5 to18. The scope of this sampling does not include early childhood education or post-secondary/adult learning. Many of the ideas for these educational areas do overlap but restricting the scope was necessary to make a sampling of materials more feasible in scale.

For the purposes of sampling for sound data gathering to produce a sufficiently comprehensive integration of relevant materials, a saturation evaluation approach was employed. In saturation evaluation, where the relevant materials may be far too vast for full inspection of every item, the goal is to assemble a representative but not necessarily exhaustive set of relevant materials. If materials from different sources contain similar information—such as regarding what brain science ideas are important for teachers—patterns and trends will begin to emerge and repeat as sources are examined.

The saturation evaluation thus captures common ground through the trend analysis. It also documents where sources diverge in substantial ways. Once sufficient sources are examined such that information collected from additional sources primarily replicates what has already been gathered, this is considered a "core" sample. For validation, sampling may continue in order to establish the body of knowledge collected as a core, through showing that few additional key ideas emerge with additional sampling, or the process may begin again with a new sampling of relevant materials to confirm a similar core emerges. The premise is that another representative though not exhaustive sampling through comparable literature would lead to a similar "core" sample. This can be addressed with additional sampling. To systematize a search of the literature, first a search for sources was undertaken, then several selection criteria were applied. The search of sources employed Harris Cooper methods for search of electronic databases followed by a search of "fugitive" or "grey" literature. Here, the electronic databases employed resources of the University of Oregon library system, which included the local university collection, the Summit U.S. Pacific Northwest collection, and the international WorldCat collection, which contained access to both extensive book collections and numerous electronic databases. Grey literature was then additionally explored as information not controlled by or disseminated through publishers, and therefore not necessarily available in the typical publishing channels, but produced by such entities as government, academia, and industry—for instance, through reports and white papers. Our search for fugitive or grey literature employed the "snowballing" approach (Miles & Huberman, 1994) by making solicitations to key researchers and by checking prior literature reviews and research syntheses (i.e., using the reference lists of prior reviews and research syntheses to identify key resources). Results of the search for sources are shown in the next section, titled "Results."

For implementing a data validation stage with clear methodology to assess and compare the quality of evidence in the materials, relevancy criteria were established for the sampling in the Harris Cooper stage 3. Drawing on the results of the search for those sources, the following five criteria were then applied:

1. *Focus Relevance:* The materials consisted of books, edited book sections, book chapters, and brain science reports intended for teachers and educators, organized to present brain science findings with at least some relationship to teaching and learning.

2. *Depth Relevance:* Information included was of sufficient technical depth supported by evidence directly citing the connection to the relevant scientific literature, with references both embedded at the appropriate point in text to make clear the connection and also fully explicated in a well-documented bibliography.

3. *Time Frame Relevance:* The time frame focused most closely on approximately the last 10 years of material in this area, with an outer limit of 15 years for some earlier resources (ultimately extended by 2 years [see "Results" section]). It also focused on selecting resources for which not only the publication dates themselves were relatively recent but predominantly the citations throughout the source were for the purpose intended relative to the research journal literature to the extent possible, since much has been learned in these areas in recent years.

4. *Developmental Relevance:* The materials selected were intended to deal with neuroscience and cognitive science research addressing primarily the needs of school-age children, in those cases where a developmental need existed to address by age 5 to 18. Also, the materials were selected to employ a reasonably sized scope to the study.

5. *Representational Relevance:* In order to employ a reasonably sized scope to the study, representational relevance was added. No more than four chapters, book sections, or brain science reports authored by the same individual scholar were selected. This was intended to allow the sample across the literature to better represent a range of perspectives within a body of work reasonably sized to analyze in this way. This added to the "saturation" characteristics of the results, while remaining within a manageable scope for analysis and interpretation of the sources.

For the analysis and interpretation stage, where the carefully scoped, collected, and evaluated data are triangulated through synthesis techniques, the sampled materials were reviewed by methods of integrative research to gather a set of core ideas that would represent both the common ground and the divergent characteristics. During this stage, and throughout the subsequent analysis, a methods-description approach was used. Here, explanations of the primary sources are used to emerge new patterns and codes throughout the data collection and analysis. This reframes the initial framework iteratively until all sources are analyzed. Finally, a posterior framework, or resulting set of patterns, is released.

Methods of integrative research (Jackson, 1980) include sampling the relevant materials and then representing the characteristics of their content and evidence. Miles and Huberman's (1994) approaches to data reduction and display were used for this portion of the literature synthesis. First, for early steps in the analysis, each relevant source was reviewed for aspects deemed important in that source for the brain science knowledge base of teachers. Guiding questions for this review process, as described by Miles and Huberman, included, What were "the main concepts, themes, issues, and questions" seen during the review (Miles & Huberman, 1994, p. 51)?

Particular attention, as Miles and Huberman describe, was paid to being explicitly mindful of the purposes of the materials and the conceptual lenses applied. In this case, the purpose of the work was (1) to gather information across multiple sources and perspectives clarifying what brain science ideas might shed the most light on teaching and learning, (2) to cast a forward-looking eye by identifying emerging areas, and (3) to focus on important gaps, if any, needing to be addressed for teachers to have a solid career-long foundation for encountering new brain science findings to inform practice on an ongoing basis. Thus, each characteristic described in the relevant source that was associated by the authors with a key idea of brain science was included in the notes for that article's review. When multiple separate characteristics were described in a source, which was the case in all the materials, each was coded as a separate "instance" of a brain science characteristic from the same study.

As Miles and Huberman ask, Given a set of codes that describe the phenomena of interest, how can the researcher then move to a second level—"one that is more general, and perhaps more explanatory" (1994, p. 69)? They describe a process of "pattern codes," which are explanatory or inferential codes that identify an emergent theme, configuration, or explanation, based on the first-level coding. The first-level coding is then a device for summarizing segments of data; the second-level pattern coding is a way of grouping these summaries into a smaller number of sets, themes, or constructs. Such pattern codes are often identified when ideas repeat in the instances, and themes begin to emerge.

Of course, the dissemination phase of the Harris Cooper methodology includes methodological and results descriptions such as these. However, the overall premise for dissemination here will draw on an idea suggested by Dr. Michael Posner (2012), a cognitive scientist who has worked extensively with brain research teams for many years and the author of numerous publications on brain research. He suggested that the dissemination contribution to the field use the results of teaching and learning meta-analysis with which we wanted to work in this book as an exercise for educators in thinking about how the findings might relate to both neuroscience research and research in cognition. Crossing these ideas allows drawing on the power of three. As Posner said, "It is all the brain after all!"

Making a practice in connection helps give educators more opportunities for multiple thought enactments, Posner said, which might help the ideas become more a part of practice depending on where a connection might be seen that is useful to teachers. This would help move discoveries from research into practice for teachers. It could also encourage instructional leadership to move in these directions as well, for policy makers and state leadership in schools.

Results

Using the techniques described, materials were identified, with the help of Columbia University for some of the key resources, from approximately a 17-year span of relevant literature, from January 1995 to May 2012, when the search stage of the project was completed. A start date of 1995 was selected to begin the identification, as some key references dated to this time. The end date coincided with the conclusion of the initial search for materials.

The scan identified 56 extended resources potentially applicable to the criteria established, including books, edited book sections by differing authors, and reports. The results are shown in Appendix B. Note that although shorter and more discrete resources, such as individual journal articles or research papers on more specific topics, are not included in the book-length resources assembled for this initial CORE sampling, as primary sources they are fully integrated into the book chapters and are used to much more extensively describe the CORE concepts. In addition to Appendix B, full referencing of all sources is shown in the Citations section at the end of each chapter. Once identified as possibly relevant, the next step, undertaken by University of Oregon researchers, was to review each of the 56 full-text resources in depth for meeting all five aspects of the relevancy criteria for this study, described previously, and then to sample from them. After identifying materials that fit the first three relevancy criteria—focus, depth, and time frame—the sources were read and analyzed to begin to categorize the various components, features, and results related to brain science deemed of importance by the authors for teachers and for learning impacts. Of the original 56 full-text resources, 35 were determined to be most relevant to the criteria and therefore included in subsequent sampling; 21 were deemed less directly relevant and therefore were removed from the subsequent sampling (see Appendix B).

With regard to collecting the components, features, and results—or Big Ideas—in the selected materials, it is important to understand that teachers are charged with helping to identify what brain science ideas are relevant to practice. They often focus on explicit features of resource materials, selecting or eliminating choices based on features they may have in mind. By providing a compendium of concepts that appear to be important based on research-synthesized evidence of what is in such materials, it is hoped to broaden the feature-focused perspective of practitioners and tie it to a body of relevant, research-based evidence, into which decision makers can easily and directly tap. While this process is begun here, the framework should not be considered complete but rather a work in progress for others to advance.

Following review of the materials as described earlier, the fourth and fifth criteria were then applied: *developmental relevance* to gauge reasonable applicability to school-age children and young adults, *and representational relevance,* calling for no more than four sources (book chapters/sections, reports, or Web-based materials) from any one author. The limit from any one author was to select a subset of materials reasonably representative of brain science materials intended to inform educators working with the identified populations.

Finally, after secondary screening of the remaining materials following application of the final two relevancy criteria, a sample of 62 separate book chapters or report sections was generated from the 35 relevant extended materials. These 62 sources became the "core" material reviewed to answer the questions posed earlier in this appendix, hereinafter to be identified as

CORE, and are shown in Appendix B. Many other references were added in each chapter. It should be remembered of course that the premise of saturation evaluation of this type is that other valid samples of materials could have been obtained, but if sufficiently representative would be expected to lead to similar conclusions regarding the Big Ideas of information contained. For the 21 sources not included in the CORE, the reasons these materials did not fully match criteria are summarized here. Full results are reported in Appendix B:

- One resource, released in 1992, was published outside of the time frame adopted here.
- Four did not meet the depth constraints for the purpose/audience here. Three of these showed references dated relative to other sources, and one did not sufficiently focus on reporting current brain science findings.
- Two additional resources showed references dated relative to other sources.
- Eight resources did not meet the focus constraints for the purpose/audience here, including being more directed to early childhood needs, post-secondary, adult learning, or parent audiences.
- Five resources were gauged as intended to present either more or less technical perspectives than identified for this purpose.
- One resource represented perspective that for this purpose was already represented by another of the author's publications in the sample.

Using this evidence, the 62 book chapters and report sections were then organized according to the Society for Neuroscience and Mind Brain Behavior Initiative topics and descriptors and additional resources were included for each chapter. They are mostly organized into five overarching categories, which also frame the chapters of this book:

1. Resources that were intended to provide an overview across the field of brain science for teachers (5 resources), and those that were more specialized primarily into one of four areas: (a) anatomy and basic brain functioning, including neural circuitry and networks; (b) information processing; (c) memory and recall; and (d) brain plasticity (21 resources)
2. What teachers often think of as mind and brain behaviors, including discussing concepts such as emotion, creativity, expertise, knowledge integration and transfer, control and judgment, and motivation (20 resources)
3. What is known about applications of these concepts to some specific areas of interest to teachers, including reading, writing, and literacy; sensory/motor, movement, and bodily health; science education, technology, and 21st century skills; the arts; and mathematics (16 resources).

Next, an initial framework and filtering criteria for evaluating claims of brain science concepts for teachers and educators was generated. This was done through a first-level coding for patterns in the CORE sources but only of the five "overview" resources as a subset of the CORE, to begin pattern identification of the key ideas and concepts. In the saturation evaluation methodology adopted here, it is important to start with some resources expected to yield an informative range of ideas. Then additional patterns are harvested in the subsequent stages as well, so that the initial patterns are helpfully exposed through a subset of perhaps the most representative resources, but do not overly impose restrictive structure on the data collection process. The selection of resources for the initial patterns thus does not ultimately "lock down" any of the results. The overview resources were selected as the most promising starting point because they were intended by a variety of different organizations around the world to capture a body of brain science information currently of importance to teachers.

The five overview resources for this stage were selected as those from different agencies that have attempted in recent years to broadly identify the landscape of brain science relevant to educators. These five were the Society for Neuroscience Brain Facts publication, a 79-page document that explores the brain and nervous system (Society for Neuroscience, 2008); the U.S. National Research Council's "Mind and Brain" chapter in the National Academy Press book for educators on *How People Learn* (National Research Council, 2000); the international Organisation for Economic Co-operation and Development (OECD) executive report chapter on *Understanding the Brain: The Birth of a Learning Science* (OECD, 2007); the "Neuroscience and Education" report of the Teaching and Learning Research Programme (TLRP), U.K.'s Economic and Social Research Council (Howard-Jones et al., 2007); and finally, to add contrast to these preceding overview resources, an *On Intelligence* book chapter discussing "A New Framework for Intelligence" (Hawkins & Blakeslee, 2004). The last resource is perhaps a more unusual choice, since it was included as representing a rather different perspective, arising out of computational neuroscience but was added to represent an additional perspective.

These resources were included for the initial pattern generation to represent a substantial body of synthesis literature from major institutions recently publishing for educators in this area. As such, the resources were expected to generally capture most of the broad patterns of interest. Deeper investigation with the full body of literature through the second-level coding in subsequent chapters expanded on this initial review, and became the focus of content for each book chapter.

To undertake the top-level pattern coding, all major brain science ideas (Big Ideas) in three of the five initial resources were identified. Not included were the U.S. NRC book chapter and the U.K. "Neuroscience and Education" report, which were held back for a validity check on the results and to add to the initial patterns, as described here.

For the three first resources, a simple framework of theme and pattern coding was assigned. The pattern coding was based on using as themes a set of topics identified by the Society for Neuroscience, matched against a set of descriptive concepts generated with representatives from Columbia University's Mortimer B. Zuckerman Mind Brain Behavior Institute (http://zuckermaninstitute.columbia.edu). The resulting themes for the purpose of this book are shown in Table A1.1.

TABLE A1.1 Themes for CORE Patterns Organized in Five Sections by Society for Neuroscience/Mind Brain Behavior Initiative Topics and Descriptors

A: Overview across the field of brain science for teachers (five resources); B: anatomy and basic brain functioning, including neural circuitry and networks, information processing, memory and recall, and brain plasticity (21 resources); C: what teachers often think of as mind and brain behaviors, including discussing concepts such as emotion, creativity, expertise, knowledge integration and transfer, control and judgment, and motivation (20 resources); D: reading, writing, and literacy; sensory/motor, movement, and bodily health; science education, technology, and 21st-century skills; the arts; and mathematics (16 resources).

Code	Society for Neuroscience Topic	Mind Brain Behavior Initiative Descriptor Aligned to Society for Neuroscience Topic, Using Examples for This Book
NNB	**overview: neuron to networks to behavior**	• What is learning and how do we do it? Learning from *neurons to networks to behavior*
KM	neuroplasticity	• Full-sized brain but not full-sized thinking—how the brain *keeps maturing* after it stops getting bigger
M	**memory**	• That sounds familiar: Neurons recall information and recode it for stronger *memories*
PR	attention	• I recognize that! How brain is wired for *pattern recognition*
NPI	**disorders**	• Common childhood *neurological/psychological illnesses* (autism, dyslexia, ADHD, mental retardation)
EAS	emotion and stress	• Feelings matter: How *emotions and stress* can interfere with learning and how motivation can enhance it
FG	play	• When learning *feels good:* How the motivation system of the brain promotes success, **as well as play**
EF	executive function	• *Executive function* (metacognition): the brain within the brain
SR	self-regulation	• Delayed gratification and *self-regulation*: Early predictors of success and what they say about the brain
DB	**drugs**	• *Deceiving the brain*: How neuroactive compounds (legal and illegal drugs, caffeine, nicotine, alcohol) affect the brain
DA	**language** (example: ELA)	• *Language* development is natural; reading acquisition is not: How the wiring of the brain naturally gives rise to speaking but not reading and writing

(Continued)

TABLE A1.1 *(Continued)*		
HH	sleep (example: Health/PE)	• *Healthy habits* for a healthy brain: sleep, exercise, good diet
SD	gender (example: Arts)	• ***Similarities and differences*** **among us: Expression and the case of space**
TU	technology (example: Science)	• ***Technology use*** **and exploring the unknown in brain science**
SI	social networks (example: Mathematics)	• ***Social interactions*** **and how they can contribute to building understanding through logic and pattern**

Miles and Huberman describe a process of reviewing for pattern coding by "loosely held chunks of meaning," with attention paid to "unfreeze and reconfigure" as the data shape up and more instances are included (Miles & Huberman, 1994, p. 70). In this case, as more sources were reviewed and instances assigned, themes began to emerge.

The Society for Neuroscience in 2009 convened a summit on neuroscience and education, inviting experts in neuroscience, cognitive science, and education to create a report. The report included a list of core brain science topics with the potential for impact on education and learning: neuroplasticity, play, attention, behavior, stress, sleep, the arts, gender, executive function, social networks, self-regulation, and technology. Initial themes for pattern coding were drawn from these Society for Neuroscience topics arrayed against the Mind Brain Behavior Initiative descriptors.

For the three initial resources, 132 key or Big Ideas were found to be present, many of which overlapped or were the same, resulting in 58 distinct patterns, or different but major brain science concepts emerging in total from the three sources. A fourth source was then analyzed and added, the U.S. NRC "Mind and Brain" chapter, in order to identify additional patterns and to see the extent to which "saturation" of new information had been achieved. The intent was to compare its key ideas to what had already emerged in the prior analysis of the other three overview resources. This next resource yielded 27 major concepts, most of which substantially overlapped with the prior 58 patterns, resulting in adding only 1 new pattern, generating less than a 2% increase in patterns, for 59 total patterns identified over the four resources.

With regard to the analysis of gaps, neither framework was found fully sufficient to cover all the patterns alone, suggesting some gaps in the overarching framework concepts. For the most part, the gaps are not major, as shown in Table A1.1, and could be addressed by the additional text added in bold in the table. These extensions point out areas of the field where additional research or brain science ideas are being suggested for teachers. Where the bold text is added, one or the other framework needed some extensions to address these conceptual gaps. Given these extensions, gaps in the literature itself are discussed in the results of Table A1.2.

TABLE A1.2 Frequencies for Themes in Four Initial Resources Examined

Pattern	Frequency	Percentage
NNB	40	25%
KM	35	22%
M	32	20%
PR	6	4%
NPI	8	5%
EAS	7	4%
FG	2	1%
EF	1	1%
SR	5	3%
DB	7	4%
DA	3	2%
HH	7	4%
SD	0	0%
TU	4	3%
SI	2	1%
Total	**159**	**100%**

Although numerous patterns were repeated across sources, all of the concepts identified in the first four sources could be aligned with the Society for Neuroscience/Mind Brain Behavior Initiative themes with extensions added (as shown in Table A1.1), by combining the Society for Neuroscience topics and the Mind Brain Behavior Initiative descriptors. For the patterns generated from the four initial CORE resources, both the Society for Neuroscience topics and the Mind Brain Behavior Initiative descriptors overlapped considerably but not completely, showing common ground but also some thinking in each that extended the other.

Summaries of the pattern percentages and topics for the four resources over themes are shown in Table A1.2. Table A1.2 gives an indication of coverage and gaps in the resources, relative to the framework ideas. For frequencies of pattern, it can be seen that the vast majority of concepts introduced in the four resources explore basic brain anatomy and circuitry, neuroplasticity and memory, which together account for about 67%, or two-thirds, of the concept coverage.

All the remaining areas together account for only one-third of the concept coverage, and are generally sparsely covered in the overview resources, although of great interest to teachers, educators, and educational policy makers. This, then, is an indication of where gaps or sparseness of coverage may exist in the teacher literature. More might be done to facilitate the needs of educators to have access to findings in these areas as well, especially as more information emerges.

In part, this book is intended to help address the "saturation" trend in these important areas. Through examining all the areas more in depth, the book chapters include the remaining CORE resources and bring other materials to bear in the chapter discussions as well.

Next Steps

Of course, the ideas here are only a small fraction of a much larger range of instructional design concepts, ideas, and experiences that educators as highly skilled professionals in their subject matter and grade-level areas bring to working effectively with children and young adults. Or perhaps these ideas are an important and fairly new emerging area about which teachers might like to know more, as discussed in the neuroethics references in Chapter 9.

As the chapters of the book fleshed out the ideas here, Miles and Huberman described the process of pattern coding as a "ladder of abstraction" (Miles & Huberman, 1994, p. 91), drawing on work from Carney (1990):

> You begin with a text, trying out coding categories on it, then moving to identify themes and trends, and then to testing hunches and findings, aiming first to delineate "deep structure" and then to integrate the data into an explanatory framework.

However, there are numerous cautions concerning the data presented here and in the book chapters. Limitations are of course inherent in any methodology, with any technique or set of techniques selected, so they need to be discussed and examined specifically for the given approaches in light of what limitations may mean both for data generation and analysis and also for interpretation.

We have attempted here to include a systematic portion of the literature, but this search should be considered an informative sample only, due to the nature of the restrictions on the approaches described. In assessing the validity of the methods in an approach such as this, one must consider whether the study was completed in "a careful enough manner so that the result can be trusted to shed light on the hypothesis of interest" (Cooper, 1998, p. 79).

To address such concerns, the saturation evaluation approach was used. It attempts to select a representative sample and examine where sources are converging and diverging, and whether sufficient replication is seen in the findings. As each new resource is added, the information function—in other words, the new information obtained for each new resource—is typically rising but at some point when sufficient resources have been examined, the function begins to flatten. This indicates that a strong degree of reiteration is being captured over the body of collected work. For the results here, although a total of 56 resources were examined for the CORE and introduced in a second stage of analysis in subsequent chapters, the first-stage analysis showed that with just three of the overview resources examined, the primary content of a fourth was well captured, with only one additional pattern among 59 total emerging.

A primary concern of evidence validation is to avoid an evaluator's potential predisposition toward outcomes. All studies can be criticized methodologically. It is even possible to unwittingly (Lord, Ross, & Lepper, 1979) point out design and analysis deficiencies in those studies or resources that run counter to some predisposition help by the evaluator, for which we acknowledge the need for cautious interpretation here. An additional concern with limitations of such techniques for evidentiary critiquing include that lists of patterns may not be complete. Pattern frameworks and guidelines such as used here through the Society of Neuroscience and Mind Brain Behavior Initiative resources can help specify an explicit set of coding criteria. But such lists may not be complete in the context of any particular data collection or set of resources to be analyzed. Addition of a methods-description approach uses examination of the primary sources to emerge new patterns and codes. This helps allow these methodological concerns to be addressed as the findings of each study emerge. The approach captures additional information, as is done here.

By mixing the two approaches of a precoded framework and allowing new codes to emerge, forms of false positive and false negative error can be identified, and study concerns documented and compared through the materials. Additionally, sources of coding error were minimized by the development and documentation of the coding sheets that emerged, such as summarized in Table A1.1.

Update to the Analysis

As an update to the analysis, we have continued to align with the Harris Cooper methodology in Synthesizing Research by following our search for grey literature with the "snowballing" approach (Miles & Huberman, 1994), seeking feedback from key researchers and by checking prior literature reviews and research syntheses (i.e., using the reference lists of prior reviews and research syntheses to identify key resources). Eight more resources were identified subsequent to the original analysis and incorporated into Appendix B for CORE inclusion, bringing the total of resources identified within the scope of the saturation evaluation to 70. In addition to this, more than 250 journal articles and other technical references have been included in the book chapters, to support the ideas described in the CORE, as well as some resources that teachers can share with students.

Conclusion

The CORE work in this appendix is meant to investigate and assemble a set of ideas that may be useful to teachers, through examining the expressions of numerous institutions and authors who have participated in this conversation over time. Preparing teachers with a core of understanding across these concepts provides a foundation for career-long educational work in the field. This is in part necessary because it is expected, as described in Chapter 1, that many more resources will appear that teachers will need to, or wish to, access and understand over time to evaluate their relevance to their own practice.

It is hoped that others will also add to this conversation. In the end, a broad swath of materials, plus the ability to *evaluate* them and to thoughtfully consider *claims* using *evidence* will be essential if teachers wish to realize potential in this area. It is also good practice for 21st-century learning, where much information is available but of limited value without the ability to judge its credibility and utility.

At a 2012 conference in San Francisco on "Educating the Whole Child/Student: Using Brain Science for Smarter, Happier and Healthier Learners," classroom teachers, school administrators, speech pathologists, counselors, and others involved in education were drawn to the topic of how the brain can support education. They attended sessions and asked questions. Many people in the audience struggled with core ideas of neuroscience and cognitive science. For instance, the idea of a baby's brain packed with neurons with some connections that get pruned away was for many a new concept (see Chapter 2).

Finding the fundamental ideas among the mix of new ideas out there, with more arriving every day through the news media and other outlets, is a challenge for teachers. Happiness, acting-out, motivation—How do they relate, or do they even relate, to what brain science can begin to help explain? To see how inspiration as well as practical help, ideas, and comments can be garnered is the goal many teachers have in mind.

As one school librarian said, "I'm trying to bring materials back with me for the teachers, but there's no way to tie it all together so that it's meaningful to them."

If you are a teacher, the intent here is that investigating a CORE principle, structured for teachers, whether pre-service or in-service, may affect what you do every day, so that at the end of each chapter you can ask, "How can I use this tomorrow in my classroom?"

Citations

Carney, T. F. (1990). *Collaboration inquiry methodology.* Windsor, Ontario, Canada: University of Windsor, Division for Instructional Development.

Cooper, H. M. (1998). *Synthesizing research: A guide for literature reviews* (3rd ed.). Thousand Oaks, CA: Sage.

Hawkins, J., & Blakeslee, S. (2004). A new framework of intelligence. *On intelligence* (pp. 85–105). New York: Times Books.

Howard-Jones, P., Pollard, A., Blakemore, S.-J., Rogers, P., Goswami, U., Butterworth, B., . . . Kaufmann, L. (2007). Neuroscience and education, issues and opportunities: A TLRP commentary. http://www.tlrp.org/pub/documents/Neuroscience Commentary FINAL.pdf

Jackson, G. B. (1980). Methods for integrative reviews. *Review of Educational Research, 50*(3), 438–460.

Lord, C., Ross, L., & Lepper, M. (1979). Biased assimilation and attitude polarization: The effects of prior theories on subsequently considered evidence. *Journal of Personality and Social Psychology, 37,* 2098–2109.

Miles, M. B., & Huberman, A. M. (1994). *Qualitative data analysis: An expanded sourcebook.* Thousand Oaks, CA: Sage.

National Research Council. (2000). 5. Mind and brain. *How people learn: Brain, mind, experience, and school: Expanded edition* (pp. 114–128). Washington, DC: The National Academies Press.

OECD. (2007). Understanding the brain: The birth of a learning science. doi: 10.1787/9789264029132-en: OECD Publishing.

Posner, M. I. (2012). Interview for neuroscience matters with Michael Posner, University of Oregon.

Scalise, K., Timms, M., Moorjani, A., Clark, L., Holtermann, K., & Irvin, P. S. (2011). Student learning in science simulations: Design features that promote learning gains. *Journal of Research in Science Teaching, 48*(9), 1050–1078.

Society for Neuroscience. (2008). *Brain facts: A primer on the brain and nervous system.* Washington, DC: Society for Neuroscience.

Summary of **Sampled Resources** of the **CORE**

(See Chapter 1 and Appendix A for additional CORE information.)

I. Core Inclusion: Identified Resources Included in the CORE Sample Selected

1. Anderson, J. R. (2000). Acquisition of memories. *Learning and memory: An integrated approach* (pp. 185–225). New York: Wiley & Sons.
2. Anderson, J. R. (2000). Retention of memories. *Learning and memory: An integrated approach* (pp. 226–264). New York: Wiley & Sons.
3. Anderson, J. R. (2000). Retrieval of memories. *Learning and memory: An integrated approach* (pp. 265–303). New York: Wiley & Sons.
4. Anderson, J. R. (2000). Skill acquisition. *Learning and memory: An integrated approach* (pp. 304–337). New York: Wiley & Sons.
5. Bigge, M. L., & Shermis, S. S. (2004). How does Bruner's cognitive-interactionist, narrative-centered cultural psychology treat learning and teaching? *Learning theories for teachers* (pp. 133–153). Boston: Pearson.
6. Carey, S. (2001). The representation of number in natural language syntax and in the language of thought: A case study of the evolution and development of representational resources. In J. Branquinho (Ed.), *The foundations of cognitive science* (pp. 23–53). Oxford: Clarendon.
7. CAST. (2003). Individual differences, teaching approaches and new media. Retrieved from http://4.17.143.133/udl/index.cfm?i=11
8. Damasio, A. R. (2001). Reflections on the neurobiology of emotion and feeling. In J. Branquinho (Ed.), *The foundations of cognitive science*. Oxford: Clarendon.

9. Damasio, H. (2001). Words and concepts in the brain. In J. Branquinho (Ed.), *The foundations of cognitive science*. Oxford: Clarendon.

10. Dehaene, S. (2009). The dyslexic brain. *Reading in the brain: The new science of how we read* (pp. 235–262). London: Penguin.

11. Dehaene, S. (2009). How do we read? *Reading in the brain: The new science of how we read* (pp. 11–52). London: Penguin.

12. Dehaene, S. (2009). Learning to read. *Reading in the brain: The new science of how we read* (pp. 195–234). London: Penguin.

13. Diamond, M., & Hopson, J. (1998). Learning not by chance. *Magic trees of the mind: How to nurture your child's intelligence, creativity, and healthy emotions from birth through adolescence* (pp. 264–284). New York: Dutton.

14. Doidge, N. (2007). Imagination: How thinking makes it so. *The brain that changes itself: Stories of personal triumph from the frontiers of brain science* (pp. 196–214). New York: Viking Penguin.

15. Doya, K., Ishii, S., Pouget, A., & Rao, R. P. N. (2011). Reading neural codes: Spike coding. *Bayesian brain: Probabilistic approaches to neural coding* (pp. 15–47). Cambridge, MA: MIT Press.

16. Eliot, L. (2010). Starting school. *Pink brain, blue brain: How small differences grow into troublesome gaps—And what we can do about it*. New York: Mariner Books.

17. Farber, I., Peterman, W., & Churchland, P. S. (2001). The view from here: The nonsymbolic structure of spatial representation. In J. Branquinho (Ed.), *The foundations of cognitive science* (pp. 55–76). Oxford: Clarendon.

18. Frith, U., & Blakemore, S.-J. (2005). *The learning brain: Lessons for education*. Malden, MA: Blackwell.

19. Gazzaniga, M. S. (2008). Is anybody there? *Human: The science behind what makes us unique* (pp. 276–321). New York: HarperCollins.

20. Gazzaniga, M. S. (2011). The way we are. *Who's in charge? Free will and the science of the brain* (pp. 7–41). New York: HarperCollins.

21. Gazzaniga, M. S. (2011). The parallel and distributed brain. *Who's in charge? Free will and the science of the brain* (pp. 43–73). New York: HarperCollins.

22. Gazzaniga, M. S. (2011). The interpreter. *Who's in charge? Free will and the science of the brain* (pp. 75–103). New York: HarperCollins.

23. Gibb, B. J. (2007). Chemical control: How legal and illegal drugs affect the brain. *The rough guide to the brain* (pp. 171–202). London: Rough Guides Ltd.

24. Gigerenzer, G., Todd, P. M., & ABC Research Group. (1999). Fast and frugal heuristics: The adaptive toolbox. *Simple heuristics that make us smart* (pp. 3–34). Oxford: Oxford University Press.

25. Goleman, D. (1995). Trauma and emotional relearning. *Emotional intelligence: Why it can matter more than IQ* (pp. 200–214). London: Bloomsbury.

26. Goleman, D. (1995). The master aptitude. *Emotional intelligence: Why it can matter more than IQ* (pp. 78–95). London: Bloomsbury.

27. Goleman, D. (1995). Anatomy of an emotional hijacking. *Emotional intelligence: Why it can matter more than IQ* (pp. 13–32). London: Bloomsbury.

28. Hawkins, J., & Blakeslee, S. (2004). A new framework of intelligence. *On intelligence* (pp. 85–105). New York: Times Books.

29. Hardiman, M. M., & Denckla, M. B. (2010). The science of education: Informing teaching and learning through the brain sciences. In The Dana Foundation (Ed.), *Cerebrum 2010: Emerging ideas in brain science*. New York: Dana Press.

30. Howard-Jones, P., Pollard, A., Blakemore, S.-J., Rogers, P., Goswami, U., Butterworth, B., . . . Kaufmann, L. (2007). Neuroscience and education, issues and opportunities: A TLRP commentary. Retrieved from http://www.tlrp.org/pub/documents/Neuroscience%20Commentary%20FINAL.pdf

31. Jensen, E. (2006). The malleable brain. *Enriching the brain: How to maximize every learner's potential* (pp. 85–112). Alexandria, VA: Association for Supervision & Curriculum Development.

32. Kandel, E. R., Jessell, T. M., & Schwartz, J. H. (2000). The anatomical organization of the central nervous system. *Principles of neural science* (4th ed.). New York: McGraw-Hill Medical.

33. Kandel, E. R., Jessell, T. M., & Schwartz, J. H. (2000). The functional organization of perception and movement. *Principles of neural science* (4th ed.). New York: McGraw-Hill Medical.

34. Kandel, E. R., Jessell, T. M., & Schwartz, J. H. (2000). Integration of sensory and motor function: The association areas of the cerebral cortex and the cognitive capabilities of the brain. *Principles of neural science* (4th ed.). New York: McGraw-Hill Medical.

35. Kandel, E. R., Jessell, T. M., & Schwartz, J. H. (2000). From nerve cells to cognition: The internal cellular representation required for perception and action. *Principles of neural science* (4th ed.). New York: McGraw-Hill Medical.

36. Klingberg, T. (2012). *The learning brain: Memory and brain development in children.* New York: Oxford University Press.

37. Koch, C. (2004). Neurons, the atoms of perception. *The quest for consciousness: A neurobiological approach* (pp. 21–48). Englewood, CO: Roberts & Company.

38. Koch, C. (2004). Introduction to the study of consciousness. *The quest for consciousness: A neurobiological approach* (pp. 1–20). Englewood, CO: Roberts & Company.

39. LeDoux, J. (2003). Building the brain. *Synaptic self: How our brains become who we are* (pp. 65–96). New York: Viking Penguin.

40. LeDoux, J. (2003). Adventures in time. *Synaptic self: How our brains become who we are* (pp. 97–133). New York: Viking Penguin.

41. McEwen, B. S. (2010). Neurobiology of stress and adaptation: Implications for health psychology, behavioral medicine, and beyond. In M. A. Gernsbacher, R. Pew, L. Hough, & J. Pomerantz (Eds.), *Psychology and the real world: Essays illustrating fundamental contributions to society.* New York: Worth.

42. Mountcastle, V. B. (1998). Cells and local networks of the neocortex. *Perceptual neuroscience: The cerebral cortex* (pp. 50–77). Cambridge, MA: Harvard University Press.

43. National Research Council. (2000). 5. Mind and brain. *How people learn: Brain, mind, experience, and school: Expanded edition* (pp. 114–128). Washington, DC: The National Academies Press.

44. OECD. (2007). Understanding the brain: The birth of a learning science. doi: 10.1787/9789264029132-en: OECD Publishing.

45. Pinker, S. (1997). Thinking machines. *How the mind works.* New York: Norton.

46. Pinker, S. (1997). Good ideas. *How the mind works.* New York: Norton.

47. Posner, M. I., & Rothbart, M. K. (2010). Applying the mechanisms of self-regulation. In M. A. Gernsbacher, R. Pew, L. Hough, & J. Pomerantz (Eds.), *Psychology and the real world: Essays illustrating fundamental contributions to society.* New York: Worth.

48. Posner, M. I., & Rothbart, M. K. (2007). Relating brain and mind. *Educating the human brain* (pp. 25–53). Washington, DC: American Psychological Association.

49. Posner, M. I., & Rothbart, M. K. (2007). Preparing for school. *Educating the human brain* (pp. 209–216). Washington, DC: American Psychological Association.

50. Posner, M. I., & Rothbart, M. K. (2007). Literacy. *Educating the human brain* (pp. 147–172). Washington, DC: American Psychological Association.

51. Posner, M. I., & Rothbart, M. K. (2007). Numeracy. *Educating the Human Brain* (pp. 173–187). Washington, DC: American Psychological Association.

52. Prensky, M. (2012). Turning on the lights. *From digital natives to digital wisdom* (pp. 55–66). Thousand Oaks, CA: Corwin.

53. Purves, D., Augustine, G. J., Fitzpatrick, D., Hall, W. C., LaMantia, A.-S., McNamara, J. O., & White, L. E. (2008). Voltage-dependent membrane permeability. *Neuroscience* (4th ed., pp. 41–60). Sunderland, MA: Sinauer Associates.

54. Purves, D., Augustine, G. J., Fitzpatrick, D., Hall, W. C., LaMantia, A.-S., McNamara, J. O., & White, L. E. (2008). Neurotransmitters and their receptors. *Neuroscience* (4th ed., pp. 119–152). Sunderland, MA: Sinauer Associates.

55. Purves, D., Augustine, G. J., Fitzpatrick, D., Hall, W. C., LaMantia, A.-S., McNamara, J. O., & White, L. E. (2008). Synaptic transmission. *Neuroscience* (4th ed., pp. 85–118). Sunderland, MA: Sinauer Associates.

56. Purves, D., Augustine, G. J., Fitzpatrick, D., Hall, W. C., LaMantia, A.-S., McNamara, J. O., & White, L. E. (2008). Channels and transporters. *Neuroscience* (4th ed., pp. 61–84). Sunderland, MA: Sinauer Associates.

57. Reisberg, D. (2010). The neural basis of cognition. *Cognition: Exploring the science of the mind* (pp. 25–55). New York: Norton.

58. Reisberg, D. (2010). The science of the mind. *Cognition: Exploring the science of the mind* (pp. 3–23). New York: Norton.

59. Restak, R., & Kim, S. (2010). Long-term memory: Imaging the future by remembering the past. *The playful brain: The surprising science of how puzzles improve the mind* (pp. 57–86). New York: Riverhead Books.

60. Rieke, F., Warland, D., de Ruyter von Steveninck, R., & Bialek, W. (1998). Foundations. *Spikes, exploring the neural code* (pp. 19–99). Cambridge, MA: The MIT Press.

61. Shenk, D. (2010). How to ruin (or inspire) a kid. *The genius in all of us* (pp. 128–143). New York: Anchor Books.

62. Society for Neuroscience. (2008). *Brain facts: A primer on the brain and nervous system*. Washington, DC: Society for Neuroscience.

63. Sousa, D. A. (2010). *Mind, brain, & education: Neuroscience implications for the classroom*. Bloomington: Solution Tree.

64. Sousa, D. A. (2005). How the brain processes information. *How the brain learns* (3rd ed.). Thousand Oaks, CA: Corwin.

65. Sousa, D. A. (2005). The power of transfer. *How the brain learns* (3rd ed.). Thousand Oaks, CA: Corwin.

66. Sousa, D. A. (2005). The brain and the arts. *How the brain learns* (3rd ed.). Thousand Oaks, CA: Corwin.

67. Sylwester, R. (2007). The arts and humanities: Going beyond reality. *The adolescent brain: Reaching for autonomy* (pp. 111–120). Thousand Oaks, CA: Corwin.

68. Sylwester, R. (2007). Productivity and vocation: Maintaining our Planet. *The adolescent brain: Reaching for autonomy* (pp. 57–67). Thousand Oaks, CA: Corwin.

69. Sylwester, R. (2010). Mastering movement: From imitation to exploration. *A child's brain: The need for nurture* (pp. 19–32). Thousand Oaks, CA: Corwin.

70. Tokuhama-Espinosa, T. (2009). *The new science of teaching and learning: Using the best of mind, brain, and education science in the classroom*. New York: Teachers College Press.

II. Identified Resources Not Included in Sample Selected

ID	Criteria Code (see key below)	Reference
1	FOCUS	Armstrong, T. (2009). *Multiple intelligences in the classroom* (3rd ed.). Alexandria, VA: Association for Supervision & Curriculum Development.
2	STYLE	Bloom, F. E. (2007). *Best of the brain from Scientific American: Mind, matter and tomorrow's brain.* New York: Dana Press.
3	FOCUS	Dickmann, M. H., & Stanford-Blair, N. (2002). A Louis moment. *Connecting leadership to the brain* (pp. 3–11). Thousand Oaks, CA: Corwin.
4	DEPTH	Erlauer, L. (2003). *The brain-compatible classroom: Using what we know about learning to improve teaching.* Alexandria, VA: Association for Supervision & Curriculum Development. Notes: 1
5	STYLE	Ferrari, M., & Vuletic, L. (Eds.). (2010). *Developmental relations among mind, brain and education (Essays in honor of Robbie Case).* New York: Springer.
6	STYLE	Gardner, H., & Traub, J. (2010). A debate on "Multiple Intelligences." In The Dana Foundation (Ed.), *Cerebrum 2010: Emerging ideas in brain science.* New York: Dana Press.
7	DEPTH, DATES	Given, B. K. (2002). *Teaching to the brain's natural learning systems.* Alexandria, VA: Association for Supervision & Curriculum Development. Notes: 2
8	DEPTH, DATES, FOCUS	Gregory, G. H., & Parry, T. (2006). *Designing brain compatible learning* (3rd ed.). Thousand Oaks, CA: Corwin.
9	DATES	Jensen, E. (2005). *Teaching with the brain in mind.* Alexandria, VA: Association for Supervision & Curriculum Development.
10	DATES	Jensen, E. (2006). *Enriching the brain.* Alexandria, VA: Association for Supervision & Curriculum Development.
11	DATES	Kotlyar, B. I. (1992). *Habituation plasticity in the nervous system* (pp. 33–48). Philadelphia, PA: Gordon and Breach Science Publishers.
12	STYLE	Ramachandran, V. S., & Blakeslee, S. (1999). *Phantoms in the brain: Probing the mysteries of the human mind.* London: Harper Perennial.
13	FOCUS	Sousa, D. A. (2003). Brain-compatible curriculum. *The leadership brain: How to lead today's schools more effectively* (pp. 90–100). Thousand Oaks, CA: Corwin.

14	FOCUS	Sprenger, M. (2005). *How to teach so students remember.* Alexandria, VA: Association for Supervision & Curriculum Development.
15	FOCUS	Sullo, B. (2009). *The motivated student: Unlocking the enthusiasm for learning.* Alexandria, VA: Association for Supervision & Curriculum Development.
16	LIMITS	Sylwester, R. (2003). *A biological brain in a cultural classroom.* Thousand Oaks, CA: Corwin.
17	FOCUS	Tilestone, D. E. (2005). *10 best teaching practices: How brain research, learning styles, and standards define teaching competencies* (2nd ed.). Thousand Oaks, CA: Corwin.
18	DEPTH, DATES	Willis, J. (2006). *Research-based strategies to ignite student learning: Insights from a neurologist and classroom teacher.* Alexandria, VA: Association for Supervision & Curriculum Development.
19	FOCUS	Willis, J. (2007). *Brain-friendly strategies for the inclusion classroom.* Alexandria, VA: Association for Supervision & Curriculum Development.
20	FOCUS	Winter, P. (2010). Engaging families in the early childhood development story—Neuroscience and early childhood development, MCEECDYA, Canberra. (Obtained from PISA 2015 Module 09 report, May 2012)
21	STYLE	Wolfe, P. (2010). *Brain matters: Translating research into classroom practice* (2nd ed.). Alexandria, VA: Association for Supervision & Curriculum Development.

▮‖ "Criteria Code" Key:

DEPTH: Depth constraints for the purpose/audience here

DATES: Dated for the purpose/audience here
- Source dated outside specified time frame
- References somewhat outside frame relative to purpose here

FOCUS: Focus constraints for the purpose/audience here
- Early childhood
- Post-secondary
- Adult learning
- Parents
- Leadership
- Not sufficiently brain science focused

- Prescriptive with insufficient brain science included for purpose
- Narrow or different focus/goal for resource relative to purpose here

STYLE: Style constraints for the purpose/audience here

- Technical language/perspective not fully interpreted or not appropriately used for audience
- Nontechnical for audience/purpose
- Narrative focus; insufficient expository emphasis for purpose

LIMITS: Chapter limits already exceeded for the given author

- For representation, CORE limited to using maximum four chapters per author
- Or perspective represented in another of the author's sources is already included

Index